Complete Java 2 Certification, 5th Edition

Sun Certified Java Programmer Exam Objectives

OBJECTIVE	CHAPTER
SECTION 1: DECLARATIONS, INITIALIZATION AND SCOPING	
1.1 Develop code that declares classes (including abstract and all forms of nested classes), interfaces, and enums, and includes the appropriate use of package and import statements (including static imports).	1, 6
1.2 Develop code that declares an interface. Develop code that implements or extends one or more interfaces. Develop code that extends an abstract class.	3
1.3 Develop code that declares, initializes, and uses primitives, arrays, enums, and objects as static, instance, and local variables. Also, use legal identifiers for variable names.	1
1.4 Develop code that declares both static and non-static methods, and—if appropriate—use method names that adhere to the JavaBeans naming standards. Also develop code that declares and uses a variable-length argument list.	3, 6
1.5 Given a code example, determine if a method is correctly overriding or overloading another method, and identify legal return values (including covariant returns), for the method.	6
1.6 Given a set of classes and superclasses, develop constructors for one or more of the classes. Given a class declaration, determine if a default constructor will be created, and if so, determine the behavior of that constructor. Given a nested or non-nested class listing, write code to instantiate the class.	6
SECTION 2: FLOW CONTROL	
2.1 Develop code that implements an if or switch statement; and identify legal argument types for these statements.	5
2.2 Develop code that implements all forms of loops and iterators, including the use of for, the enhanced for loop (for-each), do, while, labels, break, and continue; and explain the values taken by loop counter variables during and after loop execution.	5
2.3 Develop code that makes use of assertions, and distinguish appropriate from inappropriate uses of assertions.	5
2.4 Develop code that makes use of exceptions and exception handling clauses (try, catch, finally), and declares methods and overriding methods that throw exceptions.	5
2.5 Recognize the effect of an exception arising at a specified point in a code fragment. Note that the exception may be a runtime exception, a checked exception, or an error.	5

SYBEX

OBJECTIVE	CHAPTER
6.4 Develop code that makes proper use of type parameters in class/interface declarations, instance variables, method arguments, and return types; and write generic methods or methods that make use of wildcard types and understand the similarities and differences between these two approaches.	8
6.5 Use capabilities in the java.util package to write code to manipulate a list by sorting, performing a binary search, or converting the list to an array. Use capabilities in the java.util package to write code to manipulate an array by sorting, performing a binary search, or converting the array to a list. Use the java.util.Comparator and java.lang.Comparable interfaces to affect the sorting of lists and arrays. Furthermore, recognize the effect of the "natural ordering" of primitive wrapper classes and java.lang.String on sorting.	8

SECTION 7: FUNDAMENTALS

7.1 Given a code example and a scenario, write code that uses the appropriate access modifiers, package declarations, and import statements to interact with (through access or inheritance) the code in the example.	3
7.2 Given an example of a class and a command-line, determine the expected runtime behavior.	1
7.3 Determine the effect upon object references and primitive values when they are passed into methods that perform assignments or other modifying operations on the parameters.	1
7.4 Given a code example, recognize the point at which an object becomes eligible for garbage collection, and determine what is and is not guaranteed by the garbage collection system. Recognize the behaviors of System.gc and finalization.	1
7.5 Given the fully-qualified name of a class that is deployed inside and/or outside a JAR file, construct the appropriate directory structure for that class. Given a code example and a classpath, determine whether the classpath will allow the code to compile successfully.	6
7.6 Write code that correctly applies the appropriate operators including assignment operators (limited to: =, + =, -=), arithmetic operators (limited to: +, -, *, /, %, ++, --), relational operators (limited to: <, < =, >, > =, = =, !=), the instanceof operator, logical operators (limited to: &, |, ^, !, &&, ||), and the conditional operator (? :), to produce a desired result. Write code that determines the equality of two objects or two primitives.	2,4

SYBEX

OBJECTIVE	CHAPTER

SECTION 4: CONCURRENCY

4.1 Write code to define, instantiate, and start new threads using both java.lang.Thread and java.lang.Runnable.	7
4.2 Recognize the states in which a thread can exist, and identify ways in which a thread can transition from one state to another.	7
4.3 Given a scenario, write code that makes appropriate use of object locking to protect static or instance variables from concurrent access problems.	7
4.4 Given a scenario, write code that makes appropriate use of wait, notify, or notifyAll.	7

SECTION 5: OO CONCEPTS

5.1 Develop code that implements tight encapsulation, loose coupling, and high cohesion in classes, and describe the benefits.	6
5.2 Given a scenario, develop code that demonstrates the use of polymorphism. Further, determine when casting will be necessary and recognize compiler vs. runtime errors related to object reference casting.	4, 6
5.3 Explain the effect of modifiers on inheritance with respect to constructors, instance or static variables, and instance or static methods.	3, 6
5.4 Given a scenario, develop code that declares and/or invokes overridden or overloaded methods and code that declares and/or invokes superclass, overridden, or overloaded constructors.	6
5.5 Develop code that implements "is-a" and/or "has-a" relationships.	6

SECTION 6: COLLECTIONS / GENERICS

6.1 Given a design scenario, determine which collection classes and/or interfaces should be used to properly implement that design, including the use of the Comparable interface.	8
6.2 Distinguish between correct and incorrect overrides of corresponding hashCode and equals methods, and explain the difference between == and the equals method.	8
6.3 Write code that uses the generic versions of the Collections API, in particular, the Set<E>, List<E>, Queue<E> and Map<K,V> interfaces and implementation classes. Recognize the limitations of the non-generic Collections API and how to refactor code to use the generic versions.	8

SYBEX

OBJECTIVE	CHAPTER
2.6 Recognize situations that will result in any of the following being thrown: ArrayIndexOutOfBoundsException, ClassCastException, IllegalArgumentException, IllegalStateException, NullPointerException, NumberFormatException, Assertion-Error, ExceptionInInitializerError, StackOverflowError or NoClassDefFoundError.	5
2.7 Understand which of these are thrown by the virtual machine and recognize situations in which others should be thrown programatically.	5

SECTION 3: API CONTENTS

3.1 Develop code that uses the primitive wrapper classes (such as Boolean, Character, Double, Integer, etc.), and/or autoboxing & unboxing. Discuss the differences between the String, StringBuilder, and StringBuffer classes.	8
3.2 Given a scenario involving navigating file systems, reading from files, or writing to files, develop the correct solution using the following classes (sometimes in combination), from java.io: BufferedReader,BufferedWriter, File, FileReader, FileWriter and PrintWriter.	9
3.3 Develop code that serializes and/or de-serializes objects using the following APIs from java.io: DataInputStream, DataOutputStream, FileInputStream, FileOutputStream, ObjectInputStream, ObjectOutputStream and Serializable. Additionally, develop Serializable classes that correctly declare and use transient variables and private readObject and writeObject methods. Given a scenario and/or code example, recognize when, if, and which constructors will be called in an object's inheritance chain during deserialization.	9
3.4 Use standard J2SE APIs in the java.text package to correctly format or parse dates, numbers, and currency values for a specific locale; and, given a scenario, determine the appropriate methods to use if you want to use the default locale or a specific locale. Describe the purpose and use of the java.util.Locale class.	8
3.5 Write code that uses standard J2SE APIs in the java.util and java.util.regex packages to format or parse strings or streams. For strings, write code that uses the Pattern and Matcher classes and the String.split method. Recognize and use regular expression patterns for matching (limited to: . (dot), * (star), + (plus), ?, \d, \s, \w, [], ()). The use of *, +, and ? will be limited to greedy quantifiers, and the parenthesis operator will only be used as a grouping mechanism, not for capturing content during matching. For streams, write code using the Formatter and Scanner classes and the PrintWriter.format/printf methods. Recognize and use formatting parameters (limited to: %b, %c, %d, %f, %s) in format strings.	8

SYBEX

Complete Java 2
Certification
Study Guide
Fifth Edition

Complete Java® 2 Certification
Study Guide
Fifth Edition

Philip Heller

Simon Roberts

San Francisco • London

SYBEX

Publisher: Neil Edde
Acquisitions and Developmental Editor: Jeff Kellum
Production Editor: Katherine Perry
Technical Editor: James Nuzzi
Copyeditor: Linda S. Recktenwald
Compositor: Laurie Stewart, Happenstance Type-O-Rama
Graphic Illustrator: Jeffrey Wilson, Happenstance Type-O-Rama
CD Coordinator: Dan Mummert
CD Technician: Kevin Ly
Proofreaders: Jim Brook, Jennifer Larsen, Nancy Riddiough
Indexer: Ted Laux
Book Designer: Judy Fung
Cover Designer: Archer Design
Cover Illustrator/Photographer: Photodisk and Victor Arre

SYBEX

To Our Valued Readers:

Thank you for looking to Sybex for your Java certification exam prep needs. We at Sybex are proud of the reputation we've established for providing certification candidates with the practical knowledge and skills needed to succeed in the highly competitive IT marketplace.

The author, editors, and technical reviewers have worked hard to ensure that the updated fifth edition of the *Complete Java 2 Certification Study Guide* you hold in your hands is comprehensive, in-depth, and pedagogically sound. We're confident that this book will exceed the demanding standards of the certification marketplace and help you, the Java certification candidate, succeed in your endeavors.

As always, your feedback is important to us. If you believe you've identified an error in the book, please send a detailed e-mail to support@sybex.com. And if you have general comments or suggestions, feel free to drop me a line directly at nedde@sybex.com. At Sybex we're continually striving to meet the needs of individuals preparing for certification exams.

Good luck in pursuit of your Java certification!

Neil Edde
Publisher—Certification
Sybex, Inc.

Software License Agreement: Terms and Conditions

Acknowledgments

The authors would like to acknowledge the dedicated and talented people at Sybex who worked on this edition: Jeff Kellum, Katherine Perry, Linda Recktenwald, James Nuzzi, and the proofreaders, Jim Brook, Jennifer Larsen, Nancy Riddiough.

Phil would like to express his gratitude to Simon Roberts and Bryan Basham. Also to all teachers, especially Carol, Gabriel, and Pantea.

Contents at a Glance

Contents

Introduction

Tiger is a very big deal. Actually, we should say that release 5.0 of Java 2 is a very big deal. "Tiger" was the project's code name during development. Now that it's been released to the world, they've given it a number and taken away its name.

We have only good things to say about the release. It makes our lives better, because it invites us to write cleaner Java code. It also requires us to make some mental adjustments. It will do the same to you, if you haven't already adjusted. You're going to have to get used to structures like

```
enum Size { SMALL, MEDIUM, LARGE; }
```

and

```
for (String s : myVectorOfStrings)
```

and even

```
Map<String, Float> myMap = new HashMap<String, Float>();
```

Since the new Java release is a very big deal, you would expect the Sun Certified Java Programmer (SCJP) and Sun Certified Java Developer (SCJD) exams to be similarly big deals. And they are. The Programmer Exam has been extensively revised, with new objectives and questions covering new subject matter.

 At the time of this writing, Sun was keeping quiet about the Developer Exam, which is mostly a programming assignment, but you can be sure that you will be expected to know about Java's new features and to use them appropriately.(By the way, your authors are the people who created the current edition of the Developer Exam. Our non-disclosure agreements limit what we're allowed to tell you, but we can guarantee that everything we say about that exam is truthful and helpful. Other authors will claim to be able to tell you about the exam, but they don't have full access to it, and they will have to rely on guesswork.)

And since the new exams are very big deals, this edition of this book is a very big deal. When JavaSoft revises Java, you can count on Sun to revise the exams. And when Sun revises the exams, you can count on us to revise this book.

The first part of the book contains nine chapters that discuss the content of every objective of the Programmer Exam. The second part of the book contains five chapters that prepare you to write the programming assignment and take the essay exam for the SCJD certification.

There are several ways to prepare for the Java certification exams, including attending seminars and study groups, visiting websites and newsgroups, programming at home and at work, and of course, reading study guides such as this. We're glad you chose our book as one of your preparation tools, and we encourage you to exploit as many other resources as you can to ensure your success.

We believe you'll find this book particularly helpful because it was written by Java instructors and practitioners who have also taken part in the writing of the Java certification exams.

Why Become Java 2 Certified?

There are a number of reasons for becoming Java 2 certified:

- It provides proof of professional achievement.
- It increases your marketability.
- It provides greater opportunity for advancement in your field.
- It is increasingly found as a requirement for some types of advanced training.
- It raises customer confidence in you and your company's services.

Let's explore each reason in detail.

Provides Proof of Professional Achievement

Specialized certifications are the best way to stand out from the crowd. In this age of technology certifications, you will find hundreds of thousands of administrators who have successfully completed the Microsoft and Cisco certification tracks. To set yourself apart from the crowd, you need a little bit more. The Java Programmer Certification is the most basic Java certification and the Developer Certification is the most prestigious. If you pass either of these exams, you will get the recognition you deserve.

Increases Your Marketability

Almost anyone can bluff their way through an interview. Once you have been certified in Java, you will have the credentials to prove your competency. And certifications are not something that can be taken from you when you change jobs. Once certified, you can take that certification with you to any position you accept.

Provides Opportunity for Advancement

Those individuals who prove themselves as competent and dedicated are the ones who will most likely be promoted. Becoming certified is a great way to prove your skill level, and it shows your employers that you are committed to improving your skill set. Look around you at those who are certified. They are probably the ones who receive good pay raises and promotions when they come up.

Fulfills Training Requirements

Many companies have set training requirements for their staff so that they stay up-to-date on the latest technologies. Having a certification program for Sun's Java family of products provides administrators another certification path to follow when they have exhausted some of the other industry-standard certifications.

Raises Customer Confidence

As companies continue to write their production software using Java, they will undoubtedly require qualified staff to embrace this ever-changing technology. Many companies outsource the work to consulting firms with experience working with Java. Those firms that have certified staff have a definite advantage over other firms that do not.

Who Should Buy This Book?

If you want to acquire a solid foundation in Java and your goal is to prepare for the exam by learning how to program and develop in Java, this book is for you. You'll find clear explanations of the concepts you need to grasp and plenty of help to achieve the high level of professional competency you need in order to succeed in your chosen field.

If you want to become certified as a Java programmer and developer, this book is definitely for you. However, if you just want to attempt to pass the exam without really understanding Java, this study guide is not for you. It is written for people who want to acquire hands-on skills and in-depth knowledge of programming Java.

How to Become a Sun Certified Java Programmer for the Java 2 Platform 5.0

You can take the Sun Certified Java Programmer Exam whenever you like by making an appointment with Sun Educational Services. Sun contracts with third-party test centers throughout the world, so you probably won't have to travel far. The cost of taking the exam is $150.

> The U.S. telephone number for Sun Educational Services is (800) 422-8020; their URL is http://suned.sun.com. From there it will be easy to find the links you need. We hesitate to give more detailed instructions, because the site layout may change.

You can make an appointment for any time during regular business hours. When you make the appointment, ask how much time you will have. This is subject to change; on average, you'll be given two minutes per question. You will not be allowed to bring food or personal belongings into the test area. One piece of scratch paper is permitted; you will not be allowed to keep it after you have finished the exam. Most sites have security cameras.

You will be escorted to a cubicle containing a PC. The exam program will present you with randomly selected questions. Navigation buttons take you to the next or previous question for review and checking. When you have finished the test, the program will immediately present you with your score and a pass/fail indication. You will also be given feedback that indicates how well you performed in each of the dozen or so categories of the objectives. You will not be told which particular questions you got right or wrong.

Formalities of the Programmer's Exam

There are no trick questions on the exam, but every question requires careful thought. The wording of the questions is highly precise; the exam has been reviewed not just by Java experts, but also by language experts whose task was to eliminate any possible ambiguity. All you have to worry about is knowing Java; your score will not depend on your ability to second-guess the examiners.

It is not a good idea to try to second-guess the question layout. For example, do not be biased toward answer C simply because C has not come up recently. The questions are taken from a pool and presented to you in a random order, so it is entirely possible to get a run of a particular option; it is also possible to get the answers neatly spread out.

Most of the questions are multiple-choice. Some are drag-and-drop: you might be called on to arrange four lines of code into the correct order or to drop each of five technical words near the phrase that best describes it. Be aware that where multiple answers are possible, you are being asked to make a decision about each answer, almost as though the question were five individual true/false questions. This requires more effort and understanding from you, because you have to get all the pieces correct. Think carefully, and always base your answer on your knowledge of Java.

The test is taken using a windowed interface that can be driven almost entirely with the mouse. Many of the screens require scrolling. Always check the scroll bar so you can be sure you have read a question in its entirety. It would be a shame to get a question wrong because you didn't realize you needed to scroll down a few lines.

Some of the questions are easier than others, and undoubtedly you will be able to answer some more quickly than others. However, you really do need to answer all the questions if you possibly can. Unlike some exams, this one doesn't penalize you for wrong answers. If you leave a question blank, you don't have a chance. If a blind guess is your best shot, at least you have a chance. But best of all, study this book. It will prepare you so that you won't need to guess about anything— you'll know it all!

How to Become a Sun Certified Java Developer for the Java 2 Platform 5.0

The Sun Certified Java Developer Exam costs $250. You aren't allowed to register for this exam unless you are a certified Java programmer. As with the Programmer's Exam, you can register by phone or on the Web; you can use the phone number or URL given above for the Programmer's Exam.

The Developer Exam requires you to write a Java application based on a specification. You do this on your own time, not at a testing site. After you complete your assignment and submit your work, you go to a testing site to take a follow-up exam. Chapter 10, "About the Developer's Exam," gives you all the details about this process.

Conventions Used in This Book

This book uses a number of conventions to present information in as readable a manner as possible. Tips, Notes, and Warnings, shown here, appear from time to time in the text in order to call attention to specific highlights.

This is a Tip. Tips contain specific programming information.

This is a Note. Notes contain important side discussions.

This is a Warning. Warnings call attention to bugs, design omissions, and other trouble spots.

This book takes advantage of several font styles. **Bold font** in text indicates something that the user types. A `monospaced font` is used for code, output, URLs, and file and directory names. A `monospaced italic font` is used for code variables mentioned in text.

These style conventions are intended to facilitate your learning experience with this book—in other words, to increase your chances of passing the exam.

If you type, compile, and run the sample code in this book, you may observe slightly different results than what you see in the book. This is particularly true with code that has a GUI. Each platform has its own windowing system that displays buttons, check boxes, and so on differently.

How to Use This Book and the CD

We've included several testing features in both the book and on the CD bound at the back of the book. These tools will help you retain vital exam content as well as prepare to sit for the actual exam. Using our custom test engine, you can identify weak areas up front and then develop a solid studying strategy using each of these robust testing features. Our thorough `readme` will walk you through the quick and easy installation process.

Before you begin   At the beginning of the book (right after this introduction, in fact) is an assessment test that you can use to check your readiness for the actual exam. Take this test before you start reading the book. It will help you determine the areas you may need to brush up on. The answers to each assessment test question appear on a separate page after the last question of the test. Each answer also includes an explanation and a note telling you in which chapter this material appears.

Chapter review questions   To test your knowledge as you progress through the book, in Part 1 of this book there are review questions at the end of each chapter. As you finish each chapter, answer the review questions and then check to see if your answers are right—the correct answers appear on the page following the last review question. You can go back and reread the section that deals with each question you got wrong to ensure that you get the answer correctly the next time you are tested on the material.

Test engine   In addition to the assessment test and the chapter review tests, you'll find four sample exams, three that are only on the CD and one that is both printed and electronic. Take these practice exams just as if you were taking the actual exam (that is, without any reference material). When you have finished the first exam, move onto the next one to solidify your test-taking skills. If you get more than 90 percent of the answers correct, you're ready to go ahead and take the certification exam.

Real-World Scenarios and Chapter Review Labs   The chapters in Part 1 of this book have Real World Scenarios, which are small programming exercises that give you a chance to put your new knowledge to use or to explore Java's features in more depth. In the Programmer Exam part of this book you'll find Chapter Review Labs, which let you practice the techniques you've just learned. You'll find solutions to these scenarios and labs on the CD-ROM that accompanies this book, in the solutions directory. If you prefer to look on the Web, check out the book's website at www.sybex.com.

Full Text of the book in PDF   If you have to travel but still need to study for the Java 2 programming exam and you have a laptop with a CD drive, you can carry this entire book with you just by taking along the CD. The CD contains this book in PDF (Adobe Acrobat) format so it can be easily read on any computer.

About the Authors

Philip Heller is a technical author, novelist, public speaker, and consultant. He has been instrumental in the creation and maintenance of the Java Programmer and Developer exams. His popular seminars on certification have been delivered internationally. He is also the author of *Ground-Up Java* (available from Sybex), which uses interactive animated illustrations to present fundamental concepts of Java programming to new programmers.

Simon Roberts worked for Sun Microsystems for nine years as an instructor, an authority on the Java language, and the key player in the development of the entire Java certification program. He is now a consultant and instructor, specializing in Java and security. He is also a flight instructor.

Assessment Test

1. Which of the following are valid declarations? Assume `java.util.*` is imported.

    A. `Vector<Map> v;`

    B. `Set<String> s;`

    C. `Map<String> m;`

    D. `Map<String, String> m;`

2. You can determine all the keys in a Map in which of the following ways?

    A. By getting a Set object from the Map and iterating through it.

    B. By iterating through the Iterator of the Map.

    C. By enumerating through the Enumeration of the Map.

    D. By getting a List from the Map and enumerating through the List.

    E. You cannot determine the keys in a Map.

3. What keyword is used to prevent an object from being serialized?

    A. `private`

    B. `volatile`

    C. `protected`

    D. `transient`

    E. None of the above

4. An abstract class can contain methods with declared bodies.

    A. True

    B. False

5. Select the order of access modifiers from least restrictive to most restrictive.

    A. `public, private, protected,` default

    B. default`, protected, private, public`

    C. `public,` default`, protected, private`

    D. default`, public, protected, private`

    E. `public, protected,` default`, private`

6. Which access modifier allows you to access method calls in libraries not created in Java?

    A. `public`

    B. `static`

    C. `native`

    D. `transient`

    E. `volatile`

7. Which of the following statements are true? (Select all that apply.)

    A. A final object's data cannot be changed.

    B. A final class can be subclassed.

    C. A final method cannot be overloaded.

    D. A final object cannot be reassigned a new address in memory.

    E. None of the above.

8. The keyword extends refers to what type of relationship?

    A. "is a"

    B. "has a"

    C. "was a"

    D. "will be a"

    E. None of the above

9. Which of the following keywords is used to invoke a method in the parent class?

    A. this

    B. super

    C. final

    D. static

10. Given the following code, what will be the outcome?

```
public class Funcs extends java.lang.Math {
    public int add(int x, int y) {
        return x + y;
    }
    public int sub(int x, int y) {
        return x - y;
    }
    public static void main(String [] a) {
        Funcs f = new Funcs();
        System.out.println("" + f.add(1, 2));
    }
}
```

    A. The code compiles but does not output anything.

    B. "3" is printed out to the console.

    C. The code does not compile.

    D. None of the above.

11. Given the following code, what is the expected outcome?

```
public class Test {
    public static void main(String [] a) {
        int [] b = [1,2,3,4,5,6,7,8,9,0];
        System.out.println("a[2]=" + a[2]);
    }
}
```

   A. The code compiles but does not output anything.

   B. "a[2]=3" is printed out to the console.

   C. "a[2]=2" is printed out to the console.

   D. The code does not compile.

   E. None of the above.

12. What is the value of *x* after the following operation is performed?

```
x = 23 % 4;
```

   A. 23

   B. 4

   C. 5.3

   D. 3

   E. 5

13. Given the following code, what keyword must be used at line 4 in order to stop execution of the for loop?

```
1. boolean b = true;
2. for (;;) {
3.    if (b) {
4.        <insert code>
5.    }
6.    // do something
7. }
```

   A. stop

   B. continue

   C. break

   D. None of the above

14. What method call is used to tell a thread that it has the opportunity to run?

A. `wait()`

B. `notify()`

C. `start()`

D. `run()`

15. Given the following code, which of the results that follow would you expect?

```
1. package mail;
2.
3. interface Box {
4.     protected void open();
5.     void close();
6.     public void empty();
7. }
```

A. The code will not compile because of line 4.

B. The code will not compile because of line 5.

C. The code will not compile because of line 6.

D. The code will compile.

16. Assertions are used to enforce all but which of the following?

A. Preconditions

B. Postconditions

C. Exceptions

D. Class invariants

17. The developer can force garbage collection by calling `System.gc()`.

A. True

B. False

18. Select the valid primitive data types. (Select all that apply.)

A. `boolean`

B. `bit`

C. `char`

D. `float`

E. All of the above

19. How many bits does a `float` contain?

   A. 1

   B. 8

   C. 16

   D. 32

   E. 64

20. What is the value of *x* after the following line is executed?

```
x = 32 * (31 - 10 * 3);
```

   A. 32

   B. 31

   C. 3

   D. 704

   E. None of the above

21. A `StringBuffer` is slower than a `StringBuilder`, but a `StringBuffer` is threadsafe.

   A. True

   B. False

22. Select the list of primitives ordered in smallest to largest bit size representation.

   A. `boolean, char, byte, double`

   B. `byte, int, float, char`

   C. `char, short, long, float`

   D. `char, int, float, long`

   E. None of the above

23. Which class provides locale-sensitive text formatting for date and time information?

   A. `java.util.TimeFormat`

   B. `java.util.DateFormat`

   C. `java.text.TimeFormat`

   D. `java.text.DateFormat`

24. The following line of code is valid.

```
int x = 9; byte b = x;
```

   A. True

   B. False

25. Which of the following code snippets compile?

   A. `Integer i = 7;`

   B. `Integer i = new Integer(5); int j = i;`

   C. `byte b = 7;`

   D. `int i = 7; byte b = i;`

   E. None of the above

26. What will be the output of the following code?

```
public class StringTest {
   public static void main(String [] a) {
      String s1 = "test string";
      String s2 = "test string";
      if (s1 == s2) {
         System.out.println("same");
      } else {
         System.out.println("different");
      }
   }
}
```

   A. The code will compile but not run.

   B. The code will not compile.

   C. "different" will be printed out to the console.

   D. "same" will be printed out to the console.

   E. None of the above.

27. Java arrays always start at index 1.

   A. True

   B. False

28. Which of the following statements accurately describes how variables are passed to methods?

   A. Arguments are always passed by value.

   B. Arguments are always passed by reference.

   C. Arguments that are primitive type are passed by value.

   D. Arguments that are passed with the & operator are passed by reference.

29. How do you change the value that is encapsulated by a wrapper class after you have instantiated it?

   A. Use the set*XXX()* method defined for the wrapper class.

   B. Use the parse*XXX()* method defined for the wrapper class.

   C. Use the equals() method defined for the wrapper class.

   D. None of the above.

30. Suppose you are writing a class that provides custom deserialization. The class implements java.io.Serializable (and not java.io.Externalizable). What method should implement the custom deserialization, and what is its access mode?

   A. private readObject

   B. public readObject()

   C. private readExternal()

   D. public readExternal()

Answers to Assessment Test

1. A, B, D. The angle-bracket notation is part of release 5.0's generic collections. See Chapter 6 for more information.

2. A. A Map contains a Set, which is a list that does not allow duplicates. Once you acquire the Set you can iterate through the keys. See Chapter 8 for more information.

3. D. By placing the keyword `transient` before an object's declaration, that value will not be included with the serialized data of the parent object. See Chapter 9 for more information.

4. A. Abstract classes can contain methods that are defined and methods that are not defined. See Chapter 3 for more information.

5. E. The `public` access modifier means the element is available to all; `protected` lets those within the class, package, or subclass gain access to the element. The lack of a modifier, that is, "default," means that it is accessible only within the package. Finally, `private` is the most restrictive and provides access within the class only. See Chapter 3 for more information.

6. C. The `native` modifier is an indicator to the Java Virtual Machine that the method actually lives in a library outside of Java. The `System.loadLibrary()` method is required to indicate which library contains the method. See Chapter 3 for more information.

7. D. An object denoted as `final` can have its data changed; however, the address location is what is determined as unchangeable. The third statement is false because a `final` method means it cannot be overridden, and the second statement is false because a `final` class means it *cannot* be subclassed. See Chapter 3 for more information.

8. A. The keyword `extends` is used when referring to another class. The extending class will have all access to all the available methods in the extended class, and the methods may be called as though they are defined in the extending class. If the extending class defines a method that exists in the extended class, that method is said to be overridden in the extending class. Because the extending class does not have to define any of the methods available in the extended class, it is said that the subclass X "is a" Y. See Chapter 6 for more information.

9. B. The `super` keyword is used to invoke a method or constructor in a parent class. See Chapter 6 for more information.

10. C. The code does not compile because it extends the `Math` class, which has been declared as `final`. A class cannot extend a class that has been declared `final`. See Chapter 3 for more information.

11. D. The declaration of the integer array is incorrect. An array is declared by using curly braces (`{}`) instead of square brackets (`[]`). See Chapter 1 for more information.

12. D. The modulo (`%`) operator returns the leftover value after a division operation. In the given example, 23 / 4 = 5, with 3 remaining after the division. Therefore, the answer is 3. See Chapter 2 for more information.

13. C. The `break` keyword is used to stop execution of a loop. See Chapter 5 for more information.

14. B. The `notify()` method is used to tell a pool of waiting threads that one of them can run. There is no guarantee as to which thread will run, though. See Chapter 7 for more information.

15. A. All methods in an interface must be `public`. The default access modifier automatically assumes the method or constant to be `public`. See Chapter 1 for more information.

16. C. Assertions do not enforce exceptions in any way. Assertions do, however, augment the use of exceptions to ensure that code is used correctly. See Chapter 5 for more information.

17. B. Garbage collection cannot be forced by the developer. The call to `System.gc()` schedules garbage collection in the thread queue, but it is up to the Java Virtual Machine to allow the garbage collection to run. See Chapter 1 for more information.

18. A, C, D. The second option is incorrect because there is no primitive named "bit"; there is a primitive named `byte`, however. See Chapter 1 for more information.

19. D. A `float` is represented using 32 bits for data storage. See Chapter 1 for more information.

20. A. Using the order of precedence, the equation contained within the parentheses is evaluated first. Again, using the order of precedence within the parentheses, the multiplication is executed first (10 * 3 = 30) and then the subtraction (31 - 30 = 1). Once this is completed, the final equation is executed as 32 * 1, which equals 32. See Chapter 2 for more information.

21. A. The `StringBuilder` class is compatible with `StringBuffer` but is not threadsafe and is generally faster. See Chapter 8 for more information.

22. D. The sizes of the primitives are as follows: `byte`, 8 bits; `char`, 16 bits; `short`, 16 bits; `int`, 32 bits; `float`, 32 bits; `long`, 64 bits; `double`, 64 bits. The Java specification does not state the size of a `boolean`, so it is not accurate to call it the smallest primitive. See Chapter 1 for more information.

23. D. The `java.text.DateFormat` class formats date and time data into strings that are appropriate to locales. See Chapter 8 for more information.

24. B. Due to the rules of widening conversions, the integer value of *x* cannot be automatically converted to a byte. The assignment of the variable *x* to the variable *b* would require an explicit cast. This cast could result in a loss of data, though. See Chapter 4 for more information.

25. A, B, C. A and B are examples of 5.0's boxing and unboxing functionality. See Chapter 8 for details. C is a legal assignment, but D is an illegal assignment that requires a cast; see Chapter 4 for details.

26. D. Both String variables are assigned the same string, `"test string"`. Because these strings are not created using the `new String()` method, the strings are placed in the string pool, and a reference to those strings is stored in the String variables. Because the reference to the string pool is the same, the `==` comparison will return `true`. If the strings were created using the `new String()` method, the references would be different and the `==` comparison would return `false`. See Chapter 8 for more information.

27. B. Java arrays always start at index 0. See Chapter 1 for more information.

28. C.   Arguments are not always passed only by reference or only by value. It depends on the argument itself, and primitives are always passed by value. Java does not use the **&** operator to denote "pass by reference" as is done in the C programming language. See Chapter 1 for more information.

29. D.   The value encapsulated by a wrapper class is immutable. See Chapter 8 for more information.

30. A.   The `readObject()` method must be private. See Chapter 9 for more information.

The Sun Certified Java Programmer Exam

Chapter

1

Language Fundamentals

JAVA CERTIFICATION EXAM OBJECTIVES COVERED IN THIS CHAPTER:

- ✓ **1.1 Develop code that declares classes (including abstract and all forms of nested classes), interfaces, and enums, and includes the appropriate use of package and import statements (including static imports).**

- ✓ **1.3 Develop code that declares, initializes, and uses primitives, arrays, enums, and objects as static, instance, and local variables. Also, use legal identifiers for variable names.**

- ✓ **7.2 Given an example of a class and a command-line, determine the expected runtime behavior.**

- ✓ **7.3 Determine the effect upon object references and primitive values when they are passed into methods that perform assignments or other modifying operations on the parameters.**

- ✓ **7.4 Given a code example, recognize the point at which an object becomes eligible for garbage collection, and determine what is and is not guaranteed by the garbage collection system. Recognize the behaviors of System.gc and finalization.**

This book is not an introduction to Java. Since you're getting ready to take the Programmer Exam, it's safe to assume that you know how to write code, what an object is, what a constructor is, and so on. So we're going to dive right in and start looking at what you need to know to pass the exam.

This chapter covers a lot of objectives. They may seem unrelated, but they all have a common thread: they deal with the fundamentals of the language. Here you will look at Java's keywords and identifiers. Then you'll read about primitive data types and the literal values that can be assigned to them. You'll also cover some vital information about arrays, variable initialization, argument passing, and garbage collection.

Source Files

All Java source files must end with the `.java` extension. A source file should generally contain, at most, one top-level public class definition; if a public class is present, the class name should match the unextended filename. For example, if a source file contains a public class called `RayTraceApplet`, then the file must be called `RayTraceApplet.java`. A source file may contain an unlimited number of non-public class definitions.

This is not actually a language requirement, but it is an implementation requirement of many compilers, including the reference compilers from Sun. It is unwise to ignore this convention, because doing so limits the portability of your source files (but not, of course, your compiled files).

Three top-level elements known as *compilation units* may appear in a file. None of these elements is required. If they are present, then they must appear in the following order:

1. Package declaration
2. Import statements
3. Class, interface, and enum definitions

The format of the package declaration is quite simple. The keyword **package** occurs first and is followed by the package name. The package name is a series of elements separated by periods. When class files are created, they must be placed in a directory hierarchy that reflects their package names. You must be careful that each component of your package name hierarchy is a legitimate directory name on all platforms. Therefore, you must not use characters such as the space, forward slash, backslash, or other symbols. Use only alphanumeric characters in package names.

Import statements have a similar form, but you may import either an individual class from a package or the entire package. To import an individual class, simply place the fully qualified class name after the `import` keyword and finish the statement with a semicolon (;); to import an entire package, simply add an asterisk (*) to the end of the package name.

NOTE   Java's import functionality was enhanced in 5.0. For more information, see the "Importing" section later in this chapter.

White space and comments may appear before or after any of these elements.
For example, a file called `Test.java` might look like this:

```
1. // Package declaration
2. package exam.prepguide;
3.
4. // Imports
5. import java.awt.Button;  // imports a specific class
6. import java.util.*;      // imports an entire package
7.
8. // Class definition
9. public class Test {...}
```

NOTE   Sometimes you might use classes with the same name in two different packages, such as the Date classes in the packages java.util and java.sql. If you use the asterisk form of import to import both entire packages and then attempt to use a class simply called Date, you will get a compiler error reporting that this usage is ambiguous. You must either make an additional import, naming one or the other Date class explicitly, or you must refer to the class using its fully qualified name.

Keywords and Identifiers

A *keyword* is a word whose meaning is defined by the programming language. Anyone who claims to be competent in a language must at the very least be familiar with that language's keywords. Java's keywords and other special-meaning words are listed in Table 1.1.

Most of the words in Table 1.1 are keywords. Strictly speaking, `true` and `false` aren't really keywords, they are literal boolean values. Also, `goto` and `const` are *reserved words*, which means that although they have no meaning to the Java compiler, programmers may not use them as identifiers.

TABLE 1.1   Java Keywords and Reserved Words

abstract	class	extends	implements	null	strictfp	true
assert	const	false	import	package	super	try
boolean	continue	final	instanceof	private	switch	void
break	default	finally	int	protected	synchronized	volatile
byte	do	float	interface	public	this	while
case	double	for	long	return	throw	
catch	else	goto	native	short	throws	
char	enum	if	new	static	transient	

Fortunately, the exam doesn't require you to distinguish among keywords, literal booleans, and reserved words. You won't be asked trick questions like "Is goto a keyword?" You *will* be expected to know what each word in Table 1.1 does, except for strictfp, transient, and volatile.

An *identifier* is a word used by a programmer to name a variable, method, class, or label. Keywords and reserved words may not be used as identifiers. An identifier must begin with a letter, a dollar sign ($), or an underscore (_); subsequent characters may be letters, dollar signs, underscores, or digits.

Some examples are

```
foobar              // legal
BIGinterface        // legal: embedded keywords are ok
$incomeAfterTaxes   // legal
3_node5             // illegal: starts with a digit
!theCase            // illegal: bad 1st char
```

Identifiers are case sensitive—for example, radius and Radius are distinct identifiers.

The exam is careful to avoid potentially ambiguous questions that require you to make purely academic distinctions between reserved words and keywords.

Primitive Data Types

A *primitive* is a simple non-object data type that represents a single value. Java's primitive data types are

- `boolean`
- `char`
- `byte`
- `short`
- `int`
- `long`
- `float`
- `double`

The apparent bit patterns of these types are defined in the Java language specification, and their effective sizes are listed in Table 1.2.

 Variables of type `boolean` may take only the values `true` or `false`. Their representation size might vary.

TABLE 1.2   Primitive Data Types and Their Effective Sizes

Type	Effective Representation Size (bits)
byte	8
int	32
float	32
char	16
short	16
long	64
double	64

A *signed data type* is a numeric type whose value can be positive, zero, or negative. (So the number has an implicit plus *sign* or minus *sign*.) An *unsigned data type* is a numeric type whose value can only be positive or zero. The four signed integral data types are

- byte
- short
- int
- long

Variables of these types are two's-complement numbers; their ranges are given in Table 1.3. Notice that for each type, the exponent of 2 in the minimum and maximum is one less than the size of the type.

 Two's-complement is a way of representing signed integers that was originally developed for microprocessors in such a way as to have a single binary representation for the number 0. The most significant bit is used as the sign bit, where 0 is positive and 1 is negative.

TABLE 1.3   Ranges of the Integral Primitive Types

Type	Size	Minimum	Maximum
byte	8 bits	-2^7	$2^7 - 1$
short	16 bits	-2^{15}	$2^{15} - 1$
int	32 bits	-2^{31}	$2^{31} - 1$
long	64 bits	-2^{63}	$2^{63} - 1$

The char type is integral but unsigned. The range of a variable of type char is from 0 through $2^{16} - 1$. Java characters are in Unicode, which is a 16-bit encoding capable of representing a wide range of international characters. If the most significant 9 bits of a char are all 0, then the encoding is the same as 7-bit ASCII.

The two floating-point types are

- float
- double

The ranges of the floating-point primitive types are given in Table 1.4.

TABLE 1.4   Ranges of the Floating-Point Primitive Types

Type	Size	Minimum	Maximum
float	32 bits	+/–1.40239846^{-45}	+/–3.40282347^{+38}
double	16 bits	+/–4.94065645841246544^{-324}	+/–1.79769313486231570^{+308}

These types conform to the IEEE 754 specification. Many mathematical operations can yield results that have no expression in numbers (infinity, for example). To describe such non-numeric situations, both double and float can take on values that are bit patterns that do not represent numbers. Rather, these patterns represent non-numeric values. The patterns are defined in the Float and Double classes and may be referenced as follows (NaN stands for Not a Number):

- Float.NaN
- Float.NEGATIVE_INFINITY
- Float.POSITIVE_INFINITY
- Double.NaN
- Double.NEGATIVE_INFINITY
- Double.POSITIVE_INFINITY

The following code fragment shows the use of these constants:

```
1. double d = -10.0 / 0.0;
2. if (d == Double.NEGATIVE_INFINITY) {
3.    System.out.println("d just exploded: " + d);
4. }
```

In this code fragment, the test on line 2 passes, so line 3 is executed.

    All numeric primitive types are signed.

Literals

A *literal* is a value specified in the program source, as opposed to one determined at runtime. Literals can represent primitive or string variables and may appear on the right side of assignments or in method calls. You cannot assign values into literals, so they cannot appear on the left side of assignments.

In this section you'll look at the literal values that can be assigned to boolean, character, integer, floating-point, and String variables.

The only valid literals of `boolean` type are `true` and `false`. For example:

```
1. boolean isBig = true;
2. boolean isLittle = false;
```

A *chararacter literal* (`char`) represents a single Unicode character. (*Unicode* is a convention for using 16-bit unsigned numeric values to represent characters of all languages. For more on Unicode, see Chapter 9, "I/O and Streams". Usually a `char` literal can be expressed by enclosing the desired character in single quotes, as shown here:

```
char c = 'w';
```

Of course, this technique works only if the desired character is available on the keyboard at hand. Another way to express a `char` literal is as a Unicode value specified using four hexadecimal digits, preceded by \u, with the entire expression in single quotes. For example:

```
char c1 = '\u4567';
```

Java supports a few escape sequences for denoting special characters:

- `'\n'` for new line
- `'\r'` for return
- `'\t'` for tab
- `'\b'` for backspace
- `'\f'` for formfeed
- `'\''` for single quote
- `'\"'` for double quote
- `'\\'` for backslash

Integral literals may be assigned to any numeric primitive data type. They may be expressed in decimal, octal, or hexadecimal. The default is decimal. To indicate octal, prefix the literal with 0 (zero). To indicate hexadecimal, prefix the literal with `0x` or `0X`; the hex digits may be upper- or lowercase. The value 28 may thus be expressed six ways:

- `28`
- `034`
- `0x1c`
- `0x1C`
- `0X1c`
- `0X1C`

By default, an integral literal is a 32-bit value. To indicate a `long` (64-bit) literal, append the suffix L to the literal expression. (The suffix can be lowercase, but then it looks so much like a one that your readers are bound to be confused.)

A *floating-point* literal expresses a floating-point number. In order to be interpreted as a floating-point literal, a numerical expression must contain one of the following:

- A decimal point, such as `1.414`
- The letter E or e, indicating scientific notation, such as `4.23E+21`
- The suffix F or f, indicating a `float` literal, such as `1.828f`
- The suffix D or d, indicating a `double` literal, such as `1234d`

A floating-point literal with no F or D suffix defaults to `double` type.

String Literals

A *string literal* is a sequence of characters enclosed in double quotes. For example:

```
String s = "Characters in strings are 16-bit Unicode.";
```

Java provides many advanced facilities for specifying non-literal string values, including a concatenation operator and some sophisticated constructors for the `String` class. These facilities are discussed in detail in Chapter 8, "The `java.lang` and `java.util` Packages."

Arrays

A Java *array* is an ordered collection of primitives, object references, or other arrays. Java arrays are homogeneous: except as allowed by polymorphism, all elements of an array must be of the same type. That is, when you create an array, you specify the element type, and the resulting array can contain only elements that are instances of that class or subclasses of that class.

To create and use an array, you must follow three steps:

1. Declaration
2. Construction
3. Initialization

Declaration tells the compiler the array's name and what type its elements will be. For example:

```
1. int[] ints;
2. Dimension[] dims;
3. float[][] twoDee;
```

Line 1 declares an array of a primitive type. Line 2 declares an array of object references (`Dimension` is a class in the `java.awt` package). Line 3 declares a two-dimensional array—that is, an array of arrays of `floats`.

The square brackets can come before or after the array variable name. This is also true, and perhaps most useful, in method declarations. A method that takes an array of `doubles` could be declared as `myMethod(double dubs[])` or as `myMethod(double[] dubs)`; a method that returns an array of doubles may be declared as either `double[] anotherMethod()` or as `double anotherMethod()[]`. In this last case, the first form is probably more readable.

Generally, placing the square brackets adjacent to the type, rather than following the variable or method, allows the type declaration part to be read as a single unit: `int array` or `float array`, which might make more sense. However, C/C++ programmers will be more familiar with the form where the brackets are placed to the right of the variable or method declaration. Given the number of magazine articles that have been dedicated to ways to correctly interpret complex C/C++ declarations (perhaps you recall the "spiral rule"), it's probably not a bad thing that Java has modified the syntax for these declarations. Either way, you need to recognize both forms.

Notice that the declaration does not specify the size of an array. Size is specified at runtime, when the array is allocated via the **new** keyword. For example

```
1. int[] ints;          // Declaration to the compiler
2. ints = new int[25];   // Runtime construction
```

Since array size is not used until runtime, it is legal to specify size with a variable rather than a literal:

```
1. int size = 1152 * 900;
2. int[] raster;
3. raster = new int[size];
```

Declaration and construction may be performed in a single line:

```
1. int[] ints = new int[25];
```

When an array is constructed, its elements are automatically initialized to their default values. These defaults are the same as for object member variables. Numerical elements are initialized to 0; non-numeric elements are initialized to 0-like values, as shown in Table 1.5.

Arrays are actually objects, even to the extent that you can execute methods on them (mostly the methods of the `Object` class), although you cannot subclass the array class. So this initialization is exactly the same as for other objects, and as a consequence you will see this table again in the next section.

TABLE 1.5   Array Element Initialization Values

Element Type	Initial Value
byte	0
int	0
float	0.0f
char	'\u0000'
object reference	null
short	0
long	0L
double	0.0d
boolean	false

If you want to initialize an array to values other than those shown in Table 1.5, you can combine declaration, construction, and initialization into a single step. The following line of code creates a custom-initialized array of five floats:

```
1. float[] diameters = {1.1f, 2.2f, 3.3f, 4.4f, 5.5f};
```

The array size is inferred from the number of elements within the curly braces.

Of course, an array can also be initialized by explicitly assigning a value to each element, starting at array index 0:

```
1. long[] squares;
2. squares = new long[6000];
3. for (int i = 0; i < 6000; i++) {
4.    squares[i] = i * i;
5. }
```

When the array is created at line 2, it is full of default values (0L), which are replaced in lines 3–4. The code in the example works but can be improved. If you later need to change the array size (in line 2), the loop counter will have to change (in line 3), and the program could be damaged if line 3 is not taken care of. The safest way to refer to the size of an array is to append the .length member variable to the array name. Thus, our example becomes

```
1. long[] squares;
2. squares = new long[6000];
```

```
3. for (int i = 0; i < squares.length; i++) {
4.   squares[i] = i * i;
5. }
```

When an array has more than one dimension, there is more going on than you might think. Consider this declaration plus initialization:

```
int[][] myInts = new int[3][4];
```

It's natural to assume that the myInts contains 12 ints and to imagine them as organized into rows and columns, as shown in Figure 1.1.

Actually, Figure 1.1 is misleading. myInts is actually an array with three elements. Each element is a reference to an array containing 4 ints, as shown in Figure 1.2.

The subordinate arrays in a multi-dimension array don't have to all be the same length. It's possible to create an array that looks like Figure 1.3.

FIGURE 1.1　　The wrong way to think about multi-dimension arrays

1	2	3	4
91	92	93	94
2001	2002	2003	2004

FIGURE 1.2　　The right way to think about multi-dimension arrays

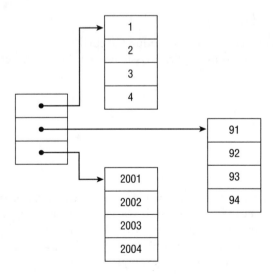

FIGURE 1.3   An irregular multi-dimension array

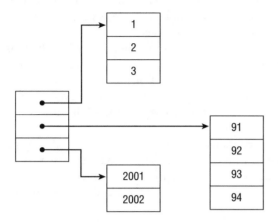

Figure 1.3 shows an array whose elements are an array of 3 ints, an array of 4 ints, and an array of 2 ints. Such an array may be created like this:

```
int[][] myInts = { {1, 2, 3}, {91, 92, 93, 94}, {2001, 2002} };
```

When you realize that the outermost array is a single-dimension array containing references, you understand that you can replace any of the references with a reference to a different subordinate array, provided the new subordinate array is of the right type. For example, you can do the following:

```
int[][] myInts = { {1, 2, 3}, {91, 92, 93, 94}, {2001, 2002} };
int[] replacement = {1, 2, 3, 4, 5, 6, 7, 8, 9, 10, 11, 12};
myInts[1] = replacement;
```

Importing

The term "import" can be confusing. In common speech, import means to bring something from abroad into one's own territory. In the Java context, it's natural to wonder what is getting brought in, and where it is getting brought into. A common mistake is to guess that importing has something to do with class loading. It's a reasonable mistake, since the class loader is the only obvious Java entity that brings something (class definitions) into somewhere (the Java Virtual Machine). However, the guess is dead wrong.

What gets brought in is the import class' name. The name is brought into the source file's *namespace*. A namespace is a kind of place—not a physical place, but an abstract place such as a directory or a source file—that contains items with unique names. The easiest example is a directory: within a directory, all filenames must be different from all other filenames. Names may be duplicated in different namespaces. For example, readme.txt may appear only once within a single directory but may appear in any other directory.

Items that appear in namespaces have short names and long names. The short name is for use within the namespace. The long name is for use outside the namespace. Suppose directory C:\MyCode\Projects contains a file named Sphinx.java. When you are working in C:\MyCode\ Projects, you can refer to the file by its short name: Sphinx.java. However, when your working directory is not C:\MyCode\Projects, you need to use the file's full name: C:\MyCode\ Projects\Sphinx.java.

The namespace of a Java source file contains the names of all classes and interfaces in the source file's package. In other words, within the source file you may refer to any class by its short name; classes outside the package must be called by their complete names. Suppose the current package contains a class named Formula. The following code creates an instance of Formula and an instance of Vector:

```
1. Formula f = new Formula();
2. java.util.Vector vec = new java.util.Vector();
```

Line 2 is a mess. The Vector class resides in the java.util package, so it must be referred to by its full name…twice! (Once in the declaration, and again in the constructor call.) If there were no workaround, the only thing worse than writing Java code would be reading Java code. Fortunately, Java provides a workaround. The source file needs an import statement:

```
import java.util.Vector;
```

Then line 2 becomes

```
2. Vector vec = new Vector();
```

This statement imports the name "Vector" into the namespace, allowing it to be used without the "java.util" prefix. When the compiler encounters a short class name, it checks the current package. If the class name is not found, the compiler then checks its import statements. In our example, the compiler will notice that there is no Vector class in the current package, but there is an import statement. The import tells the compiler, "When I say Vector, I really mean java.util.Vector."

Java's static import facility, which was introduced in rev 5.0, allows you to import static data and methods, as well as classes. In other words, you may refer to static data and methods in external classes without using full names. For example, the java.awt.Color class contains static data members names RED, GREEN, BLUE, and so on. Suppose you want to set myColor to GREEN. Without static imports, you have to do the following:

```
import java.awt.Color;
...
myColor = Color.GREEN;
```

With a static import, you can import the name "GREEN" into your namespace:

```
import static java.awt.Color.GREEN;
...
myColor = GREEN;
```

Note that the `import` keyword is followed by `static`. This tells the compiler to import the name of a static element of a class, rather than a class name.

Static imports eliminate the nuisance of constant interfaces. Constant interfaces are fairly common, since before rev 5.0 there was no good alternative. Many packages or applications define constants that are needed by more than one source file. For example, an application that uses both English and metric weights might need the following:

```
public static float LBS_PER_KG = 2.2f;
public static float KGS_PER_LB = 1 / LBS_PER_KG;
```

Now the question is, where do these lines belong? The general answer to this question is that they belong in the most appropriate class or interface. Unfortunately, "most appropriate" doesn't always mean most convenient. Suppose you put our two lines in a class called `Scales`. Since the constants are in the namespace of `Scales`, they may appear there without prefix. For example, `Scales` might contain

```
massInPounds = massInKgs * LBS_PER_KG;
```

However, other classes must go to more trouble. Any class except `Scales` has to do the following:

```
massInPounds = massInKgs * Scales.LBS_PER_KG;
```

Many programmers, wishing to avoid the inconvenience of prefixing, have discovered the trick of creating an interface (known as a *constant interface*) to contain constants. This trick has two benefits. First, you don't have to decide which class to put the constants in; they go in the interface. Second, in any class that implements the constant interface, you don't have to prefix the constants. In our example, you might be tempted to place the constant definitions in an interface called `Conversion`. Then the `Scales` class, and all other classes that convert between pounds and kilos, can implement `Conversion`.

Unfortunately, constant interfaces have several drawbacks. In the first place, to say that a class implements an interface really means that the class exposes the public methods listed in the interface. Interfaces are for defining types and should be used exclusively for that purpose. Constant interfaces only contain data, so they definitely don't define types.

The second disadvantage is a bit more complicated. Suppose someone you work with writes some code that uses an instance of `Scales`. This person can legally reference that instance with a variable of type `Conversion`, even though doing so would be quite inappropriate. Later, if you wanted to eliminate the `Conversion` interface, you couldn't do so, because your misguided colleague would be relying on the existence of the interface.

With static imports, you have an alternative to constant interfaces. To use static imports, you first locate your constants in the classes where they belong. Let's assume you put LBS_PER_KG and KGS_PER_LB in the Scales class. Now any other source file can use the following syntax:

```
import static Scales.LBS_PER_KG;
import static Scales.KGS_PER_LB;
```

Any source file that uses these statements may refer to LBS_PER_KG and KGS_PER_LB, rather than Scales.LBS_PER_KG and Scales.KGS_PER_LB.

The static import facility is aware of packages and access modes. To do a static import from a class in a different package, you have to prefix the class name with its package path. For example, to import the constant NORTH from class java.awt.BorderLayout, you would use

```
import static java.awt.BorderLayout.NORTH;
```

Only public data may be imported from classes in external packages. Data imported from other classes in the same package may be public, protected, or default, but not private. These rules are consistent with the meanings of public, protected, default, and private.

Java's access modes are discussed in detail in Chapter 3, "Modifiers."

You can use the star notation to import all accessible constants from a class. The line

```
import static pkga.pkgb.AClassName.*;
```

will import all non-private constants if AClassName is in the current package or all public constants if AClassName is in a different package.

Static importing gives you access to static methods as well as static data. Suppose class measure.Scales has a method called poundsToMicrograms() that looks like this:

```
public static float poundsToMicrograms(float pounds) {
    return pounds * KGS_PER_LB * 1.0e6f;
}
```

Any source file can import this method as follows:

```
import static measure.Scales.poundsToMicrograms();
```

A source file that performs this import may invoke the method as (for example)

```
float ugs = poundsToMicrograms(lbs);
```

This is a bit more convenient than

```
float ugs = Scales.poundsToMicrograms(lbs);
```

As with ordinary imports, static imports have only a slight compile-time cost and zero run-time cost. Many programmers are unclear on this point, perhaps because the word "import" feels like such an active verb; it seems as if surely the class loader or some other mechanism must be hard at work. Remember that importing does nothing more than bring a name into the local namespace. So importing and static importing are quite inexpensive.

Class Fundamentals

Java is all about classes, and a review of the exam objectives will show that you need to be intimately familiar with them. Classes are discussed in detail in Chapter 6, "Objects and Classes." For now, let's examine a few fundamentals.

Class Paths

When the Java compiler or the Virtual Machine needs a classfile, it searches all the locations listed in its classpath. The classpath is formed by merging the CLASSPATH environment variable and any locations specified in -classpath or -cp command line arguments. The members of a classpath may be directories or jar files.

Let's take an example. Suppose the compiler is looking for class sgsware.sphinx.Domain. The package structure sgsware.sphinx requires that the Domain.class file must be in a directory called sphinx, which must be in a directory called sgsware. So the compiler checks each class-path member to see if it contains sgsware\sphinx\Domain.class.

On Windows platforms, directories and jar files in a classpath are separated by a semicolon (";"). On UNIX platforms the separator is a colon (":").

The *main()* Method

The main() method is the entry point for standalone Java applications. To create an application, you write a class definition that includes a main() method. To execute an application, type **java** at the command line, followed by the name of the class containing the main() method to be executed.

The signature for main() is

```
public static void main(String[] args)
```

The main() method must be public so that the JVM can call it. It is static so that it can be executed without the necessity of constructing an instance of the application class. The return type must be void.

The argument to main() is a single-dimension array of Strings, containing any arguments that the user might have entered on the command line. For example, consider the following command line:

```
% java Mapper France Belgium
```

With this command line, the args[] array has two elements: France in args[0], and Belgium in args[1]. Note that neither the class name (Mapper) nor the command name (java) appears in the array. Of course, the name args is purely arbitrary: any legal identifier may be used, provided the array is a single-dimension array of String objects.

Variables and Initialization

Java supports variables of three different lifetimes:

Member variable A *member variable* of a class is created when an instance is created, and it is destroyed when the object is destroyed. Subject to accessibility rules and the need for a reference to the object, member variables are accessible as long as the enclosing object exists.

Automatic variable An *automatic variable* of a method is created on entry to the method and exists only during execution of the method, and therefore it is accessible only during the execution of that method. (You'll see an exception to this rule when you look at inner classes, but don't worry about that for now.)

Class variable A *class variable* (also known as a *static variable*) is created when the class is loaded and is destroyed when the class is unloaded. There is only one copy of a class variable, and it exists regardless of the number of instances of the class, even if the class is never instantiated.

All member variables that are not explicitly assigned a value upon declaration are automatically assigned an initial value. The initialization value for member variables depends on the member variable's type. Values are listed in Table 1.6.

The values in Table 1.6 are the same as those in Table 1.5; member variable initialization values are the same as array element initialization values.

A member value may be initialized in its own declaration line:

```
1. class HasVariables {
2.    int x = 20;
3.    static int y = 30;
```

When this technique is used, nonstatic instance variables are initialized just before the class constructor is executed; here x would be set to 20 just before invocation of any HasVariables constructor. Static variables are initialized at class load time; here y would be set to 30 when the HasVariables class is loaded.

Automatic variables (also known as *method local variables* are not initialized by the system; every automatic variable must be explicitly initialized before being used. For example, this method will not compile:

```
1. public int wrong() {
2.    int i;
3.    return i+5;
4. }
```

The compiler error at line 3 is, "Variable i may not have been initialized." This error often appears when initialization of an automatic variable occurs at a lower level of curly braces than the use of that variable. For example, the following method returns the fourth root of a positive number:

```
1. public double fourthRoot(double d) {
2.    double result;
3.       if (d >= 0) {
4.          result = Math.sqrt(Math.sqrt(d));
5.       }
6.       return result;
7. }
```

Here the result is initialized on line 4, but the initialization takes place within the curly braces of lines 3 and 5. The compiler will flag line 6, complaining that "Variable result may not have been initialized." A common solution is to initialize result to some reasonable default as soon as it is declared:

```
1. public double fourthRoot(double d) {
2.    double result = 0.0;  // Initialize
3.       if (d >= 0) {
4.          result = Math.sqrt(Math.sqrt(d));
5.       }
6.       return result;
7. }
```

Now result is satisfactorily initialized. Line 2 demonstrates that an automatic variable may be initialized in its declaration line. Initialization on a separate line is also possible.

Class variables are initialized in the same manner as for member variables.

TABLE 1.6   Initialization Values for Member Variables

Element Type	Initial Value	Element Type	Initial Value
byte	0	short	0
int	0	long	0L
float	0.0f	double	0.0d
char	'\u0000'	boolean	false
object reference	null		

Argument Passing: By Reference or by Value

When Java passes an argument into a method call, a *copy* of the argument is actually passed. Consider the following code fragment:

```
1. double radians = 1.2345;
2. System.out.println("Sine of " + radians +
3.                    " = " + Math.sin(radians));
```

The variable radians contains a pattern of bits that represents the number 1.2345. On line 2, a copy of this bit pattern is passed into the method-calling apparatus of the JVM.

When an argument is passed into a method, changes to the argument value by the method do not affect the original data. Consider the following method:

```
1. public void bumper(int bumpMe) {
2.   bumpMe += 15;
3. }
```

Line 2 modifies a copy of the parameter passed by the caller. For example

```
1. int xx = 12345;
2. bumper(xx);
3. System.out.println("Now xx is " + xx);
```

On line 2, the caller's xx variable is copied; the copy is passed into the bumper() method and incremented by 15. Because the original xx is untouched, line 3 will report that xx is still 12345.

This is also true when the argument to be passed is an object rather than a primitive. However, it is crucial for you to understand that the effect is very different. In order to understand the process, you have to understand the concept of the *object reference*.

Java programs do not deal directly with objects. When an object is constructed, the constructor returns a value—a bit pattern—that uniquely identifies the object. This value is known as a *reference* to the object. For example, consider the following code:

```
1. Button btn;
2. btn = new Button("Ok");
```

In line 2, the Button constructor returns a reference to the just-constructed button—not the actual button object or a copy of the button object. This reference is stored in the variable btn. In some implementations of the JVM, a reference is simply the address of the object; however, the JVM specification gives wide latitude as to how references can be implemented. You can think of a reference as simply a pattern of bits that uniquely identifies an individual object.

How to Create a Reference to a Primitive

This is a useful technique if you need to create the effect of passing primitive values by reference. Simply pass an array of one primitive element over the method call, and the called method can now change the value seen by the caller. To do so, use code like this:

```
1. public class PrimitiveReference {
2.    public static void main(String args[]) {
3.       int [] myValue = { 1 };
4.       modifyIt(myValue);
5.       System.out.println("myValue contains " +
6.                          myValue[0]);
7.    }
8.    public static void modifyIt(int [] value) {
9.       value[0]++;
10.   }
11. }
```

In most JVMs, the reference value is actually the address of an address. This second address refers to the real data. This approach, called *double indirection*, allows the garbage collector to relocate objects to reduce memory fragmentation.

When Java code appears to store objects in variables or pass objects into method calls, the object references are stored or passed.

Consider this code fragment:

```
1. Button btn;
2. btn = new Button("Pink");
3. replacer(btn);
4. System.out.println(btn.getLabel());
5.
6. public void replacer(Button replaceMe) {
7.    replaceMe = new Button("Blue");
8. }
```

Line 2 constructs a button and stores a reference to that button in `btn`. In line 3, a copy of the reference is passed into the `replacer()` method. Before execution of line 7, the value in `replaceMe` is a reference to the Pink button. Then line 7 constructs a second button and stores a reference to the second button in `replaceMe`, thus overwriting the reference to the Pink button.

However, the caller's copy of the reference is not affected, so on line 4 the call to `btn.getLabel()` calls the original button; the string printed out is "Pink".

You have seen that called methods cannot affect the original value of their arguments—that is, the values stored by the caller. However, when the called method operates on an object via the reference value that is passed to it, there are important consequences. If the method modifies the object via the reference, as distinguished from modifying the method argument—the reference—then the changes will be visible to the caller. For example

```
1. Button btn;
2. btn = new Button("Pink");
3. changer(btn);
4. System.out.println(btn.getLabel());
5.
6. public void changer(Button changeMe) {
7.    changeMe.setLabel("Blue");
8. }
```

In this example, the variable `changeMe` is a copy of the reference `btn`, just as before. However, this time the code uses the copy of the reference to change the actual original object rather than trying to change the reference. Because the caller's object is changed rather than the callee's reference, the change is visible and the value printed out by line 4 is "Blue".

Arrays are objects, meaning that programs deal with references to arrays, not with arrays themselves. What gets passed into a method is a copy of a reference to an array. It is therefore possible for a called method to modify the contents of a caller's array.

Garbage Collection

Most modern languages permit you to allocate data storage during a program run. In Java, this is done directly when you create an object with the **new** operation and indirectly when you call a method that has local variables or arguments. Method locals and arguments are allocated space on the stack and are discarded when the method exits, but objects are allocated space on the heap and have a longer lifetime.

 Each process has its own stack and heap, and they are located on opposite sides of the process address space. The sizes of the stack and heap are limited by the amount of memory that is available on the host running the program. They may be further limited by the operating system or user-specific limits.

It is important to recognize that objects are always allocated on the heap. Even if they are created in a method using code like

```
public void aMethod() {
    MyClass mc = new MyClass();
}
```

the local variable mc is a reference, allocated on the stack, whereas the object to which that variable refers, an instance of MyClass, is allocated on the heap.

In this discussion, we are concerned with recovery of space allocated on the heap. The increased lifetime raises the question of when storage allocation on the heap can be released. Some languages require that you, the programmer, explicitly release the storage when you have finished with it. This approach has proven seriously error-prone, because you might release the storage too soon (causing corrupted data if any other reference to the data is still in use) or forget to release it altogether (causing a memory shortage). Java's garbage collection solves the first of these problems and greatly simplifies the second.

How to Cause Leaks in a Garbage Collection System

The nature of automatic garbage collection has an important consequence: you can still get memory leaks. If you allow live, accessible references to unneeded objects to persist in your programs, then those objects cannot be garbage collected. Therefore, it may be a good idea to explicitly assign null into a variable when you have finished with it. This issue is particularly noticeable if you are implementing a collection of some kind.

In this example, assume the array storage is being used to maintain the storage of a stack. This pop() method is inappropriate:

```
1. public Object pop() {
2.     return storage[index--];
3. }
```

If the caller of this pop() method abandons the popped value, it will not be eligible for garbage collection until the array element containing a reference to it is overwritten. This might take a long time. You can speed up the process like this:

```
1. public Object pop() {
2.     Object returnValue = storage[index];
3.     storage[index--] = null;
4.     return returnValue;
5. }
```

In Java, you never explicitly free memory that you have allocated; instead, Java provides automatic garbage collection. The runtime system keeps track of the memory that is allocated and is able to determine whether that memory is still useable. This work is usually done in the background by a low-priority thread that is referred to as the *garbage collector*. When the garbage collector finds memory that is no longer accessible from any live thread (the object is out of scope), it takes steps to release it back into the heap for re-use. Specifically, the garbage collector calls the class destructor method called `finalize()` (if it is defined) and then frees the memory.

Garbage collection can be done in a number of different ways; each has advantages and disadvantages, depending on the type of program that is running. A real-time control system, for example, needs to know that nothing will prevent it from responding quickly to interrupts; this application requires a garbage collector that can work in small chunks or that can be interrupted easily. On the other hand, a memory-intensive program might work better with a garbage collector that stops the program from time to time but recovers memory more urgently as a result. At present, garbage collection is hardwired into the Java runtime system; most garbage collection algorithms use an approach that gives a reasonable compromise between speed of memory recovery and responsiveness. In the future, you will probably be able to plug in different garbage-collection algorithms or buy different JVMs with appropriate collection algorithms, according to your particular needs.

This discussion leaves one crucial question unanswered: When is storage recovered? The best answer is that storage is not recovered unless it is definitely no longer in use. That's it. Even though you are not using an object any longer, you cannot say if it will be collected in 1 millisecond, in 100 milliseconds, or even if it will be collected at all. The methods `System.gc()` and `Runtime.gc()` look as if they run the garbage collector, but even these cannot be relied upon in general, because some other thread might prevent the garbage-collection thread from running. In fact, the documentation for the `gc()` methods states:

> Calling this method suggests that the Java Virtual Machine expends effort toward recycling unused objects.

Summary

This chapter has covered a variety of topics. You learned that a source file's elements must appear in this order:

1. Package declaration
2. Import statements
3. Class, interface, and enum definitions

Imports may be static. There should be, at most, one public class definition per source file; the filename must match the name of the public class.

You also learned that an identifier must begin with a letter, a dollar sign, or an underscore; subsequent characters may be letters, dollar signs, underscores, or digits. Java has four signed integral primitive data types: byte, short, int, and long; all four types display the behavior of two's-complement representation. Java's two floating-point primitive data types are float and double; the char type is unsigned and represents a Unicode character; the boolean type may take on only the values true and false.

In addition, you learned that arrays must be (in order)

1. Declared

2. Constructed

3. Initialized

Default initialization is applied to member variables, class variables, and array elements, but not automatic variables. The default values are 0 for numeric types, the null value for object references, the null character for char, and false for boolean. The length member of an array gives the number of elements in the array. A class with a main() method can be invoked from the command line as a Java application. The signature for main() is public static void main(String[] args). The args[] array contains all command-line arguments that appeared after the name of the application class.

You should also understand that method arguments are copies, not originals. For arguments of primitive data type, this means that modifications to an argument within a method are not visible to the caller of the method. For arguments of object type (including arrays), modifications to an argument value within a method are still not visible to the caller of the method; however, modifications in the object or array to which the argument refers *do* appear to the caller.

Finally, Java's garbage-collection mechanism may recover only memory that is definitely unused. It is not possible to force garbage collection reliably. It is not possible to predict when a piece of unused memory will be collected, only to say when it becomes *eligible* for collection. Garbage collection does not prevent memory leaks; they can still occur if unused references are not cleared to null or destroyed.

Exam Essentials

Recognize and create correctly constructed source files.   You should know the various kinds of compilation units and their required order of appearance.

Recognize and create correctly constructed declarations.   You should be familiar with declarations of packages, classes, interfaces, methods, and variables.

Recognize Java keywords.   You should recognize the keywords and reserved words listed in Table 1.1.

Distinguish between legal and illegal identifiers.   You should know the rules that restrict the first character and the subsequent characters of an identifier.

Know all the primitive data types and the ranges of the integral data types.   These are summarized in Tables 1.2 and 1.3.

Recognize correctly formatted literals.   You should be familiar with all formats for literal characters, strings, and numbers.

Know how to declare and construct arrays.   The declaration includes one empty pair of square brackets for each dimension of the array. The square brackets can appear before or after the array name. Arrays are constructed with the keyword new.

Know the default initialization values for all possible types of class variables and array elements. Know when data is initialized.   Initialization takes place when a class or array is constructed. The initialization values are 0 for numeric type arrays, false for boolean arrays, and null for object reference type arrays.

Understand importing and static importing.   Be aware of the difference between traditional importing and the new static import facility.

Know the contents of the argument list of an application's main() method, given the command line that invoked the application.   Be aware that the list is an array of Strings containing everything on the command line except the java command, command-line options, and the name of the class.

Know that Java passes method arguments by value.   Changes made to a method argument are not visible to the caller, because the method argument changes a copy of the argument. Objects are not passed to methods; only references to objects are passed.

Understand memory reclamation and the circumstances under which memory will be reclaimed. If an object is still accessible to any live thread, that object will certainly not be collected. This is true even if the program will never access the object again—the logic is simple and cannot make inferences about the semantics of the code. No guarantees are made about reclaiming available memory or the timing of reclamation if it does occur. A standard JVM has no entirely reliable, platform-independent way to force garbage collection. The System and Runtime classes each have a gc() method, and these methods make it more likely that garbage collection will run, but they provide no guarantee.

Review Questions

1. A signed data type has an equal number of non-zero positive and negative values available.

    A. True

    B. False

2. Choose the valid identifiers from those listed here. (Choose all that apply.)

    A. `BigOlLongStringWithMeaninglessName`

    B. `$int`

    C. `bytes`

    D. `$1`

    E. `finalist`

3. Which of the following signatures are valid for the `main()` method entry point of an application? (Choose all that apply.)

    A. `public static void main()`

    B. `public static void main(String arg[])`

    C. `public void main(String [] arg)`

    D. `public static void main(String[] args)`

    E. `public static int main(String [] arg)`

4. If all three top-level elements occur in a source file, they must appear in which order?

    A. Imports, package declarations, classes/interfaces/enums

    B. Classes/interfaces/enums, imports, package declarations

    C. Package declaration must come first; order for imports and class/interfaces/enum definitions is not significant

    D. Package declaration, imports, class/interface/enum definitions.

    E. Imports must come first; order for package declarations and class/interface/enum definitions is not significant

5. Consider the following line of code:

    ```
    int[] x = new int[25];
    ```

    After execution, which statements are true? (Choose all that apply.)

    A. `x[24]` is 0

    B. `x[24]` is undefined

    C. `x[25]` is 0

    D. `x[0]` is `null`

    E. `x.length` is 25

6.   Consider the following application:

```
1. class Q6 {
2.   public static void main(String args[]) {
3.     Holder h = new Holder();
4.     h.held = 100;
5.     h.bump(h);
6.     System.out.println(h.held);
7.   }
8. }
9.
10. class Holder {
11.   public int held;
12.   public void bump(Holder theHolder) {
13.     theHolder.held++; }
14.   }
15. }
```

What value is printed out at line 6?

A. 0

B. 1

C. 100

D. 101

7.   Consider the following application:

```
1. class Q7 {
2.   public static void main(String args[]) {
3.     double d = 12.3;
4.     Decrementer dec = new Decrementer();
5.     dec.decrement(d);
6.     System.out.println(d);
7.   }
8. }
9.
10. class Decrementer {
11.   public void decrement(double decMe) {
12.     decMe = decMe - 1.0;
13.   }
14. }
```

What value is printed out at line 6?

A. 0.0

B. 1.0

C. 12.3

D. 11.3

8. How can you force garbage collection of an object?

   A. Garbage collection cannot be forced.

   B. Call `System.gc()`.

   C. Call `System.gc()`, passing in a reference to the object to be garbage-collected.

   D. Call `Runtime.gc()`.

   E. Set all references to the object to new values (`null`, for example).

9. What is the range of values that can be assigned to a variable of type `short`?

   A. Depends on the underlying hardware

   B. 0 through $2^{16} - 1$

   C. 0 through $2^{32} - 1$

   D. -2^{15} through $2^{15} - 1$

   E. -2^{31} through $2^{31} - 1$

10. What is the range of values that can be assigned to a variable of type `byte`?

    A. Depends on the underlying hardware

    B. 0 through $2^8 - 1$

    C. 0 through $2^{16} - 1$

    D. -2^7 through $2^7 - 1$

    E. -2^{15} through $2^{15} - 1$

11. Suppose a source file contains a large number of `import` statements. How do the imports affect the time required to compile the source file?

    A. Compilation takes no additional time.

    B. Compilation takes slightly more time.

    C. Compilation takes significantly more time.

12. Suppose a source file contains a large number of `import` statements and one class definition. How do the imports affect the time required to load the class?

    A. Class loading takes no additional time.

    B. Class loading takes slightly more time.

    C. Class loading takes significantly more time.

13. Which of the following are legal `import` statements?

    A. import java.util.Vector;

    B. static import java.util.Vector.*;

    C. import static java.util.Vector.*;

    D. import java.util.Vector static;

14. Which of the following may be statically imported? (Choose all that apply.)

    A. Package names

    B. Static method names

    C. Static field names

    D. Method-local variable names

15. What happens when you try to compile and run the following code?

```
public class Q15 {
  static String s;
  public static void main(String[] args) {
    System.out.println(">>" + s + "<<");
  }
}
```

    A. The code does not compile

    B. The code compiles, and prints out >><<

    C. The code compiles, and prints out >>null<<

16. Which of the following are legal? (Choose all that apply.)

    A. int a = abcd;

    B. int b = ABCD;

    C. int c = 0xabcd;

    D. int d = 0XABCD;

    E. int e = 0abcd;

    F. int f = 0ABCD;

17. Which of the following are legal? (Choose all that apply.)

    A. double d = 1.2d;

    B. double d = 1.2D;

    C. double d = 1.2d5;

    D. double d = 1.2D5;

18. Which of the following are legal?

    A. `char c = 0x1234;`

    B. `char c = \u1234;`

    C. `char c = '\u1234';`

19. Consider the following code:

```
1. StringBuffer sbuf = new StringBuffer();
2. sbuf = null;
3. System.gc();
```

Choose all true statements:

    A. After line 2 executes, the `StringBuffer` object is garbage collected.

    B. After line 3 executes, the `StringBuffer` object is garbage collected.

    C. After line 2 executes, the `StringBuffer` object is eligible for garbage collection.

    D. After line 3 executes, the `StringBuffer` object is eligible for garbage collection.

20. Which of the following are true? (Choose all that apply.)

    A. Primitives are passed by reference.

    B. Primitives are passed by value.

    C. References are passed by reference.

    D. References are passed by value.

Answers to Review Questions

1. B. The range of negative numbers is greater by one than the range of positive numbers.

2. A, B, C, D, E. All of the identifiers are valid. An identifier begins with a letter, a dollar sign, or an underscore; subsequent characters may be letters, dollar signs, underscores, or digits. And of course keywords and their kin may not be identifiers.

3. B, D. All the choices are valid method signatures. However, in order to be the entry point of an application, a `main()` method must be public, static, and void; it must take a single argument of type `String[]`.

4. D. Package declaration must come first, followed by imports, followed by class/interface/enum definitions.

5. A, E. The array has 25 elements, indexed from 0 through 24. All elements are initialized to 0.

6. D. A holder is constructed on line 3. A reference to that holder is passed into method `bump()` on line 5. Within the method call, the holder's `held` variable is bumped from 100 to 101.

7. C. The `decrement()` method is passed a copy of the argument d; the copy gets decremented, but the original is untouched.

8. A. Garbage collection cannot be forced. Calling `System.gc()` or `Runtime.gc()` is not 100 percent reliable, because the garbage-collection thread might defer to a thread of higher priority; thus options B and D are incorrect. Option C is incorrect because the two `gc()` methods do not take arguments; in fact, if you still have a reference to pass into any method, the object is not yet eligible to be collected. Option E will make the object eligible for collection the next time the garbage collector runs.

9. D. The range for a 16-bit `short` is -2^{15} through $2^{15} - 1$. This range is part of the Java specification, regardless of the underlying hardware.

10. D. The range for an 8-bit `byte` is -2^7 through 2^7-1. Table 1.3 lists the ranges for Java's integral primitive data types.

11. B . Importing slightly increases compilation time.

12. A.. Importing is strictly a compile-time function. It has no effect on class loading or on any other run-time function.

13. A, C. The `import` keyword may optionally be followed by the `static` keyword.

14. B, C. You may statically import method and field names.

15. C. The code compiles without error. At static initialization time, s is initialized to null (and not to a reference to an empty string, as suggested by C).

16. C, D. The characters a–f and A–F may be combined with the digits 0–9 to create a hexadecimal literal, which must begin with `0x`.

17. A, B. The d suffix in option A and the D suffix in option B are optional. Options C and D are illegal because the notation requires e or E, not d or D.

18. C. A Unicode literal character must be enclosed in single quotes and must begin with \u.

19. C.. After line 2 executes, there are no references to the `StringBuffer` object, so it becomes eligible for garbage collection.

20. B, D. In Java, all arguments are passed by value.

Chapter

2

Operators and Assignments

JAVA CERTIFICATION EXAM OBJECTIVES COVERED IN THIS CHAPTER:

✓ 7.6 Write code that correctly applies the appropriate operators including assignment operators (limited to: =, + =, -=), arithmetic operators (limited to: +, -, *, /, %, ++, --), relational operators (limited to: <, < =, >, > =, = =, !=), the instanceof operator, logical operators (limited to: &, |, ^, !, &&, ||), and the conditional operator (? :), to produce a desired result. Write code that determines the equality of two objects or two primitives.

Java provides a full set of operators, most of which are taken from C and C++. However, Java's operators differ in some important aspects from their counterparts in these other languages, and you need to understand clearly how Java's operators behave. This chapter describes all the operators. Some are described briefly, whereas operators that sometimes cause confusion are described in more detail. You will also learn about the behavior of expressions under conditions of arithmetic overflow. In this chapter, we will first look at the different Java operators. The rest of this chapter examines each of these operators. But before we start, let's consider the general issue of evaluation order.

Overview of the Java Operators

Java's operators, which are shown in Table 2.1, perform traditional arithmetic and logical operations, as well as the object-oriented cast and `instanceof` operations. They are listed in precedence order, with the highest precedence at the top of the table. Each group has been given a name for reference purposes; that name is shown in the left column of the table. Arithmetic and comparison operators are each split further into two subgroupings because they have different levels of precedence. We'll discuss these groupings later.

TABLE 2.1   Operators in Java, in Descending Order of Precedence

Category	Operators
Unary	`++  --  +  -  !  ~  (type)`
Arithmetic	`*  /  %`
	`+  -`
Shift	`<<  >>  >>>`
Comparison	`<  <=  >  >=  instanceof`
	`==  !=`

TABLE 2.1   Operators in Java, in Descending Order of Precedence *(continued)*

Category	Operators
Bitwise	& ^ |
Short-circuit	&& ||
Conditional	?:
Assignment	= *op=*

Evaluation Order

In Java, the order of evaluation of operands in an expression is fixed. Consider this code fragment:

```
1. int [] a = { 4, 4 };
2. int b = 1;
3. a[b] = b = 0;
```

In this case, it might be unclear which element of the array is modified: Which value of b is used to select the array element, 0 or 1? An evaluation from left to right requires that the leftmost expression, a[b], be evaluated first, so it is a reference to the element a[1]. Next, b is evaluated, which is simply a reference to the variable called b. The constant expression 0 is evaluated next, which clearly does not involve any work. Now that the operands have been evaluated, the operations take place. This is done in the order specified by precedence and associativity. For assignments, associativity is right to left, so the value 0 is first assigned to the variable called b; then the value 0 is assigned into the last element of the array a.

We will look at each of these operators in more detail in the rest of this chapter.

Although Table 2.1 shows the precedence order, the degree of detail in this precedence ordering is rather high. It is generally better style to keep expressions simple and to use redundant bracketing to make it clear how any particular expression should be evaluated. This approach reduces the chance that less-experienced programmers will have difficulty trying to read or maintain your code. Bear in mind that the code generated by the compiler will be the same despite redundant brackets.

The Unary Operators

The first group of operators in Table 2.1 consists of the *unary operators*. Most operators take two operands. When you multiply, for example, you work with two numbers. Unary operators, on the other hand, take only a single operand and work just on that. Java provides seven unary operators:

- The increment and decrement operators: ++ and --
- The unary plus and minus operators: + and -
- The bitwise inversion operator: ~
- The **boolean** complement operator: !
- The cast: ()

 Strictly speaking, the cast is not an operator. However, we discuss it as if it were for simplicity, because it fits well with the rest of our discussion.

The Increment and Decrement Operators: ++ and --

The ++ and -- operators modify the value of an expression by adding or subtracting 1. So, for example, if an int variable x contains 10, then ++x results in 11. Similarly, --x, again applied when x contains 10, gives a value of 9. In this case, the expression --x itself describes storage (the value of the variable x), so the resulting value is stored in x.

The preceding examples show the operators positioned before the expression (known as *pre-increment* or *pre-decrement*). They can, however, be placed after the expression instead (known as *post-increment* or *post-decrement*). To understand how the position of these operators affects their operation, you must appreciate the difference between the value stored by these operators and the result value they give. Both x++ and ++x cause the same result in x. However, the value of the expression itself is different. For example, if you say y = x++;, then the value assigned to y is the original value of x. If you say y = ++x;, then the value assigned to y is 1 more than the original value of x. In both cases, the value of x is incremented by 1.

Table 2.2 shows the values of x and y before and after particular assignments using these operators.

TABLE 2.2   Examples of Pre-and Post- Increment and Decrement Operations

Initial Value of *x*	Expression	Final Value of *y*	Final Value of *x*
5	y = x++	5	6
5	y = ++x	6	6

TABLE 2.2   Examples of Pre-and Post- Increment and Decrement Operations *(continued)*

Initial Value of x	Expression	Final Value of y	Final Value of x
5	y = x--	5	4
5	y = --x	4	4

The Unary Plus and Minus Operators: + and -

The unary operators + and - are distinct from the more common binary + and - operators, which are usually just referred to as add and subtract. Both the programmer and the compiler are able to determine which meaning these symbols should have in a given context.

Unary + has no effect beyond emphasizing the positive nature of a numeric literal. Unary - negates an expression. So, you might make a block of assignments like this:

```
1. x = -3;
2. y = +3;
3. z = -(y + 6);
```

In such an example, the only reasons for using the unary + operator are to make it explicit that y is assigned a positive value and perhaps to keep the code aligned more pleasingly. At line 3, notice that these operators are not restricted to literal values but can be applied to expressions equally well, so the value of z is initialized to –9.

The Bitwise Inversion Operator: ~

The ~ operator performs *bitwise inversion* on integral types. For each primitive type, Java uses a virtual machine representation that is platform independent. This means that the bit pattern used to represent a particular value in a particular variable type is always the same. This feature makes bit-manipulation operators even more useful, because they do not introduce platform dependencies. The ~ operator works by inverting all the 1 bits in a binary value to 0s and all the 0 bits to 1s.

For example, applying this operator to a byte containing 00001111 would result in the value 11110000. The same simple logic applies, no matter how many bits there are in the value being operated on. This operator is often used in conjunction with shift operators (<<, >>, and >>>) to perform bit manipulation, for example, when driving I/O ports.

The *Boolean* Complement Operator: *!*

The ! operator inverts the value of a boolean expression. So !true gives false and !false gives true. This operator is often used in the test part of an if() statement. The effect is to change the value of the boolean expression. In this way, for example, the body of the if() and else parts can be swapped. Consider these two equivalent code fragments:

```
1. public Object myMethod(Object x) {
2.   if (x instanceof String) {
3.     // do nothing
4.   }
5.   else {
6.     x = x.toString();
7.   }
8.   return x;
9. }
```

and

```
1. public Object myMethod(Object x) {
2.   if (!(x instanceof String)) {
3.     x = x.toString();
4.   }
5.   return x;
6. }
```

   In the first fragment, a test is made at line 2, but the conversion and assignment, at line 6, occur only if the test failed. This is achieved by the somewhat cumbersome technique of using only the else part of an if/else construction. The second fragment uses the complement operator so that the overall test performed at line 2 is reversed; it may be read as, "If it is false that x is an instance of a string," or more likely, "If x is not a string." Because of this change to the test, the conversion can be performed at line 3 in the situation that the test has succeeded; no else part is required, and the resulting code is cleaner and shorter.

This is a simple example, but such usage is common. This level of understanding will leave you well armed for the Certification Exam.

The Cast Operator: *(type)*

Casting is used for explicit conversion of the type of an expression. This is possible only for plausible target types. The compiler and the runtime system check for conformance with typing rules, which are described in Chapter 4, "Converting and Casting."

   Casts can be applied to change the type of primitive values—for example, forcing a double value into an int variable like this:

```
int circum = (int)(Math.PI * diameter);
```

If the cast, which is represented by the (int) part, were not present, the compiler would reject the assignment; a double value, such as is returned by the arithmetic here, cannot be represented accurately by an int variable. The cast is the programmer's way to say to the compiler, "I know you think this is risky, but trust me—I'm an engineer." Of course, if the result loses value or precision to the extent that the program does not work properly, then you are on your own. Casts can also be applied to object references. This often happens when you use containers, such as the Vector object. If you put, for example, String objects into a Vector, then when you extract them, the return type of the elementAt() method is simply Object. To use the recovered value as a String reference, a cast is needed, like this:

```
1. Vector v = new Vector();
2. v.add ("Hello");
3. String s = (String)v.get(0);
```

The cast here occurs at line 3, in the form (String). Although the compiler allows this cast, checks occur at runtime to determine if the object extracted from the Vector really is a String.

Chapter 4, "Converting and Casting," covers casting, the rules governing which casts are legal and which are not, and the nature of the runtime checks that are performed on cast operations.

Now that we have considered the unary operators, which have the highest precedence, we will discuss the five arithmetic operators.

The Arithmetic Operators

Next highest in precedence, after the unary operators, are the *arithmetic operators*. This group includes, but is not limited to, the four most familiar operators, which perform addition, subtraction, multiplication, and division. Arithmetic operators are split into two further subgroupings, as shown in Table 2.1. In the first group are *, /, and %; in the second group, at a lower precedence, are + and -. The following sections discuss these operators and also what happens when arithmetic goes wrong.

The Multiplication and Division Operators: * and /

The * and / operators perform multiplication and division on all primitive numeric types and char. Integer division will generate an ArithmeticException when attempting to divide by zero.

You probably understand multiplication and division quite well from years of rote learning at school. In programming, of course, some limitations are imposed by the representation of numbers in a computer. These limitations apply to all number formats, from byte to double, but are perhaps most noticeable in integer arithmetic.

If you multiply or divide two integers, the result will be calculated using integer arithmetic in either int or long representation. If the numbers are large enough, the result will be bigger than the maximum number that can be represented, and the final value will be meaningless. This condition is referred to as *overflow*. For example, byte values can represent a range of −128 to +127, so if two particular bytes have the values 64 and 4, then multiplying them should, arithmetically, give a value of 256 (100000000 in binary—note that this value has nine digits). Actually, when you store the result in a byte variable, you will get a value of 0, because only the low-order eight bits of the result can be represented.

On the other hand, when you divide with integer arithmetic, the result is forced into an integer and, typically, a lot of information that would have formed a fractional part of the answer is lost. This condition is referred to as *underflow*. For example, 7 / 4 should give 1.75, but integer arithmetic will result in a value of 1. You therefore have a choice in many expressions: multiply first and then divide, which risks overflow, or divide first and then multiply, which risks underflow. Conventional wisdom says that you should multiply first and then divide, because this at least might work perfectly, whereas dividing first almost definitely loses precision. Consider this example:

```
1. int a = 12345, b = 234567, c, d;
2. long e, f;
3.
4. c = a * b / b; // this should equal a, that is, 12345
5. d = a / b * b; // this should also equal a
6. System.out.println("a is " + a +
7.    "\nb is " + b +
8.    "\nc is " + c +
9.    "\nd is " + d);
10.
11. e = (long)a * b / b;
12. f = (long)a / b * b;
13. System.out.println(
14.    "\ne is " + e +
15.    "\nf is " + f);
```

The output from this code is

```
a is 12345
b is 234567
c is -5965
d is 0
e is 12345
f is 0
```

Do not worry about the exact numbers in this example. The important feature is that in the case where multiplication is performed first, the calculation overflows when performed with int values, resulting in a nonsense answer. However, the result is correct if the representation is wide enough—as when using the long variables. In both cases, dividing first has a catastrophic effect on the result, regardless of the width of the representation.

The Modulo Operator: %

Although multiplication and division are generally familiar operations, the % operator is perhaps less well known. The modulo operator gives a value that is related to the remainder of a division. It is generally applied to two integers, although it can be applied to floating-point numbers, too. In school, we learned that 7 divided by 4 gives 1, remainder 3. In Java, we say x = 7 % 4; and expect that x will have the value 3.

This is the simple behavior of the modulo operator, but additional concerns appear if you use negative or floating-point operands. In such cases, follow this procedure:

1. Reduce the magnitude of the left operand by the magnitude of the right one.

2. Repeat until the magnitude of the result is less than the magnitude of the right operand.

This gives the result of the modulo operator. Figure 2.1 shows some examples of this process.

Note that the sign of the result is entirely determined by the sign of the left operand. When the modulo operator is applied to floating-point types, the effect is to perform an integral number of subtractions, leaving a floating-point result that might well have a fractional part.

A useful rule of thumb for dealing with modulo calculations that involve negative numbers is this: Simply drop any negative signs from either operand and calculate the result. Then, if the original left operand was negative, negate the result. The sign of the right operand is irrelevant.

FIGURE 2.1   Calculating the result of the modulo operator for a variety of conditions

17 % 5

$17 - 5 \rightarrow 12$
$12 - 5 \rightarrow 7$
$7 - 5 \rightarrow 2$

$2 < 5$ so $17 \% 5 = \underline{\underline{2}}$

21 % 7

$21 - 7 = 14$
$14 - 7 = 7$
$7 - 7 = 0$

$0 < 7$ so $21 \% 7 = \underline{\underline{0}}$

7.6 % 2.9

$7.6 - 2.9 = 4.7$
$4.7 - 2.9 = 1.8$

$1.8 < 2.9$ so $7.6 \% 2.9 = \underline{1.8}$

−5 % 2

Here, to reduce absolute value by 2, we must <u>add</u>

$-5 + 2 = -3$
$-3 + 2 = -1$

Absolute value of −1 is 1 and $1 < 2$

so $-5 \% 2 = \underline{\underline{-1}}$

−5 % −2

Again, we must reduce absolute value of −5 by the absolute value of −2 which is 2

$-5 - (-2) = -3$
$-3 - (-2) = -1$

so again, $-5 \% -2 = \underline{\underline{-1}}$

The modulo operation involves division during execution. As a result, it can throw an `ArithmeticException` if it's applied to integral types and the second operand is 0.

You might not have learned about the modulo operator in school, but you will certainly recognize the + and - operators. Although basically familiar, the + operator has some capabilities beyond simple addition.

The Addition and Subtraction Operators: **+** and **-**

The operators + and - perform addition and subtraction. They apply to operands of any numeric type but, uniquely, + is also permitted where either operand is a `String` object. Java does not allow the programmer to perform operator overloading, but the + operator is overloaded by the language. This is not surprising, because in most languages that support multiple arithmetic types, the arithmetic operators (+, -, *, /, and so forth) are overloaded to handle these different types. Java, however, further overloads the + operator to support *concatenation*—that is, joining together—of `String` objects. The use of + with `String` arguments also performs conversions, and these can be succinct and expressive if you understand them. First, we will consider the use of the + operator in its conventional role of numeric addition.

Overloading is the term given when the same name is used for more than one piece of code, and the code that is to be used is selected by the argument or operand types provided. For example, the `println()` method can be given a `String` argument or an `int`. These two uses actually refer to entirely different methods; only the name is reused. Similarly, the + symbol is used to indicate addition of `int` values, but the exact same symbol is also used to indicate the addition of `float` values. These two forms of addition require entirely different code to execute; again, the operand types are used to decide which code is to be run. Where an operator can take different operand types, we refer to *operator overloading*. Some languages, but not Java, allow you to use operator overloading to define multiple uses of operators for your own types. Overloading is described in detail in Chapter 6, "Objects and Classes."

Where the + operator is applied to purely numeric operands, its meaning is simple and familiar. The operands are added together to produce a result. Of course, some promotions might take place, according to the normal rules, and the result might overflow. Generally, however, numeric addition behaves as you would expect.

Promotions are discussed in a later section, "Arithmetic Promotion of Operands."

If overflow or underflow occurs during numeric addition or subtraction, then data is lost but no exception occurs. A more detailed description of behavior in arithmetic error conditions appears in a later section, "Arithmetic Error Conditions." Most of the new understanding to be gained about the + operator relates to its role in concatenating text.

Where either of the operands of a + expression is a `String` object, the meaning of the operator is changed from numeric addition to string concatenation. In order to achieve this result, both operands must be handled as text. If both operands are in fact `String` objects, this is simple. If, however, one of the operands is not a `String` object, then the non-`String` operand is converted to a `String` object before the concatenation takes place.

For object types, conversion to a `String` object is performed by invoking the `toString()` method of that object. The `toString()` method is defined in `java.lang.Object`, which is the root of the class hierarchy, and therefore all objects inherit a `toString()` method. Sometimes, the effect of the `toString()` method is to produce rather cryptic text that is suitable only for debugging output, but it definitely exists and may legally be called.

Conversion of an operand of primitive type to a `String` is typically achieved by using, indirectly, the conversion utility methods in the wrapper classes. So, for example, an `int` value is converted by the static method `Integer.toString()`.

The `toString()` method in the `java.lang.Object` class produces a `String` that contains the name of the object's class and some identifying value—typically its reference value, separated by the at symbol (@). For example, this `String` might look like `java.lang.Object@1cc6dd`. This behavior is inherited by subclasses unless they deliberately override it.

It is a good idea to define a helpful `toString()` method in all your classes, even if you do not require it as part of the class behavior. Code the `toString()` method so that it represents the state of the object in a fashion that can assist in debugging; for example, output the names and values of the main instance variables.

To prepare for the Certification Exam questions, and to use the + operator effectively in your own programs, you should understand the following points:

- For a + expression with two operands of primitive numeric type, the result
  - Is of a primitive numeric type.
  - Is at least `int`, because of normal promotions.
  - Is of a type at least as wide as the wider of the two operands.
  - Has a value calculated by promoting the operands to the result type and then performing the addition using that type. This might result in overflow or loss of precision.
- For a + expression with any operand that is not of primitive numeric type,
  - At least one operand must be a `String` object or literal; otherwise, the expression is illegal.
  - Any remaining non-`String` operands are converted to `String`, and the result of the expression is the concatenation of all operands.
- To convert an operand of some object type to a `String`, the conversion is performed by invoking the `toString()` method of that object.
- To convert an operand of a primitive type to a `String`, the conversion is performed by a static method in a container class, such as `Integer.toString()`.

> If you want to control the formatting of the converted result, you should use the facilities in the `java.text` package.

Now that you understand arithmetic operators and the concatenation of text using the + operator, you should realize that sometimes arithmetic does not work as intended—it could result in an error of some kind. The next section discusses what happens under such error conditions.

Arithmetic Error Conditions

We expect arithmetic to produce "sensible" results that reflect the mathematical meaning of the expression being evaluated. However, because the computation is performed on a machine with specific limits on its ability to represent numbers, calculations can sometimes result in errors. You saw, in the section on the multiplication and division operators, that overflow and underflow can occur if the operands are too large or too small. In exceptional conditions, the following rules apply:

- Integer division by zero, including modulo (%) operation, results in an `ArithmeticException`.

- No other arithmetic causes any exception. Instead, the operation proceeds to a result, even though that result might be arithmetically incorrect.

- Floating-point calculations represent out-of-range values using the IEEE 754 infinity, minus infinity, and Not a Number (NaN) values. Named constants representing these are declared in both the `Float` and `Double` classes.

- Integer calculations, other than division by zero, that cause overflow or a similar error simply leave the final, typically truncated bit pattern in the result. This bit pattern is derived from the operation and the number representation and might even be of the wrong sign. Because the operations and number representations do not depend upon the platform, neither do the result values under error conditions.

These rules describe the effect of error conditions, but some additional significance is associated with the NaN values. NaN values are used to indicate that a calculation has no result in ordinary arithmetic, such as some calculations involving infinity or the square root of a negative number.

Some floating-point calculations can return a NaN. This occurs, for example, as a result of calculating the square root of a negative number. Two NaN values are defined in the `java.lang` package (`Float.NaN` and `Double.NaN`) and are considered non-ordinal for comparisons. This means that for *any* value of x, including NaN itself, all of the following comparisons will return false:

```
x < Float.NaN
x <= Float.NaN
x == Float.NaN
x > Float.NaN
x >= Float.NaN
```

In fact, the test

```
Float.NaN != Float.NaN
```

and the equivalent with `Double.NaN` return true, as you might deduce from the fact that `x ==` `Float.NaN` gives false even if `x` contains `Float.NaN`.

The most appropriate way to test for a NaN result from a calculation is to use the `Float` `.isNaN(float)` or `Double.isNaN(double)` static method provided in the `java.lang` package.

Arithmetic Promotion of Operands

Arithmetic promotion of operands takes place before any binary operator is applied so that all numeric operands are at least `int` type. This promotion has an important consequence for the unsigned right-shift operator when applied to values that are narrower than `int`.

The diagram in Figure 2.2 shows the process by which a `byte` is shifted right. First the `byte` is promoted to an `int`, which is done treating the `byte` as a signed quantity. Next, the shift occurs, and 0 bits are indeed propagated into the top bits of the result—but these bits are not part of the original `byte`. When the result is cast down to a `byte` again, the high-order bits of that `byte` appear to have been created by a signed shift right, rather than an unsigned one. This is why you should generally not use the logical right-shift operator with operands smaller than an `int`: It is unlikely to produce the result you expected.

FIGURE 2.2   Unsigned right shift of a byte

Calculation for –64 >>> 4.

Original data (–64 decimal)		11000000	
Promote to `int` gives:	11111111	11111111 11111111	11000000
Shift right unsigned 4 bits gives:	00001111	11111111 11111111	11111100
Truncate to byte gives:			11111100
Expected result was:			00001100

The Comparison Operators

Comparison operators—<, <=, >, >=, ==, and !=—return a `boolean` result; the relation as written is either true or it is false. In addition, the `instanceof` operator determines whether or not a given object is an instance of a particular class. These operators are commonly used to form conditions, such as in `if()` statements or in loop control. There are three types of comparison: *Ordinal* comparisons test the relative value of numeric operands. *Object-type comparisons* determine whether the run-time type of an object is of a particular type or a subclass of that particular type. *Equality comparisons* test whether two values are the same and may be applied to values of non-numeric types.

The Ordinal Comparisons Operators: <, <=, >, and >=

The ordinal comparison operators are

- Less than: <
- Less than or equal to: <=
- Greater than: >
- Greater than or equal to: >=

These are applicable to all numeric types and to `char` and produce a `boolean` result.
So, for example, given the following declarations,

```
int p = 9;
int q = 65;
int r = -12;
float f = 9.0F;
char c = 'A';
```

the following tests all return true:

```
p < q
f < q
f <= c
c > r
c >= q
```

Notice that arithmetic promotions are applied when these operators are used. This is entirely according to the normal rules discussed in Chapter 4. For example, although it would be an error to attempt to assign, say, the `float` value 9.0F to the `char` variable c, it is perfectly acceptable to compare the two. To achieve the result, Java promotes the smaller type to the larger type; hence the `char` value 'A' (represented by the Unicode value 65) is promoted to a `float` 65.0F. The comparison is then performed on the resulting `float` values.

Although the ordinal comparisons operate satisfactorily on dissimilar numeric types, including `char`, they are not applicable to any non-numeric types. They cannot take `boolean` or any class-type operands.

The *instanceof* Operator

The `instanceof` operator tests the class of an object at runtime. The left argument can be any object reference expression, usually a variable or an array element, whereas the right operand must be a class, interface, or array type. You cannot use a `java.lang.Class` object reference or a `String` representing the name of the class as the right operand. A compiler error results if the left operand cannot be cast to the right operand.

Casting is discussed in Chapter 4.

This code fragment shows an example of how `instanceof` may be used. Assume that a class hierarchy exists with `Person` as a base class and `Parent` as a subclass:

```
1. public class Classroom {
2.    private Hashtable inTheRoom = new Hashtable();
3.    public void enterRoom(Person p) {
4.       inTheRoom.put(p.getName(), p);
5.    }
6.    public Person getParent(String name) {
7.       Object p = inTheRoom.get(name);
8.       if (p instanceof Parent) {
9.         return (Parent)p;
10.      }
11.      else {
12.         return null;
13.      }
14.   }
15. }
```

The method `getParent()` at lines 6–14 checks to see if the `Hashtable` contains a parent with the specified name. This is done by first searching the `Hashtable` for an entry with the given name and then testing to see if the entry that is returned is actually a `Parent`. The `instanceof` operator returns true if the class of the left argument is the same as, or is some subclass of, the class specified by the right operand.

The right operand may equally well be an interface. In such a case, the test determines whether the object at the left argument implements the specified interface.

You can also use the `instanceof` operator to test whether a reference refers to an array. Because arrays are themselves objects in Java, this is natural enough, but the test that is performed actually checks two things: First, it checks whether the object is an array, and then it checks whether the element type of that array is some subclass of the element type of the right argument. This is a logical extension of the behavior that is shown for simple types and reflects the idea that an array of, say, `Button` objects is an array of `Component` objects, because a `Button` is a `Component`. A test for an array type looks like this:

```
if (x instanceof Component[])
```

Note, however, that you cannot simply test for "any array of any element type," as the syntax. This line is not legal:

```
if (x instanceof [])
```

Neither is it sufficient to test for arrays of `Object` element type like this

```
if (x instanceof Object [])
```

because the array might be of a primitive base type, in which case the test will fail.

 Although it is not required by the Certification Exam, you might find it useful to know that you can determine whether an object is in fact an array without regard to the base type. You can do this using the `isArray()` method of the `Class` class. For example, this test returns true if the variable `myObject` refers to an array: `myObject.getClass().isArray()`.

If the left argument of the `instanceof` operator is a `null` value, the `instanceof` test simply returns false; it does not cause an exception.

The Equality Comparison Operators: == and !=

The operators `==` and `!=` test for equality and inequality, respectively, returning a `boolean` value. For primitive types, the concept of equality is quite straightforward and is subject to promotion rules so that, for example, a `float` value of 10.0 is considered equal to a `byte` value of 10. For variables of object type, the "value" is taken as the reference to the object—typically, the memory address. You should not use these operators to compare the contents of objects, such as strings, because they will return true if two references refer to the same object, rather than if the two objects have equivalent value. *Object comparisons* compare the data of two objects, whereas *reference comparisons* compare the memory locations of two objects.

To achieve a content or semantic comparison, for example, so that two different `Double` objects containing the value 1234 are considered equal, you must use the `equals()` method rather than the `==` or `!=` operator.

To operate appropriately, the `equals()` method must have been defined for the class of the objects you are comparing. To determine whether it has, check the documentation supplied with the JDK or, for third-party classes, produced by Javadoc. The documentation should report that an `equals()` method is defined for the class and overrides `equals()` in some superclass. If this is not indicated, then you should assume that the `equals()` method will not produce a useful content comparison. You also need to know that `equals()` is defined as accepting an `Object` argument, but the actual argument must be of the same type as the object upon which the method is invoked—that is, for `x.equals(y)`, the test `y instanceof the-type-of-x` must be true. If this is not the case, then `equals()` must return false.

The Bitwise Operators

The *bitwise operators*—`&`, `^`, and `|`—provide bitwise AND, eXclusive-OR (XOR), and OR operations, respectively. They are applicable to integral types. Collections of bits are sometimes used to save storage space where several `boolean` values are needed or to represent the states of a collection of binary inputs from physical devices.

Defining an *equals()* Method

This information is not required for the Certification Exam but is generally of value when writing real programs. If you define an equals() method in your own classes, you should be careful to observe three rules, or else your classes might behave incorrectly in some specific circumstances.

First, the argument to the equals() method is an Object; you must avoid the temptation to make the argument to equals() specific to the class you are defining. If you do this, you will have overloaded the equals() method, not overridden it, and functionality in other parts of the Java APIs that depends on the equals() method will fail. Perhaps most significant, lookup methods in containers, such as containsKey() and get() in the HashMap, will fail.

The second rule is that the equals() method should be commutative: The result of x.equals(y) should always be the same as the result of y.equals(x).

The final rule is that if you define an equals() method, you should also define a hashCode() method. This method should return the same value for objects that compare equal using the equals() method. Again, this behavior is needed to support the containers and other classes. A minimal but acceptable behavior for the hashCode() method is simply to return 1. Doing so removes any efficiency gains that hashing would give, forcing a HashMap to behave like a linked list when storing such objects, but at least the behavior is correct.

The bitwise operations calculate each bit of their results by comparing the corresponding bits of the two operands on the basis of these three rules:

- For AND operations, 1 AND 1 produces 1. Any other combination produces 0.
- For XOR operations, 1 XOR 0 produces 1, as does 0 XOR 1. (All these operations are commutative.) Any other combination produces 0.
- For OR operations, 0 OR 0 produces 0. Any other combination produces 1.

The names AND, XOR, and OR are intended to be mnemonic for these operations. You get a 1 result from an AND operation if both the first operand *and* the second operand are 1. An XOR gives a 1 result if one *or* the other operand, but not both (this is the *exclusiveness*), is 1. In the OR operation, you get a 1 result if either the first operand *or* the second operand (*or* both) is 1. These rules are represented in Tables 2.3 through 2.5.

Compare the rows of each table with the corresponding rule for the operations listed in the previous bullets. You will see that for the AND operation, the only situation that leads to a 1 bit as the result is when both operands are 1 bits. For XOR, a 1 bit results when one or the other (but not both) of the operands is a 1 bit. Finally, for the OR operation, the result is a 1 bit, except when both operands are 0 bits. Now let's see how this concept works when applied to whole binary numbers, rather than just single bits. The approach can be applied to any size of integer, but we will look at bytes because they serve to illustrate the idea without putting so many digits on the page as to cause confusion. Consider this example:

```
          00110011
          11110000
    AND   --------
          00110000
```

TABLE 2.3   The AND Operation

Op1	Op2	Op1 AND Op2
0	0	0
0	1	0
1	0	0
1	1	1

TABLE 2.4   The XOR Operation

Op1	Op2	Op1 XOR Op2
0	0	0
0	1	1
1	0	1
1	1	0

TABLE 2.5   The OR Operation

Op1	Op2	Op1 OR Op2
0	0	0
0	1	1

TABLE 2.5   The OR Operation *(continued)*

Op1	Op2	Op1 OR Op2
1	0	1
1	1	1

Observe that each bit in the result is calculated solely on the basis of the two bits appearing directly above it in the calculation. Take a look at the least significant bit:

```
            00110011
            11110000
    AND     --------
            00110000
```

This result bit is calculated as 1 and 0, which gives 0.
Now observe the fourth bit from the left:

```
            00110011
            11110000
    AND     --------
            00110000
```

This result bit is calculated as 1 AND 1, which gives 1. All the other bits in the result are calculated in the same fashion, using the two corresponding bits and the rules stated earlier.

Exclusive-OR operations are done by using the same bit-by-bit approach, using the appropriate rules for calculating the individual bits, as the following calculations show:

```
          00110011                00110011
          11110000                11110000
    XOR   --------        XOR     --------
          11000011                11000011
```

The indicated bit positions above are calculated as either 1 XOR 0 or as 0 XOR 1, producing 1 in either case.

```
            00110011
            11110000
    XOR     --------
            11000011
```

In the previous calculation, the result bit is 0 because both operand bits were 1.

```
            00110011
            11110000
    XOR     --------
            11000011
```

And here, the 0 operand bits also result in a 0 result bit.

The OR operation again takes a similar approach, but with its own rules for calculating the result bits. Consider this example:

```
        00110011
        11110000
OR    --------
        11110011
```

Here, the two operand bits are 1 and 0, so the result is 1.

```
        00110011
        11110000
OR    ----+---
        11110011
```

However, in this calculation, both operand bits are 0, which is the condition that produces a 0 result bit for the OR operation.

Although programmers usually apply these operators to the bits in integer variables, it is also permitted to apply them to Boolean operands.

Boolean Operations

The comparison operators behave in fundamentally the same way when applied to arguments of boolean, rather than integral, types. However, instead of calculating the result on a bit-by-bit basis, the boolean values are treated as single bits, with true corresponding to a 1 bit and false to a 0 bit. The general rules discussed in the previous section may be modified like this when applied to boolean values:

- For AND operations, true AND true produces true. Any other combination produces false.
- For XOR operations, true XOR false produces true, and false XOR true produces true. Other combinations produce false.
- For OR operations, false OR false produces false. Any other combination produces true.

These rules are represented in Tables 2.6 through 2.8.

Again, compare these tables with the rules stated in the bulleted list. Also compare them with Tables 2.3 through 2.5, which describe the same operations on bits. You will see that 1 bits are replaced by true, and 0 bits are replaced by false.

TABLE 2.6   The AND Operation on *boolean* Values

Op1	Op2	Op1 AND Op2
false	false	false
false	true	false

TABLE 2.6   The AND Operation on *boolean* Values *(continued)*

Op1	Op2	Op1 AND Op2
true	false	false
true	true	true

TABLE 2.7   The XOR Operation on *boolean* Values

Op1	Op2	Op1 XOR Op2
false	false	false
false	true	true
true	false	true
true	true	false

TABLE 2.8   The OR Operation on *boolean* Values

Op1	Op2	Op1 OR Op2
false	false	false
false	true	true
true	false	true
true	true	true

As with all operations, the two operands must be of compatible types. So, if either operand is of `boolean` type, both must be. Java does not permit you to cast any type to `boolean`; instead you must use comparisons or methods that return `boolean` values.

The next section covers the short-circuit logical operators. These operators perform logical AND and OR operations but are slightly different in implementation from the operators just discussed.

The Short-Circuit Logical Operators

The short-circuit logical operators—&& and ||—provide logical AND and OR operations on boolean types. Note that no XOR operation is provided. Superficially, these operators are similar to the & and | operators, with the limitation of being applicable only to boolean values and not integral types. However, the && and || operations have a valuable additional feature: the ability to "short circuit" a calculation if the result is definitely known. This feature makes these operators central to a popular null-reference-handling idiom in Java programming. They can also improve efficiency.

The main difference between the & and && and between the | and || operators is that the right operand might not be evaluated in the latter cases. We will look at how this happens in the rest of this section. This behavior is based on two mathematical rules that define conditions under which the result of a boolean AND or OR operation is entirely determined by one operand without regard for the value of the other:

- For an AND operation, if one operand is false, the result is false, without regard to the other operand.

- For an OR operation, if one operand is true, the result is true, without regard to the other operand.

To put it another way, for any boolean value X,

- false AND X = false

- true OR X = true

Given these rules, if the left operand of a boolean AND operation is false, then the result is definitely false, whatever the right operand. It is therefore unnecessary to evaluate the right operand. Similarly, if the left operand of a boolean OR operation is true, the result is definitely true and the right operand need not be evaluated.

Consider a fragment of code intended to print out a String if that String exists and is longer than 20 characters:

```
1. if (s != null) {
2.    if (s.length() > 20) {
3.       System.out.println(s);
4.    }
5. }
```

However, the same operation can be coded very succinctly like this:

```
1. if ((s != null) && (s.length() > 20)) {
2.    System.out.println(s);
3. }
```

If the String reference s is null, then calling the s.length() method would raise a NullPointerException. In both of these examples, however, the situation never arises. In the second example, avoiding execution of the s.length() method is a direct consequence of the short-circuit behavior of the && operator. If the test (s != null) returns false (if s is in fact null), then the whole test expression is guaranteed to be false. Where the first operand is false, the && operator does not evaluate the second operand; so, in this case, the expression (s.length() > 20) is not evaluated.

Although these shortcuts do not affect the result of the operation, side effects might well be changed. If the evaluation of the right operand involves a side effect, then omitting the evaluation will change the overall meaning of the expression in some way. This behavior distinguishes these operators from the bitwise operators applied to boolean types. Consider these fragments:

```
//first example:
1. int val = (int)(2 * Math.random());
2. boolean test = (val == 0) || (++val == 2);
3. System.out.println("test = " + test + "\nval = " + val);
//second example:
1. int val = (int)(2 * Math.random());
2. boolean test = (val == 0) | (++val == 2);
3. System.out.println("test = " + test + "\nval = " + val);
```

The first example will sometimes print

```
test = true
val = 0
```

and sometimes it will print

```
test = true
val = 2
```

The second example will sometimes print

```
test = true
val = 1
```

and sometimes it will print

```
test = true
val = 2
```

The point is that in the case of the short-circuit operator, if val starts out at 0, then the second part of the expression (++val) is never executed, and val remains at 0. Alternatively, val starts at 1 and is incremented to 2. In the second case, the non-short-circuit version, the increment always occurs, and val ends up as either 1 or 2, depending on the original value returned by the random() method. In all cases, the value of test is true, because either val starts out at 0, or it starts at 1 and the test (++val == 2) is true.

So, the essential points about the && and || operators are as follows:

- They accept boolean operands.

- They evaluate the right operand only if the outcome is not certain based solely on the left operand. This is determined using these identities:

  - false AND X = false

  - true OR X = true

The next section discusses the conditional, or ternary, operator. Like the short-circuit logical operators, this operator may be less familiar than others, especially to programmers without a background in C, C++, or C#.

The Conditional Operator

The *conditional operator*—?:— (also known as a *ternary operator*, because it takes three operands) provides a way to code simple conditions (if/else) into a single expression. The (boolean) expression to the left of the ? is evaluated. If true, the result of the whole expression is the value of the expression to the left of the colon; otherwise, it is the value of the expression to the right of the colon. The expressions on either side of the colon must be assignment-compatible with the result type.

For example, if a, b, and c are int variables, and x is a boolean, then the statement a = x ? b : c; is directly equivalent to the textually longer version:

```
1. if (x) {
2.    a = b;
3. }
4. else {
5.    a = c;
6. }
```

Of course x, a, b, and c can all be complex expressions if you desire.

Many people do not like the conditional operator, and in some companies its use is prohibited by the local style guide. This operator does keep source code more concise, but in many cases an optimizing compiler will generate equally compact and efficient code from the longer, and arguably more readable, if/else approach. One particularly effective way to abuse the conditional operator is to nest it, producing expressions of the form a = b ? c ? d : e ? f : g : h ? i : j ? k : l;. Whatever your feelings or corporate mandate, you should at least be able to read this operator, because you will find it used by other programmers.

Here are the points you should review for handling conditional operators in an exam question, or to use them properly in a program. In an expression of the form a = x ? b : c;

- The types of the expressions b and c should be compatible and are made identical through conversion.

- The type of the expression x should be boolean.

- The types of the expressions b and c should be assignment-compatible with the type of a.

- The value assigned to a will be b if x is true or will be c if x is false.

Now that we have discussed the conditional (ternary) operator, only one group of operators remains: the assignment operators.

The Assignment Operators

*Assignment operators—= and*op=— set the value of a variable or expression to a new value. Assignments are supported by a battery of operators. Simple assignment uses =. Operators such as += and *= provide compound "calculate and assign" functions. These compound operators take a general form *op=*, where *op* can be any of the binary non-boolean operators already discussed. In general, for any compatible expressions *x* and *y*, the expression x *op=* y is a shorthand for x = x *op* y. However, there are two differences you must know. First, be aware that side effects in the expression *x* are evaluated exactly once, not twice, as the expanded view might suggest. The second issue is that the assignment operators include an implicit cast. Consider this situation:

```
1. byte x = 2;
2. x += 3;
```

If this had been written using the longhand approach

```
1. byte x = 2;
2. x = (byte)(x + 3);
```

the cast to byte would have been necessary because the result of an integer addition is at least an int. In the first case, using the assignment operator, this cast is implied. This is one of two situations where Java allows down-casting without explicit programmer intervention. (The other situation is in combined declaration and initialization.) Be sure to compare this with the general principles of assignment and casting laid out in Chapter 4.

The statement x += 2; involves typing two fewer characters but is otherwise no more effective than the longer version x = x + 2; and is neither more nor less readable. However, if x is a complex expression, such as target[temp .calculateOffset(1.9F) + depth++].item, it is definitely more readable to express incrementing this value by 2 using the += 2 form. This is because these operators define that the exact same thing will be read on the right side as is written on the left side. So the maintainer does not have to struggle to decide whether the two complex expressions are actually the same, and the original programmer avoids some of the risk of mistyping a copy of the expression.

All the operators discussed up to this point have produced a value as a result of the operation. The expression 1 ? 2, for example, results in a value 3, which can then be used in some further way—perhaps assignment to a variable. The assignment operators in Java are considered to be operators because they have a resulting value. So, given three int variables a, b, and c, the statement a = b = c = 0; is entirely legal. It is executed from right to left, so that first 0 is assigned into the variable c. After it has been executed, the expression c = 0 takes the value that was assigned to the left side—that is, 0. Next, the assignment of b takes place, using the value of the expression to the right of the equal sign—again, 0. Similarly, that expression takes the value that was assigned, so finally the variable a is also set to 0.

Although *execution order* is determined by precedence and associativity, *evaluation order* of the arguments is not. Be sure you understand the points made in the section "Evaluation Order" at the start of this chapter.

As a general rule, avoid writing expressions that are complex enough for these issues to matter. A sequence of simply constructed expressions is easier to read and is less likely to cause confusion or other errors than complex ones. You are also likely to find that the compiler will optimize multiple simple expressions just as well as it would a single, very complex one.

Summary

We have covered a lot of material in this chapter, so let's recap some of the key points.

The unary operators were the first topics we covered. Recall that they take only a single operand. The seven unary operators are ++, --, +, -, !, ~, and (). Their key points are as follows:

- The ++ and -- operators increment and decrement expressions. The position of the operator (either prefix or suffix) is significant.

- The + operator has no effect on an expression other than to make it clear that a literal constant is positive. The - operator negates an expression's value.

- The ! operator inverts the value of a boolean expression.

- The ~ operator inverts the bit pattern of an integral expression.

- The (*type*) operator is used to persuade the compiler to permit certain assignments that the programmer believes are appropriate, but that break the normal, rigorous rules of the language. Its use is subject to extensive checks at compile time and runtime.

Next we covered arithmetic operators. We discussed in detail the four most familiar operators, which perform addition, subtraction, multiplication, and division. Recall that this group is further split into two subgroupings. There are five arithmetic operators:

- Multiplication: *

- Division: /

- Modulo: %
- Addition and `String` concatenation: +
- Subtraction: –

The arithmetic operators can be applied to any numeric type. Also, the + operator performs text concatenation if either of its operands is a `String` object. Under the conditions where one operand in a + expression is a `String` object, the other is forced to be a `String` object, too. Conversions are performed as necessary. They might result in cryptic text, but they are definitely legal.

Under conditions of arithmetic overflow or similar errors, accuracy is generally lost silently. Only integer division by zero can throw an exception. Floating-point calculations can produce NaN—indicating Not a Number (that is, the expression has no meaning in normal arithmetic)—or infinity as their result under error conditions.

We also discussed bitwise operators, which are sometimes used to save storage space, for instance. There are three bitwise operators: &, ^, and |. They are usually named AND, eXclusive-OR (XOR), and OR, respectively. For these operators, the following points apply:

- In bitwise operations, each result bit is calculated on the basis of the two bits from the same, corresponding position in the operands.
- For the AND operation, a 1 bit results if the first operand bit and the second operand bit are both 1.
- For the XOR operation, a 1 bit results only if exactly one operand bit is 1.
- For the OR operation, a 1 bit results if either the first operand bit or the second operand bit is 1.

For `boolean` operations, the arguments and results are treated as single-bit values with true represented by 1 and false by 0.

We described assignment operators, which set the value of a variable or expression to a new value. The key points about the assignment operators are as follows:

- Simple assignment, using =, assigns the value of the right operand to the left operand.
- The value of an object is its reference, not its contents.
- The right operand must be a type that is assignment-compatible with the left operand. Assignment compatibility and conversions are discussed in detail in Chapter 4.
- The assignment operators all return a value so that they can be used within larger expressions. The value returned is the value that was assigned to the left operand.
- The compound assignment operators, of the form *op=*, when applied in an expression like a *op=* b; , appear to behave like a = a *op* b;, except that the expression a and any of its side effects are evaluated only once.

Compound assignment operators exist for all binary, non-`boolean` operators: *=, /=, %=, +=, –=, &=, ^=, and |=. We have now discussed all the operators provided by Java.

The ternary operator ?: (also referred to as the conditional operator) requires three operands and provides the programmer with a more compact way to write an `if/else` statement.

The short-circuit Boolean operators **&&** and **||** are binary operators that allow the programmer to circumvent evaluating one or more expressions, thereby making the code more efficient at runtime.

The remainder of the operators discussed in this chapter are the comparison operators <, <=, >, >=, and `instanceof`. These binary operators compare the left operand with the right operand and return a Boolean result of either `true` or `false`.

Exam Essentials

Understand the functionality of all the operators discussed in this chapter.   These operators are unary operators, the cast operator, binary arithmetic operators, comparison operators, bitwise operators, short-circuit operators, the conditional operator, and assignment operators.

Understand when arithmetic promotion takes place.   You should know the type of the result of unary and binary arithmetic operations performed on operands of any type.

Understand the difference between object equality and reference equality.   Object equality checks the data of two possibly distinct objects. Reference equality checks whether two references point to the same object.

Know the functionality of the `equals()` **method of the** `Object`, `Boolean`, **and** `String` **classes.** The `Object` version uses a reference equality check; the `Boolean` and `String` versions compare encapsulated data.

Review Questions

1. After execution of the following code fragment, what are the values of the variables x, a, and b?

    ```
    1. int x, a = 6, b = 7;
    2. x = a++ + b++;
    ```

    A. x = 15, a = 7, b = 8
    B. x = 15, a = 6, b = 7
    C. x = 13, a = 7, b = 8
    D. x = 13, a = 6, b = 7

2. Which of the following expressions are legal? (Choose all that apply.)

    A. `int x = 6; x = !x;`
    B. `int x = 6; if (!(x > 3)) {}`
    C. `int x = 6; x = ~x;`

3. Which of the following expressions results in a positive value in x?

    A. `int x = -1; x = x >>> 5;`
    B. `int x = -1; x = x >>> 32;`
    C. `byte x = -1; x = x >>> 5;`
    D. `int x = -1; x = x >> 5;`

4. Which of the following expressions are legal? (Choose all that apply.)

    A. `String x = "Hello"; int y = 9; x += y;`
    B. `String x = "Hello"; int y = 9; if (x == y) {}`
    C. `String x = "Hello"; int y = 9; x = x + y;`
    D. `String x = "Hello"; int y = 9; y = y + x;`

5. What is -8 % 5?

    A. -3
    B. 3
    C. -2
    D. 2

6. What is 7 % -4?

    A. -3
    B. 3
    C. -4
    D. 4

7.   What results from running the following code?

```
1. public class Xor {
2.    public static void main(String args[]) {
3.       byte b = 10; // 00001010 binary
4.       byte c = 15; // 00001111 binary
5.       b = (byte)(b ^ c);
6.       System.out.println("b contains " + b);
7.    }
8. }
```

   A. The output: b contains 10

   B. The output: b contains 5

   C. The output: b contains 250

   D. The output: b contains 245

8.   What results from attempting to compile and run the following code?

```
1. public class Conditional {
2.    public static void main(String args[]) {
3.       int x = 4;
4.       System.out.println("value is " +
5.          ((x > 4) ? 99.99 : 9));
6.    }
7. }
```

   A. The output: value is 99.99

   B. The output: value is 9

   C. The output: value is 9.0

   D. A compiler error at line 5

9.   What does the following code do?

```
Integer i = null;
if (i != null  &  i.intValue() == 5)
  System.out.println("Value is 5");
```

   A. Prints "Value is 5".

   B. Throws an exception.

10. Is it possible to define a class called Thing so that the following method can return true under certain circumstances?

```
boolean weird(Thing s) {
  Integer x = new Integer(5);
  return s.equals(x);
}
```

   A. Yes

   B. No

11. Suppose ob1 and ob2 are references to instances of java.lang.Object. If (ob1 == ob2) is false, can ob1.equals(ob2) ever be true?

   A. Yes

   B. No

12. When a byte is added to a char, what is the type of the result?

   A. byte

   B. char

   C. int

   D. short

   E. You can't add a byte to a char.

13. When a short is added to a float, what is the type of the result?

   A. short

   B. int

   C. float

   D. You can't add a short to a float.

14. Which statement is true about the following method?

```
int selfXor(int i) {
  return i ^ i;
}
```

   A. It always returns 0.

   B. It always returns 1.

   C. It always an int where every bit is 1.

   D. The returned value varies depending on the argument.

15. Which of the following operations might throw an `ArithmeticException`?

    A. >>

    B. >>>

    C. <<

    D. None of these

16. Which of the following operations might throw an `ArithmeticException`?

    A. +

    B. -

    C. *

    D. /

    E. None of these

17. What is the return type of the `instanceof` operator?

    A. A reference

    B. A class

    C. An `int`

    D. A `boolean`

18. Which of the following may appear on the left-hand side of an `instanceof` operator?

    A. A reference

    B. A class

    C. An interface

    D. A variable of primitive type

19. Which of the following may appear on the right-hand side of an `instanceof` operator? (Choose all that apply.)

    A. A reference

    B. A class

    C. An interface

    D. A variable of primitive type

    E. The name of a primitive type

20. What is `-50 >> 1`?

    A. A negative number with very large magnitude.

    B. A positive number with very large magnitude.

    C. -100

    D. -25

    E. 100

    F. 25

Answers to Review Questions

1. C. The assignment statement is evaluated as if it were

```
x = a + b; a = a + 1; b = b + 1;
```

So the assignment to x is made using the sum of 6 + 7, giving 13. After the addition, the values of a and b are incremented; the new values, 7 and 8, are stored in the variables.

2. B, C. In option A, the use of ! is illegal because x is of int type, not boolean. In option B, the comparison operation is valid, because the expression (x > 3) is a boolean type and the ! operator can properly be applied to it. In option C, the bitwise inversion operator is legally applied to an integral type.

3. A. Option A uses the unsigned right shift, so 0s are shifted into the most significant positions; any two's-complement number with a 0 in the most significant position is positive. Option B shifts by 32 % 32 = 0 positions, so there is no effect. Option C doesn't compile, because "x >>> 5" is an int, which can't be assigned to a byte. Option D applies the signed shift to a negative operand, so the result is negative.

4. A, C. Options A and C are equivalent. They both add a String to an int; the resulting String is assigned to x, whose type is String, so the code is legal. Option B doesn't compile because an int and a String may not be compared. C is illegal because the last statement tries to assign a String to an int.

5. A. When doing modulo arithmetic with a negative left-hand operand, the result is the negative of what it would be if both operands were positive. So -8 % 5 is the negative of 8 % 5.

6. B. When doing modulo arithmetic with a negative right-hand operand, the result is the same as it would be if the right-hand operand were positive. So 7 % -4 is the same as 7 % 4.

7. B. The XOR operator produces a 1 bit in any position where the operand bits are different. So 00001010 ^ 00001111 is 00000101, which is 5.

8. C. In this code, the optional result values for the conditional operator, 99.99 (a double) and 9 (an int), are of different types. The result type of a conditional operator must be fully determined at compile time, and in this case the type chosen, using the rules of promotion for binary operands, is double. Because the result is a double, the output value is printed in a floating-point format.

If the two possible argument types had been entirely incompatible—for example, (x > 4) ? "Hello" : 9—then the compiler would have issued an error at that line.

9. B. The & operator does not short circuit. Even though the left-hand operand is null, the right-hand operand is still evaluated. Attempting to call the intValue() method on null results in a NullPointerException.

10. A. The Thing class is free to override equals() to do anything it likes. The method can even return true when comparing the current instance to an instance of Integer.

11. B. The `Object` class' `equals()` method just does an `==` check, so if (`ob1` `==` `ob2`) is `false`, then `ob1.equals(ob2)` will always be `false`.

12. C. `Byte`, `short`, and `char` operands are widened to `int`s before the addition is performed. The result type is the same as the operands: `int`.

13. C. When a short is added to a float, the narrower data type (short) is widened to match the wider type (float), and the result is a float.

14. A. Any value XOR itself is always 0.

15. D. Only non-floating division can throw an `ArithmeticException`.

16. D. Only non-floating division can throw an `ArithmeticException`.

17. D. The `instanceof` operator generates a `boolean` value.

18. A. Only references may be the left-hand operands of `instanceof`.

19. B, C. Classes, interfaces, arrays of classes, and arrays of interfaces may be the right-hand operands of `instanceof`.

20. D. `>>` is the signed right-shift operator, so the result has the same sign as the left-hand operand. Right-shifting by n bit positions is equivalent to dividing by 2-to-the-n, so the result is -50 / 2, which is -25.

Chapter

3

Modifiers

JAVA CERTIFICATION EXAM OBJECTIVES COVERED IN THIS CHAPTER:

✓ 1.2 Develop code that declares an interface. Develop code that implements or extends one or more interfaces. Develop code that extends an abstract class.

✓ 1.4 Develop code that declares both static and non-static methods, and - if appropriate - use method names that adhere to the JavaBeans naming standards. Also develop code that declares and uses a variable-length argument list.

✓ 5.3 Explain the effect of modifiers on inheritance with respect to constructors, instance or static variables, and instance or static methods.

✓ 7.1 Given a code example and a scenario, write code that uses the appropriate access modifiers, package declarations, and import statements to interact with (through access or inheritance) the code in the example.

When you create a class, a variable, or a method, you have some control over how it will behave under certain situations, such as access from external classes, multi-threaded contention, or serialization. You enforce this control by using modifiers.

In this chapter you will learn about all of Java's modifiers as they apply to top-level classes. Inner classes are not discussed here but are covered in Chapter 6, "Objects and Classes."

Modifier Overview

Modifiers are Java keywords that give the compiler information about the nature of code, data, or classes. Modifiers specify, for example, that a particular feature is static, final, or transient. (A *feature* is a class, a method, or a variable.) A group of modifiers, called *access modifiers*, dictates which classes are allowed to use a feature. Other modifiers can be used in combination to describe the attributes of a feature.

The most common modifiers are the access modifiers:

- `public`
- `private`
- `protected`

The remaining modifiers do not fall into any clear categorization. They are

- `final`
- `abstract`
- `static`
- `native`
- `transient`
- `synchronized`
- `volatile`

In the following sections, we will first look at the access modifiers, and then look at the other modifiers.

The Access Modifiers

Access modifiers control which classes may use a feature. A class's features are

- The class itself
- Its member variables
- Its methods and constructors
- Its nested classes

 Since nested (or inner) classes are not presented until Chapter 6, this discussion concerns only access modifiers as they apply to regular classes, member variables, methods, and constructors.

Note that, with rare exceptions, the only variables that may be controlled by access modifiers are class-level variables. The variables that you declare and use within a class's methods may not have access modifiers. This makes sense; a method variable can be used only within its method.

The access modifiers are

- public
- private
- protected

The only access modifier permitted to non-nested classes is public; there is no such thing as a protected or private top-level class.

A feature may have at most one access modifier. If a feature has no access modifier, its access defaults to a mode that, unfortunately, has no standardized name. The default access mode is known variously as *friendly*, *package*, or *default*. In this book, we use the term *default*. Be aware that Sun is encouraging us to avoid the use of *friendly*, due to confusion with a somewhat similar concept in C++.

The following declarations are all legal (provided they appear in an appropriate context):

```
class Parser { ... }
public class EightDimensionalComplex { ... }
private int i;
Graphics offScreenGC;
protected double getChiSquared() { ... }
private class Horse { ... }
```

The following declarations are illegal:

```
public protected int x;      // At most 1 access modifier
default Button getBtn() {...} //  default  isn't a keyword
```

public

The most generous access modifier is public. A *public* class, variable, or method may be used in any Java program without restriction. Any public method may be overridden by any subclass. An application declares its main() method to be public so that main() can be invoked from any Java runtime environment.

private

The least generous access modifier is private. Top-level (that is, not inner) classes may not be declared private. A *private* variable or method may be used only by an instance of the class that declares the variable or method. For an example of the private access modifier, consider the following code:

```
1. class Complex {
2.    private double real, imaginary;
3.
4.    public Complex(double r, double i) {
5.       real = r; imaginary = i;
6.    }
7.    public Complex add(Complex c) {
8.       return new Complex(real + c.real,
9.       imaginary + c.imaginary);
10.   }
11. }
12.
13. class Client {
14.    void useThem() {
15.       Complex c1 = new Complex(1, 2);
16.       Complex c2 = new Complex(3, 4);
17.       Complex c3 = c1.add(c2);
18.       double d = c3.real;   // Illegal!
19.    }
20. }
```

On line 17, a call is made to c1.add(c2). Object c1 will execute the method using object c2 as a parameter. In line 8, c1 accesses its own private variables as well as those of c2. There is nothing wrong with this. Declaring real and imaginary to be private means that they can be accessed only by instances of the Complex class, but they can be accessed by any instance of Complex. Thus c1 may access its own real and imaginary variables, as well as the real and imaginary of any other instance of Complex. Access modifiers dictate which *classes*, not which *instances*, may access features.

Line 18 is illegal and will cause a compiler error. The error message says, "Variable real in class Complex not accessible from class Client." The private variable real may be accessed only by an instance of Complex.

Private data can be hidden from the very object that owns the data. If class Complex has a subclass called SubComplex, then every instance of SubComplex will inherit its own real and imaginary variables. Nevertheless, no instance of SubComplex can ever access those variables. Once again, the private features of Complex can be accessed only within the Complex class; an instance of a subclass is denied access. Thus, for example, the following code will not compile:

```
1.  class Complex {
2.    private double real, imaginary;
3.  }
4.
5.
6.  class SubComplex extends Complex {
7.    SubComplex(double r, double i) {
8.      real = r;              // Trouble!
9.    }
10. }
```

In the constructor for class SubComplex (on line 8), the variable real is accessed. This line causes a compiler error, with a message that is very similar to the message of the previous example: "Undefined variable: real." The private nature of variable real prevents an instance of SubComplex from accessing one of its own variables!

Default

Default is the name of the access of classes, variables, and methods if you don't specify an access modifier. A class's data and methods may be default, as well as the class itself. A class's default features are accessible to any class in the same package as the class in question. A default method may be overridden by any subclass that is in the same package as the superclass.

Default is not a Java keyword; it is simply a name that is given to the access level that results from not specifying an access modifier.

It would seem that default access is of interest only to people who are in the business of making packages. This is technically true, but actually everybody is always making packages, even if they aren't aware of it. The result of this behind-the-scenes package making is a degree of convenience for programmers that deserves investigation.

When you write an application that involves developing several different classes, you probably keep all your .java sources and all your .class class files in a single working directory. When you execute your code, you do so from that directory. The Java runtime environment considers that all class files in its current working directory constitute a package.

Imagine what happens when you develop several classes in this way and don't bother to provide access modifiers for your classes, data, or methods. These features are neither public nor private nor protected. They result in default access, which means they are accessible to any other classes in the package. Because Java considers that all the classes in the directory actually make up a package, all your classes get to access one another's features. This makes it easy to develop code quickly without worrying too much about access.

Now imagine what happens if you are deliberately developing your own package. A little extra work is required: You have to put a package statement in your source code, and you have to compile with the -d option. Any features of the package's classes that you do not explicitly mark with an access modifier will be accessible to all the members of the package, which is probably what you want. Fellow package members have a special relationship, and it stands to reason that they should get access not granted to classes outside the package. Classes outside the package may not access the default features, because the features are default, not public. Classes outside the package may subclass the classes in the package (you do something like this, for example, when you write an applet); however, even the subclasses may not access the default features, because the features are default, not protected or public. Figure 3.1 illustrates default access both within and outside a package.

FIGURE 3.1   Default access

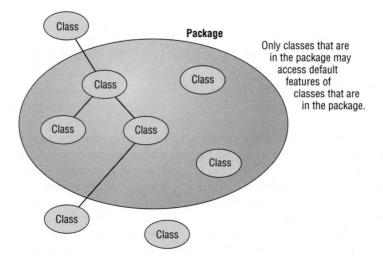

Only classes that are in the package may access default features of classes that are in the package.

protected

The name *protected* is a bit misleading. From the sound of it, you might guess that protected access is extremely restrictive—perhaps the next closest thing to private access. In fact, protected features are even more accessible than default features.

Only variables and methods may be declared protected. A protected feature of a class is available to all classes in the same package, just like a default feature. Moreover, a protected feature of a class can be available in certain limited ways to all subclasses of the class that owns the protected feature. This access is provided even to subclasses that reside in a different package from the class that owns the protected feature.

It's important to be aware that different-package subclasses don't have unlimited access to protected superclass features. In fact, different-package subclasses have only the following privileges:

- They may override protected methods of the superclass.

- An instance may read and write protected fields that it inherits from its superclass. However, the instance may not read or write protected inherited fields of other instances.

- An instance may call protected methods that it inherits from its superclass. However, the instance may not call protected methods of other instances.

As an example of the protected access modifier, consider the following code:

```
1. package sportinggoods;
2. class Ski {
3.    void applyWax() { . . . }
4. }
```

The applyWax() method has default access. Now consider the following subclass:

```
1. package sportinggoods;
2. class DownhillSki extends Ski {
3.    void tuneup() {
4.       applyWax();
5.       // other tuneup functionality here
6.    }
7. }
```

The subclass calls the inherited method applyWax(). This is not a problem as long as both the Ski and DownhillSki classes reside in the same package. However, if either class were to be moved to a different package, DownhillSki would no longer have access to the inherited applyWax() method, and compilation would fail. The problem would be fixed by making applyWax() protected on line 3:

```
1. package adifferentpackage;    // Class Ski now in
                                 // a different package
2. class Ski {
3.    protected void applyWax() { . . . }
4. }
```

Real World Scenario

Protected Access in Depth

In this exercise you will look at how protected data can be accessed from a subclass that belongs to a different package. Because access is enforced at compile time, you will not be writing code that is intended to be executed. Rather, you will write several simple classes and see which ones compile.

Begin by creating a public superclass called Bird, in a package called birdpack. This superclass should have a single data member: a protected int called nFeathers. Then create four subclasses of Bird, all of which reside in a package called duckpack. Thus you will have subclasses whose package is different from their superclass' package; this is exactly the situation for which protected access is designed.

The first subclass, called Duck1, should have a method that accesses the nFeathers variable of the current instance of Duck1. Before compiling Duck1.java, ask yourself if the code should compile.

The second subclass, called Duck2, should have a method that constructs a new instance of Duck2 and accesses the nFeathers variable of the new instance. Before compiling Duck2.java, ask yourself if the code should compile.

The third subclass, called Duck3, should have a method that constructs an instance of Bird (the superclass) and accesses the nFeathers variable of the Bird instance. Before compiling Duck3.java, ask yourself if the code should compile.

The fourth and last subclass, called Swan, should have a method that constructs a new instance of Duck1 and accesses the nFeathers variable of that instance. Before compiling Swan.java, ask yourself if the code should compile.

Sample solutions appear on your CD-ROM in the directory solutions\Chapter_03.

A note on compilation: When a source file contains a package declaration, it is generally most convenient to compile with the -d option. Doing so will ensure creation of an appropriate package directory hierarchy, with class files installed correctly. Thus, for example, the easiest way to compile Bird.java is with the following command line:

```
javac -d . Bird.java
```

Subclasses and Method Privacy

Java specifies that methods may not be overridden to be more private. For example, most applets provide an init() method, which overrides the do-nothing version inherited from the java.applet.Applet superclass. The inherited version is declared public, so declaring the subclass version to be private, protected, or default would result in a compiler error. The error message says, "Methods can't be overridden to be more private."

Figure 3.2 shows the legal access types for subclasses. A method with some particular access type may be overridden by a method with a different access type, provided there is a path in the figure from the original type to the new type.

FIGURE 3.2   Legal overridden method access

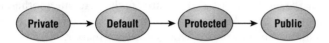

The rules for overriding can be summarized as follows:

- A private method may be overridden by a private, default, protected, or public method.
- A default method may be overridden by a default, protected, or public method.
- A protected method may be overridden by a protected or public method.
- A public method may be overridden only by a public method.

Figure 3.3 shows the illegal access types for subclasses. A method with some particular access type may not be shadowed by a method with a different access type, if there is a path in the figure from the original type to the new type.

FIGURE 3.3   Illegal overridden method access

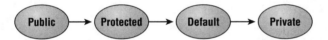

The illegal overriding combinations can be summarized as follows:

- A default method may not be overridden by a private method.
- A protected method may not be overridden by a default or private method.
- A public method may not be overridden by a protected, default, or private method.

Other Modifiers

In this section, we will discuss Java's other modifiers, namely:

- `final`
- `abstract`
- `static`
- `native`
- `transient`
- `volatile`
- `synchronized`

The transient and volatile modifiers are not mentioned in the Certification Exam objectives, so they are just touched on briefly in this chapter. In addition, the synchronized modifier is discussed in more detail in Chapter 7, "Threads."

Unlike the access modifiers, the modifiers listed above are unrelated to one another. Each one relates to a distinct programming concept. A feature may have more than one of these modifiers; in this situation the order of appearance of the keywords does not matter.

Not every modifier can be applied to every kind of feature. Table 3.2, at the end of this chapter, summarizes which modifiers apply to which features.

final

The *final* modifier applies to classes, variables, and methods. The meaning of final varies from context to context, but the essential idea is the same: final features may not be changed.

A final class cannot be subclassed. For example, the following code will not compile, because the java.lang.Math class is final:

```
class SubMath extends java.lang.Math { }
```

The compiler error says, "Can't subclass final classes."

A final variable cannot be modified once it has been assigned a value. In Java, final variables play the same role as consts in C++ and #define constants in C. For example, the java.lang.Math class has a final variable, of type double, called PI. Obviously, pi is not the sort of value that should be changed during the execution of a program.

If a final variable is a reference to an object, it is the reference that must stay the same, not the object. This is shown in the following code:

```
1.   class Walrus {
2.     int weight;
3.     Walrus(int w) { weight = w; }
4.   }
5.
6.   class Tester {
7.     final Walrus w1 = new Walrus(1500);
8.     void test() {
9.       w1 = new Walrus(1400);     // Illegal
10.      w1.weight = 1800;          // Legal
11.    }
12.  }
```

Here the final variable is w1, declared on line 7. Because it is final, w1 cannot receive a new value; line 9 is illegal. However, the data inside w1 is not final, and line 10 is perfectly legal. In other words,

- You may *not* change a final object reference variable.

- You *may* change data owned by an object that is referred to by a final object reference variable.

A final method may not be overridden. For example, the following code will not compile:

```
1. class Mammal {
2.    final void getAround() { }
3. }
4.
5. class Dolphin extends Mammal {
6.    void getAround() { }
7. }
```

Dolphins get around in a very different way from most mammals, so it makes sense to try to override the inherited version of getAround(). However, getAround() is final, so the only result is a compiler error at line 6 that says, "Final methods can't be overridden."

abstract

The *abstract* modifier can be applied to classes and methods.

A class that is abstract may not be instantiated (that is, you may not call its constructor). Abstract classes provide a way to defer implementation to subclasses. Consider the class hierarchy shown in Figure 3.4.

The designer of class Animal has decided that every subclass should have a travel() method. Each subclass has its own unique way of traveling, so it is not possible to provide travel() in the superclass and have each subclass inherit the same parental version. Instead, the Animal superclass declares travel() to be abstract. The declaration looks like this:

```
abstract void travel();
```

At the end of the line is a semicolon where you would expect to find curly braces containing the body of the method. The method body—its implementation—is deferred to the subclasses. The superclass provides only the method name and signature. Any subclass of Animal must provide an implementation of travel() or declare itself to be abstract. In the latter case, implementation of travel() is deferred yet again, to a subclass of the subclass.

If a class contains one or more abstract methods, the compiler insists that the class must be declared abstract. This is a great convenience to people who will be using the class: they need to look in only one place (the class declaration) to find out if they are allowed to instantiate the class directly or if they have to build a subclass.

FIGURE 3.4 A class hierarchy with abstraction

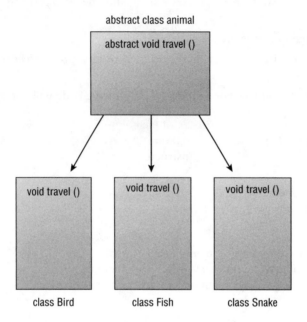

In fact, the compiler insists that a class must be declared abstract if any of the following conditions is true:

- The class has one or more abstract methods.

- The class inherits one or more abstract methods (from an abstract parent) for which it does not provide implementations.

- The class declares that it implements an interface but does not provide implementations for every method of that interface.

These three conditions are very similar to one another. In each case, there is an incomplete class. Some part of the class's functionality is missing and must be provided by a subclass.

 In a way, abstract is the opposite of final. A final class, for example, may not be subclassed; an abstract class *must* be subclassed.

static

The *static* modifier can be applied to variables, methods, and even a strange kind of code that is not part of a method. You can think of static features as belonging to a class, rather than being associated with an individual instance of the class.

The following example shows a simple class with a single static variable:

```
1. class Ecstatic{
2.    static int x = 0;
3.    Ecstatic() { x++; }
4. }
```

Variable x is static; this means that there is only one x, no matter how many instances of class Ecstatic might exist at any moment. There might be one Ecstatic instance, or many, or even none, yet there is always precisely one x. The 4 bytes of memory occupied by x are allocated when class Ecstatic is loaded. The initialization to 0 (line 2) also happens at class-load time. The static variable is incremented every time the constructor is called, so it is possible to know how many instances have been created.

You can reference a static variable two ways:

- Via a reference to any instance of the class
- Via the class name

The first method works, but it can result in confusing code and is considered bad form. The following example shows why:

```
1. Ecstatic e1 = new Ecstatic();
2. Ecstatic e2 = new Ecstatic();
3. e1.x = 100;
4. e2.x = 200;
5. reallyImportantVariable = e1.x;
```

If you didn't know that x is static, you might think that reallyImportantVariable gets set to 100 in line 5. In fact, it gets set to 200, because e1.x and e2.x refer to the same (static) variable.

A better way to refer to a static variable is via the class name. The following code is identical to the previous code:

```
1. Ecstatic e1 = new Ecstatic();
2. Ecstatic e2 = new Ecstatic();
3. Ecstatic.x = 100;    // Why did I do this?
4. Ecstatic.x = 200;
5. reallyImportantVariable = Ecstatic.x;
```

Now it is clear that line 3 is useless, and the value of reallyImportantVariable gets set to 200 in line 5. Referring to static features via the class name rather than an instance results in source code that more clearly describes what will happen at runtime.

Methods, as well as data, can be declared static. Static methods are not allowed to use the nonstatic features of their class (although they are free to access the class's static data and call its other static methods). Thus, static methods are not concerned with individual instances of a class. They may be invoked before even a single instance of the class is constructed. Every Java application is an example, because every application has a main() method that is static:

```
1. class SomeClass {
2.    static int i = 48;
3.    int j = 1;
4.
5.    public static void main(String args[]) {
6.      i += 100;
7.      // j *= 5; Lucky for us this is commented out!
8.    }
9. }
```

When this application is started (that is, when somebody types **java SomeClass** on a command line), no instance of class SomeClass exists. At line 6, the i that gets incremented is static, so it exists even though there are no instances. Line 7 would result in a compiler error if it were not commented out, because j is nonstatic.

Instance methods have an implicit variable named this, which is a reference to the object executing the method. In nonstatic code, you can refer to a variable or method without specifying which object's variable or method you mean. The compiler assumes you mean this. For example, consider the following code:

```
1. class Xyzzy {
2.    int w;
3.
4. void bumpW() {
5.      w++;
6.    }
7. }
```

On line 5, the programmer has not specified which object's w is to be incremented. The compiler assumes that line 5 is an abbreviation for this.w++;.

With static methods, there is no this. If you try to access an instance variable or call an instance method within a static method, you will get an error message that says, "Undefined variable: this." The concept of "the instance that is executing the current method" does not mean anything, because there is no such instance. Like static variables, static methods are not associated with any individual instance of their class.

If a static method needs to access a nonstatic variable or call a nonstatic method, it must specify which instance of its class owns the variable or executes the method. This situation is familiar to anyone who has ever written an application with a GUI:

```
1.    import java.awt.*;
2.
3.    public class MyFrame extends Frame {
```

```
4.    MyFrame() {
5.      setSize(300, 300);
6.    }
7.
8.    public static void main(String args[]) {
9.      MyFrame theFrame = new MyFrame();
10.     theFrame.setVisible(true);
11.   }
12. }
```

In line 9, the static method main() constructs an instance of class MyFrame. In the next line, that instance is told to execute the (nonstatic) method setVisible(). This technique bridges the gap from static to nonstatic, and it is frequently seen in applications.

The following code, for example, will not compile:

```
1. class Cattle {
2.   static void foo() {}
3. }
4.
5. class Sheep extends Cattle {
6.   void foo() {}
7. }
```

The compiler flags line 6 with the message, "Static methods can't be overridden." If line 6 were changed to static void foo() { }, then compilation would succeed. Static methods can appear to be overridden—a superclass and a subclass can have static methods with identical names, argument lists, and return types—but technically this is not considered overriding because the methods are static.

To summarize static methods:

- A static method may access only the static data of its class; it may not access nonstatic data.
- A static method may call only the static methods of its class; it may not call nonstatic methods.
- A static method has no this.
- A static method may not be overridden to be nonstatic.

Static Initializers

It is legal for a class to contain static code that does not exist within a method body. A class may have a block of initializer code that is simply surrounded by curly braces and labeled static. For example:

```
1.  public class StaticExample {
2.    static double d = 1.23;
```

```
3.
4.    static {
5.      System.out.println("Static code: d=" + d++);
6.    }
7.
8.    public static void main(String args[]) {
9.      System.out.println("main: d = " + d++);
10.   }
11. }
```

Something seems to be missing from line 4. You might expect to see a complete method declaration there: `static void printAndBump()`, for example, instead of just `static`. In fact, line 4 is perfectly valid; it is known as *static initializer* code. The code inside the curlies is executed exactly once, at the time the class is loaded. At class-load time, all static initialization (such as line 2) and all free-floating static code (such as lines 4–6) are executed in order of appearance within the class definition.

The output from this code is:

```
Static code: d=1.23
main: d = 2.23
```

Free-floating initializer code should be used with caution because it can easily become difficult to read. The compiler supports multiple initializer blocks within a class, but there is rarely a good reason for having more than one such block.

Static Imports and Access

You saw in Chapter 1, "Language Fundamentals," that static features of a class can be imported, using Java 1.5's `static import` facility. Static data and methods may have any of the four access modes discussed earlier in this chapter: `public`, `private`, `protected`, and default. A feature's access mode dictates which source files may statically import that feature.

When you think about how access mode affects static importing, you don't have to consider class/subclass relationships (which you have to do, for example, when thinking about protected features). This is because static imports appear in source files just after package declarations, before any classes are defined. Remember, you import into the namespace of a source file, not into the definition of a class. A source file may contain one, several, or many class definitions, or it may contain no class definitions at all.

So the interaction between access mode and static importing is very simple: any nonprivate feature may be statically imported into a source file of the same package; only a public feature may be statically imported into a source file in a different package. This is summarized in Table 3.1.

TABLE 3.1   Access and Static Imports

Feature Access Mode	Feature May Be Statically Imported into Same-Package Source File	Feature May Be Statically Imported into Different-Package Source File
Public	Yes	Yes
Protected	Yes	No
Default	Yes	No
Private	No	No

native

The *native* modifier can refer only to methods. Like the `abstract` modifier, `native` indicates that the body of a method is to be found elsewhere. In the case of abstract methods, the body is in a subclass; with native methods, the body lies entirely outside the Java Virtual Machine (JVM), in a library.

Native code is written in a non-Java language, typically C or C++, and compiled for a single target machine type. (Thus Java's platform independence is violated.) People who port Java to new platforms implement extensive native code to support GUI components, network communication, and a broad range of other platform-specific functionality. However, it is rare for application and applet programmers to need to write native code.

One technique, however, is of interest in light of the last section's discussion of static code. When a native method is invoked, the library that contains the native code ought to be loaded and available to the JVM; if it is not loaded, there will be a delay. The library is loaded by calling `System.loadLibrary ("library_name")` and, to avoid a delay, it is desirable to make this call as early as possible. Often programmers will use the technique shown in the following code sample, which assumes the library name is `MyNativeLib`:

```
1. class NativeExample {
2.    native void doSomethingLocal(int i);
3.
4.    static {
5.      System.loadLibrary("MyNativeLib");
6.    }
7. }
```

Notice the `native` declaration on line 2, which declares that the code that implements `doSomethingLocal()` resides in a local library. Lines 4–6 are static initializer code, so they are executed at the time that class `NativeExample` is loaded; this ensures that the library will be available by the time somebody needs it.

Callers of native methods do not have to know that the method is native. The call is made in exactly the same way as if it were nonnative:

```
1. NativeExample natex;
2. natex = new NativeExample();
3. natex.doSomethingLocal(5);
```

Many common methods are native, including the clone() and notify() methods of the Object class.

transient

The *transient* modifier applies only to variables. A transient variable is not stored as part of its object's persistent state. (If you're not familiar with object persistence, it is covered in Chapter 12, "Input and Output".)

Many objects (specifically, those that implement the Serializable or Externalizable interfaces) can have their state serialized and written to some destination outside the JVM. This is done by passing the object to the writeObject() method of the ObjectOutputStream class. If the stream is chained to a FileOutputStream, then the object's state is written to a file. If the stream is chained to a socket's OutputStream, then the object's state is written to the network. In both cases, the object can be reconstituted by reading it from an ObjectInputStream.

Sometimes an object contains extremely sensitive information. Consider the following class:

```
1. class WealthyCustomer
2. extends Customer implements Serializable {
3.    private float $wealth;
4.    private String accessCode;
5. }
```

Once an object is written to a destination outside the JVM, none of Java's elaborate security mechanisms is in effect. If an instance of this class were to be written to a file or to the Internet, somebody could snoop the access code. Line 4 should be marked with the transient keyword:

```
1. class WealthyCustomer
2. extends Customer implements Serializable {
3.    private float $wealth;
4.    private transient String accessCode;
5. }
```

Now the value of accessCode will not be written out during serialization.

volatile

The *volatile modifier* is not in common use. Only variables may be volatile; declaring them so indicates that such variables might be modified asynchronously, so the compiler takes special precautions. Volatile variables are of interest in multiprocessor environments.

synchronized

The *synchronized* modifier is used to control access to critical code in multithreaded programs. Multithreading is an extensive topic in its own right and is covered in Chapter 7.

Modifiers and Features

Not all modifiers can be applied to all features. Top-level classes may not be protected. Methods may not be transient. Static is so general that you can apply it to free-floating blocks of code.

Table 3.2 shows all the possible combinations of features and modifiers. Note that classes here are strictly top-level (that is, not inner) classes. (Inner classes are covered in Chapter 6.)

TABLE 3.2   All Possible Combinations of Features and Modifiers

Modifier	Class	Variable	Method	Constructor	Free-Floating Block
public	yes	yes	yes	yes	no
protected	no	yes	yes	yes	no
(default)*	yes	yes	yes	yes	yes
private	no	yes	yes	yes	no
final	yes	yes	yes	no	no
abstract	yes	no	yes	no	no
static	no	yes	yes	no	yes
native	no	no	yes	no	no
transient	no	yes	no	no	no
volatile	no	yes	no	no	no
synchronized	no	no	yes	no	yes

Default is not a modifier; it is just the name of the access if no modifier is specified.

Summary

The focus of this chapter was to understand how all of the modifiers work and how they *can* or *cannot* work together. Some modifiers can be used in combination. Java's access modifiers are:

- public
- protected
- private

If a feature does not have an access modifier, its access is "default."
   Java's other modifiers are:

- final
- abstract
- static
- native
- transient
- synchronized
- volatile

Exam Essentials

Understand the four access modes and the corresponding keywords.   You should know the significance of public, private, protected, and default access when applied to data and methods.

Know the effect of declaring a final class, variable, or method.   A final class cannot be subclassed; a final variable cannot be modified after initialization; a final method cannot be overridden.

Know the effect of declaring an abstract class or method.   An abstract class cannot be instantiated; an abstract method's definition is deferred to a subclass.

Understand the effect of declaring a static variable or method.   Static variables belong to the class; static methods have no this pointer and may not access nonstatic variables and methods of their class.

Know how to reference a static variable or method.   A static feature may be referenced through the class name—the preferred method—or through a reference to any instance of the class.

Be able to recognize static initializer code.   Static initializer code appears in curly brackets with no method declaration. Such code is executed once, when the class is loaded.

Review Questions

1. Which of the following declarations are illegal? (Choose all that apply.)

    A. `default String s;`

    B. `transient int i = 41;`

    C. `public final static native int w();`

    D. `abstract double d;`

    E. `abstract final double hyperbolicCosine();`

2. Which of the following statements is true?

    A. An abstract class may not have any final methods.

    B. A final class may not have any abstract methods.

3. What is the minimal modification that will make this code compile correctly?

    ```
    1. final class Aaa
    2. {
    3.     int xxx;
    4.     void yyy() { xxx = 1; }
    5. }
    6.
    7.
    8. class Bbb extends Aaa
    9. {
    10.     final Aaa finalref = new Aaa();
    11.
    12.     final void yyy()
    13.     {
    14.         System.out.println("In method yyy()");
    15.         finalref.xxx = 12345;
    16.     }
    17. }
    ```

    A. On line 1, remove the `final` modifier.

    B. On line 10, remove the `final` modifier.

    C. Remove line 15.

    D. On lines 1 and 10, remove the `final` modifier.

    E. The code will compile as is. No modification is needed.

4. Which of the following statements is true?

   A. Transient methods may not be overridden.

   B. Transient methods must be overridden.

   C. Transient classes may not be serialized.

   D. Transient variables must be static.

   E. Transient variables are not serialized.

5. Which statement is true about this application?

```
1. class StaticStuff
2. {
3.     static int x = 10;
4.
5.     static { x += 5; }
6.
7.     public static void main(String args[])
8.     {
9.         System.out.println("x = " + x);
10.     }
11.
12.     static {x /= 5; }
13. }
```

   A. Lines 5 and 12 will not compile because the method names and return types are missing.

   B. Line 12 will not compile because you can only have one static initializer.

   C. The code compiles and execution produces the output x = 10.

   D. The code compiles and execution produces the output x = 15.

   E. The code compiles and execution produces the output x = 3.

6. Which statement is true about this code?

```
1. class HasStatic
2. {
3.     private static int x = 100;
4.
5.     public static void main(String args[])
6.     {
7.         HasStatic hs1 = new HasStatic();
8.         hs1.x++;
9.         HasStatic hs2 = new HasStatic();
10.         hs2.x++;
```

```
11.          hs1 = new HasStatic();
12.          hs1.x++;
13.          HasStatic.x++;
14.          System.out.println("x = " + x);
15.     }
16. }
```

A. Line 8 will not compile because it is a static reference to a private variable.

B. Line 13 will not compile because it is a static reference to a private variable.

C. The program compiles and the output is x = 102.

D. The program compiles and the output is x = 103.

E. The program compiles and the output is x = 104.

7. Given the following code, and making no other changes, which combination of access modifiers (public, protected, or private) can legally be placed before aMethod() on line 3 and be placed before aMethod() on line 8?

```
1. class SuperDuper
2. {
3.     void aMethod() { }
4. }
5.
6. class Sub extends SuperDuper
7. {
8.     void aMethod() { }
9. }
```

A. line 3: public; line 8: private

B. line 3: protected; line 8: private

C. line 3: default; line 8: private

D. line 3: private; line 8: protected

E. line 3: public; line 8: protected

8. Which modifier or modifiers should be used to denote a variable that should not be written out as part of its class's persistent state? (Choose the shortest possible answer.)

A. private

B. protected

C. private protected

D. transient

E. volatile

9. This question concerns the following class definition:

```
1. package abcde;
2.
3. public class Bird {
4.    protected static int referenceCount = 0;
5.    public Bird() { referenceCount++; }
6.    protected void fly() { /* Flap wings, etc. */ }
7.    static int getRefCount() { return referenceCount; }
8. }
```

Which statement is true about class `Bird` and the following class `Parrot`?

```
1. package abcde;
2.
3. class Parrot extends abcde.Bird {
4.    public void fly() {
5.       /* Parrot-specific flight code. */
6.    }
7.    public int getRefCount() {
8.       return referenceCount;
9.    }
10. }
```

- **A.** Compilation of `Parrot.java` fails at line 4 because method `fly()` is protected in the superclass, and classes `Bird` and `Parrot` are in the same package.
- **B.** Compilation of `Parrot.java` fails at line 4 because method `fly()` is protected in the superclass and public in the subclass, and methods may not be overridden to be more public.
- **C.** Compilation of `Parrot.java` fails at line 7 because method `getRefCount()` is static in the superclass, and static methods may not be overridden to be nonstatic.
- **D.** Compilation of `Parrot.java` succeeds, but a runtime exception is thrown if method `fly()` is ever called on an instance of class `Parrot`.
- **E.** Compilation of `Parrot.java` succeeds, but a runtime exception is thrown if method `getRefCount()` is ever called on an instance of class `Parrot`.

10. This question concerns the following class definition:

```
1. package abcde;
2.
3. public class Bird {
4.    protected static int referenceCount = 0;
5.    public Bird() { referenceCount++; }
6.    protected void fly() { /* Flap wings, etc. */ }
```

```
7.    static int getRefCount() { return referenceCount; }
8. }
```

Which statement is true about class `Bird` and the following class `Nightingale`?

```
1. package singers;
2.
3. class Nightingale extends abcde.Bird {
4.    Nightingale() { referenceCount++; }
5.
6.    public static void main(String args[]) {
7.       System.out.print("Before: " + referenceCount);
8.       Nightingale florence = new Nightingale();
9.       System.out.println("  After: " + referenceCount);
10.       florence.fly();
11.    }
12. }
```

- **A.** The program will compile and execute. The output will be `Before: 0  After: 2.`
- **B.** The program will compile and execute. The output will be `Before: 0  After: 1.`
- **C.** Compilation of `Nightingale` will fail at line 4 because static members cannot be overridden.
- **D.** Compilation of `Nightingale` will fail at line 10 because method `fly()` is protected in the superclass.
- **E.** Compilation of `Nightingale` will succeed, but an exception will be thrown at line 10, because method `fly()` is protected in the superclass.

11. Suppose class Supe, in package `packagea`, has a method called `doSomething()`. Suppose class Subby, in package `packageb`, overrides `doSomething()`. What access modes may Subby's version of the method have? (Choose all that apply.)

- **A.** `public`
- **B.** `protected`
- **C.** Default
- **D.** `private`

12. Which of the following statements are true?

- **A.** An abstract class may be instantiated.
- **B.** An abstract class must contain at least one abstract method.
- **C.** An abstract class must contain at least one abstract data field.
- **D.** An abstract class must be overridden.
- **E.** An abstract class must declare that it implements an interface.
- **F.** None of the above.

13. Suppose interface Inty defines five methods. Suppose class Classy declares that it implements Inty but does not provide implementations for any of the five interface methods. Which is/are true?

    A. The class will not compile.

    B. The class will compile if it is declared public.

    C. The class will compile if it is declared abstract.

    D. The class may not be instantiated.

14. Which of the following may be declared final? (Choose all that apply.)

    A. Classes

    B. Data

    C. Methods

15. Which of the following may follow the static keyword? (Choose all that apply.)

    A. Class definitions

    B. Data

    C. Methods

    D. Code blocks enclosed in curly brackets

16. Suppose class A has a method called doSomething(), with default access. Suppose class B extends A and overrides doSomething(). Which access modes may apply to B's version of doSomething()? (Choose all that apply.)

    A. public

    B. private

    C. protected

    D. Default

17. True or false: If class Y extends class X, the two classes are in different packages, and class X has a protected method called abby(), then any instance of Y may call the abby() method of any other instance of Y.

    A. True

    B. False

18. Which of the following statements are true?

    A. A final class must be instantiated.

    B. A final class must contain at least one final method.

    C. A final class must contain at least one final data field.

    D. A final class may not be extended.

    E. None of the above.

19. Which of the following statements are true?

   A. A final class must be instantiated.

   B. A final class may only contain final methods.

   C. A final class may not contain non-final data fields.

   D. A final class may not be extended.

   E. None of the above.

20. What does the following code print?

```
public class A
{
  static int x;

  public static void main(String[] args) {
    A that1 = new A();
    A that2 = new A();
    that1.x = 5;
    that2.x = 1000;
    x = -1;
    System.out.println(x);
}
  }
```

   A. 0

   B. 5

   C. 1000

   D. -1

Answers to Review Questions

1. A, D, E. A is illegal because "default" is not a keyword. B is a legal transient declaration. C is strange but legal. D is illegal because only methods and classes may be abstract. E is illegal because abstract and final are contradictory.

2. B. Any class with abstract methods must itself be abstract, and a class may not be both abstract and final. Statement A says that an abstract class may not have final methods, but there is nothing wrong with this. The abstract class will eventually be subclassed, and the subclass must avoid overriding the parent's final methods. Any other methods can be freely overridden.

3. A. The code will not compile because on line 1, class Aaa is declared final and may not be subclassed. Lines 10 and 15 are fine. The instance variable finalref is final, so it may not be modified; it can reference only the object created on line 10. However, the data within that object is not final, so nothing is wrong with line 15.

4. E. A, B, and C don't mean anything because only variables may be transient, not methods or classes. D is false because transient variables need not be static, and in fact they very rarely are.. E is a good one-sentence definition of transient.

5. E. Multiple static initializers (lines 5 and 12) are legal. All static initializer code is executed at class-load time, so before main() is ever run, the value of x is initialized to 10 (line 3), then bumped to 15 (line 5), and then divided by 5 (line 12).

6. E. The program compiles fine; the "static reference to a private variable" stuff in answers A and B is nonsense. The static variable x gets incremented four times, on lines 8, 10, 12, and 13.

7. D. The basic principle is that a method may not be overridden to be more private. (See Figure 3.2 in this chapter.) All choices except D make the access of the overriding method more private.

8. D. A and B are access modifiers. C is an illegal combination of two access modifiers. E ("volatile") is used for certain multi-threaded situations, and is not covered in the Exam.

9. C. Static methods may not be overridden to be nonstatic. B is incorrect because it states the case backward: methods can be overridden to be more public, not more private. Answers A, D, and E make no sense.

10. A. There is nothing wrong with Nightingale. The static referenceCount is bumped twice: once on line 4 of Nightingale and once on line 5 of Bird. (The no-argument constructor of the superclass is always implicitly called at the beginning of a class's constructor, unless a different superclass constructor is requested. This has nothing to do with modifiers; see Chapter 6.) Because referenceCount is bumped twice and not just once, answer B is wrong. C says that statics cannot be overridden, but no static method is being overridden on line 4; all that is happening is an increment of an inherited static variable. D is wrong because protected is precisely the access modifier you want Bird.fly() to have: you are calling Bird.fly() from a subclass in a different package. Answer E is ridiculous, but it uses credible terminology.

11. A, B. Since the method in the superclass is overridden in a different package, the superclass version must be public or protected. (Default methods may be overridden only if the subclass is in the same package as the superclass; private methods may not be overridden at all.) An overriding method's access mode must be the same as, or more open than, the superclass version's access mode.

12. F. A is false because the compiler forbids construction of an abstract class. B is false because abstract classes need not contain any abstract methods (though if a class *does* contain any abstract methods, it *must* be abstract). C is false because there is no such thing as an abstract data field. D is false because, when you really think about it, it doesn't make any sense; the compiler compiles classes one at a time and has no interest in whether or not a class is overridden. E is false because there is no compiler requirement that an abstract class must declare that it implements any interface.

13. C, D. If a class does not provide implementations for all methods of all interfaces that the class declares it implements, that class must be declared abstract. Abstract classes may not be instantiated.

14. A, B, C. Classes, data, and methods can be declared final. Variables cannot.

15. B, C, D. Classes may not be static. Data and methods may be static, and often they are. When the `static` keyword is followed by a code block, the block is a static initializer and is executed when the class is loaded.

16. A, C, D. An overriding method's access mode must be the same as, or more open than, the superclass version's access mode.

17. B. An object that inherits a protected method from a superclass in a different package may call that method on itself but not on other instances of the same class.

18. D. There is only one restriction on a final class: A final class may not be extended.

19. D. There is only one restriction on a final class: A final class may not be extended.

20. D. Since x is static, there is only one variable, which is shared by all instances along with the class. Thus the last assignment wins.

Chapter

4

Converting and Casting

JAVA CERTIFICATION EXAM OBJECTIVE COVERED IN THIS CHAPTER:

- ✓ 5.2 Given a scenario, develop code that demonstrates the use of polymorphism. Further, determine when casting will be necessary and recognize compiler vs. runtime errors related to object reference casting.

- ✓ 7.6 Write code that correctly applies the appropriate operators including assignment operators (limited to: =, + =, -=), arithmetic operators (limited to: +, -, *, /, %, ++, --), relational operators (limited to: <, < =, >, > =, = =, !=), the instanceof operator, logical operators (limited to: &, |, ^, !, &&, ||), and the conditional operator (? :), to produce a desired result. Write code that determines the equality of two objects or two primitives.

Every Java variable has a type. Primitive data types include `int`, `long`, and `double`. Object reference data types may be classes (such as `Vector` or `Graphics`) or interfaces (such as `LayoutManager` or `Runnable`). There can also be arrays of primitives, objects, or arrays.

This chapter discusses the ways that a data value can change its type. Values can change type either implicitly or explicitly; that is, they change either at the system's initiative or at your request. These two styles of type change are technically known as converting and casting. Java places a lot of importance on type, and successful Java programming requires that you be aware of type changes.

Explicit and Implicit Type Changes

You can explicitly change the type of a value by *casting*. To cast an expression to a new type, just prefix the expression with the new type name in parentheses. For example, the following line of code retrieves an element from a vector, casts that element to type `Button`, and assigns the result to a variable called `btn`:

```
Button btn = (Button) (myVector.elementAt(5));
```

Of course, the sixth element of the vector must be capable of being treated as a `Button`. Compile-time rules and runtime rules must be observed. This chapter will familiarize you with those rules.

In some situations, the system implicitly changes the type of an expression without your explicitly performing a cast. For example, suppose you have a variable called `myColor` that refers to an instance of `Color`, and you want to store `myColor` in a vector. You would probably do the following:

```
myVector.add(myColor);
```

There is more to this code than meets the eye. The `add()` method of class `Vector` is declared with a parameter of type `Object`, not of type `Color`. As the argument is passed to the method, it undergoes an implicit type change. Such automatic, nonexplicit type changing is known as *conversion*. Conversion, like casting, is governed by rules. Unlike the casting rules, all conversion rules are enforced at compile time.

The number of casting and conversion rules is rather large, due to the large number of cases to be considered. (For example, can you cast a `char` to a `double`? Can you convert an interface to a final class? Yes to the first, no to the second.) The good news is that most of the rules accord with common sense, and most of the combinations can be generalized into rules of thumb. By the end of this chapter, you will know when you can explicitly cast and when the system will implicitly convert on your behalf.

Primitives and Conversion

The two broad categories of Java data types are primitives and objects. *Primitive* data types include `ints`, `floats`, `booleans`, and so on. (There are eight primitive data types in all; see Chapter 1, "Language Fundamentals," for a complete explanation of Java's primitives.) *Object* data types (or more properly, *object reference* data types) are the hundreds of classes and interfaces provided with the JDK, plus the infinitude of classes and interfaces to be invented by Java programmers.

Both primitive values and object references can be converted and cast, so you must consider four general cases:

- Conversion of primitives
- Casting of primitives
- Conversion of object references
- Casting of object references

The simplest topic is implicit conversion of primitives. All conversion of primitive data types takes place at compile time; this is the case because all the information needed to determine whether the conversion is legal is available at compile time.

Conversion of a primitive might occur in three contexts or situations:

- Assignment
- Method call
- Arithmetic promotion

The following sections deal with each of these contexts in turn.

Primitive Conversion: Assignment

Assignment conversion happens when you assign a value to a variable of a different type from the original value. For example

```
1. int i;
2. double d;
3. i = 10;
4. d = i;  // Assign an int value to a double variable
```

Obviously, d cannot hold an integer value. At the moment that the fourth line of code is executed, the integer 10 that is stored in variable i gets converted to the double-precision value 10.0000000000000 (remaining zeros omitted for brevity).

The previous code is perfectly legal. Some assignments, on the other hand, are illegal. For example

```
1. double d;
2. short s;
3. d = 1.2345;
4. s = d;   // Assign a double value to a short variable
```

This code will not compile. (The error message says, "Incompatible type for =.") The compiler recognizes that trying to cram a double value into a short variable is like trying to pour a quart of milk into an eight-ounce cup, as shown in Figure 4.1. It can't be done without mess and loss. If you see someone trying to do it, you might be tempted to say, "Are you sure you know what you're doing? Shouldn't you do that in the sink?" In other words, you would want some reassurance that the other person wanted the result they were about to get.

When the compiler notices that you are trying to cram a big value into a little variable, it goes through a similar process. Line 4 above could easily be a mistake, so the compiler needs to be convinced that it's really what you want. To convince the compiler, you must use an explicit cast, which will be explained in the following section.

FIGURE 4.1   Illegal conversion of a quart to a cup, with loss of data

The general rules for primitive assignment conversion can be stated as follows:

- A `boolean` cannot be converted to any other type.

- A non-`boolean` can be converted to another non-`boolean` type, provided the conversion is a *widening conversion.*

- A non-`boolean` cannot be converted to another non-`boolean` type if the conversion would be a *narrowing conversion.*

Widening conversions change a value to a type that accommodates a wider range of values than the original type can accommodate. In most cases, the new type has more bits than the original and can be visualized as being "wider" than the original, as shown in Figure 4.2.

Widening conversions do not lose information about the magnitude of a value. In the first example in this section, an `int` value was assigned to a `double` variable. This conversion was legal because `double`s are wider (represented by more bits) than `int`s, so there is room in a `double` to accommodate the information in an `int`. Java's widening conversions are

- From a `byte` to a `short`, an `int`, a `long`, a `float`, or a `double`

- From a `short` to an `int`, a `long`, a `float`, or a `double`

- From a `char` to an `int`, a `long`, a `float`, or a `double`

- From an `int` to a `long`, a `float`, or a `double`

- From a `long` to a `float` or a `double`

- From a `float` to a `double`

Figure 4.3 illustrates all the widening conversions. The arrows can be taken to mean "can be widened to." To determine whether it is legal to convert from one type to another, find the first type in the figure and see if you can reach the desired type by following the arrows.

FIGURE 4.2   Widening conversion of a positive value

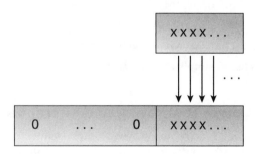

FIGURE 4.3   Widening conversions

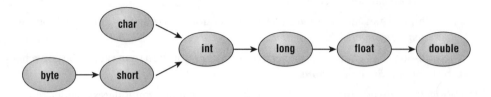

The figure shows, for example, that it is perfectly legal to assign a byte value to a float variable, because you can trace a path from byte to float by following the arrows (byte to short to int to long to float). You cannot, on the other hand, trace a path from long to short, so it is not legal to assign a long value to a short variable.

Figure 4.3 is easy to memorize. The figure consists mostly of the numeric data types in order of size. The only extra piece of information is char, but that goes in the only place it could go: a 16-bit char "fits inside" a 32-bit int. (Note that you can't convert a byte to a char or a char to a short, even though it seems reasonable to do so.)

Any conversion between primitive types that is not represented by a path of arrows in Figure 4.3 is a narrowing conversion. These conversions lose information about the magnitude of the value being converted and are not allowed in assignments. It is graphically impossible to portray the narrowing conversions in a diagram like Figure 4.3, but they can be summarized as follows:

- From a byte to a char
- From a short to a byte or a char
- From a char to a byte or a short
- From an int to a byte, a short, or a char
- From a long to a byte, a short, a char, or an int
- From a float to a byte, a short, a char, an int, or a long
- From a double to a byte, a short, a char, an int, a long, or a float

You do not really need to memorize this list. It simply represents all the conversions not shown in Figure 4.3, which is easier to memorize.

Assignment Conversion, Narrower Primitives, and Literal Values

Java's assignment conversion rule is sometimes inconvenient when a literal value is assigned to a primitive. By default, a numeric literal is either a double or an int, so the following line of code generates a compiler error:

```
float f = 1.234;
```

The literal value 1.234 is a double, so it cannot be assigned to a float variable.

You might assume that assigning a literal `int` to some narrower integral type (`byte`, `short`, or `char`) would fail to compile in a similar way. For example, it would be reasonable to assume that all of the following lines generate compiler errors:

```
byte  b = 1;
short s = 2;
char  c = 3;
```

In fact, all three of these lines compile without error. The reason is that Java relaxes its assignment conversion rule when a literal `int` value is assigned to a narrower primitive type (`byte`, `short`, or `char`), provided the literal value falls within the legal range of the primitive type.

This relaxation of the rule applies only when the assigned value is an integral literal. Thus the second line of the following code will *not* compile:

```
int i = 12;
byte b = I
```

Primitive Conversion: Method Call

Another kind of conversion is *method-call conversion*. A method-call conversion happens when you pass a value of one type as an argument to a method that expects a different type. For example, the `cos()` method of the `Math` class expects a single argument of type `double`. Consider the following code:

```
1. float frads;
2. double d;
3. frads = 2.34567f;
4. d = Math.cos(frads);  // Pass float to method
                         // that expects double
```

The `float` value in `frads` is automatically converted to a `double` value before it is handed to the `cos()` method. Just as with assignment conversions, strict rules govern which conversions are allowed and which conversions will be rejected by the compiler. The following code quite reasonably generates a compiler error (assuming there is a vector called `myVector`):

```
1. double d = 12.0;
2. Object ob = myVector.elementAt(d);
```

The compiler error message says, "Incompatible type for method. Explicit cast needed to convert double to int." This means the compiler can't convert the `double` argument to a type that is supported by a version of the `elementAt()` method. It turns out that the only version of `elementAt()` is the version that takes an integer argument. Thus a value can be passed to `elementAt()` only if that value is an `int` or can be converted to an `int`.

Fortunately, the rule that governs which method-call conversions are permitted is the same rule that governs assignment conversions. Widening conversions (as shown in Figure 4.3) are permitted; narrowing conversions are forbidden.

Primitive Conversion: Arithmetic Promotion

The last kind of primitive conversion to consider is *arithmetic promotion*. Arithmetic-promotion conversions happen within arithmetic statements while the compiler is trying to make sense out of many different possible kinds of operand.

Consider the following fragment:

```
1. short s = 9;
2. int i = 10;
3. float f = 11.1f;
4. double d = 12.2;
5. if (-s * i  >=  f / d)
6.    System.out.println(">=");
7. else
8.    System.out.println("<");
```

The code on line 5 multiplies a negated `short` by an `int`; then it divides a `float` by a `double`; finally, it compares the two results. Behind the scenes, the system is doing extensive type conversion to ensure that the operands can be meaningfully incremented, multiplied, divided, and compared. These conversions are all widening conversions. Thus they are known as *arithmetic-promotion conversions* because values are *promoted* to wider types.

The rules that govern arithmetic promotion distinguish between unary and binary operators. Unary operators operate on a single value. Binary operators operate on two values. Figure 4.4 shows Java's unary and binary arithmetic operators.

For unary operators, two rules apply, depending on the type of the single operand:

- If the operand is a `byte`, a `short`, or a `char`, it is converted to an `int` (unless the operator is `++` or `--`, in which case no conversion happens).

- Else there is no conversion.

FIGURE 4.4   Unary and binary arithmetic operators

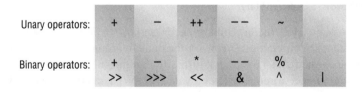

For binary operators, there are four rules, depending on the types of the two operands:

- If one of the operands is a `double`, the other operand is converted to a `double`.
- Else if one of the operands is a `float`, the other operand is converted to a `float`.
- Else if one of the operands is a `long`, the other operand is converted to a `long`.
- Else both operands are converted to `int`s.

With these rules in mind, it is possible to determine what really happens in the code example given at the beginning of this section:

1. The `short s` is promoted to an `int` and then negated.

2. The result of step 1 (an `int`) is multiplied by the `int i`. Because both operands are of the same type, and that type is not narrower than an `int`, no conversion is necessary. The result of the multiplication is an `int`.

3. Before `float f` is divided by `double d`, `f` is widened to a `double`. The division generates a double-precision result.

4. The result of step 2 (an `int`) is to be compared to the result of step 3 (a `double`). The `int` is converted to a `double`, and the two operands are compared. The result of a comparison is always of type `boolean`.

Primitives and Casting

So far, this chapter has shown that Java is perfectly willing to perform widening conversions on primitives. These conversions are implicit and behind the scenes; you don't need to write any explicit code to make them happen.

Casting is explicitly telling Java to make a conversion. A casting operation may widen or narrow its argument. To cast, just precede a value with the parenthesized name of the desired type. For example, the following lines of code cast an `int` to a `double`:

```
1. int i = 5;
2. double d = (double)i;
```

Of course, the cast is not always necessary. The following code, in which the cast has been omitted, would do an assignment conversion on `i`, with the same result as the previous example:

```
1. int i = 5;
2. double d = i;
```

Casts are required when you want to perform a narrowing conversion. Such conversion will never be performed implicitly; you have to program an explicit cast to convince the compiler that what you really want is a narrowing conversion. Narrowing runs the risk of losing information; the cast tells the compiler that you accept the risk.

For example, the following code generates a compiler error:

```
1. short s = 259;
2. byte b = s;    // Compiler error
3. System.out.println("s = " + s + ", b = " + b);
```

The compiler error message for the second line will say (among other things), "Explicit cast needed to convert short to byte." Adding an explicit cast is easy:

```
1. short s = 259;
2. byte b = (byte)s;     // Explicit cast
3. System.out.println("b = " + b);
```

When this code is executed, the number 259 (binary 100000011) must be squeezed into a single byte. This is accomplished by preserving the low-order byte of the value and discarding the rest. The code prints out the (perhaps surprising) message:

```
b = 3
```

The 1 bit in bit position 8 is discarded, leaving only 3, as shown in Figure 4.5. Narrowing conversions can result in radical value changes; this is why the compiler requires you to cast explicitly. The cast tells the compiler, "Yes, I really want to do it."

Casting a value to a wider value (as shown in Figure 4.3) is always permitted but never required; if you omit the cast, an implicit conversion will be performed on your behalf. However, explicitly casting can make your code a bit more readable. For example

```
  1. int i = 2;
  2. double radians;
       .        // Hundreds of
       .        // lines of
       .        // code
600. radians = (double)i;
```

The cast in the last line is not required, but it serves as a good reminder to any readers (including yourself) who might have forgotten the type of radians.

Two simple rules govern casting of primitive types:

- You can cast any non-boolean type to any other non-boolean type.

- You cannot cast a boolean to any other type; you cannot cast any other type to a boolean.

Note that although casting is ordinarily used when narrowing, it is perfectly legal to cast when widening. The cast is unnecessary, but it provides a bit of clarity.

Real World Scenario

Legal and Illegal Casts

Write an application that illustrates legal and illegal casts. Work with the following class/interface hierarchy:

```
class Fruit
class Apple extends Fruit
interface Squeezable
class Citrus extends Fruit implements Squeezable
class Orange extends Citrus
```

You will have to define the classes and the interface, but the definitions can be empty. Your application should construct one instance of each of the following classes:

- Object
- Fruit
- Apple
- Citrus
- Orange

Try to cast each of these objects to the following types:

- Fruit
- Apple
- Squeezable
- Citrus
- Orange

For each attempted cast, print out a message stating whether the cast succeeded. (A ClassCastException is thrown if the cast failed; if no exception is thrown, the cast succeeded.) A fragment of the output of the sample solution (Caster.java on the CD-ROM) looks like this:

```
Checking casts for FruitFruit: OKApple: NOSqueezable: NOCitrus: NOOrange: NO
Checking casts for AppleFruit: OKApple: OKSqueezable: NOCitrus: NOOrange: NO
```

FIGURE 4.5   Casting a short to a byte

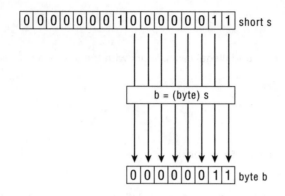

Object Reference Conversion

Object reference variables, like primitive values, participate in assignment conversion, method-call conversion, and casting. (There is no arithmetic promotion of object references, because references cannot be arithmetic operands.) Object reference conversion is more complicated than primitive conversion, because there are more possible combinations of old and new types—and more combinations mean more rules.

Reference conversion, like primitive conversion, takes place at compile time, because the compiler has all the information it needs to determine whether the conversion is legal. Later you will see that this is not the case for object casting.

The following sections examine object reference assignment, method-call, and casting conversions.

Object Reference Assignment Conversion

Object reference assignment conversion happens when you assign an object reference value to a variable of a different type. There are three general kinds of object reference type:

- A class type, such as `Button` or `FileWriter`

- An interface type, such as `Cloneable` or `LayoutManager`

- An array type, such as `int[][]` or `TextArea[]`

Generally speaking, assignment conversion of a reference looks like this:

```
1. Oldtype x = new Oldtype();
2. Newtype y = x;    // reference assignment conversion
```

This is the general format of an assignment conversion from an `Oldtype` to a `Newtype`. Unfortunately, `Oldtype` can be a class, an interface, or an array; `Newtype` can also be a class, an interface, or an array. Thus there are nine (= 3 ∴ 3) possible combinations to consider. Figure 4.6 shows the rules for all nine cases.

It would be difficult to memorize the nine rules shown in Figure 4.6. Fortunately, there is a rule of thumb.

Recall that with primitives, conversions were permitted, provided they were widening conversions. The notion of widening does not really apply to references, but a similar principle is at work. In general, object reference conversion is permitted when the direction of the conversion is "up" the inheritance hierarchy; that is, the old type should inherit from the new type. This rule of thumb does not cover all nine cases, but it is a helpful way to look at things.

The rules for object reference conversion can be stated as follows:

- An interface type can be converted only to an interface type or to `Object`. If the new type is an interface, it must be a superinterface of the old type.

- A class type can be converted to a class type or to an interface type. If converting to a class type, the new type must be a superclass of the old type. If converting to an interface type, the old class must implement the interface.

- An array may be converted to the class `Object`, to the interface `Cloneable` or `Serializable`, or to an array. Only an array of object reference types can be converted to an array, and the old element type must be convertible to the new element type.

To illustrate these rules, consider the inheritance hierarchy shown in Figure 4.7 (assume there is an interface called `Squeezable`).

FIGURE 4.6   The rules for object reference assignment conversion

Converting `Oldtype` to `Newtype`:

	`Oldtype` is a class	`Oldtype` is an interface	`Oldtype` is an array
`Newtype` is a class	`Oldtype` must be a subclass of `Newtype`	`Newtype` must be `Object`	`Newtype` must be `Object`
`Newtype` is an interface	`Oldtype` must implement interface `Newtype`	`Oldtype` must be a subinterface of `Newtype`	`Newtype` must be `Cloneable` or `Serializable`
`Newtype` is an array	Compiler error	Compiler error	`Oldtype` must be an array of some object reference type that can be converted to whatever `Newtype` is an array of

FIGURE 4.7   A simple class hierarchy

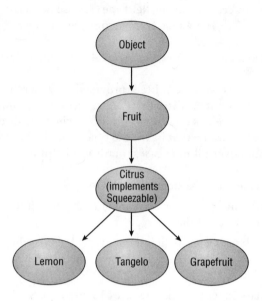

As a first example, consider the following code:

```
1. Tangelo tange = new Tangelo();
2. Citrus cit = tange;
```

This code is fine. A Tangelo is being converted to a Citrus. The new type is a superclass of the old type, so the conversion is allowed. Converting in the other direction ("down" the hierarchy tree) is not allowed:

```
1. Citrus cit = new Citrus();
2. Tangelo tange = cit;
```

This code will result in a compiler error.

What happens when one of the types is an interface?

```
1. Grapefruit g = new Grapefruit();
2. Squeezable squee = g;    // No problem
3. Grapefruit g2 = squee;   // Error
```

The second line ("No problem") changes a class type (Grapefruit) to an interface type. This is correct, provided Grapefruit really implements Squeezable. A glance at Figure 4.7 shows that this is indeed the case, because Grapefruit inherits from Citrus, which implements Squeezable. The third line is an error, because an interface can never be implicitly converted to any reference type other than Object.

Finally, consider an example with arrays:

```
1. Fruit fruits[];
2. Lemon lemons[];
3. Citrus citruses[] = new Citrus[10];
4. for (int i = 0; i < 10; i++) {
5.   citruses[i] = new Citrus();
6. }
7. fruits = citruses;     // No problem
8. lemons = citruses;     // Error
```

Line 7 converts an array of Citrus to an array of Fruit. This is fine, because Fruit is a super-class of Citrus. Line 8 converts in the other direction and fails, because Lemon is not a superclass of Citrus.

Object Method-Call Conversion

Fortunately, the rules for method-call conversion of object reference values are the same as the rules described earlier for assignment conversion of objects. The general rule of thumb is that converting to a superclass is permitted and converting to a subclass is not permitted.

To see how the rules make sense in the context of method calls, consider the extremely useful java.lang.Vector class. You can store anything you like in a vector (anything nonprimitive, that is) by calling the method add (Object ob). For example, the following code stores a Tangelo in a vector:

```
1. Vector myVec = new Vector();
2. Tangelo tange = new Tangelo();
3. myVec.add (tange);
```

The tange argument will automatically be converted to type Object. The automatic conversion means that the people who wrote the java.lang.Vector class didn't have to write a separate method for every possible type of object that anyone might conceivably want to store in a vector. This is fortunate: the Tangelo class was developed years after the invention of the vector, so the developer of the Vector class could not possibly have written specific Tangelo-handling code. An object of any class (and even an array of any type) can be passed into the single add (Object ob) method.

Object Reference Casting

Object reference casting is like primitive casting: by using a cast, you convince the compiler to let you do a conversion that otherwise might not be allowed.

Any kind of conversion that is allowed for assignments or method calls is allowed for explicit casting. For example, the following code is legal:

```
1. Lemon lem = new Lemon();
2. Citrus cit = (Citrus)lem;
```

The cast is legal but not needed; if you leave it out, the compiler will do an implicit assignment conversion. The power of casting appears when you explicitly cast to a type that is not allowed by the rules of implicit conversion.

To understand how object casting works, it is important to understand the difference between objects and object reference variables. Every object (well, nearly every object—there are some obscure cases) is constructed via the **new** operator. The class name following **new** determines for all time the true class of the object. For example, if an object is constructed by calling **new** Color(222, 0, 255), then throughout that object's lifetime, its class will be Color.

Java programs do not deal directly with objects. They deal with references to objects. For example, consider the following code:

```
Color purple = new Color(222, 0, 255);
```

The variable purple is not an object; it is a reference to an object. The object itself lives in memory somewhere in the Java Virtual Machine (JVM). The variable purple contains something similar to the address of the object. This address is known as a *reference* to the object. The difference between a reference and an object is illustrated in Figure 4.8. References are stored in variables, and variables have types that are specified by the programmer at compile time. Object reference variable types can be classes (such as Graphics or FileWriter), interfaces (such as Runnable or LayoutManager), or arrays (such as int[][] or Vector[]).

FIGURE 4.8   Reference and object

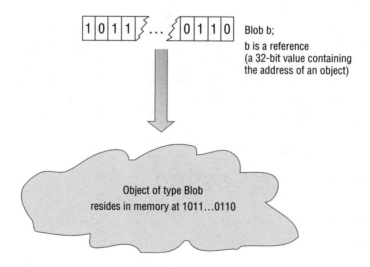

Although an object's class is unchanging, it may be referenced by variables of many different types. For example, consider a stack. It is constructed by calling new Stack( ), so its class really is Stack. Yet at various moments during the lifetime of this object, it may be referenced by variables of type Stack (of course), or of type Vector (because Stack inherits from Vector), or of type Object (because everything inherits from Object). It may even be referenced by variables of type Serializable, which is an interface, because the Stack class implements the Serializable interface. This situation is shown in Figure 4.9.

FIGURE 4.9   Many variable types, one class

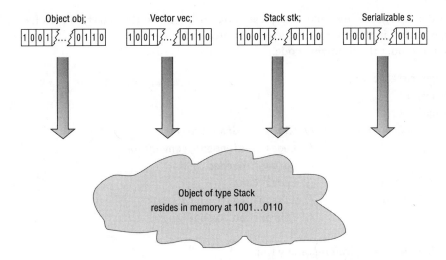

The type of a reference variable is obvious at compile time. However, the class of an object referenced by such a variable cannot be known until runtime. This lack of knowledge is not a shortcoming of Java technology; it results from a fundamental principle of computer science. The distinction between compile-time knowledge and runtime knowledge was not relevant to our discussion of conversions; however, the difference becomes important with reference value casting. The rules for casting are a bit broader than those for conversion. Some of these rules concern reference type and can be enforced by the compiler at compile time; other rules concern object class and can be enforced only during execution.

Quite a few rules govern object casting because a large number of obscure cases must be covered. For the exam, the important rules to remember when casting from Oldtype to Newtype are as follows:

- When both Oldtype and Newtype are classes, one class must be a subclass of the other.

- When both Oldtype and Newtype are arrays, both arrays must contain reference types (not primitives), and it must be legal to cast an element of Oldtype to an element of Newtype.

- You can always cast between an interface and a nonfinal object.

Assuming that a desired cast survives compilation, a second check must occur at runtime. The second check determines whether the class of the object being cast is compatible with the new type. (This check could not be made at compile time, because the object being cast did not exist then.) Here, *compatible* means that the class can be converted according to the conversion rules discussed in the previous two sections. The following rules cover the most common runtime cases:

- If Newtype is a class, the class of the expression being converted must be Newtype or must inherit from Newtype.

- If Newtype is an interface, the class of the expression being converted must implement Newtype.

It is definitely time for some examples! Look once again at the Fruit/Citrus hierarchy that you saw earlier in this chapter, which is repeated in Figure 4.10.

First, consider the following code:

```
1. Grapefruit g, g1;
2. Citrus c;
3. Tangelo t;
4. g = new Grapefruit(); // Class is Grapefruit
5. c = g;                // Legal assignment conversion,
                         // no cast needed
6. g1 = (Grapefruit)c;   // Legal cast
7. t = (Tangelo)c;       // Illegal cast
                         // (throws an exception)
```

FIGURE 4.10   Fruit hierarchy (reprise)

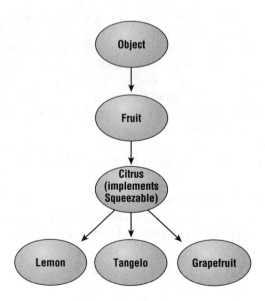

This code has four references but only one object. The object's class is Grapefruit, because Grapefruit's constructor is called on line 4. The assignment c = g on line 5 is a perfectly legal assignment conversion ("up" the inheritance hierarchy), so no explicit cast is required. In lines 6 and 7, the Citrus is cast to a Grapefruit and to a Tangelo. Recall that for casting between class types, one of the two classes (it doesn't matter which one) must be a subclass of the other. The first cast is from a Citrus to its subclass Grapefruit; the second cast is from a Citrus to its subclass Tangelo. Thus both casts are legal—at compile time. The compiler cannot determine the class of the object referenced by c, so it accepts both casts and lets fate determine the outcome at runtime.

When the code is executed, eventually the JVM attempts to execute line 6: g1 = (Grapefruit)c;. The class of c is determined to be Grapefruit, and there is no objection to converting a Grapefruit to a Grapefruit.

Line 7 attempts (at runtime) to cast c to type Tangelo. The class of c is still Grapefruit, and a Grapefruit cannot be cast to a Tangelo. In order for the cast to be legal, the class of c would have to be Tangelo itself or some subclass of Tangelo. Because this is not the case, a runtime exception (java.lang.ClassCastException) is thrown.

Now take an example where an object is cast to an interface type. Begin by considering the following code fragment:

```
1. Grapefruit g, g1;
2. Squeezable s;
3. g = new Grapefruit();
4. s = g;        // Convert Grapefruit to Squeezable (OK)
5. g1 = s;       // Convert Squeezable to Grapefruit
                 // (Compile error)
```

This code will not compile. Line 5 attempts to convert an interface (Squeezable) to a class (Grapefruit). It doesn't matter that Grapefruit implements Squeezable. Implicitly converting an interface to a class is never allowed; it is one of those cases where you have to use an explicit cast to tell the compiler that you really know what you're doing. With the cast, line 5 becomes

```
5. g1 = (Grapefruit)s;
```

Adding the cast makes the compiler happy. At runtime, the JVM checks whether the class of s (which is Grapefruit) can be converted to Grapefruit. It certainly can, so the cast is allowed.

For a final example, involving arrays, look at the following code:

```
1. Grapefruit g[];
2. Squeezable s[];
3. Citrus c[];
4. g = new Grapefruit[500];
5. s = g;             // Convert Grapefruit array to
                      // Squeezable array (OK)
6. c = (Citrus[])s;  // Cast Squeezable array to Citrus
                      // array (OK)
```

Line 6 casts an array of **Squeezables** (**s**) to an array of **Citruses** (**c**). An array cast is legal if casting the array element types is legal (and if the element types are references, not primitives). In this example, the question is whether a **Squeezable** (the element type of array **s**) can be cast to a **Citrus** (the element type of the cast array). The previous example showed that this is a legal cast.

Summary

Primitive values and object references are very different kinds of data. Both can be converted (implicitly) or cast (explicitly). Primitive type changes are caused by assignment conversion, method-call conversion, arithmetic-promotion conversion, or explicit casting.

Primitives can be converted only if the conversion widens the data. Primitives can be narrowed by casting, as long as neither the old nor the new type is **boolean**.

Object references can be converted or cast; the rules that govern these activities are extensive because many combinations of cases must be covered. In general, going "up" the inheritance tree can be accomplished implicitly through conversion; going "down" the tree requires explicit casting. Object reference type changes are caused by assignment conversion, method-call conversion, or explicit casting.

Exam Essentials

Understand when primitive conversion takes place.   Assignment and method-call conversion take place when the new data type is the same as or wider than the old type. Type widths are summarized in Figure 4.3.

Understand when arithmetic promotion takes place.   You should know the type of result of unary and binary arithmetic operations performed on operands of any type.

Understand when primitive casting is required.   Casting is required when the new data type is neither the same as nor wider than the old type.

Understand when object reference conversion takes place.   The rules are summarized in Figure 4.6. The most common case is when the new type is a parent class of the old type.

Understand when object reference casting is required.   The most common case is when the new type inherits from the old type.

Review Questions

1. Which of the following statements is correct? (Choose one.)

    A. Only primitives are converted automatically; to change the type of an object reference, you have to do a cast.

    B. Only object references are converted automatically; to change the type of a primitive, you have to do a cast.

    C. Arithmetic promotion of object references requires explicit casting.

    D. Both primitives and object references can be both converted and cast.

    E. Casting of numeric types may require a runtime check.

2. Which one line in the following code will not compile?

    ```
    1. byte b = 5;
    2. char c = '5';
    3. short s = 55;
    4. int i = 555;
    5. float f = 555.5f;
    6. b = s;
    7. i = c;
    8. if (f > b)
    9.    f = i;
    ```

    A. Line 1

    B. Line 2

    C. Line 3

    D. Line 4

    E. Line 5

    F. Line 6

    G. Line 7

    H. Line 8

    I. Line 9

3. Will the following code compile?

    ```
    1. byte b = 2;
    2. byte b1 = 3;
    3. b = b * b1;
    ```

    A. Yes

    B. No

4.   In the following code, what are the possible types for variable `result`? (Choose the most complete true answer.)

```
1. byte b = 11;
2. short s = 13;
3. result = b * ++s;
```

A. byte, short, int, long, float, double

B. boolean, byte, short, char, int, long, float, double

C. byte, short, char, int, long, float, double

D. byte, short, char

E. int, long, float, double

5.   Consider the following class:

```
1.  class Cruncher {
2.    void crunch(int i) {
3.      System.out.println("int version");
4.    }
5.    void crunch(String s) {
6.      System.out.println("String version");
7.    }
8.
9.    public static void main(String args[]) {
10.     Cruncher crun = new Cruncher();
11.     char ch = 'p';
12.     crun.crunch(ch);
13.   }
14. }
```

Which of the following statements is true? (Choose one.)

A. Line 5 will not compile, because `void` methods cannot be overridden.

B. Line 12 will not compile, because no version of `crunch()` takes a `char` argument.

C. The code will compile but will throw an exception at line 12.

D. The code will compile and produce the following output: `int version`.

E. The code will compile and produce the following output: `String version`.

6. Which of the following statements is true? (Choose one.)

   A. Object references can be converted in assignments but not in method calls.

   B. Object references can be converted in method calls but not in assignments.

   C. Object references can be converted in both method calls and assignments, but the rules governing these conversions are very different.

   D. Object references can be converted in both method calls and assignments, and the rules governing these conversions are identical.

   E. Object references can never be converted.

7. Consider the following code. Which line will not compile?

```
1. Object ob = new Object();
2. String[] stringarr = new String[50];
3. Float floater = new Float(3.14f);
4. ob = stringarr;
5. ob = stringarr[5];
6. floater = ob;
7. ob = floater;
```

   A. Line 4

   B. Line 5

   C. Line 6

   D. Line 7

Questions 8–10 refer to the class hierarchy shown in the graphic below.

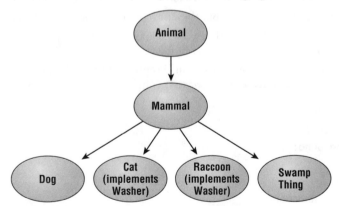

8. Consider the following code:

```
1. Dog       rover, fido;
2. Animal    anim;
3.
```

```
4. rover = new Dog();
5. anim = rover;
6. fido = (Dog)anim;
```

Which of the following statements is true? (Choose one.)

A. Line 5 will not compile.

B. Line 6 will not compile.

C. The code will compile but will throw an exception at line 6.

D. The code will compile and run.

E. The code will compile and run, but the cast in line 6 is not required and can be eliminated.

9. Consider the following code:

```
1. Cat sunflower;
2. Washer wawa;
3. SwampThing pogo;
4.
5. sunflower = new Cat();
6. wawa = sunflower;
7. pogo = (SwampThing)wawa;
```

Which of the following statements is true? (Choose one.)

A. Line 6 will not compile; an explicit cast is required to convert a `Cat` to a `Washer`.

B. Line 7 will not compile, because you cannot cast an interface to a class.

C. The code will compile and run, but the cast in line 7 is not required and can be eliminated.

D. The code will compile but will throw an exception at line 7, because runtime conversion from an interface to a class is not permitted.

E. The code will compile but will throw an exception at line 7, because the runtime class of `wawa` cannot be converted to type `SwampThing`.

10. Consider the following code:

```
1. Raccoon rocky;
2. SwampThing pogo;
3. Washer w;
4.
5. rocky = new Raccoon();
6. w = rocky;
7. pogo = w;
```

Which of the following statements is true? (Choose one.)

A. Line 6 will not compile; an explicit cast is required to convert a `Raccoon` to a `Washer`.

B. Line 7 will not compile; an explicit cast is required to convert a `Washer` to a `SwampThing`.

C. The code will compile and run.

D. The code will compile but will throw an exception at line 7, because runtime conversion from an interface to a class is not permitted.

E. The code will compile but will throw an exception at line 7, because the runtime class of `w` cannot be converted to type `SwampThing`.

11. Which of the following may legally appear as the new type (between the parentheses) in a cast operation?

A. Classes

B. Interfaces

C. Arrays of classes

D. Arrays of interfaces

E. All of the above

12. Which of the following may legally appear as the new type (between the parentheses) in a cast operation?

A. Abstract classes

B. Final classes

C. Primitives

D. All of the above

13. Suppose the declared type of x is a class, and the declared type of y is an interface. When is the assignment x = y; legal?

A. When the type of x is `Object`

B. When the type of x is an array

C. Always

D. Never

14. Suppose the type of xarr is an array of XXX, and the type of yarr is an array of YYY. When is the assignment `xarr = yarr;` legal?

A. Sometimes

B. Always

C. Never

15. When is x & y an `int`? (Choose one).

  A. Always

  B. Sometimes

  C. When neither x nor y is a float, a long, or a double

16. What are the legal types for `whatsMyType`?

```
short s = 10;
whatsMyType = !s;
```

  A. `short`

  B. `int`

  C. There are no possible legal types.

17. When a negative `long` is cast to a byte, what are the possible values of the result?

  A. Positive

  B. Zero

  C. Negative

  D. All of the above

18. When a negative `byte` is cast to a `long`, what are the possible values of the result?

  A. Positive

  B. Zero

  C. Negative

19. Which of the following operators can perform promotion on their operands? (Choose all that apply.)

  A. +

  B. –

  C. ++

  D. --

  E. ~

  F. !

20. What is the difference between the rules for method-call conversion and the rules for assignment conversion?

  A. There is no difference; the rules are the same.

  B. Method-call conversion supports narrowing, assignment conversion does not.

  C. Assignment conversion supports narrowing, method-call conversion does not.

  D. Method-call conversion supports narrowing if the method declares that it throws `ClassCastException`.

Answers to Review Questions

1. D. D is correct because in Java primitives and object references can be both converted and cast. A and B are wrong because they contradict D. C is wrong because objects do not take part in arithmetic operations. E is wrong because only casting of object references potentially requires a runtime check.

2. F. The code b = s will not compile, because converting a short to a byte is a narrowing conversion, which requires an explicit cast. The other assignments in the code are widening conversions.

3. B. Surprisingly, the code will fail to compile at line 3. The two operands, which are originally bytes, are converted to ints before the multiplication. The result of the multiplication is an int, which cannot be assigned to byte b.

4. E. The result of the calculation on line 2 is an int (because all arithmetic results are ints or wider). An int can be assigned to an int, long, float, or double.

5. D. At line 12, the char argument ch is widened to type int (a method-call conversion) and passed to the int version of method crunch().

6. D. Method-call and assignment conversions are governed by the same rules concerning the legal relationships between the old and new types.

7. C. Changing an Object to a Float is going "down" the inheritance hierarchy tree, so an explicit cast is required.

    Questions 8–10 refer to the class hierarchy shown in the graphic below.

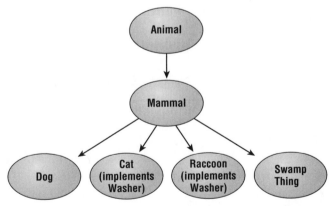

8. D. 80The code will compile and run. The cast in line 6 is required, because changing an Animal to a Dog is going "down" the tree.

9. E. The cast in line 7 is required. Answer D is a preposterous statement expressed in a tone of authority.

10. B. The conversion in line 6 is fine (class to interface), but the conversion in line 7 (interface to class) is not allowed. A cast in line 7 will make the code compile, but then at runtime a `ClassCastException` will be thrown, because `Washer` and `SwampThing` are incompatible.

11. E. Any type may appear inside the parentheses of a cast.

12. E. Any type, including classes with any kind of modifier, may appear inside the parentheses of a cast.

13. A. An interface may be converted only to a class, and the class must be `Object`.

14. A. An array may be converted to another array, provided the element types of the arrays are compatible. This is sometimes, but not always, the case.

15. B. The result is an `int` whenever the operands are `bytes`, `shorts`, `chars`, or `ints`. C is wrong because it does not account for the situation where both operands are `booleans`.

16. C. The expression `!s` won't compile, because the `!` operator may be applied only to `booleans`.

17. D. When a `long` is cast to a `byte`, all but the least-significant 8 bits are discarded. The remaining bits might represent a positive number, zero, or a negative number.

18. C. When a numeric primitive is cast or converted to a wider type, the original value is preserved, so naturally the original sign cannot change.

19. A, B, E. All numeric operators promote. `!`, which is strictly `boolean`, does not promote.

20. A. Method-call conversion and assignment conversion are governed by the same rules.

Chapter 5

Flow Control, Assertions, and Exception Handling

JAVA CERTIFICATION EXAM OBJECTIVES COVERED IN THIS CHAPTER:

- ✓ 2.1 Develop code that implements an if or switch statement; and identify legal argument types for these statements.

- ✓ 2.2 Develop code that implements all forms of loops and iterators, including the use of for, the enhanced for loop (for-each), do, while, labels, break, and continue; and explain the values taken by loop counter variables during and after loop execution.

- ✓ 2.3 Develop code that makes use of assertions, and distinguish appropriate from inappropriate uses of assertions.

- ✓ 2.4 Develop code that makes use of exceptions and exception handling clauses (try, catch, finally), and declares methods and overriding methods that throw exceptions.

- ✓ 2.5 Recognize the effect of an exception arising at a specified point in a code fragment. Note that the exception may be a runtime exception, a checked exception, or an error.

- ✓ 2.6 Recognize situations that will result in any of the following being thrown: ArrayIndexOutOfBoundsException, ClassCast-Exception, IllegalArgumentException, IllegalState-Exception, NullPointerException, NumberFormatException, Assertion-Error, ExceptionInInitializerError, StackOverflow-Error or NoClassDefFoundError. Understand which of these are thrown by the virtual machine and recognize situations in which others should be thrown programatically.

Programming is the art of getting program execution to flow to the right place at the right time. Java lets you control program flow with traditional features such as loops, conditionals, and switches. Java also supports two more modern flow-control constructs: exceptions and assertions. Moreover, Java has enhanced the for-loop syntax to make it more closely integrated with collections.

In this chapter you'll look at both the traditional and the new facilities for controlling program flow.

The Loop Constructs

Java provides three loop constructions. Taken from C and C++, these are the while(), do, and for() constructs. Each provides the facility for repeating the execution of a block of code until some condition occurs.

The *while()* Loop

The general form of the while() loop is

```
1. while (boolean_condition)
2.     repeated_statement_or_block
```

In such a construct, the element *boolean_condition* must be an expression that returns a boolean result. Notice that this differs from C and C++, where a variety of types may be used: In Java you can use *only* a boolean expression. Typically, you might use a comparison of some kind, such as x > 5.

The *repeated_statement_or_block* will be executed again and again as long as the *boolean_condition* is true. If the condition never becomes false, then the loop will repeat forever. In practice, this really means that the loop will repeat until the program is stopped or the machine is turned off.

Notice that we've described the loop body as a "repeated statement or block." We need to make two important points here. The first is one of coding style, and as such is not directly related to the Programmer's Exam (although it might be relevant to the Developer's Exam when you take that). The second is the strict interpretation of the language specification, and as such might be needed in the Programmer's Exam. The two issues are related, so we will discuss them over the next few paragraphs.

The first point is that you would be well advised always to write a block to contain the code for the body of a loop or an `if()` statement. That is, always use a pair of braces so your code will look like this:

```
1. while (boolean_condition) {
2.    statement(s);
3. }
```

You should do so even where the loop contains only a single statement. The reason is that in many situations, you will change from a single line to multiple lines, and if the braces are in position already, that is one less thing to forget. One typical situation where this arises is when you add debug output to the middle of a loop to see how many times the loop is executed. It's very frustrating to realize after 20 minutes of messing about that the loop was executed 10 times, although the message was printed only on exit from the loop. It's perhaps worse to see the message printed 10 times but to have moved the proper body of the loop outside of it entirely.

The second point is that, from the position of strict correctness, you need to know that a single statement without braces is allowed in loops and `if` statements. So, the following code is correct and prints "five times" five times, but "once" only once:

```
1.   int i = 0;
2.   while (i++ < 5)
3.      System.out.println("five times");
4.   System.out.println("once");
```

It is highly unlikely that you will be presented with code that uses a single nonblocked statement as the body of a loop or the conditional part of an `if` statement, but if you do, you need to recognize how it will behave and that it is not incorrect.

The exact position of the opening curly brace that marks a block of code is a matter of near-religious contention. Some programmers put it at the end of a line, as in most of the examples in this book. Others put it on a line by itself. Provided it is otherwise placed in the correct sequence, it does not matter how many space, tab, and newline characters are placed before or after the opening curly brace. In other words, this positioning is not relevant to syntactic correctness. You should be aware, however, that the style used in presenting the exam questions, as well as that used for the code in the developer-level exam, is the style shown here, where the opening brace is placed at the end of the line.

Observe that if the *boolean_condition* is already false when the loop is first encountered, then the body of the loop will never be executed. This fact relates to the main distinguishing feature of the do loop, which we will discuss next.

The *do* Loop

The general form of the do loop is

```
1. do
2.    repeated_statement_or_block
3. while (boolean_condition);
```

It is similar to the `while()` loop just discussed, and as before, it is best to have a loop body formed with a block:

```
1. do {
2.    do_something
3.    do_more
4. } while (boolean_condition);
```

Again, repetition of the loop is terminated when the `boolean_condition` becomes false. The significant difference is that this loop always executes the body of the loop at least once, because the test is performed at the end of the body.

Notice that the do loop (as opposed to the `while` loop) is guaranteed to run at least once, regardless of the value of the conditional expression. The do loop is probably used less frequently than the `while()` loop, but the third loop format is perhaps the most common. The third form is the `for()` loop, which we will discuss next.

The *for()* Loop

A common requirement in programming is to perform a loop so that a single variable is incremented over a range of values between two limits. This ability is frequently provided by a loop that uses the keyword `for`. Java's `while()` loop can achieve this effect, but it is most commonly achieved using the `for()` loop. However, as with C and C++, using the `for()` loop is more general than simply providing for iteration over a sequence of values.

The general form of the `for()` loop is

```
1. for (statement ; condition ; expression)
2.    loop_body
```

Again, a block should normally be used as the *loop_body* part, like this:

```
1. for (statement ; condition ; expression) {
2.    do_something
3.    do_more
4. }
```

The keys to this loop are in the three parts contained in the brackets following the for keyword:

- The *statement* is executed immediately before the loop itself is started. It is often used to set up starting conditions. You will see shortly that it can also contain variable declarations.

- The *condition* must be a boolean expression and is treated exactly the same as in the while() loop. The body of the loop will be executed repeatedly until the condition ceases to be true. As with the while() loop, it is possible that the body of a for() loop might never be executed. This occurs if the condition is already false at the start of the loop.

- The *expression* (short for "iteration expression") is executed immediately after the body of the loop, just before the test is performed again. Commonly, it is used to increment a loop counter.

If you have already declared an int variable x, you can code a simple sequence-counting loop like this:

```
1. for (x = 0; x < 10; x++) {
2.    System.out.println(" value is "  + x);
3. }
```

This code would result in 10 lines of output, starting with

```
value is 0
```

and ending with

```
value is 9
```

In fact, because for() loops commonly need a counting variable, you are allowed to declare variables in the *statement* part. The scope of such a variable is restricted to the statement or block following the for() statement and the for() part itself. This limitation protects loop counter variables from interfering with each other and prevents leftover loop count values from accidental re-use. The result is code like this:

```
1. for (int x = 0; x < 10; x++) {
2.    System.out.println("value is " + x);
3. }
```

It might be useful to look at the equivalent of this code implemented using a while() loop:

```
1. {
2.    int x = 0;
3.    while (x < 10) {
4.       System.out.println("value is "  + x);
5.       x++;
6.    }
7. }
```

This version reinforces a couple of points. First, the scope of the variable x, declared in the *statement* part of the for() loop, is restricted to the loop and its control parts (that is, the *statement*, *condition*, and *expression*). Second, the *expression* is executed after the rest of the loop body, effectively before control comes back to the test condition.

Empty *for()* Loops

Any part of a for() loop's control may be omitted if you wish. Omitting the test is equivalent to a perpetually true test, so the construct

```
for(;;) {}
```

creates a loop that repeats forever. Notice that both semicolons must still be included for correct syntax, even though the statement, condition, and expression are omitted.

The *for()* Loop and the Comma Separator

The for() loop allows the use of the comma separator in a special way. The *statement* and *expression* parts described previously can contain a sequence of expressions rather than just a single one. If you want such a sequence, you should separate those expressions, not with a semicolon (which would be mistaken as the separator between the three parts of the for() loop control structure), but with a comma. This behavior is borrowed from C and C++, where the comma is an operator; in Java the comma serves only as a special case separator for conditions where the semicolon would be unsuitable. This example demonstrates:

```
1. int j, k;
2. for (j = 3, k = 6; j + k < 20; j++, k +=2) {
3.   System.out.println("j is " + j + " k is " + k);
4. }
```

Note that although you can use the comma to separate several expressions, you cannot mix expressions with variable declarations, nor can you have multiple declarations of different types. So these would be illegal:

```
1. int i = 7;
2. for (i++, int j = 0; i < 10; j++) { } // illegal!
```

```
1. for (int i = 7, long j = 0; i < 10; j++) { } // illegal!
```

A final note on this issue is that the use of the comma to separate multiple declarations of a single type is allowed, like this:

```
1. for (int i = 7, j = 0; i < 10; j++) { }
```

This line declares two int variables, i and j, and initializes them to 7 and 0 respectively. This, however, is a standard feature of declarations and is not specific to the for() loop.

Enhanced *for* Loops

Java's for loops were enhanced in release 1.5 to work more easily with arrays and collections. Collections and their for loop enhancements are discussed in Chapter 8, "The java.lang and java.util Packages." Here we will just look at how arrays work with enhanced for loops.

You often want to perform identical processing on every element of an array. For example, the following method returns the sum of the squares of the members of an array of floats:

```java
float sumOfSquares(float[] floats) {
  float sum = 0;
  for (int i=0; i<floats.length; i++)
    sum += floats[i];
  return sum;
}
```

With enhanced for loops, this method can be rewritten as

```java
float sumOfSquares(float[] floats) {
  float sum = 0;
  for (float f:floats)
    sum += f;
  return sum;
}
```

The new version eliminates the loop counter. The new syntax is

```java
for (type variable_name:array)
```

The type must be compatible with the array type. The colon is pronounced "in," so if you were reading the new for line out loud you would say, "for float f in floats." The loop executes once for each member of the array, with the variable taking on each array member value in turn.

The array may contain primitives or references. The next example is a method that computes the sum of the lengths of an array of strings:

```java
int sumOfLengths(String[] strings) {
  int totalLength = 0;
  for (String s:strings)
    totalLength += s.length();
  return totalLength;
}
```

In Chapter 8 you will see how the enhanced for loop can iterate over collection members as well as array members.

We have now discussed the loop constructions in their basic forms. The next section looks at more advanced flow control in loops, specifically the use of the `break` and `continue` statements.

The *break* and *continue* Statements in Loops

Sometimes you need to abandon execution of the body of a loop—or perhaps a number of nested loops. Java provides two statements, `break` and `continue`, which can be used to achieve this effect. The `break` statement terminates execution of a loop. The `continue` statement terminates the current pass through a loop. Let's look in more detail at these two keywords.

Using *continue*

Suppose you have a loop that is processing an array of items that each contain two `String` references. The first `String` is always non-`null`, but the second might not be present. To process this, you might decide that you want, in pseudocode, something along these lines:

```
for each element of the array
  process the first String
  if the second String exists
    process the second String
  endif
endfor
```

You will recognize that this can be coded easily by using an `if` block to control processing of the second `String`. However, you can also use the `continue` statement like this:

```
1. for (int i = 0; i < array.length; i++) {
2.   // process first string
3.   if (array[i].secondString == null) {
4.     continue;
5.   }
6.   // process second string
7. }
```

In this case, the example is sufficiently simple that you probably do not see any advantage over using the `if()` condition to control the execution of the second part. If the second `String` processing was long, and perhaps heavily indented in its own right, you might find that the use of `continue` was slightly simpler visually.

The real strength of `continue` is that it is able to skip out of multiple levels of loop. Suppose the example, instead of being two `String` objects, is two-dimensional arrays of `char` values. Now you will need to nest your loops. Consider this sample:

```
1. mainLoop: for (int i = 0; i < array.length; i++) {
2.   for (int j = 0; j < array[i].length; j++) {
3.     if (array[i][j] == '\u0000') {
```

```
4.       continue mainLoop;
5.     }
6.   }
7. }
```

Notice particularly the label `mainLoop` that has been applied to the `for()` on line 1. The fact that this is a label is indicated by the trailing colon. You typically apply labels of this form to the opening loop statements: `while()`, `do`, or `for()`.

Here, when the processing of the second array comes across a 0 value, it abandons the whole processing not just for the inner loop but for the current object in the main array. This is equivalent to jumping to the statement `i++` in the first `for()` statement.

You might still think this is not really any advantage over using `if()` statements, but imagine that further processing was done between lines 6 and 7, and that finding the 0 character in the array was required to avoid that further processing. To achieve that without using `continue`, you would have to set a flag in the inner loop and use it to abandon the outer loop processing. It can be done, but it is rather messy.

Using *break*

The `break` statement, when applied to a loop, is somewhat similar to the `continue` statement. However, instead of prematurely completing the current iteration of a loop, `break` causes the entire loop to be abandoned. Consider this example:

```
1. for (int j = 0; j < array.length; j++) {
2.   if (array[j] == null) {
3.     break; //break out of inner loop
4.   }
5.   // process array[j]
6. }
```

In this case, instead of simply skipping some processing for `array[j]` and proceeding directly to processing `array[j+1]`, this version quits the entire inner loop as soon as a `null` element is found.

You can also use labels on `break` statements, and as before, you must place a matching label on one of the enclosing blocks. The `break` and `continue` statements provide a convenient way to make parts of a loop conditional, especially when used in their labeled formats.

The next section discusses the `if()/else` and `switch()` constructions, which provide the normal means of implementing conditional code.

The Selection Statements

Java provides a choice of two selection constructs: the `if()/else` and `switch()` mechanisms. You can easily write simple conditional code for a choice of two execution paths based on the value of a `boolean` expression using `if()/else`. If you need more complex choices between multiple execution paths, and if an integral argument is available to control the choice, then you can use switch(); otherwise you can use either nests or sequences of if()/else.

The *if()/else* Construct

The if()/else construct takes a boolean argument as the basis of its choice. Often you will use a comparison expression to provide this argument. For example

```
1. if (x > 5) {
2.    System.out.println("x is more than 5");
3. }
```

This sample executes line 2, provided the test (x > 5) in line 1 returns true. Notice that we used a block even though there is only a single conditional line, just as we suggested you should generally do with the loops discussed earlier.

You can use an else block to give code that is executed under the conditions that the test returns false. For example

```
1. if (x > 5) {
2.    System.out.println("x is more than 5");
3. }
4. else {
5.    System.out.println("x is not more than 5");
6. }
```

You can also use if()/else in a nested fashion, refining conditions to more specific, or narrower, tests at each point.

The if()/else construction makes a test between only two possible paths of execution. However, you can also use the if()/else construction to choose between multiple possible execution paths by using the if()/else if() variation of the construction. For example

```
1. if (hours > 1700) {
2.    System.out.println("good evening");
3. }
4. else if (hours > 1200){
5.    System.out.println("good afternoon");
6. }
7. else {
8.    System.out.println("good morning");
9. }
```

The code snippet above can be rewritten using the switch() statement. The next section discusses the switch() statement, which allows a single value to select between multiple possible execution paths.

The *switch()* Construct

If you need to make a choice between multiple alternative execution paths, and the choice can be based upon an `int` value, you can use the `switch()` construct. Consider this example:

```
1. switch (x) {
2.    case 1:
3.       System.out.println("Got a 1");
4.       break;
5.    case 2:
6.    case 3:
7.       System.out.println("Got 2 or 3");
8.       break;
9.    default:
10.      System.out.println("Not a 1, 2, or 3");
11.      break;
12. }
```

Note that, although you cannot determine the fact by inspection of this code, the variable x must be either `byte`, `short`, `char`, or `int`. It must not be `long`, either of the floating-point types, `boolean`, or an object reference. Strictly, the value must be "assignment compatible" with `int`.

The comparison of values following `case` labels with the value of the expression supplied as an argument to `switch()` determines the execution path. The arguments to `case` labels must be constants, or at least constant expressions that can be fully evaluated at compile time. You cannot use a variable or an expression involving variables.

Each `case` label takes only a single argument, but when execution jumps to one of these labels, it continues downward until it reaches a `break` statement. This occurs even if execution passes another `case` label or the `default` label. So, in the previous example, if x has the value 2, execution goes through lines 1, 5, 6, 7, and 8 and continues beyond line 12. This requirement for `break` to indicate the completion of the `case` part is important. More often than not, you do not want to omit the `break`, because you do not want execution to "fall through." However, to achieve the effect shown in the example, where more than one particular value of x causes execution of the same block of code, you use multiple `case` labels with only a single `break`.

The `default` statement is comparable to the `else` part of an `if()`/`else` construction. Execution jumps to the `default` statement if none of the explicit `case` values matches the argument provided to `switch()`. Although the `default` statement is shown at the end of the `switch()` block in the example (and this is both a conventional and reasonably logical place to put it), no rule requires this placement.

Now that you have examined the constructions that provide for iteration and selection under normal program control, let's look at the flow of control under exception conditions—that is, conditions when some runtime problem has arisen.

Exceptions

Occasionally when a program is executing something occurs that is not quite normal from the point of view of the goal at hand. For example, a user might type an invalid filename; a file might contain corrupted data; a network link could fail; or a bug in the program might cause it to try to make an illegal memory access, such as referring to an element beyond the end of an array.

Circumstances of this type are called *exception conditions* in Java and are represented using objects. An extensive class hierarchy descending from `java.lang.Throwable` is dedicated to describing them.

Most new Java programmers first encounter exceptions when they try to call a useful method that they read about in the API pages. Usually it's the pages for the `java.io` package, whose methods throw lots of exceptions. For example, you might decide to call the `getCanonicalFile()` method of an instance of `java.io.File`. (Don't worry about what the method actually *does*! We're here to study exceptions, not file I/O.)

If you don't know anything about exceptions, you might try to do the following:

```
myFile.getCanonicalFile();
```

Unfortunately, this doesn't compile. The compiler error says something like

```
unreported exception java.io.IOException; must be caught or declared to be
thrown
```

On closer inspection of the API page for the `File` class, you see that the `getCanonicalFile()` method declaration includes the words "throws IOException." Whenever you see "throws" in a method description on an API page, you can't just call the method. You need to deal with the exception in one of two ways: you can catch it or you can declare it. These options are explained in the next two sections.

Catching Exceptions

One way to call a method that throws an exception is to create a `try` block and a `catch` block. The structure looks like this:

```
try {
  // Exception-throwing code
}
catch (Exception_type name) {
  // Exception-handling code
}
```

The `try` block contains code that throws exceptions. Code that doesn't throw exceptions may also be included.

The `catch` keyword is followed by a declaration, which appears in parentheses. Like any declaration, this consists of a type followed by a name. The type must match the type of the exception being thrown in the `try` block. (Well, not exactly, but it's a good enough explanation for now.) The name may be anything you like; it has scope within the curlies ({ }) of the `catch` block. To make sense of all this, let's see what happens when an exception is thrown. We'll continue the example of the previous section.

```
1.  File myFile = getMyFile();
2.
3.  try {
4.    System.out.println("About to call.");
5.    myFile.getCanonicalFile();
6.    System.out.println("Call succeeded.");
7.  }
8.
9.  catch (IOException xceptn) {
10.   System.out.println("File stress! " + xceptn.getMessage());
11.   xceptn.printStackTrace();
12. }
13.
14. System.out.println("Life goes on.");
```

Line 1 is just setup. The `try` block is lines 3–7. Note that only line 5 can throw an exception. (Recall that the API explanation for `getCanonicalFile()` says, "throws IOException.") Lines 9–12 are the `catch` block.

When this code executes, there are two possible scenarios, because the `getCanonicalFile()` call might or might not find itself in an abnormal condition. When a method declares that it throws an exception type, it doesn't mean that an exception is thrown every time the method is called. It just means that an exception *might* get thrown, if the method gets into trouble.

In the simpler scenario, no exception is thrown. Execution starts on line 1 and then enters the `try` block. Lines 4, 5, and 6 execute. The `catch` block is skipped, and execution continues at line 14.

In the more interesting scenario, execution runs as before until the `getCanonicalFile()` call on line 5 gets into trouble. Then the `getCanonicalFile()` method throws an `IOException`. (You'll see a little later how methods throw exceptions.) In Java, exceptions are objects, and so in our example an instance of `IOException` is created (somehow, somewhere) and given to the Java Virtual Machine (JVM). The current execution of the `try` block is abandoned, so line 6 does not execute. Instead, execution jumps into the `catch` block. Within the block (lines 10 and 11 in our example) `xceptn` is a reference to the exception object.

All exceptions descend from the `java.lang.Throwable` superclass, from which they inherit two very useful methods. When an exception object is constructed, a text message is stored inside it. This message describes the circumstances that caused the exception to be thrown. It can be retrieved by calling `getMessage()` on the exception, as in line 10. Often the way to handle an exception is to display the message to the user and let the user figure out what to do next. The second useful method is `printStackTrace()`, as seen on line 11, which displays a snapshot of the JVM's call stack at the moment the exception was created. The stack trace tells you on what line of what source file the exception was created. It also tells you from where (line number and source filename) the method containing that line was called. And it also tells from where the method containing *that* line was called, and so on, up and up until you get to a line in main(). So the stack trace tells you who called the code that called the code that called the code, et cetera, which is extremely useful for debugging.

As useful as stack traces are for debugging, they are inappropriate for deployed code, since they expose users to information they shouldn't have to worry about.

A try block may contain code that throws different exception types. This can even happen if the block contains only a single line of code, because a method is allowed to throw different types to indicate different kinds of trouble. When multiple exception types are thrown, you use multiple catch blocks. Here's an example of a try block that throws two different exception types, with one catch block for each type:

```
1. File myFile = getMyFile();
2. String s = getStringAndHopeForAllDigits();
3.
4. try {
5.    System.out.println("About to call.");
6.    int x = Integer.parseInt(s);
7.    myFile.getCanonicalFile();
8.    System.out.println("Call succeeded.");
9. }
10.
11. catch (NumberFormatException xceptn) {
12.    System.out.println("Bad text! " + xceptn.getMessage());
13.    xceptn.printStackTrace();
14. }
15.
16. catch (IOException xceptn) {
17.    System.out.println("File stress! " + xceptn.getMessage());
18.    xceptn.printStackTrace();
19. }
20.
21. System.out.println("Life goes on.");
```

The first catch block, on lines 11–14, handles the NumberFormatException that parseInt() throws. The second catch block, on lines 16–19, is the same as the one from the previous example, handling the IOException thrown by the getCanonicalFile() call.

If no exception is thrown, the try block runs to completion, and then execution continues at the first line after the last catch block. If an exception is thrown, the appropriate catch block executes, and then execution continues at the first line after the last catch block.

There is more to say about catch blocks, but first let's look at a way to handle exceptions without using catch blocks at all.

Declaring Exceptions

There is a way to call exception-throwing methods without enclosing the calls in try blocks. A method declaration may end with the throws keyword, followed by an exception type, or by multiple exception types followed by commas. A throws declaration may be combined without restriction with any other modifiers. Here are some examples:

```
public void throwsOne() throws IOException {

...

}


private static synchronized int throwsTwo()
    throws IOException, AWTException {

...

}
```

When a method declares that it throws exceptions, any method call that throws exception types listed in the method declaration does not need to appear in a try block. So in the examples above, throwsOne() may contain calls to methods that throw IOException, without enclosing those calls in try blocks. Similarly, within throwsTwo(), any calls to methods that throw IOException or AWTException need not appear in try blocks.

Of course, methods that call throwsOne() or throwsTwo() must either enclose those calls in try blocks or declare that they, too, throw the exception types.

How the JVM Dispatches Exceptions

When a method throws an exception, an exception object is (somehow) created and (somehow) handed off to the JVM. We'll examine these *somehows* in the next section. For now, it's time to see what really happens when the JVM needs to process an exception.

The JVM begins by checking whether the exception came from code in a try block. If so, each catch block following that try block is checked, in order of appearance, for compatibility with the exception. A catch block is compatible if the exception is an instance of the class declared at the beginning of the catch block. The check is made using the instanceof operator. So, for example, if a catch block looks like this

```
catch (IOException x) { ... }
```

then the block will handle any `IOException` instance and also (because that's how `instanceof` works) any instance of any subclass of `IOException`.

If the exception is not compatible with any `catch` block, or if it wasn't thrown from a `try` block, the JVM checks the exception types declared to be thrown by the current method. If a compatible type is found (again using `instanceof`), then the JVM's attention turns to the method that called the current method, and this entire process repeats...possibly many times, if the exception is to be handled far up the calling chain.

If there simply isn't a compatible `catch` block for the exception, then the JVM prints out the exception's stack trace and then terminates itself. The compiler makes every possible effort to prevent you from writing code in which this happens.

Notice that if a `try` block throws 15 different exception types, and all the types are subclasses of, for example, `IOException`, then you don't need 15 `catch` blocks. You can have a single `catch (IOException x)` block, because every exception that can possibly be thrown will be an `instanceof IOException`. You would do this if every different exceptional condition required the same processing.

Two Kinds of Exception

Java has two kinds of exception: checked and runtime. A good way to understand the difference is to look at some exception class names. All of Java's exception classes have names that are somewhat long and quite descriptive. (It's a worthwhile trade-off.) For example, there's `ArrayIndexOutOfBoundsException`. It's obvious what condition that one indicates. There's also `FileNotFoundException`, which is equally obvious.

There's an important difference between an array index that's too large and a file that can't be found. The array index problem is completely avoidable: there is no reason why anyone should ever ship code that tries to index nonexistent array elements. On the other hand, the existence or nonexistence of files out on a disk is not something over which the program or the programmer has any control. At the time you write your code, you can't possibly have knowledge about what files will exist on all disks attached to all computers that will run your program at any time in the infinite future.

To put it bluntly, an out-of-bounds array index is all your fault. An absent file is nobody's fault.

In Java terminology, the avoidable exceptions that are your fault are known as *runtime exceptions*. The term isn't very descriptive; you might want to think of it as an abbreviation for "these-should-never-happen-at-runtime" exceptions. Other runtime exceptions include `ArithmeticException`, which as you've seen indicates division by zero, and `NegativeArraySizeException`, which is thrown when you construct an array with—you guessed it—negative length.

The right time to deal with runtime exceptions is when you're designing, developing, and debugging your code. Since runtime exceptions should never be thrown in finished code, it's not appropriate to deal with them in `catch` blocks. In fact, runtime exceptions are exempt from all the rules we've discussed so far. You are free to call methods that throw runtime exceptions, without enclosing the calls in `try` blocks or adding `throws` to the declaration of your enclosing methods. (If it weren't for this exemption, Java source would be all but impossible to read.

Every expression that uses division, every array construction, and every array access would need an exception-handling mechanism.)

The compiler and JVM define runtime exceptions to be the `java.lang.RuntimeException` class, as well as all its subclasses. Figure 5.1 shows the big picture of the exception hierarchy.

Any exception class that doesn't descend from `RuntimeException` is known as a *checked exception*. It is the checked exceptions that must be handled by either the `try-catch` mechanism or the `throws-declaration` mechanism. The compiler ensures that every checked exception has a handler somewhere.

Errors, which appear on the right side of the figure, behave just like other checked exceptions. However, programmers should never throw or catch errors, which mostly are reserved for indicating trouble in JVM. The only errors that programmers are ever likely to see are assertion errors, which are discussed later in this chapter.

FIGURE 5.1   The Exception Inheritance Hierarchy

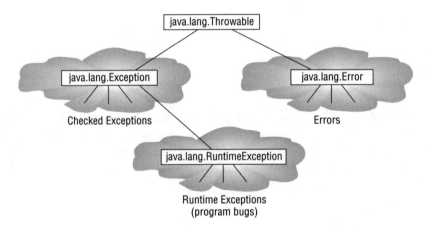

The *finally* Block

The last `catch` block associated with a `try` block may be followed by a `finally` block. This is a block of code, enclosed in curlies ({ }) and preceded by the keyword `finally`. Here's an example:

```
1. File myFile = getMyFile();
2. String s = getStringAndHopeForAllDigits();
3.
4. try {
5.   System.out.println("About to call.");
6.   int x = Integer.parseInt(s);
7.   myFile.getCanonicalFile();
```

```
 8.    System.out.println("Call succeeded.");
 9. }
10.
11. catch (NumberFormatException xceptn) {
12.    System.out.println("Bad text! " + xceptn.getMessage());
13.    xceptn.printStackTrace();
14. }
15.
16. catch (IOException xceptn) {
17.    System.out.println("File stress! " + xceptn.getMessage());
18.    xceptn.printStackTrace();
19. }
20.
21. finally {
22.    System.out.println("In the finally block.");
23. }
24.
25. System.out.println("Life goes on.");
```

The finally block's code is guaranteed to execute in nearly all circumstances. If the block throws its own exception, execution jumps to the corresponding exception handler, and so the finally block doesn't run to completion. Aside from that it almost takes a catastrophe to prevent a finally block from running to completion. Here's what it takes:

- The death of the current thread
- Execution of System.exit()
- Turning off the computer

At first glance, finally blocks don't seem very useful. After all, won't the first line of code after the try/catch/finally stuff run in all circumstances? In most cases this is so, but it's possible to create code that never gets to that line. For example, a catch block might call a method that throws an exception out of the current method; in that case execution will never get around to the first line after the try/catch/finally code.

Throwing Exceptions

The methods that you write can throw exceptions. To throw your own exception, first decide whether the exception should be checked at runtime. Then choose the appropriate exception type. Check the API pages. An easy way is to check the exceptions listing for the major packages (java.lang, java.util, etc.). If you find a class whose name describes the situation you want to signal, use that class. If you don't, you'll have to create your own exception class, as described in the next section.

At the point where you want your method to throw, construct an instance of your chosen exception type. Then use the `throw` keyword as shown in the example below:

```
IOException x = new IOException("Phaser bank lockup.");
throw x;
```

All the exception classes in the core packages have two constructors. One is a `no-args` constructor. It's bad form to use that one. It's much more helpful to pass a descriptive string into the constructor. This string becomes the text that is returned when someone catches your exception and calls its `getMessage()` method.

The moment an exception is constructed, the current thread's call stack is recorded in the exception object, where it can be retrieved by a `printStackTrace()` call. It's good practice to throw an exception as soon as possible after construction, so that the stack trace will nearly reflect the thread's status at the moment the exception was thrown.

All checked exception types thrown from a method must be represented in the method's "throws" list. To be properly represented, an exception type must either appear on the list or descend from a type that appears on the list.

Creating Your Own Exception Classes

Creating your own exception classes is easy. First, decide whether you want a checked or a runtime exception. Checked exceptions should extend `java.lang.Exception` or one of its subclasses. Runtime exceptions should extend `java.lang.RuntimeException` or one of its subclasses. Choose a descriptive name for your class; it should end with `exception`.

The class doesn't need any methods, unless you see a special need for them. It should have three constructors. The argument list of these constructors should include

- A message
- A cause
- A message and a cause

A message is a string that is retrieved by the `getMessage()` call. A cause is another exception. Causes come into play when a method handles an exception by throwing a different exception type, one that will have more meaning to that method's callers. The code that catches the new exception might need information embedded in the original exception: the cause or the stack trace might be especially useful.

To retrieve an exception's cause, call its `getCause()` method. The return type is actually `Throwable`, which allows `throwables` and errors to have causes. A cause might have its own cause, and so on; this structure is known as *exception chaining*.

All you need to do with the message and the cause is pass them to the superclass constructor. Here's an example:

```
public class PhaserBankException extends Exception {
  public PhaserBankException(String message) {
    super(message);
```

```
  }

  public PhaserBankException(Throwable cause) {
    super(cause);
  }

  public PhaserBankException(String message, Throwable cause) {
    super(message);
  }
}
```

Custom exception types are always the right choice when the core classes don't contain an exception whose name describes your situation.

Exceptions and Overriding

When you extend a class and override a method, the Java compiler insists that all exception classes thrown by the new method must be the same as, or subclasses of, the exception classes thrown by the original method. Consider these examples (assume they are declared in separate source files; the line numbers are simply for reference):

```
1. public class BaseClass {
2.    public void method() throws IOException {
3.    }
4. }
5.
6. public class LegalOne extends BaseClass {
7.    public void method() throws IOException {
8.    }
9. }
10.
11. public class LegalTwo extends BaseClass {
12.    public void method() {
13.    }
14. }
15.
16. public class LegalThree extends BaseClass {
17.    public void method()
18.    throws EOFException, MalformedURLException {
19.    }
20. }
21.
```

```
22. public class IllegalOne extends BaseClass {
23.    public void method()
24.    throws IOException, IllegalAccessException {
25.    }
26. }
27.
28. public class IllegalTwo extends BaseClass {
29.    public void method()
30.    throws Exception {
31.    }
32. }
```

Notice that the original method() in BaseClass is declared as throwing an IOException. This declaration allows it, and any overriding method defined in a subclass, to throw an IOException or any object that is a subclass of IOException. Overriding methods cannot, however, throw any checked exceptions that are not subclasses of IOException.

Given these rules, you will see that line 7 in LegalOne is correct, because method() is declared exactly the same way as the original that it overrides. Similarly, line 18 in LegalThree is correct, because both EOFException and MalformedURLException are subclasses of IOException—so this adheres to the rule that nothing may be thrown that is not a subclass of the exceptions already declared. Line 12 in LegalTwo is correct, because it throws no exceptions and therefore cannot throw any exceptions that are not subclasses of IOException.

The methods at lines 23 and 29 are not permissible, because both of them throw checked exceptions that are not subclasses of IOException. In IllegalOne, IllegalAccessException is a subclass of Exception; in IllegalTwo, Exception itself is a superclass of IOException. Both IllegalAccessException and Exception are checked exceptions, so the methods that attempt to throw them are illegal as overriding methods of method() in BaseClass.

The point of this rule relates to the use of base class variables as references to objects of sub-class type. Chapter 4, "Converting and Casting," explains that you can declare a variable of a class X and then use that variable to refer to any object that is of class X or any subclass of X.

Imagine that in the examples just described, you declared a variable myBaseObject of class BaseClass; you can use it to refer to objects of any of the classes LegalOne, LegalTwo, and LegalThree. (You can't use it to refer to objects of class IllegalOne or IllegalTwo, because those objects cannot be created in the first place: their code won't compile.) The compiler imposes checks on how you call myBaseObject.method(). Those checks ensure that for each call, either you have enclosed the call in a try block and provided a corresponding catch block or you have declared that the calling method itself might throw an IOException. Now suppose that at runtime, the variable myBaseObject was used to refer to an object of class IllegalOne. Under these conditions, the compiler would still believe that the only exceptions that must be dealt with are of class IOException, because it believes that myBaseObject refers to an object of class BaseClass. The compiler would therefore not insist that you provide a try/catch construct that catches the IllegalAccessException, nor that you declare the calling method as throwing that exception. Thus if the class IllegalOne were permitted, overriding methods would be able to bypass the enforced checks for checked exceptions.

It is important to consider the likely needs of subclasses whenever you define a class. Recall that it is entirely permissible to declare that a method throws an exception even if no code exists to actually throw that exception. Now that you know an overriding method cannot throw exceptions that were not declared in the parent method, you will recognize that some parent classes need to declare exceptions in methods that do not in fact throw any exceptions. For example, the `InputStream` class cannot, of itself, actually throw any exceptions, because it doesn't interact with real devices that could fail. However, it is used as the base class for a whole hierarchy of classes that do interact with physical devices: `FileInputStream` and so forth. It is important that the `read()` methods of those subclasses be able to throw exceptions, so the corresponding `read()` methods in the `InputStream` class itself must be declared as throwing `IOException`.

We have now looked at all the aspects of exception handling that you will need to prepare for the Programmer's Exam and to make effective use of exceptions in your programs.

Assertions

A new facility called assertions was introduced in the Java 1.4 release. Assertions provide a convenient mechanism for verifying that a class's methods are called correctly. This mechanism can be enabled or disabled at runtime. The intention is that assertions typically will be enabled during development and disabled in the field.

The new `assert` keyword has the following syntax:

```
assert Expression1;
assert Expression1:Expression2;
```

Expression1 must have `boolean` type. *Expression2* may have any type. If assertions are disabled at runtime (the default state), the `assert` statement does absolutely nothing. If assertions are enabled at runtime (via a command-line argument to the JVM), then *Expression1* is evaluated. If its value is true, no further action is taken. If its value is false, then an `AssertionError` is thrown. If *Expression2* is present, it is passed into the constructor of the `AssertionError`, where it is converted to a `String` and used as the error's message.

If you want to use assertions, you need to understand three concepts: how to compile them, how to enable them at runtime, and how to use them appropriately. We'll look at these concepts in the next three sections.

Assertions and Compilation

Sun is generally reluctant to expand the Java language, and with good reason. Unbridled language expansion would compromise Java's simplicity and could also create compatibility problems with existing code.

For example, the introduction of the `assert` keyword in release 1.4 was inconvenient for developers who had used `assert` as an identifier in pre-1.4 code (perhaps to implement their own home-grown assertion facility). Thus it was necessary to introduce a compiler flag to control whether `assert` should be treated as an identifier or as a keyword. To treat it as a keyword (that is, to take advantage of the new facility), you had to compile with `-source 1.4` as in the following example:

```
javac -source 1.4 UsefulApplication.java
```

If the flag was omitted, the 1.4 compiler treated source code as if the `assert` keyword did not exist; thus `assert` could be used as an identifier.

Release 5.0 automatically treats assert as a keyword, so it is no longer necessary to compile with a `-source` flag.

Runtime Enabling of Assertions

Assertions are disabled by default. To enable assertions at runtime, use the `-enableassertions` or `-ea` flag on the Java command line, as in the following example:

```
java -ea UsefulApplication
```

Additional runtime flags enable or disable assertions at the class level, but they are beyond the scope of the exam and of this book. If assertions are disabled, `assert` statements have no effect.

The `-ea` flag means that code can be developed with heavy reliance on assertions for debugging. The code can be shipped without removing the `assert` statements from the source files.

Using Assertions

Assertions are commonly used to check *preconditions*, *postconditions*, and *class invariants*. Before going further, we should define these terms.

A precondition is a constraint that must be met on entry of a method. If a method's preconditions are not met, the method should terminate at once before it can do any damage. A method's preconditions are typically functions of its arguments and the state of its object. Argument range checking at the start of a method is a common form of precondition testing.

A postcondition is a constraint that must be met on return from a method. If a method's postconditions are not met, the method should not be allowed to return. A method's postconditions are typically functions of its return value and the state of its object. In a general sense, if a precondition fails, the problem lies in the method's caller, whereas if a postcondition fails, the problem lies in the method itself.

A class invariant is a constraint on a class's state that must be met before and after execution of any non-private method of a class. (Private methods might be used to restore the required state after execution of a non-private method.)

To see how assertions can be used to enforce pre- and postconditions, imagine a class called `Library` that models a library (not a software library, but the kind where you can borrow books). Such a class might have a method called `reserveACopy()` that reserves a copy of a book on behalf of a library member. This method might look as follows, assuming the existence of classes Member (representing a person who is a member of the library) and Book (representing a single copy of a book):

```
1. private Book reserveACopy(String title, Member member) {
2.    assert isValidTitle(title);
3.
4.    Book book = getAvailableCopy(title);
5.    reserve(book, member);
6.
7.    assert bookIsInStock(book);
8.    return book;
9. }
```

Line 2 enforces a precondition. If the title is not valid (perhaps someone accidentally typed "Moby-Duck"), then the method should terminate as soon as possible, before any damage can be done. In fact, if the precondition fails, the failure indicates that the class needs more work. The code that called reserveACopy() with bad arguments needs to be fixed. The assertion failed (we hope) during in-house testing. Eventually the Library class would be debugged so that reserveACopy() would never be called with bad arguments. At this point (and not before this point), the class would be ready for shipment to the field, where assertions would be disabled.

Line 7 enforces a postcondition. The body of the method is supposed to find an available copy of the desired book. If the book that was found is not available after all, then a problem exists with the method's algorithm. The method should be terminated immediately before the library's data gets hopelessly corrupted, and the method should be debugged. When the author of the method has faith in the algorithm's correctness, the method can be shipped to an environment where assertions can be disabled.

There is a subtle point to be made about the appropriateness of using assertions to check preconditions of public methods. Note that the method in our example was private, so it could be called only from within its own class. Thus if the assertion on line 2 failed, you could point the finger of blame only at yourself or at a colleague down the hall; nobody else could call reserveACopy(). However, if the method were public, it could be called by anyone, including a customer who bought the class for re-use in a separate product. Such a programmer is beyond the control of your quality assurance system. A call to reserveACopy() with bad arguments would not necessarily indicate an internal problem with the Library class. So, if the reserveACopy() method were public, preconditions would have to be checked without the assertion mechanism, because the bad call would happen in the field with assertions disabled. The following code shows how to use an exception to indicate precondition failure:

```
1. public Book reserveACopy(String title, Member member) {
2.    if (!isValidTitle(title))
3.       throw new IllegalArgumentException("Bad title: " + title);
4.
5.    Book book = getAvailableCopy(title);
```

```
6.    reserve(book, member);
7.
8.    assert bookIsInStock(book);
9.    return book;
10. }
```

IllegalArgumentException is a runtime exception, so reserveACopy() does not need a throws clause and callers do not need to use the try/catch mechanism.

This previous example demonstrates that assertions are not appropriate for checking preconditions in public methods.

 Real World Scenario

Practicing with Assertions

In this exercise, you will modify a very simple class to take advantage of assertions. The original code, which appears in the AssertCheckStarting.java file on the CD-ROM, is as follows:

```java
public class AssertCheckStarting
{
    private final static int     SUIT_CLUBS    = 0;
    private final static int     SUIT_DIAMONDS = 1;
    private final static int     SUIT_HEARTS   = 2;
    private final static int     SUIT_SPADES   = 3;

    private final static String[]   suitNames =
    {
      "Clubs", "Diamonds", "Hearts", "Spades"
    };

    private static String suitToName(int suitNum)
    {
      return suitNames[suitNum];
    }

    public static void explainSuitNum(int suitNum)
    {
      System.out.println("Suit #" + suitNum + " is " +
        suitToName(suitNum));
    }
```

```
    public static void main(String[] args)
    {
      int suitNum = Integer.parseInt(args[0]);
      explainSuitNum(suitNum);
    }
}
```

The explainSuitToName()method is public, presumably so that it can be called from other classes; it calls suitToName(), which is appropriately private, since it uses knowledge of the way the class internally represents suit names.

Your assignment is to modify suitToName(), explainSuitToName(), or both, so that they appropriately check their preconditions. One possible solution appears in the file AssertCheckFinal.java on the CD-ROM. The method comments explain the solution.

Summary

This chapter covered various aspects of flow control in Java.

We began by discussing Java's three loop constructions: while(), do, and for(). These can be used with traditional syntax, but Java has expanded them by adding labeled break and continue statements, as well as the enhanced-for syntax.

We then covered Java's two selection constructs: the if()/else and switch() statements which provide ways to conditionally execute code.

The chapter ended with a discussion of exceptions and assertions. Exceptions indicate abnormal termination of try blocks or methods, and must be dealt with programmatically. Assertions indicate bugs.

Exam Essentials

Understand the operation of Java while, do, and for loops. Understand labeled loops, labeled breaks, and labeled continues in these loops.   You should be able to construct each kind of loop and know when blocks are executed and conditions are evaluated. Know how flow control proceeds in each of these structures.

Know the syntax of the enhanced for loop.   The syntax is for (type variable_name:array).

Know the legal argument types for if and switch() statements.   The argument of an if statement must be of type boolean. The argument of a switch() must be of type byte, short, char, or int.

Recognize and create correctly constructed switch() **statements.**   You should be able to create regular and default cases, with or without break statements.

Analyze code that uses a try block, and understand the flow of control no matter what exception types are thrown.   You should be completely familiar with all the functionality of the try, catch, and finally blocks.

Understand the difference between checked exceptions and runtime exceptions.   Know the inheritance of these families of exception types and know which kinds must be explicitly handled in your code.

Understand all of your exception-handling options when calling methods that throw checked exceptions.   You should know how to create try blocks and how to declare that a method throws exceptions.

Know what exception types may be thrown when you override a method that throws exceptions.   You need to be familiar with the required relationships between the superclass version's exception types and the subclass version's exception types.

Know how to use the assertions facility.   You need to know the syntax of assert statements and behavior when the boolean statement is true or false. You also need to know how to enable assertions at compile- and runtime.

Review Questions

1.   Consider the following code:

```
1. for (int i = 0; i < 2; i++) {
2.    for (int j = 0; j < 3; j++) {
3.       if (i == j) {
4.          continue;
5.       }
6.       System.out.println("i = " + i + " j = " + j);
7.    }
8. }
```

Which lines would be part of the output? (Choose all that apply.)

   A. i = 0 j = 0

   B. i = 0 j = 1

   C. i = 0 j = 2

   D. i = 1 j = 0

   E. i = 1 j = 1

   F. i = 1 j = 2

2.   Consider the following code:

```
1. outer: for (int i = 0; i < 2; i++) {
2.    for (int j = 0; j < 3; j++) {
3.       if (i == j) {
4.          continue outer;
5.       }
6.       System.out.println("i = " + i + " j = " + j);
7.    }
8. }
```

Which lines would be part of the output? (Choose all that apply.)

   A. i = 0 j = 0

   B. i = 0 j = 1

   C. i = 0 j = 2

   D. i = 1 j = 0

   E. i = 1 j = 1

   F. i = 1 j = 2

3. Which of the following are legal loop constructions? (Choose all that apply.)

A.
```java
while (int i<7) {
    i++;
    System.out.println("i is " + i);
}
```

B.
```java
int i = 3;
while (i) {
    System.out.println("i is " + i);
}
```

C.
```java
int j = 0;
for (int k=0, j+k != 10; j++,k++) {
    System.out.println("j=" + j + ", k=" + k);
}
```

D.
```java
int j=0;
do {
    System.out.println("j=" + j++);
    if (j==3)
        continue loop;
} while (j<10);
```

4. What would be the output from this code fragment?

```java
1. int x = 0, y = 4, z = 5;
2. if (x > 2) {
3.    if (y < 5) {
4.       System.out.println("message one");
5.    }
6.    else {
7.       System.out.println("message two");
8.    }
9. }
10. else if (z > 5) {
11.    System.out.println("message three");
12. }
13. else {
14.    System.out.println("message four");
15. }
```

A. message one

B. message two

C. message three

D. message four

5.   Which statement is true about the following code fragment?

```
1. int j = 2;
2. switch (j) {
3.    case 2:
4.       System.out.println("value is two");
5.    case 2 + 1:
6.       System.out.println("value is three");
7.       break;
8.    default:
9.       System.out.println("value is " + j);
10.      break;
11. }
```

A.   The code is illegal because of the expression at line 5.

B.   The acceptable types for the variable j, as the argument to the switch() construct, could be any of byte, short, int, or long.

C.   The output would be the text value is two.

D.   The output would be the text value is two followed by the text value is three.

E.   The output would be the text value is two, followed by the text value is three, followed by the text value is 2.

6.   Consider the following class hierarchy and code fragment:

```
                    java.lang.Exception
                           \
                    java.io.IOException
                       /           \
  java.io.StreamCorruptedException    java.net.MalformedURLException
```

```
1. try {
2.    // assume s is previously defined
3.    URL u = new URL(s);
4.    // in is an ObjectInputStream
5.    Object o = in.readObject();
6.    System.out.println("Success");
7. }
8. catch (MalformedURLException e) {
9.    System.out.println("Bad URL");
10. }
11. catch (StreamCorruptedException e) {
12.    System.out.println("Bad file contents");
13. }
14. catch (Exception e) {
15.    System.out.println("General exception");
```

```
16. }
17. finally {
18.   System.out.println("Doing finally part");
19. }
20. System.out.println("Carrying on");
```

What lines are output if the constructor at line 3 throws a MalformedURLException? (Choose all that apply.)

A. Success

B. Bad URL

C. Bad file contents

D. General exception

E. Doing finally part

F. Carrying on

7. Consider the following class hierarchy and code fragment:

```
                    java.lang.Exception
                              \
                       java.io.IOException
                        /              \
  java.io.StreamCorruptedException    java.net.MalformedURLException
```

```
1. try {
2.    // assume s is previously defined
3.    URL u = new URL(s);
4.    // in is an ObjectInputStream
5.    Object o = in.readObject();
6.    System.out.println("Success");
7. }
8. catch (MalformedURLException e) {
9.    System.out.println("Bad URL");
10. }
11. catch (StreamCorruptedException e) {
12.    System.out.println("Bad file contents");
13. }
14. catch (Exception e) {
15.    System.out.println("General exception");
16. }
17. finally {
18.    System.out.println("Doing finally part");
19. }
20. System.out.println("Carrying on");
```

What lines are output if the methods at lines 3 and 5 complete successfully without throwing any exceptions? (Choose all that apply.)

A. Success

B. Bad URL

C. Bad file contents

D. General exception

E. Doing finally part

F. Carrying on

8. Consider the following class hierarchy and code fragment:

```
                  java.lang.Throwable
                  /              \
      java.lang.Error        java.lang.Exception
          /                           \
java.lang.OutOfMemoryError       java.io.IOException
                                  /              \
    java.io.StreamCorruptedException    java.net.MalformedURLException
```

```
1. try {
2.     // assume s is previously defined
3.     URL u = new URL(s);
4.     // in is an ObjectInputStream
5.     Object o = in.readObject();
6.     System.out.println("Success");
7. }
8. catch (MalformedURLException e) {
9.     System.out.println("Bad URL");
10. }
11. catch (StreamCorruptedException e) {
12.     System.out.println("Bad file contents");
13. }
14. catch (Exception e) {
15.     System.out.println("General exception");
16. }
17. finally {
18.     System.out.println("Doing finally part");
19. }
20. System.out.println("Carrying on");
```

What lines are output if the method at line 5 throws an `OutOfMemoryError`? (Choose all that apply.)

A. Success

B. Bad URL

C. Bad file contents

D. General exception

E. Doing finally part

F. Carrying on

9. Which of the following are appropriate situations for assertions?

    A. Preconditions of a public method

    B. Postconditions of a public method

    C. Preconditions of a private method

    D. Postconditions of a private method

10. Consider the following code:

```
1. public class Assertification {
2.   public static void main(String[] args) {
3.     assert args.length == 0;
4   }
5. }
```

Which of the following conditions must be true in order for the code to throw an `AssertionError`? Assume you are using release 5.0. (Choose all that apply.)

    A. The source code must be compiled with the `-source 1.5` flag.

    B. The application must be run with the `-enableassertions` flag or another assertion-enabling flag.

    C. The `args` array must have exactly zero elements.

    D. The `args` array must have one or more elements.

11. Which of the following is the most appropriate way to handle invalid arguments in a public method?

    A. Throw `java.lang.InvalidArgumentException`.

    B. Throw `java.lang.IllegalArgumentException`.

    C. Check for argument validity in an `assert` statement, which throws `AssertionError` when the arguments are invalid.

    D. Use non-`assert` code to check for argument validity. If invalid arguments are detected, explicitly throw `AssertionError`.

12. Suppose `salaries` is an array containing floats. Which of the following are valid loop control statements for processing each element of `salaries`?

A. `for (float f:salaries)`

B. `for (int i:salaries)`

C. `for (float f::salaries)`

D. `for (int i::salaries)`

13. Which of the following are legal? (Choose all that apply.)

A. `for (int i=0, j=1; i<10; i++, j++)`

B. `for (int i=0, j=1;; i++, j++)`

C. `for (int i=0, float j=1; ; i++, j++)`

D. `for (String s = ""; s.length()<10; s += '!')`

14. Suppose a method called `finallyTest()` consists of a `try` block, followed by a `catch` block, followed by a `finally` block. Assuming the JVM doesn't crash and the code does not execute a `System.exit()` call, under what circumstances will the `finally` block *not* begin to execute?

A. The `try` block throws an exception, and the `catch` block also throws an exception.

B. The `try` block throws an exception that is not handled by the `catch` block.

C. The `try` block throws an exception, and the `catch` block calls `finallyTest()` in a way that causes another exception to be thrown.

D. If the JVM doesn't crash and the code does not execute a `System.exit()` call, the `finally` block will always execute.

15. Which of the following are legal loop definitions? (Choose all that apply.)

A. `while (int a = 0) { /* whatever */ }`

B. `while (int a == 0) { /* whatever */ }`

C. `do { /* whatever */ } while (int a = 0)`

D. `do { /* whatever */ } while (int a == 0)`

E. `for (int a==0; a<100; a++) { /* whatever */ }`

F. None of them are legal.

16. Which of the following are legal argument types for a `switch` statement?

A. `byte`

B. `int`

C. `long`

D. `float`

E. `char`

F. `String`

17. When is it appropriate to pass a cause to an exception's constructor?

   A. Always

   B. When the exception is being thrown in response to catching of a different exception type

   C. When the exception is being thrown from a public method

   D. When the exception is being thrown from a private method

18. Which of the following should always be caught?

   A. Runtime exceptions

   B. Checked exceptions

   C. Assertion errors

   D. Errors other than assertion errors

19. When does an exception's stack trace get recorded in the exception object?

   A. When the exception is constructed

   B. When the exception is thrown

   C. When the exception is caught

   D. When the exception's `printStackTrace()` method is called

20. When is it appropriate to write code that constructs and throws an error?

   A. When a public method's preconditions are violated

   B. When a public method's postconditions are violated

   C. When a nonpublic method's preconditions are violated

   D. When a nonpublic method's postconditions are violated

   E. Never

Answers to Review Questions

1. B, C, D, F. The loops iterate i from 0 to 1 and j from 0 to 2. However, the inner loop executes a `continue` statement whenever the values of i and j are the same. Because the output is generated inside the inner loop, after the `continue` statement, no output is generated when the values are the same. Therefore, the outputs suggested by options A and E are skipped.

2. D. It seems that the variable i will take the values 0 and 1, and for each of these values, j will take values 0, 1, and 2. However, whenever i and j have the same value, the outer loop is continued before the output is generated. Because the outer loop is the target of the `continue` statement, the whole of the inner loop is abandoned. Therefore, the only line to be output is that shown in option D.

3. C. In A, the variable declaration for i is illegal. This type of declaration is permitted only in the first part of a `for()` loop. In B, the loop control expression—the variable i in this case—is of type `int`. A `boolean` expression is required. C is valid. Despite the complexity of declaring one value inside the `for()` construction and one outside (along with the use of the comma operator in the end part), this code is entirely legitimate. D would be correct, except that the label has been omitted from the 2nd line, which should read `loop: do {`.

4. D. The first test at line 2 fails, which immediately causes control to skip to line 10, bypassing both the possible tests that might result in the output of `message one` or `message two`. So, even though the test at line 3 would be true, it is never made; A is not correct. At line 10, the test is again false, so the message at line 11 is skipped, but `message four`, at line 14, is output.

5. D. A is incorrect because the code is legal despite the expression at line 5; the expression itself is a constant. B is incorrect because it states that the `switch()` part can take a `long` argument. Only `byte`, `short`, `char`, and `int` are acceptable. The output results from the value 2 like this: first, the option `case 2:` is selected, which outputs `value is two`. However, there is no `break` statement between lines 4 and 5, so the execution falls into the next `case` and outputs `value is three` from line 6. The `default:` part of a `switch()` is executed only when no other options have been selected, or if no `break` precedes it. Neither of these situations holds true, so the output consists only of the two messages listed in D.

6. B, E, F. The exception causes a jump out of the `try` block, so the message `Success` from line 6 is not printed. The first applicable `catch` is at line 8, which is an exact match for the thrown exception. This results in the message at line 9 being printed, so B is one of the required answers. Only one `catch` block is ever executed, so control passes to the `finally` block, which results in the message at line 18 being output; so E is part of the correct answer. Execution continues after the `finally` block. This results in the output of the message at line 20, so F is also part of the correct answer.

7. A, E, F. With no exceptions, the `try` block executes to completion, so the message `Success` from line 6 is printed and A is part of the correct answer. No `catch` is executed, so B, C, and D are incorrect. Control then passes to the `finally` block, which results in the message at line 18 being output, so E is part of the correct answer. Because no exception was thrown, execution continues after the `finally` block, resulting in the output of the message at line 20; so F is also part of the correct answer.

8. E. The thrown error prevents completion of the `try` block, so the message `Success` from line 6 is not printed. No `catch` is appropriate, so B, C, and D are incorrect. Control then passes to the `finally` block, which results in the message at line 18 being output; so option E is part of the correct answer. Because the error was not caught, execution exits the method and the error is rethrown in the caller of this method; so F is not part of the correct answer.

9. B, C, D. Assertions should not be used to check preconditions of a public method.

10. A, B, D. The 1.4 compiler only treated `assert` as a keyword (and not an ordinary identifier) if the `-source 1.4` flag appeared in the command line. However, 5.0 does not require a `-source` flag. So A is not a requirement. If the application is not run with assertions explicitly enabled, all `assert` statements will be ignored. If the `args` array does not have exactly zero arguments, no `AssertionError` will be thrown.

11. B. Assertions should not be used to check preconditions in a public method. Some kind of runtime exception should be thrown, and `IllegalArgumentException` is the most appropriate class name for this situation. There is no such thing as `java.lang.InvalidArgumentException`.

12. A. Option A demonstrates the correct syntax of an enhanced `for` loop, traversing the elements of an array of floats.

13. A, B, D. A and B demonstrate multiple initialization and increment parts, which are legal. In B, the test part is empty, so the loop will run forever unless it hits a break statement, throws an exception, or does something equally catastrophic. C is illegal because only one type may be declared in the initialization. D is unusual because it uses strings rather than the more commonly seen `int`s, but it is perfectly legal.

14. D. Unless execution terminates abnormally, the `finally` block will always eventually execute.

15. F. A through D are all illegal because only `for` loops allow loop variables to be declared in the loop control code. E is illegal because the variable must be initialized with =, not ==.

16. A, B, E. The argument of a `switch` statement must be a `byte`, `char`, `short`, `int`, or `enum`. Enums are discussed in Chapter 6, "Objects and Classes."

17. B. Exception chaining is appropriate when an exception is being thrown in response to catching a different exception type.

18. B. Runtime exceptions don't have to be caught. Errors should never be caught.

19. A. The stack trace is recorded when the exception is constructed.

20. E. It is never appropriate for application programmers to construct and throw errors.

Chapter

6

Objects and Classes

JAVA CERTIFICATION EXAM OBJECTIVES COVERED IN THIS CHAPTER:

✓ 1.1 Develop code that declares classes (including abstract and all forms of nested classes), interfaces, and enums, and includes the appropriate use of package and import statements (including static imports).

✓ 1.4 Develop code that declares both static and non-static methods, and - if appropriate - use method names that adhere to the JavaBeans naming standards. Also develop code that declares and uses a variable-length argument list.

✓ 1.5 Given a code example, determine if a method is correctly overriding or overloading another method, and identify legal return values (including covariant returns), for the method.

✓ 1.6 Given a set of classes and superclasses, develop constructors for one or more of the classes. Given a class declaration, determine if a default constructor will be created, and if so, determine the behavior of that constructor. Given a nested or non-nested class listing, write code to instantiate the class.

✓ 5.1 Develop code that implements tight encapsulation, loose coupling, and high cohesion in classes, and describe the benefits.

✓ 5.2 Given a scenario, develop code that demonstrates the use of polymorphism. Further, determine when casting will be necessary and recognize compiler vs. runtime errors related to object reference casting.

✓ 5.3 Explain the effect of modifiers on inheritance with respect to constructors, instance or static variables, and instance or static methods.

✓ **5.4 Given a scenario, develop code that declares and/or invokes overridden or overloaded methods and code that declares and/or invokes superclass, overridden, or overloaded constructors.**

✓ **5.5 Develop code that implements "is-a" and/or "has-a" relationships.**

✓ **6.2 Distinguish between correct and incorrect overrides of corresponding** hashCode() **and** equals() **methods, and explain the difference between** == **and the** equals() **method.**

✓ **7.5 Given the fully-qualified name of a class that is deployed inside and/or outside a JAR file, construct the appropriate directory structure for that class. Given a code example and a classpath, determine whether the classpath will allow the code to compile successfully.**

This chapter discusses the object-oriented features of Java. Good coding in Java requires a sound understanding of the object-oriented (OO) paradigm, and this in turn requires a good grasp of the language features that implement objects and classes. The many benefits of object orientation have been the subject of considerable public debate, but for many programmers these benefits have not been realized. In most cases, the reason the promise has not been fulfilled is simply that programmers have not been writing objects. Instead, many programmers have been writing hybrid applications with a mixture of procedural and object-oriented code. Unfortunately, while such an approach has given rise to *some* of the benefits of OO, it has also engendered *all* the disadvantages of both styles. So you can see why the designers of the exam believe that it is important to understand object-oriented concepts.

This chapter assumes that you know what classes and interfaces are. However, you may not be familiar with enums, which were introduced in release 5.0. Enums are also presented in detail in this chapter.

Benefits of Object-Oriented Implementation

As a Java programmer and developer, you should have an understanding of the benefits of object-oriented design. These benefits accrue from two particular features of the OO paradigm. The first of these, and perhaps the most important, is the notion of *encapsulation*; the second and perhaps better known is the extensibility provided by *inheritance*.

Encapsulation

Encapsulation is really just a fancy name for the aggregation of data and behavior. Consider the primitive data types of any programming language you have ever used. You do not know how these data items are stored and, for the most part, you do not care. What matters are the operations that you can perform on these data items and the boundary conditions within which you can expect those operations to properly work. These primitive types are in fact reference types, albeit not user-defined.

Your first goal in defining a good class should be to clearly define the data members that describe instances of that class, keeping in mind that this should be done only with variables of private accessibility. Next, consider how to represent the behavior associated with these data.

All behavior should be accessed only via methods. By insisting that the variables inside an object are inaccessible outside the object, you ensure that the nature of those variables is irrelevant outside the object. This in turn means that you can freely change the nature of the storage for maintenance purposes, performance improvement, or any other reason. This is the essence of encapsulation.

Sometimes, perhaps as a consequence of the way you have stored the state in a class, boundary conditions must be applied to its methods. A *boundary condition* is a limit on the range of arguments for which a method can operate properly. As examples, a square-root function cannot operate on a negative number unless imaginary numbers are included in its range; an add operation cannot operate if both of its arguments are more than half the maximum value for the operation's return type.

When you encounter a boundary condition that results from your choice of storage format, you must make a choice. If you consider that the boundary conditions are reasonable, then you should do two things. First, document the boundary condition. Next, test the boundary conditions at the entry to the method and, if the boundary condition has been exceeded, throw a runtime exception of some kind. Alternatively, you might decide that the boundary condition is not acceptable, in which case you should redesign the storage used in the class.

Now, consider this: if you had allowed access to any of the variables used to represent the object state, then redefining the way the object's state is stored would immediately cause any other code that uses these variables to have to be rewritten. However, by using only private member variables, you have insisted that all interaction with this object is made through methods and never by direct variable access—so you have eliminated this problem. In consequence, you are able to redesign your internal storage freely and, provided the signatures of all the methods remain the same, no other code needs to change.

Re-use

We discussed how tight encapsulation can make code that is more reliable and robust. Now we will consider the second most significant advantage of object-oriented programming: code re-use.

Writing good, encapsulated classes usually requires more work in the initial stages than would be required to produce the same functionality with a traditional programming approach. However, you will normally find that using rigorous OO techniques will actually reduce the overall time required to produce finished code. This is the case for two reasons. First, the robust classes you produce require less time to integrate into the final program and less time to fix bugs. Second, with careful design, you can re-use classes even in some circumstances that are different from the original intent of the class.

This re-use is possible in two ways, using either composition (the "has a" relation) or inheritance (the "is a" relation). Composition is probably safer and easier to control, although inheritance—perhaps because it is perceived as "pure OO"—seems to be more interesting and appealing to most programmers.

As a certified Java programmer, you don't really need to know the details of object-oriented design techniques or the relative merits and weaknesses of composition versus inheritance.

However, you should appreciate one significant sequence of facts: if a class is well encapsulated, it will be easier to re-use successfully. The more a class is re-used, the better tested it will be and the fewer bugs it will have. Better-tested, less-buggy classes are easier to re-use. This sequence leads to a positive spiral of quality because the better the class, the easier and safer it becomes to re-use. All these benefits come from tight encapsulation.

Coupling and Cohesion

After object-oriented programming had been in practice for a while, the research community coined the terms "coupling" and "cohesion" to describe two related qualities of object-oriented programs. The Programmer's Exam requires you to be familiar with these concepts.

Coupling is an object's reliance on knowledge of the internals of another entity's implementation. When object A is tightly coupled to object B, a programmer who wants to use or modify A is required to have an inappropriately extensive expertise in how to use B.

The best insurance against coupling between classes is good encapsulation. However, Java's access model makes it possible to create coupling between two instances of the same class, even if that class is well encapsulated. Recall from Chapter 3, "Modifiers," that an object's private data and methods may be accessed by any instance of that object's class. If an instance uses another instance's private data or methods, the result is tight coupling.

Cohesion is the degree to which a class or method resists being broken down into smaller pieces. Cohesion is desirable and is easy to recognize in its absence.

Consider a `Telescope` class with methods that aim and focus a telescope and other methods that process the images that the scope captures. If you were modeling the Hubble, your class would have a lot of methods of each type. If you looked at the class' source, you would probably find that the aiming and focusing methods might call each other, but they wouldn't call the image-processing methods or access the image-processing data. The converse would also be true: the image-processing code wouldn't have much contact with the aiming/focusing code.

A class like `Telescope` that can easily be split into distinct elements probably models not one but two (or more!) real-world objects. Such a class ought to be divided into its natural constituents.

Methods as well as classes can have or lack cohesion. A low-cohesion method can often be spotted by the presence of "and" in its name. For example, if you're reading the source code for a Java-based guitar-playing robot, you might come across a method named `tuneDStringAndPlayDMinorScale()`. Obviously this method performs two different tasks; the only reason they are together is that playing a scale on a string is often done right after tuning that string. But *often* isn't *always*. If you separate the code into `tuneDString()` and `playDMinorScale()`, then people have the option of playing a different scale, or not playing a scale at all, after they tune the string.

Now that we've discussed why you would want to write object-oriented code, let's look at how this is achieved.

Implementing Object-Oriented Relationships

This section considers the implementation of classes for which you have been given a basic description.

There are two phrases that are commonly used when describing a class in plain English: "is a" and "has a." As a working simplification, they are used to describe the superclass and member variables, respectively. For example, consider this description:

"A home is a house that has a family and a pet."

This description would give rise to the outline of a Java class in this form:

```
1. public class Home extends House {
2.     Family inhabitants;
3.     Pet thePet;
4. }
```

Notice the direct correspondence between the "is a" clause and the `extends` clause. In this example, a direct correspondence also exists between the items listed after "has a" and the member variables. Such a correspondence is representative in simple examples and in a test situation; however, you should be aware that in real examples, there are other ways you can provide a class with attributes. Probably the most important of these alternatives is the approach taken by JavaBeans, which is to supply accessor and mutator methods that operate on private data members.

 The example shown is simplified to focus on the knowledge and understanding that is required by the exam. In a real situation, the variables should generally be private (or at least some specific rationale should apply to whatever accessibility they have), and some methods will be needed in the class.

Methods, Overloading and Overriding

As you construct classes and add methods to them, in some circumstances you will want to re-use the same name for a method. You can do so two ways with Java. Re-using the same method name with different arguments and perhaps a different return type is known as *overloading*. Using the same method name with identical arguments and return type is known as *overriding*.

A method name can be re-used anywhere, as long as certain conditions are met:

- In an unrelated class, no special conditions apply, and the two methods are not considered related in any way.

- In the class that defines the original method, or a subclass of that class, the method name can be re-used if the argument list differs in terms of the type of at least one argument. This is overloading. It is important to realize that a difference in return type or list of thrown exceptions is insufficient to constitute an overload and is illegal.

- In a strict subclass of the class that defines the original method, the method name can be re-used with identical argument types and order and with identical return type. This is overriding. In this case, additional restrictions apply to the accessibility of, and exceptions that may be thrown by, the method.

In general, a class is considered to be a subclass of itself. That is, if classes A, B, and C are defined so that C extends B and B extends A, then the subclasses of A are A, B, and C. The term *strict subclass* is used to describe the subclasses excluding the class itself. So the strict subclasses of A are only B and C.

Now let's take a look at these ideas in detail. First, we will consider overloading method names.

Overloading Method Names

In Java, a method is uniquely identified by the combination of its fully qualified class name, the method name, and the exact sequence of its argument types. Overloading is the re-use of a method name in the one class or subclass for a different method. It is not related to object orientation, although a purely coincidental correlation shows that object-oriented languages are more likely to support overloading. Notice that overloading is essentially a trick with names; hence this section's title is "Overloading Method Names" rather than "Overloading Methods." The following are all different methods:

```
1. public void aMethod(String s) { }
2. public void aMethod() { }
3. public void aMethod(int i, String s) { }
4. public void aMethod(String s, int i) { }
```

These methods all have identical return types and names, but their argument lists are different either in the types of the arguments that they take or in the order. Only the argument *types* are considered, not their names, so a method such as

```
public void aMethod(int j, String name) { }
```

would *not* be distinguished from the method defined in line 3.

What Is Overloading For?

Why is overloading useful? Sometimes you will be creating several methods that perform closely related functions under different conditions. For example, imagine methods that calculate the area of a triangle. One such method might take the Cartesian coordinates of the three vertices, and another might take the polar coordinates. A third method might take the lengths of all three sides, whereas a fourth might take three angles and the length of one side. These methods would all be performing the same essential function, so it is entirely proper to use the same name for the methods. In languages that do not permit overloading, you would have to think up four different method names, such as

```
areaByCoord(Point p, Point q, Point r)
areaByPolarCoord(PolarPt p, PolarPt q, PolarPt r)
areaBySideLengths(int l1, int l2, int l3)
areaByAnglesAndASide(int l1, int angle1, int angle2, int angle3)
```

Overloading is really nothing new. Almost every language that has a type system has used overloading in a way, although most have not allowed the programmer free use of it. Consider the arithmetic operators +, -, *, and /. In most languages, they can be used with integer or floating-point operands. The implementation of, say, multiplication for integer and floating-point operands generally involves completely different code, and yet the compiler permits the same symbol to be used. Because the operand types are different, the compiler can decide which version of the operation should be used. This process is known as *operator overloading* and is the same principle as method overloading.

It is quite useful, for thinking up method names and for improving program readability, to be able to use one method name for several related methods requiring different implementations. However, you should restrict your use of overloaded method names to situations where the methods really are performing the same basic function with different data sets. Methods that perform different jobs should have different names.

One last point to consider is the return type of an overloaded method. The language treats methods with overloaded names as totally different methods, and as such they *can* have different return types (you will see shortly that overriding methods do not have this freedom).

Invoking Overloaded Methods

When you write multiple methods that perform the same basic function with different arguments, you often find that it would be useful to call one of these methods as support for another version. Consider a method called `printRJ()` that is to be provided in versions that take a `String` or an `int` value. The version that takes an `int` could most easily be coded so that it converts the `int` to a `String` and then calls the version that operates on `String` objects.

You can do this easily. Remember that the compiler decides which method to call simply by looking at the argument list and that the various overloaded methods are in fact unrelated. All you have to do is write the method call exactly as normal—the compiler will do the rest. Consider this example:

```
1. public class RightJustify {
2.    // Declare a String of 80 spaces
3.    private static final String padding =
4.       "                        " +
5.       "                        " +
6.       "                        " +
7.       "                        ";
```

```
8.    public static void printRJ(String s, int w) {
9.      System.out.print(
10.        padding.substring(0, w - s.length()));
11.      System.out.print(s);
12.    }
13.    public static void printRJ(int i, int w) {
14.      printRJ("", w);
15.    }
16. }
```

At line 14, the `int` argument is converted to a `String` object by adding it to an empty `String`. The method call at this same line is then seen by the compiler as a call to a method called `print()` that takes a `String` as the first argument, which results in selection of the method at line 8.

To summarize, these are the key points about overloading methods:

- The identity of a method is determined by the combination of its fully qualified class; its name; and the type, order, and count of arguments in the argument list.

- Two or more methods in the same class (including methods inherited from a superclass) with the same name but different argument lists are called *overloaded*.

- Methods with overloaded names are effectively independent methods—using the same name is really just a convenience to the programmer. Return type, accessibility, and exception lists may vary freely.

Now that we have considered overloading thoroughly, let's look at overriding.

Method Overriding

You have just seen that overloading is essentially a trick with names, effectively treating the argument list as part of the method identification. Overriding is somewhat more subtle, relating directly to subclassing and hence to the object-oriented nature of a language.

When you extend one class to produce a new one, you inherit and have access to certain non-private methods of the original class (as dictated by access modifiers and package relationships). Sometimes, however, you might need to modify the behavior of one of these methods to suit your new class. In this case, you actually want to redefine the method, and this is the essential purpose of overriding.

There are a number of key distinctions between overloading and overriding:

- Overloaded methods supplement each other; an overriding method replaces the method it overrides.

- Overloaded methods can exist, in any number, in the same class. Each method in a parent class can be overridden at most once in any one subclass.

- Overloaded methods must have *different* argument lists; overriding methods must have argument lists of *identical* type and order (otherwise they are simply treated as over-loaded methods).

- The return type of an overloaded method may be chosen freely; the return type of an overriding method must be *identical* to that of the method it overrides.

- The exception list of an overloaded method may be chosen according to the rules defined earlier in this chapter.

- The access modifiers of an overloaded method may be chosen according to the rules defined earlier in this chapter.

What Is Overriding For?

Overloading allows multiple implementations of the same essential functionality to use the same name. Overriding, on the other hand, modifies the implementation of a particular piece of behavior for a subclass.

Consider a class that describes a rectangle. Imaginatively, we'll call it Rectangle. We're talking about an abstract rectangle here, so no visual representation is associated with it. This class has a method called setSize(), which is used to set width and height values. In the Rectangle class, the implementation of the setSize() method simply sets the value of the private width and height variables for later use. Now, imagine you create a DisplayedRectangle class that is a subclass of the original Rectangle. When the setSize() method is called, you need to arrange a new behavior. Specifically, the width and height variables must be changed, but also the visual representation must be redrawn. This is achieved by overriding.

If you define a method that has exactly the same name and exactly the same argument types as a method in a parent class, then you are overriding the method. Under these conditions, the method must also have the identical return type and follow the accessibility and exception list rules for that of the method it overrides. Consider this example:

```
1. class Rectangle {
2.    int x, y, w, h;
3.
4.    public void setSize(int w, int h) {
5.      this.w = w; this.h = h;
6.    }
7. }
8. class DisplayedRectangle extends Rectangle {
9.    public void setSize(int w, int h) {
10.      this.w = w; this.h = h;
11.      redisplay(); // implementation
12.    }
13.    public void redisplay() {
14.      // implementation not shown
15.    }
16. }
17.
```

```
18. public class TestRectangle {
19.   public static void main(String args[]) {
20.     Rectangle [] recs = new Rectangle[4];
21.     recs[0] = new Rectangle();
22.     recs[1] = new DisplayedRectangle();
23.     recs[2] = new DisplayedRectangle();
24.     recs[3] = new Rectangle();
25.     for (int r=0; r<4; r++) {
26.       int w = ((int)(Math.random() * 400));
27.       int h = ((int)(Math.random() * 200));
28.       recs[r].setSize(w, h);
29.     }
30.   }
31. }
```

Clearly this example is incomplete, because no code exists to cause the display of the DisplayedRectangle objects, but it is complete enough for us to discuss.

At line 20, the array recs is created as an array of Rectangle objects; yet at lines 21–24, the array is used to hold not only two instances of Rectangle but also two instances of DisplayedRectangle. Subsequently, when the setSize() method is called, it will be important that the executed code be the code associated with the actual object referred to by the array element, rather than always being the code of the Rectangle class. This is exactly what Java does, and this is the essential point of overriding methods. It is as if you ask an object to perform certain behavior, and that object makes its own interpretation of the request. C++ programmers should take particular note of this point, because it differs significantly from the default behavior of overriding methods in that language.

In order for any particular method to override another correctly, some requirements must be met. Some of them have been mentioned before in comparison with overloading, but all are listed here for completeness:

- The method name and the type and order of arguments must be identical to those of a method in a parent class. If this is the case, then the method is an attempt to override the corresponding parent class method, and the remaining points listed here must be adhered to or a compiler error arises. If these criteria are not met, then the method is not an attempt to override and the following rules are irrelevant.

- The return type must be the same as, or a subclass of, the superclass version's return type.

- Methods marked final may not be overridden.

- The accessibility must not be more restrictive than that of the original method.

- The method may throw only checked exception types that are the same as, or subclasses of, exception types thrown by the original method.

The second rule is new in release 5.0. Prior to 5.0, an overriding method's return type had to exactly match the superclass version's return type. Now the rule has been expanded, to support *covariant return types.* A covariant return type of an overriding method is a subclass of the return type of the superclass version. Here's an example:

```
class TheSuperclass {
  Number getValue() {
    return new Long(33);
  }
}

class TheSubclass extends TheSuperclass {
  Float getValue() {
    return new Float(1.23f);
  }
}
```

The superclass version returns a Number. The subclass version returns a Float, which extends Number. This would be illegal without covariant return types.

The accessibility of an overriding method must not be less than that of the method it overrides, simply because it is considered to be the replacement method in conditions like those of the rectangles example earlier. So, imagine that the setSize() method of DisplayedRectangle was inaccessible from the main() method of the TestRectangle class. The calls to recs[1].setSize() and recs[2].setSize() would be illegal, but the compiler would be unable to determine this because it knows only that the elements of the array are Rectangle objects. The extends keyword literally requires that the subclass be an extension of the parent class: if methods could be removed from the class or made less accessible, then the subclass would not be a simple extension but would potentially be a reduction. Under those conditions, the idea of treating DisplayedRectangle objects as being Rectangle objects when used as method arguments or elements of a collection would be severely flawed.

A similar logic gives rise to the final rule relating to checked exceptions. Checked exceptions are those that the compiler ensures are handled in the source you write. As with accessibility, it must be possible for the compiler to make correct use of a variable of the parent class even if that variable really refers to an object of a derived class. For checked exceptions, this requirement means that an overriding method must not be able to throw exceptions that would not be thrown by the original method.

 Chapter 5, "Flow Control, Assertions, and Exception Handling," discussed checked exceptions and this rule in more detail.

Late Binding

Normally, when a compiler for a non-object-oriented language comes across a method (or function or procedure) invocation, it determines exactly what target code should be called and builds machine language to represent that call. In an object-oriented language, this behavior is not possible because the proper code to invoke is determined based upon the class of the object being used to make the call, not the type of the variable. Instead, code is generated that will allow the decision to be made at runtime. This delayed decision-making is variously referred to as *late binding* (*binding* is one term for the job a linker does when it glues various bits of machine code together to make an executable program file).

The Java Virtual Machine (JVM) has been designed from the start to support an object-oriented programming system, so there are machine-level instructions for making method calls. The compiler needs only to prepare the argument list and produce one method invocation instruction; the job of identifying and calling the proper target code is performed by the JVM.

If the JVM is to be able to decide what code should be invoked by a particular method call, it must be able to determine the class of the object upon which the call is based. Again, the JVM design has supported this process from the beginning. Unlike traditional languages or runtime environments, every time the Java system allocates memory, it marks that memory with the type of the data that it has been allocated to hold. So, given any object, and without regard to the type associated with the reference variable acting as a handle to that object, the runtime system can determine the real class of that object by inspection. This process is the basis of the `instanceof` operator, which allows you to program a test to determine the actual class of an object at runtime.

 The `instanceof` operator was described in Chapter 2, "Operators and Assignments."

Invoking Overridden Methods

When we discussed overloading methods, you saw how to invoke one version of a method from another. It is also useful to be able to invoke an overridden method from the method that overrides it. Consider that when you write an overriding method, that method entirely replaces the original method. However, sometimes you wish only to add a little extra behavior and want to retain all the original behavior. This goal can be achieved, although it requires a small trick of syntax to perform. Look at this example:

```
1. class Rectangle {
2.    private int x, y, w, h;
3.    public String toString() {
4.       return "x = " + x + ", y = " + y +
5.          ", w = " + w + ", h = " + h;
6.    }
7. }
8. class DecoratedRectangle extends Rectangle {
9.    private int borderWidth;
10.    public String toString() {
```

```
11.      return super.toString() + ", borderWidth = " +
12.      borderWidth;
13.   }
14. }
```

At line 11, the overriding method in the DecoratedRectangle class uses the parental toString() method to perform the greater part of its work. Because the variables x, y, w, and h in the Rectangle class are marked as private, it would have been impossible for the overriding method in DecoratedRectangle to achieve its work directly.

A call of the form super.*xxx()* always invokes the behavior that would have been used if the current overriding method had not been defined. It does not matter whether the parental method is defined in the immediate superclass or in some ancestor class further up the hierarchy: super invokes the version of this method that is "next up the tree."

To summarize, these are the key points about overriding methods:

- A method that has an identical name and identical number, types, and order of arguments as a method in a parent class is an overriding method.

- Each parent class method may be overridden once at most in any one subclass. (That is, you cannot have two identical methods in the same class.)

- An overriding method must return exactly the same type as the method it overrides.

- An overriding method must not be less accessible than the method it overrides.

- An overriding method must not throw any checked exceptions (or subclasses of those exceptions) that are not declared for the overridden method.

- An overridden method is completely replaced by the overriding method unless the overridden method is deliberately invoked from within the subclass.

This is quite a lot to think about, so you might like to take a break before you move on to the next topic: constructors.

Variable-Length Argument Lists

Prior to release 5.0, a method declaration specified an exact number of arguments. Release 5.0 allows a method to declare that its argument list includes a variable number of args of a particular type. This is done by appending three dots (...) after the type. For example, here's a method declaration that accepts a variable number of Strings:

```
void xyz(String … stringies)
```

Callers may invoke this method with any number of String arguments (even none at all). Within the method, stringies appears as an array of Strings.

Many methods of the core Java classes accept variable argument lists, so keep your eye out for the three dots in method descriptions in the API pages.

Constructors and Subclassing

Inheritance generally makes the code and data defined in a parent class available for use in a subclass. This is subject to accessibility controls so that, for example, private items in the parent class are not directly accessible in the methods of the subclass, even though they exist. In fact, constructors are not inherited in the normal way but must be defined for each class in the class itself.

A constructor is invoked with a call of the form new MyClass(arg1, arg2, ...). If the argument list is empty, the constructor is called a *no-arguments* (or *no-args*) *constructor*. If you do not explicitly code any constructors for a class, the compiler automatically creates a default constructor that does nothing except invoke the superclass' default constructor, via a mechanism described in the next section. This "freebie" constructor is called the *default constructor*. It has public access if the class is public; otherwise its access mode is default.

Often you will define a constructor that takes arguments and will want to use those arguments to control the construction of the parent part of the object. You can pass control to a constructor in the parent class by using the keyword super. To control the particular constructor that is used, you simply provide the appropriate arguments. Consider this example:

```
1. class Base {
2.    public Base(String s) {
3.      // initialize this object using s
4.    }
5.    public Base(int i) {
6.      // initialize this object using i
7.    }
8. }
9.
10. class Derived extends Base {
11.    public Derived(String s) {
12.      // pass control to Base constructor at line 2
13.      super(s);
14.    }
15.    public Derived(int i) {
16.      // pass control to Base constructor at line 5
17.      super(i);
18.    }
19. }
```

The code at lines 13 and 17 demonstrates the use of super() to control the construction of the parent class part of an object. The definitions of the constructors at lines 11 and 15 select an appropriate way to build their inherited part by invoking super() with an argument list that matches one of the constructors for the parent class. It is important to know that the superclass constructor must be called before any reference is made to any part of this object. This rule is imposed to guarantee that nothing is ever accessed in an uninitialized state. Generally, the rule means that if super() is to appear at all in a constructor, then it must be the first statement.

Although the example shows the invocation of parental constructors with argument lists that match those of the original constructor, this is not a requirement. It would be perfectly acceptable, for example, if line 17 read

```
17.     super("Value is " + i);
```

This would have caused control to be passed to the constructor at line 2, which takes a String argument, rather than the one at line 5.

Overloading Constructors

Although you just saw that constructors are not inherited in the same way as methods, the overloading mechanisms apply quite normally. In fact, the example discussing the use of super() to control the invocation of parental constructors showed overloaded constructors. You saw earlier how you could invoke one method from another that overloads its name simply by calling the method with an appropriate parameter list. There are also times when it's useful to invoke one constructor from another. Imagine you have a constructor that takes five arguments and does considerable processing to initialize the object. You wish to provide another constructor that takes only two arguments and sets the remaining three to default values. It would be nice to avoid re-coding the body of the first constructor and instead simply set up the default values and pass control to the first constructor. You can do so using a small trick of syntax.

Usually, you would invoke a method by using its name followed by an argument list in parentheses, and you would invoke a constructor by using the keyword new, followed by the name of the class, followed again by an argument list in parentheses. Thus you might try to use the new ClassName(args) construction to invoke another constructor of your own class. Unfortunately, although this is legal syntax, it results in an entirely separate object being created. The approach Java takes is to provide another meaning for the keyword this. Look at this example:

```
1. public class AnyClass {
2.     public AnyClass(int a, String b, float c, Date d) {
3.         // complex processing to initialize
4.         // based on arguments
5.     }
6.     public AnyClass(int a) {
7.         this(a, "default", 0.0F, new Date());
8.     }
9. }
```

The constructor at line 6 takes a single argument and uses that, along with three other default values, to call the constructor at line 2. The call is made using the this() construction at line 7. As with super(), this() must be positioned as the first statement of the constructor.

We have said that any use of either super() or this() in a constructor must be placed at the first line. Clearly, you cannot put both on the first line. If you write a constructor that has neither a call to super() nor a call to this(), then the compiler automatically inserts a call to the parent class constructor with no arguments. If an explicit call to another constructor is made using this(), then the superclass constructor is not called until the other constructor runs. It is permitted for that other constructor to start with a call to either this() or super(), if desired. Java insists that the object is initialized from the top of the class hierarchy downward; that is why the call to super() or this() must occur at the start of a constructor. This point has an important consequence. We just said that if there is no call to either this() or super(), then the compiler puts in a call to the no-argument constructor in the parent. As a result, if you try to extend a class that does not have a no-argument constructor, then you *must* explicitly call super() with one of the argument forms that are supported by constructors in the parent class.

Let's summarize the key points about constructors before we move on to inner classes:

- Constructors are not inherited in the same way as normal methods. You can create an object only if the class defines a constructor with an argument list that matches the one your new call provides.

- If you define no constructors in a class, then the compiler provides a default that takes no arguments. If you define even a single constructor, this default is not provided.

- It is common to provide multiple overloaded constructors—that is, constructors with different argument lists. One constructor can call another using the syntax this(*arguments*).

- A constructor delays running its body until the parent parts of the class have been initialized. This commonly happens because of an implicit call to super() added by the compiler. You can provide your own call to super(*arguments*) to control the way the parent parts are initialized. If you do so, it must be the first statement of the constructor.

- A constructor can use overloaded constructor versions to support its work. These are invoked using the syntax this(*arguments*) and if supplied, this call must be the first statement of the constructor. In such conditions, the initialization of the parent class is performed in the overloaded constructor.

Inner Classes

The material we have looked at so far has been part of Java since its earliest versions. Inner classes are a feature added with the release of JDK 1.1. *Inner classes*, which are sometimes called *nested classes*, can give your programs additional clarity and make them more concise.

Fundamentally, an inner class is the same as any other class but is declared inside (that is, between the opening and closing curly braces of) some other class. In fact, you can declare nested classes in any block, including blocks that are part of a method. Classes defined inside a method differ slightly from the more general case of inner classes that are defined as members of a class; we'll look at these differences in detail later. For now, when we refer to a "member class," we mean a class that is *not* defined in a method but rather in a class. In this context, the use of the term *member* is closely parallel to its use in the context of member variables and member methods.

The complexity of inner classes relates to scope and access—particularly access to variables in enclosing scopes. Before we consider these matters, let's look at the syntax of a basic inner class, which is really quite simple. Consider this example:

```
1. public class OuterOne {
2.    private int x;
3.    public class InnerOne {
4.       private int y;
5.       public void innerMethod() {
6.          System.out.println("y is " + y);
7.       }
8.    }
9.    public void outerMethod() {
10.      System.out.println("x is " + x);
11.   }
12.   // other methods...
13. }
```

In this example, there is no obvious benefit in having declared the class called InnerOne as an inner class; so far we are only looking at the syntax. When an inner class is declared like this, the enclosing class name becomes part of the fully qualified name of the inner class. In this case, the two classes' full names are OuterOne and OuterOne.InnerOne. This format is reminiscent of a class called InnerOne declared in a package called OuterOne. This point of view is not entirely inappropriate, because an inner class belongs to its enclosing class in a fashion similar to the way a class belongs to a package. It is illegal for a package and a class to have the same name, so there can be no ambiguity.

WARNING   Although the dotted representation of inner class names works for the declaration of the type of an identifier, it does not reflect the filename of the class. If you try to load this class using the Class.forName() method, the call will fail. On the disk, and from the point of view of the Class class and class loaders, the name of the class is OuterOne$InnerOne. The dollar-separated name is also used if you print out the class name by using the methods getClass().getName() on an instance of the inner class. You probably recall that classes are located in directories that reflect their package names. The dollar-separated convention is adopted for inner class names to ensure that there is no ambiguity on the disk between inner classes and package members. It also reduces conflicts with file systems and shell interpreters that treat the dot character as special, perhaps limiting the number of characters that can follow it.

Real World Scenario

Inner Class Details

Here is a simple public interface:

```
public interface Reporter {
  public void report();
}
```

Write an application that answers the following two questions:

1. Suppose an enclosing class contains a non-anonymous inner class, which implements Reporter. Suppose the enclosing class has a method called getReporter() with return type Reporter that returns an instance of the inner class. How useful is the returned object? Can it be used outside of the class where it is defined? The external called doesn't own the definition of the inner class and doesn't even know that the return type is an instance of the inner class; it knows only that it's going to get *something* that implements Reporter. So the situation seems reasonable. Verify for yourself whether it works. To go further, experiment with different access modes for the inner class.

2. What if the inner class in part 1 is anonymous?

One possible solution, with explanatory comments, appears on the CD-ROM in the file \solutions\Chapter_06\InnerClassTest.java.

Although for the purpose of naming, being able to define a class inside another class provides some organizational benefit, but this is not the end of the story. Objects that are instances of the inner class generally retain the ability to access the members of the outer class. This behavior is discussed in the next section.

The Enclosing *this* Reference and Construction of Inner Classes

When an instance of an inner class is created, normally a preexisting instance of the outer class must act as context. This instance of the outer class will be accessible from the inner object. Consider this example, which is expanded from the earlier one:

```
1. public class OuterOne {
2.    private int x;
3.    public class InnerOne {
4.       private int y;
5.       public void innerMethod() {
```

```
6.        System.out.println("enclosing x is " + x);
7.        System.out.println("y is " + y);
8.      }
9.    }
10.   public void outerMethod() {
11.      System.out.println("x is " + x);
12.   }
13.   public void makeInner() {
14.      InnerOne anInner = new InnerOne();
15.      anInner.innerMethod();
16.   }
17.   // other methods...
18. }
```

You will see two changes in this code when you compare it to the earlier version. First, innerMethod() now not only outputs the value of y, which is defined in InnerOne, but also, at line 6, outputs the value of x, which is defined in OuterOne. The second change is that in lines 13–16, the code creates an instance of the InnerOne class and invokes innerMethod() upon it.

The accessibility of the members of the enclosing class is crucial and very useful. It is possible because the inner class has a hidden reference to the outer class instance that was the current context when the inner class object was created. In effect, it ensures that the inner class and the outer class belong together, rather than the inner instance being just another member of the outer instance.

Sometimes you might want to create an instance of an inner class from a static method or in some other situation where no this object is available. The situation arises in a main() method or if you need to create the inner class from a method of some object of an unrelated class. You can achieve this by using the new operator as though it were a member method of the outer class. Of course, you still must have an instance of the outer class. The following code, which is a main() method in isolation, could be added to the code seen so far to produce a complete example:

```
1. public static void main(String args[]) {
2.   OuterOne.InnerOne i = new OuterOne().new InnerOne();
3.   i.innerMethod();
4. }
```

From the point of view of the inner class instance, this use of two new statements on the same line is a compacted way of doing the following:

```
1. public static void main(String args[]) {
2.   OuterOne o = new OuterOne();
3.   OuterOne.InnerOne i = o.new InnerOne();
4.   i.innerMethod();
5. }
```

If you attempt to use the new operation to construct an instance of an inner class without a prefixing reference to an instance of the outer class, the implied prefix this. is assumed. This behavior is identical to that which you find with ordinary member accesses and method invocations. As with member access and method invocation, it is important that the this reference be valid when you try to use it. A static method contains no this reference, which is why you must take special efforts in these conditions.

Member Classes

To this point, we have not distinguished between classes defined directly in the scope of a class—that is, *member classes*—and classes defined inside methods. There are important distinctions between these two scopes that you will need to have clear in your mind. First, we'll look at the features that are unique to member classes.

Access Modifiers

Members of a class, whether they are variables, methods, or nested classes, may be marked with modifiers that control access to those members. This means that member classes can be marked private, public, protected, or default access. The meaning of these access modifiers is the same for member classes as it is for other members, and therefore we won't spend time on those issues here. Instead, refer to Chapter 3 if you need to revisit these concepts.

Static Inner Classes

Just like any other member, a member inner class may be marked static. When applied to a variable, static means that the variable is associated with the class, rather than with any particular instance of the class. When applied to an inner class, the meaning is similar. Specifically, a static inner class does *not* have any reference to an enclosing instance. As a result, methods of a static inner class cannot use the keyword this (either implied or explicit) to access instance variables of the enclosing class; those methods can, however, access static variables of the enclosing class. This is just the same as the rules that apply to static methods in ordinary classes. As you would expect, you can create an instance of a static inner class without the need for a current instance of the enclosing class. The syntax for this construction is very simple; just use the long name of the inner class—that is, the name that includes the name of the outer class, as in the underlined part of line 5:

```
1. public class MyOuter {
2.    public static class MyInner {
3.    }
4.    public static void main(String [] args) {
5.       MyInner aMyInner = new MyOuter.MyInner();
6.    }
7. }
```

The net result is that a static inner class is really just a top-level class with a modified naming scheme. In fact, you can use static inner classes as an extension to packaging.

Not only can you declare a class inside another class, but you can also declare a class inside a method of another class. We will discuss this next.

Classes Defined inside Methods

In the opening of this chapter, we said that nested classes can be declared in any block and that this means you can define a class inside a method. This is superficially similar to what you have already seen, but in this case there are three particular points to be considered.

The first point is that anything declared inside a method is not a member of the class but is local to the method. The immediate consequence is that classes declared in methods are private to the method and cannot be marked with any access modifier; neither can they be marked as static. If you think about this, you'll recognize that these are just the same rules as for any variable declaration you might make in a method.

The second point is that an object created from an inner class within a method can have some access to the variables of the enclosing method. We'll look at how this is done and the restrictions that apply to this access in a moment.

Finally, it is possible to create an anonymous class—literally, a class with no specified name—and doing so can be very eloquent when working with event listeners. We will discuss this technique after covering the rules governing access from an inner class to method variables in the enclosing blocks.

Accessing Method Variables

The rule that governs access to the variables of an enclosing method is simple. Any variable, either a local variable or a formal parameter, can be accessed by methods within an inner class, provided that variable is marked final. A final variable is effectively a constant, so this might seem to be quite a severe restriction, but the point is simply this: an object created inside a method is likely to outlive the method invocation. Because local variables and method arguments are conventionally destroyed when their method exits, these variables would be invalid for access by inner class methods after the enclosing method exits. By allowing access only to final variables, it becomes possible to copy the values of those variables into the object, thereby extending their lifetimes. The other possible approaches to this problem would be writing to two copies of the same data every time it was changed or putting method local variables onto the heap instead of the stack. Either of these approaches would significantly degrade performance.

Let's look at an example:

```
1. public class MOuter {
2.    private int m = (int)(Math.random() * 100);
3.    public static void main(String args[]) {
4.      MOuter that = new MOuter();
5.      that.go((int)(Math.random() * 100),
6.        (int)(Math.random() * 100));
```

```
7.   }
8.
9.   public void go(int x, final int y) {
10.      int a = x + y;
11.      final int b = x - y;
12.      class MInner {
13.        public void method() {
14.          System.out.println("m is " + m);
15. //         System.out.println("x is " + x); //Illegal!
16.          System.out.println("y is " + y);
17. //         System.out.println("a is " + a); //Illegal!
18.          System.out.println("b is " + b);
19.        }
20.      }
21.
22.      MInner that = new MInner();
23.      that.method();
24.   }
25. }
```

In this example, the class MInner is defined in lines 12–20. Within it, method() has access to the member variable m in the enclosing class (as with the previous examples) but also to the final variables of go(). The commented-out code on lines 15 and 17 would be illegal, because it attempts to refer to nonfinal variables in go(); if these lines were included in the source proper, they would cause compiler errors.

Anonymous Classes

Some classes that you define inside a method do not need a name. A class defined in this way without a name is called an *anonymous class*. Anonymous classes can be declared to extend another class or to implement a single interface. The syntax does not allow you to do both at the same time or to implement more than one interface explicitly (of course, if you extend a class and the parent class implements interfaces, then so does the new class). If you declare a class that implements a single explicit interface, then it is a direct subclass of java.lang.Object.

Because you do not know the name of an anonymous inner class, you cannot use the new keyword in the usual way to create an instance of that class. In fact, the definition, construction, and first use (often in an assignment) of an anonymous class all occur in the same place. The next example shows a typical creation of an anonymous inner class that implements a single interface, in this case ActionListener. The essential parts of the declaration and construction are on lines 3–7:

```
1. public void aMethod() {
2.   theButton.addActionListener(
3.     new ActionListener() {
```

```
4.        public void actionPerformed(ActionEvent e) {
5.          System.out.println("The action has occurred");
6.        }
7.      }
8.    );
9.  }
```

In this fragment, the variable used at line 2, theButton, is a reference to a Button object. Notice that the action listener attached to the button is defined in lines 3–7. The entire declaration forms the argument to the addActionListener() method call at line 2; the closing parenthesis that completes this method call is on line 8.

The declaration and construction both start on line 3. Notice that the name of the interface is used immediately after the new keyword. This pattern is used for both interfaces and classes. The class has no visible name of its own in the source but is referred to simply using the class or interface name from which the new anonymous class is derived. The effect of this syntax is to state that you are defining a class and you do not want to think up a name for that class. Further, the class implements the specified interface or extends the specified class without using either the implements or extends keyword.

An anonymous class gives you a convenient way to avoid having to think up trivial names for classes, but the facility should be used with care. Clearly, you cannot instantiate objects of this class anywhere except in the code shown. Further, anonymous classes should be small. If the class defines methods other than those of a simple, well-known interface such as an AWT event listener, it probably should not be anonymous. Similarly, if the class has methods containing more than one or two lines of straightforward code or if the entire class has more than about 10 lines, it probably should not be anonymous. These are not absolute rules; rather, the point here is that if you do not give the class a name, you have only the "self-documenting" nature of the code to explain what it is for. If, in fact, the code is not simple enough to be genuinely self-documenting, then you probably should give it a descriptive name.

When the compiler comes across an anonymous inner class, it creates a separate class file for it called *EnclosingClassName*$n.class, where *EnclosingClassName* is the name of the class that contains the anonymous inner class, and *n* is the integer counter for the anonymous inner classes in the enclosing class (starting at 1).

Construction and Initialization of Anonymous Inner Classes

You need to understand a few points about the construction and initialization of anonymous inner classes to succeed in the Certification Exam and in real life. Let's look at these issues.

As you have already seen, the class is instantiated and declared in the same place. This means that anonymous inner classes are unique to method scopes; you cannot have anonymity with a member class.

You cannot define any specific constructor for an anonymous inner class. This is a direct consequence of the fact that you do not specify a name for the class, and therefore you cannot use that name to specify a constructor. However, an inner class can be constructed with arguments under some conditions, and an inner class can have an initializer if you wish.

Anonymous Class Declarations

As you have already seen, the structure of the code that declares and constructs an anonymous inner class is

```
new Xxxx() { /* class body. */ }
```

where *Xxxx* is a class or interface name. It is important to grasp that code of this form is an *expression* that returns a reference to an object. Thus the previous code is incomplete by itself but can be used wherever you can use an object reference. For example, you might assign the reference to the constructed object into a variable, like this:

```
Xxxx anXxxx = new Xxxx () { /* class body. */ };
```

Notice that you must be sure to make a complete statement, including the closing semicolon. Alternatively, you might use the reference to the constructed object as an argument to a method call. In that case, the overall appearance is like this:

```
someMethod(new Xxxx () { /* class body. */ });
```

Passing Arguments into the Construction of an Anonymous Inner Class

If the anonymous inner class extends another class, and that parent class has constructors that take arguments, then you can arrange for one of these constructors to be invoked by specifying the argument list to the construction of the anonymous inner class. An example follows:

```
// Assume this code appears in some method
Button b = new Button("Anonymous Button") {
  // behavior for the button
};
// do things with the button b...
...
```

In this situation, the compiler will build a constructor for your anonymous inner class that effectively invokes the superclass constructor with the argument list provided, something like this:

```
// This is not code you write! This exemplifies what the
// compiler creates internally when asked to compile
// something like the previous anonymous example
class AnonymousButtonSubclass extends Button {
  public AnonymousButtonSubclass(String s) {
    super(s);
  }
}
```

Note that this isn't the actual code that would be created—specifically, the class name is made up—but it conveys the general idea.

Initializing an Anonymous Inner Class

Sometimes you will want to perform some kind of initialization when an inner class is constructed. In normal classes, you would create a constructor. In an anonymous inner class, you cannot do this, but you can use the initializer feature that was added to the language at JDK 1.1. If you provide an unnamed block in class scope, then it will be invoked as part of the construction process, like this:

```
public MyClass {
  { // initializer
    System.out.println("Creating an instance");
  }
}
```

This is true of any class, but the technique is particularly useful with anonymous inner classes, where it is the only tool you have that provides some control over the construction process.

A Complex Example of Anonymous Inner Classes

Now let's look at a complete example following the pattern of the earlier example using a `Button`. This example uses two anonymous inner classes, one nested inside the other; an initializer; and a constructor that takes an argument:

```
1.  import java.awt.*;
2.  import java.awt.event.*;
3.
4.  public class X extends Frame {
5.    public static void main(String args[]) {
6.      X x = new X();
7.      x.pack();
8.      x.setVisible(true);
9.    }
10.
11.   private int count;
12.
13.   public X() {
14.     final Label l = new Label("Count = " + count);
15.     add(l, BorderLayout.SOUTH);
16.
17.     add(
18.       new Button("Hello " + 1) {
19.         // initializer
20.           addActionListener(
21.             new ActionListener() {
```

```
22.                 public void actionPerformed(
23.                   ActionEvent ev) {
24.                   count++;
25.                   l.setText("Count = " + count);
26.                 }
27.               }
28.             );
29.           }
30.       }, BorderLayout.NORTH
31.     );
32.   }
33. }
```

Lines 19–29 form the initializer and set up a listener on the Button. The listener is another anonymous inner class; as we said earlier, you can arbitrarily nest these things. Notice how the label variable declared at line 14 is final; this allows it to be accessed from the inner classes and, specifically, from the listener defined in the initializer of the first anonymous inner class.

Contracts and Naming Conventions

In programming, as in life, a contract is an agreement about behavior; each party agrees to act in certain predictable ways and gains the right to expect certain predictable behavior from the other party. More precisely, a Java *contract* is an agreement that prescribes the behavior of some of a class' methods. Any class that honors the contract can expect to interact predictably with other classes.

Java's two most common contracts are the equals contract and the hash code contract. They describe the expected behavior of any equals() or hashCode() method. If a class' equals() and hashCode() methods honor the contracts, the class can take advantage of many useful Java features, the most important of which is the Collections framework is described in Chapter 8, "The *java.lang* and *java.util* Packages."

The equals contract is described in detail on the API page for java.lang.Object, in the equals() method description. It has several parts, of which the most important are

- Any object should be equal to itself.
- If x equals y, then y equals x.
- If x equals y and y equals z, then x equals z.

The version of equals() inherited from Object uses the == operator to test for equality. If you override this behavior, the compiler has no way to know whether your new version honors the contract. Your choices are to make sure it does or to forego the benefits of, for example, the Collections framework. If you violate the contract and use collections anyway, the resulting bugs could be very difficult to track down. (This is useful information: If you have an elusive bug related to storing your class in a collection, check out your equals() and hashCode() methods to make sure they obey their contracts.)

The hash code contract specifies behavior of the hashCode() method. A *hash code* is an int that represents the uniqueness of an object; it is used by classes that need an efficient way to determine whether two objects contain different values. The contract is specified on the API page for java.lang.Object, in the hashCode() method description. It requires that if two objects are equal according to their equals() methods, then they must have equal hash codes. Note that the converse is not part of the contract: it's okay for two unequal objects to have the same hash code.

Consider a class called Point3D, representing a point in three-dimensional space. A reasonable implementation would be

```java
public class Point3d {
  private int x, y, z;

  public boolean equals(Object ob) {
    Point3D that = (Point3D ob);
    return this.x == that.x  &&
           this.y == that.y  &&
           this.z == that.z;
  }

  public int hashCode() {
    return x + y + z;
  }
}
```

Two instances of this class are equal if their x, y, and z values match. Clearly the hash code contract is honored. Note that it is possible for unequal instances to have equal hash codes. For example, one instance might have values (100, 200, 300) while another has values (600, 1, -1). This is acceptable. However, be aware that collection classes might slow down when dealing with unequal objects with equal hash codes.

A hash code algorithm should strike a reasonable balance between detecting uniqueness and running efficiently. You can avoid slowing down collections by writing hashCode() methods that are scrupulous about uniqueness, but it does you no good to speed up collection efficiency if your scrupulous hashCode() methods are inefficient. For example, you might wonder about the following alternative hashCode() version for Point3D:

```java
public int hashCode() {
  return (int)(Math.pow(2, x) +
               Math.pow(3, y) +
               Math.pow(5, z));
}
```

This version is very unlikely to return equal hash codes for unequal objects, so collections containing Point3D instances will be efficient, but those three power operations and the cast will make the hashCode() method itself run too slowly.

A *naming convention* is a contract that specifies how a method's name relates to its behavior. Java's most important naming convention is the JavaBeans convention (it has nothing to do with *Enterprise* JavaBeans).

The JavaBeans naming convention concerns properties of objects. A property is a quality that is represented by one or more of an object's variables. The convention specifies a discipline for choosing names for properties and the methods that access and modify them. Specifically,

- A property name begins with a lowercase letter. All subsequent letters are lowercase except for the first letter of a new word. Underscores are not used. Examples: bear, innerClass, normalizedRotationalInertia

- A method that returns the value of a property is named getXxx(), where xxx is the property name. Example: getInnerClass()

- A method that modifies the value of a property is named setXxx(), where xxx is the property name. Example: setNormalizedRotationalInertia()

If you develop the habit of using the JavaBeans naming convention, the habit will serve you well if you decide to pursue the various technologies of J2EE.

Enums

5.0 introduces the *enum*, which is a class with certain added functionality and also certain restrictions. Enums are subclasses of java.lang.Enum. They address a problem that is best explained by example. Suppose you are programming a Java-based automatic car. One of the car's tasks will be to respond to an oncoming traffic light. So you decide to create a TrafficLight class to encapsulate a light's red/yellow/green status. Here is one approach:

```
public class TrafficLight {
  private int state;   // 1 means red
                       // 2 means yellow
                       // 3 means green

  public int getState() {
    return state;
  }
}
```

Assume that the class also contains timing code to change the state at appropriate intervals. That code isn't relevant here.

This class is extremely prone to error. Anyone who modifies the class or calls getState() has to know that 1 means red, 2 means yellow, and 3 means green. If anyone's code gets confused even for a moment about which value means which color, the resulting bug could be very difficult to track down.

The common solution is to introduce constants:

```
public class TrafficLight {
    public final static int RED    = 1;
    public final static int YELLOW = 2;
    public final static int GREEN  = 3;

    private int state;

    public int getState() {
        return state;
    }
}
```

That's a bit better. In fact, prior to release 5.0 it was the best possible approach short of writing about a page of tedious support code. However, this version of TrafficLight still has problems. You can hope that everybody who calls getState() will treat the return value appropriately, like this:

```
switch (nextTrafficLight.getState()) {
    case TrafficLight.RED:
        stop();
        break;
    case TrafficLight.YELLOW:
        floorIt();
        break;
    case TrafficLight.GREEN:
        proceed();
        break;
    default:
        assert false: "Strange-colored light";
}
```

This code compares the light's state only to constants defined in the TrafficLight class, never to literal integer values. You can *hope* people who call getState() use this approach; you can *insist* they do so in daily e-mail memos; but you can't *guarantee* they will do so.

Our code so far has numerous drawbacks, especially these:

- It is possible to assign an out-of-range value to a light's state.

- Printing a light's state is not very informative.

A more robust approach is shown here:

```
1.  public class LightState {
2.     protected final String     name;
3.
4.     public final static LightState RED = new LightState("red");
5.     public final static LightState YELLOW = new LightState("yellow");
6.     public final static LightState GREEN = new LightState("green");
7.
8.     private LightState(String s) {
9.       name = s;
10.    }
11.
12.    public String name() {
13.      return name;
14.    }
15. }
```

The new approach represents states by using instances of the LightState class, rather than ints. Note that the constructor is private, so you can never construct any instances from outside the class or its subclasses; the only instances you will ever need are constructed statically. You can't use the new class as a switch statement argument as you could with the ints of the previous example, but that's a small price to pay. Our original switching code becomes

```
LightState state = nextTrafficLight.getState();
if (state == LightState.RED)
  stop();
else if (state == LightState.YELLOW)
  floorIt();
else if (state == LightState.GREEN)
  proceed();
else
  assert false : "null light state.";
```

This design ensures that the only possibly unexpected state value for a traffic light is null. Also, debugging code can print out any LightState instance and produce an informative result. In fact, this approach is so useful that it has a name: the *typesafe enumeration* design pattern. It is considered typesafe because there is a dedicated type whose sole purpose is to encode a few enumerated states, thus avoiding the dangers of using arbitrarily assigned int values. (Arbitrarily assigned ints or other primitives are knows as *enumerated constants*.) Some programming languages (Pascal, for example) have built-in support for typesafe enumerations. Java did not, until 1.5.

There is only one disadvantage to the typesafe enumeration pattern: it requires a lot of coding. The LightState class shown above is easy enough to create, but a large program with lots of formalized states might require dozens of enumeration classes, and even seasoned developers might be tempted to cut corners.

Java 5.0's typesafe enumeration support provides all the benefits of the LightState class with very little programming effort. The similarities between traditional classes and enums include the following:

- You can declare an enum anywhere you can declare a class.

- Compiling an enum generates a .class file whose name is derived from the enum's name.

- Enums inherit data and methods from Object.

- Enums may be converted and cast according to the same rules that govern any class that extends Object.

- Enums may have main() methods and can be invoked as applications.

- Enums that have no explicit constructors get default no-args constructors.

Enums have restricted functionality. They are *unlike* traditional classes in the following ways:

- Enums are declared with the enum keyword rather than the class keyword.

- Enums may not be instantiated.

- Enums may not extend anything and may not be extended.

- Enums may be arguments in switch statements.

- Enums have built-in name() and toString() methods, both of which return the name of the current instance.

The first statement of an enum has a special format, as shown below. Here is LightState rewritten as an enum:

```
public enum LightState {
  RED, YELLOW, GREEN;
}
```

Notice the first (and only) statement, which is a comma-separated list of identifiers, terminated by a semicolon. When an enum is class-loaded, one instance is created for each identifier in the list; you can think of the identifiers as the names of the instances. The names become public static final members of the enum, so you can refer to the instances as, for example, LightState.YELLOW. The instances are called the enum's *constants*.

The code that follows shows how to use the LightState enum. Assume the getState() method now returns a LightState rather than an int:

```
switch (nextTrafficLight.getState()) {
  case LightState.RED:
    stop();
    break;
```

```
  case LightState.YELLOW:
    floorIt();
    break;
  case LightState.GREEN:
    proceed();
    break;
  default:
    assert false: "null light state";
}
```

This code is almost identical to the original version. The main difference is that RED, YELLOW, and GREEN are now defined in LightState rather than in TrafficLight. This is a more appropriate place for them. The only other difference is the message printed by the assert statement (the original version printed "Strange-colored light"). With enums, the light cannot have a strange color. The compiler ensures that the only instances of TrafficLight that can ever exist are RED, YELLOW, and GREEN. If the value returned by getState() is not one of these values, then it must be null.

Often a simple enum containing only a name list is all you need. However, you can add data, methods, and constructors to an enum. Here is an example that adds all three. Suppose you want to create an enum to represent the suits of a deck of cards. You might begin like this:

```
public enum Suit {
  CLUB, DIAMOND, HEART, SPADE;
}
```

That's fine until you realize that suits are colored, and it is appropriate for a suit to know its own color. Here is a version of Suit that supports colors:

```
1. enum Suit {
2.   DIAMOND(true), HEART(true), CLUB(false), SPADE(false);
3.
4.   private boolean red;
5.
6.   Suit(boolean b) {
7.     red = b;
8.   }
9.
10.  public boolean isRed() {
11.    return red;
12.  }
13.
14.  public String toString() {
15.    String s = name();
```

```
16.    s += red ? ":red"  : ":black";
17.    return s;
18.  }
19.}
```

The name list on line 2 must appear before all other elements of the enum. Line 4 is an ordinary data declaration. Lines 6–8 are an ordinary constructor and lines 10–12 are an ordinary accessor method. You would expect to see such code in any class with a private `boolean` variable called `red`.

The `boolean`s in parens on line 2 (after each name) are constructor arguments. If there is no argument list following an instance name, that instance is constructed using the enum's no-args constructor. (As with traditional classes, an enum with no explicit constructor gets a default no-args constructor.) However, if an instance name is followed by an argument list, there must be a constructor with a compatible arg list. In our example, the constructor on lines 6–8 is compatible.

Line 16 calls `name()`, which is a final method inherited from `java.lang.Enum`. The `name()` method returns an instance's name as it appears in the instance name list. `toString()` also returns the instance's name but is not final. So your enums can override `toString()` to provide extra information, relying on a call to `name()`.

As you can see, enums are very easy to use, thanks to functionality provided by the compiler and inherited from the `java.lang.Enum` superclass. If you get in the habit of using enums instead of enumerated constants in all appropriate situations, you will spare yourself countless debugging headaches.

Summary

We have covered a lot of material in this chapter, but all of it is important. Let's look again at the key points.

We began by covering object-oriented design and implementation. The benefits of object-oriented design and implementation include reusability (through composition and inheritance) and data protection (through encapsulation). We discussed the concept of overloading methods, which allows the programmer to write several methods by the same name in the same class with different argument lists, return types, accessibility modifiers, and lists of exceptions to be thrown. We also discussed overriding methods, which allows the programmer to define new behavior in a subclass method that differs from that of the superclass method. Late binding ensures that the correct behavior is executed at runtime.

We defined when and how constructors are defined with respect to subclassing. Constructors are not inherited, but a single default constructor is provided by the compiler for all classes, including subclasses. A constructor in a subclass can call a constructor in its superclass (by using the `super()` reference) or another constructor in the same class (by using the `this()` reference).

Inner classes can give your programs additional clarity and make them more concise. An inner class in class scope can have any accessibility, including private. Inner classes defined as local to a block may not be static. However, an inner class declared local to a block (for example, in a method) must not have any access modifier. Such a class is effectively private to the block. Classes defined in methods can be anonymous, in which case they must be instantiated at the same point they are defined. Anonymous inner classes can implement an interface or extend a class, but they cannot have any explicit constructors.

Contracts are agreements among programmers regarding class behavior. Classes that honor contracts will interact predictably with other classes.

Finally, we looked at enums, which are specialized classes that provide a robust alternative to enumerated constants. Enums are never explicitly constructed.

Exam Essentials

Be familiar with the way the Java language realizes the "is a" and "has a" relationships. The "is a" relationship implies class extension. The "has a" relationship implies ownership of a reference to a different object.

Be able to identify legally overloaded methods and constructors.   The methods/constructors must have different argument lists.

Be able to identify legally overridden methods.   The methods must have the same name, argument list, and return type.

Know the legal return types for overloaded and overridden methods.   There are no restrictions for an overloaded method; an overriding method must have the same return type as the overridden version.

Know that the compiler generates a default constructor when a class has no explicit constructors. When a class has constructor code, no default constructor is generated.

Understand the chain of calls to parental constructors.   Each constructor invocation begins by invoking a parental constructor.

Know how to create a constructor that invokes a nondefault parental constructor.   Understand the use of the super keyword.

Be able to identify correctly constructed inner classes, including inner classes in methods and anonymous inner classes.   The syntax for each of these forms is explained in previous sections of this chapter.

Know which data and methods of an enclosing class are available to an inner class. Understand that the inner class can access all data and methods of its enclosing class.

Understand the restrictions on static inner classes.   Understand that a static inner class cannot access nonstatic features of its enclosing class.

Know how to use a nonstatic inner class from a static method of the enclosing class.   Be able to recognize the new `Outer().new Inner()` format.

Know how to use enums, and know when it is appropriate to use them.   Enums are classes that are intended to replace enumerated constants. You should be able to recognize an (old-style) group of enumerated constants and know how to create appropriate enums to replace the constants.

Review Questions

1. Consider this class:

```
1. public class Test1 {
2.    public float aMethod(float a, float b) {
3.    }
4.
5. }
```

Which of the following methods would be legal if added (individually) at line 4? (Choose all that apply.)

A. `public int aMethod(int a, int b) { }`

B. `public float aMethod(float a, float b) { }`

C. `public float aMethod(float a, float b, int c) throws Exception { }`

D. `public float aMethod(float c, float d) { }`

E. `private float aMethod(int a, int b, int c) { }`

2. Consider these classes, defined in separate source files:

```
1. public class Test1 {
2.    public float aMethod(float a, float b)
3.                  throws IOException {...
4.    }
5. }
```

```
1. public class Test2 extends Test1 {
2.
3. }
```

Which of the following methods would be legal (individually) at line 2 in class Test2? (Choose all that apply.)

A. `float aMethod(float a, float b) {...}`

B. `public int aMethod(int a, int b) throws Exception {...}`

C. `public float aMethod(float a, float b) throws  Exception {...}`

D. `public float aMethod(float p, float q) {...}`

3. You have been given a design document for a veterinary registration system for implementation in Java. It states:

    "A pet has an owner, a registration date, and a vaccination-due date. A cat is a pet that has a flag indicating whether it has been neutered, and a textual description of its markings."

    Given that the Pet class has already been defined, which of the following fields would be appropriate for inclusion in the Cat class as members? (Choose all that apply.)

    A. `Pet thePet;`

    B. `Date registered;`

    C. `Date vaccinationDue;`

    D. `Cat theCat;`

    E. `boolean neutered;`

    F. `String markings;`

4. You have been given a design document for a veterinary registration system for implementation in Java. It states:

    "A pet has an owner, a registration date, and a vaccination-due date. A cat is a pet that has a flag indicating if it has been neutered, and a textual description of its markings."

    Given that the Pet class has already been defined and you expect the Cat class to be used freely throughout the application, how would you make the opening declaration of the Cat class, up to but not including the first opening brace? Use only these words and spaces: `boolean`, `Cat`, `class`, `Date`, `extends`, `Object`, `Owner`, `Pet`, `private`, `protected`, `public`, `String`.

    A. `protected class Cat extends Owner`

    B. `public class Cat extends Object`

    C. `public class Cat extends Pet`

    D. `private class Cat extends Pet`

5. Consider the following classes, declared in separate source files:

    ```
    1. public class Base {
    2.   public void method(int i) {
    3.     System.out.print("Value is " + i);
    4.   }
    5. }
    ```
    ```
    1. public class Sub extends Base {
    2.   public void method(int j) {
    3.     System.out.print("This value is " + j);
    ```

```
4.    }
5.    public void method(String s) {
6.       System.out.print("I was passed " + s);
7.    }
8.    public static void main(String args[]) {
9.       Base b1 = new Base();
10.      Base b2 = new Sub();
11.      b1.method(5);
12.      b2.method(6);
13.   }
14. }
```

What output results when the main method of the class Sub is run?

A. Value is 5Value is 6

B. This value is 5This value is 6

C. Value is 5This value is 6

D. This value is 5Value is 6

E. I was passed 5I was passed 6

6. Consider the following class definition:

```
1. public class Test extends Base {
2.    public Test(int j) {
3.    }
4.    public Test(int j, int k) {
5.       super(j, k);
6.    }
7. }
```

Which of the following are legitimate calls to construct instances of the Test class? (Choose all that apply.)

A. Test t = new Test();

B. Test t = new Test(1);

C. Test t = new Test(1, 2);

D. Test t = new Test(1, 2, 3);

E. Test t = (new Base()).new Test(1);

7. Consider the following class definition:

```
1. public class Test extends Base {
2.    public Test(int j) {
3.    }
4.    public Test(int j, int k) {
5.      super(j, k);
6.    }
7. }
```

Which of the following forms of constructor must exist explicitly in the definition of the Base class? Assume Test and Base are in the same package. (Choose all that apply.)

A. Base() { }

B. Base(int j) { }

C. Base(int j, int k) { }

D. Base(int j, int k, int l) { }

8. Consider the following definition:

```
1. public class Outer {
2.    public int a = 1;
3.    private int b = 2;
4.    public void method(final int c) {
5.      int d = 3;
6.      class Inner {
7.        private void iMethod(int e) {
8.
9.        }
10.     }
11.   }
12. }
```

Which variables can be referenced at line 8? (Choose all that apply.)

A. a

B. b

C. c

D. d

E. e

9. Which of the following statements are true? (Choose all that apply.)

A. Given that `Inner` is a nonstatic class declared inside a public class `Outer` and that appropriate constructor forms are defined, an instance of `Inner` can be constructed like this: `new Outer().new Inner()`

B. If an anonymous inner class inside the class `Outer` is defined to implement the interface `ActionListener`, it can be constructed like this: `new Outer().new ActionListener()`

C. Given that `Inner` is a nonstatic class declared inside a public class `Outer` and that appropriate constructor forms are defined, an instance of `Inner` can be constructed in a static method like this: `new Inner()`

D. An anonymous class instance that implements the interface `MyInterface` can be constructed and returned from a method like this:

```
1. return new MyInterface(int x) {
2.    int x;
3.    public MyInterface(int x) {
4.      this.x = x;5.    }6. };
```

10. Which of the following are legal enums?

A. `enum Animals { LION, TIGER, BEAR }`

B.
```
enum Animals {
    int age;
    LION, TIGER, BEAR;
}
```

C.
```
enum Animals {
    LION, TIGER, BEAR;
    int weight;
}
```

D.
```
enum Animals {
    LION(450), TIGER(450), BEAR;
    int weight;

    Animals(int w) {
      weight = w;
    }
}
```

E.
```
enum Animals {
    LION(450), TIGER(450), BEAR;
    int weight;

    Animals() { }

    Animals(int w) {
      weight = w;
    }
}
```

11. Which of the following may override a method whose signature is `void xyz(float f)`?

    A. `void xyz(float f)`

    B. `public void xyz(float f)`

    C. `private void xyz(float f)`

    D. `public int xyz(float f)`

    E. `private int xyz(float f)`

12. Which of the following are true? (Choose all that apply.)

    A. An enum definition should declare that it extends `java.lang.Enum`.

    B. An enum may be subclassed.

    C. An enum may contain public method definitions.

    D. An enum may contain private data.

13. Which of the following are true? (Choose all that apply.)

    A. An enum definition may contain the `main()` method of an application.

    B. You can call an enum's `toString()` method.

    C. You can call an enum's `wait()` method.

    D. You can call an enum's `notify()` method.

14. Suppose x and y are of type `TrafficLightState`, which is an enum. What is the best way to test whether x and y refer to the same constant?

    A. `if (x == y)`

    B. `if (x.equals(y))`

    C. `if (x.toString().equals(y.toString()))`

    D. `if (x.hashCode() == y.hashCode())`

15. Which of the following restrictions apply to anonymous inner classes?

    A. They must be defined inside a code block.

    B. They may only read and write final variables of the enclosing class.

    C. They may only call final methods of the enclosing class.

    D. They may not call the enclosing class' synchronized methods.

16. Given the following code, which of the following will compile?

    ```
    enum Spice { NUTMEG, CINNAMON, CORIANDER, ROSEMARY; }
    ```

    A. `Spice sp = Spice.NUTMEG; Object ob = sp;`

    B. `Spice sp = Spice.NUTMEG; Object ob = (Object)sp;`

    C. `Object ob = new Object(); Spice sp = object;`

    D. `Object ob = new Object(); Spice sp = (Spice)object;`

17. Which of the following are true?

   A. An anonymous inner class may implement at most one interface.

   B. An anonymous inner class may implement arbitrarily many interfaces.

   C. An anonymous inner class may extend a parent class other than `Object`.

   D. An anonymous inner class that implements one interface may extend a parent class other than `Object`.

   E. An anonymous inner class that implements several interfaces may extend a parent class other than `Object`.

18. Which methods return an enum constant's name?

   A. `getName()`

   B. `name()`

   C. `toString()`

   D. `nameString()`

   E. `getNameString()`

19. Suppose class X contains the following method:

```
void doSomething(int a, float b)  { … }
```

   Which of the following methods may appear in class Y, which extends X?

   A. `public void doSomething(int a, float b) { … }`

   B. `private void doSomething(int a, float b) { … }`

   C. `public void doSomething(int a, float b)`
   `    throws java.io.IOException { … }`

   D. `private void doSomething(int a, float b)`
   `    throws java.io.IOException { … }`

20. This question involves `IOException`, `AWTException`, and `EOFException`. They are all checked exception types. `IOException` and `AWTException` extend `Exception`, and `EOFException` extends `IOException`. Suppose class X contains the following method:

```
void doSomething() throws IOException{ … }
```

   Which of the following methods may appear in class Y, which extends X?

   A. `void doSomething() { … }`

   B. `void doSomething() throws AWTException { … }`

   C. `void doSomething() throws EOFException { … }`

   D. `void doSomething() throws IOException, EOFException { … }`

Answers to Review Questions

1.   A, C, E. In each of these answers, the argument list differs from the original, so the method is an overload. Overloaded methods are effectively independent, and there are no constraints on the accessibility, return type, or exceptions that may be thrown. B would be a legal overriding method, except that it cannot be defined in the same class as the original method; rather, it must be declared in a subclass. D is also an override, because the *types* of its arguments are the same: changing the parameter names is not sufficient to count as overloading.

2.   B, D. A is illegal because it is less accessible than the original method; the fact that it throws no exceptions is perfectly acceptable. B is legal because it overloads the method of the parent class, and as such it is not constrained by any rules governing its return value, accessibility, or argument list. The exception thrown by C is sufficient to make that method illegal. D is legal because the accessibility and return type are identical, and the method is an override because the types of the arguments are identical—remember that the names of the arguments are irrelevant. The absence of an exception list in D is not a problem: An overriding method may legitimately throw fewer exceptions than its original, but it may not throw more.

3.   E, F. The Cat class is a subclass of the Pet class, and as such should extend Pet, rather than contain an instance of Pet. B and C should be members of the Pet class and as such are inherited into the Cat class; therefore, they should not be declared in the Cat class. D would declare a reference to an instance of the Cat class, which is not generally appropriate inside the Cat class (unless, perhaps, you were asked to give the Cat a member that refers to its mother). Finally, the neutered flag and markings descriptions, E and F, are the items called for by the specification; these are correct items.

4.   C. The class should be public, because it is to be used freely throughout the application. The statement "A cat is a pet" tells you that the Cat class should subclass Pet. The other words offered are required for the body of the definitions of either Cat or Pet—for use as member variables—but are not part of the opening declaration.

5.   C. The first message is produced by the Base class when b1.method(5) is called and is therefore Value is 5. Despite the fact that variable b2 is declared as being of the Base class, the behavior that results when method() is invoked upon it is the behavior associated with the class of the actual object, not with the type of the variable. Because the object is of class Sub, not of class Base, the second message is generated by line 3 of class Sub: This value is 6.

6.   B, C. Because the class has explicit constructors defined, the default constructor is suppressed, so A is not possible. B and C have argument lists that match the constructors defined at lines 2 and 4 respectively, and so they are correct constructions. D has three integer arguments, but there are no constructors that take three arguments of any kind in the Test class, so D is incorrect. Finally, E is a syntax used for construction of inner classes and is therefore wrong.

7. A, C. The constructor at lines 2 and 3 includes no explicit call to either this() or super(), which means that the compiler will generate a call to the no-args superclass constructor, as in A. The explicit call to super() at line 5 requires that the Base class must have a constructor as in C. This requirement has two consequences. First, C must be one of the required constructors and therefore one of the answers. Second, the Base class must have at least that constructor defined explicitly, so the default constructor is not generated but must be added explicitly. Therefore the constructor of A is also required and must be a correct answer. At no point in the Test class is there a call to either a superclass constructor with one or three arguments, so B and D need not explicitly exist.

8. A, B, C, E. Because Inner is not a static inner class, it has a reference to an enclosing object, and all the variables of that object are accessible. Therefore A and B are correct, despite the fact that b is marked private. Variables in the enclosing method are accessible only if those variables are marked final, so the method argument c is correct, but the variable d is not. Finally, the parameter e is of course accessible, because it is a parameter to the method containing line 8.

9. A. Construction of a normal (that is, a named and nonstatic) inner class requires an instance of the enclosing class. Often this enclosing instance is provided via the implied this reference, but an explicit reference can be used in front of the new operator, as shown in A. Anonymous inner classes can be instantiated only at the same point they are declared, so B is illegal. C is illegal because Inner is a nonstatic inner class, and so it requires a reference to an enclosing instance when it is constructed. D is illegal because it attempts to use arguments to the constructor of an anonymous inner class that implements an interface.

10. C, E. A is illegal because the list of names must be terminated by a semicolon. B is illegal because the list of names must be the first element in the enum body. C is a legal enum that contains, in addition to its name list, a variable. D is illegal because the declaration of Bear requires the existence of a no-args constructor. E fixes the bug in D by adding a no-args constructor.

11. A, B. A uses the original method's signature verbatim, which is legal. B makes the subclass version more accessible, which is legal. C makes the subclass version less accessible, which is not legal. D and E change the return type, which is not legal.

12. C, D. Enums may not extend or be extended. They may contain methods and data just like ordinary classes.

13. A, B, C, D. Enums may contain public static void main() methods and may serve as application main classes. Enums inherit from Object, so they have toString(), wait(), and notify() methods.

14. A. It is never possible to have two instances of an enum that represent the same value. So the == operator is reliable, and it's faster than any method call.

15. A. An anonymous inner class must appear inside a block of code. There are no restrictions preventing an anonymous inner class from accessing the enclosing class' non-final data or methods or calling the enclosing class' synchronized methods.

16. A, B, D. Enums may be converted to Object, just like other objects. So A and B are legal, though the cast in B is not necessary. Assigning an Object reference to an enum requires a cast, so C is illegal, but D is legal.

17. A, C. An anonymous inner class may either implement a single interface or extend a parent class other than Object, but not both.

18. B, C. Both name() and toString() return a constant's name. name() is final, but toString() can be overridden.

19. A. A method with default access may be overridden to have default, protected, or public access but not private access, because a method may not be overridden with more restrictive access. An overriding method may not declare that it throws exception types that do not appear in the superclass version.

20. A, C, D. An overriding method may throw an unlimited number of exception types, provided all types are the same as, or are descended from, the types that appear in the overridden version's declared list of thrown exception types.

Chapter

7

Threads

Threads are Java's way of making a single Java Virtual Machine (JVM) look like many machines, all running at the same time. This effect, usually, is an illusion: there is only one JVM and usually only one CPU, but the CPU switches among the JVM's various threads to give the impression that there are multiple CPUs. JVM threads work behind the scenes on your behalf, listening for user input, managing garbage collection, and performing a variety of other tasks.

As a Java programmer, you can choose between a *single-threaded* and a *multithreaded* programming paradigm. A single-threaded Java program has one entry point (the main() method) and one exit point. All instructions are run serially, from start to finish. A multithreaded program has a *first* entry point (the main() method), followed by multiple entry and exit points for other methods that may be scheduled to run concurrently with the main() method.

Java provides you with tools for creating and managing threads. Threads are valuable tools for allowing unrelated, loosely related, or tightly related work to be programmed separately and executed concurrently.

The Certification Exam objectives require that you be familiar with Java's thread support, including the mechanisms for creating, controlling, and communicating between threads. This chapter begins with some fundamentals of thread programming. After that you'll learn about basic thread control techniques, and then move on to the real heart of the matter: monitor programming.

Thread Fundamentals

Java's thread support resides in three places:

- The java.lang.Thread class
- The java.lang.Object class
- The Java language and JVM

In this section you'll learn some of the underlying concepts of thread programming, including what really happens when a thread executes, what happens after execution ends, basic thread states, priorities, and daemon threads.

What a Thread Executes

To make a thread execute, you call its start() method. Doing so registers the thread with a piece of system code called the *thread scheduler*. The scheduler might be part of the JVM or of the host operating system. The scheduler determines which thread is running on each available CPU at any given time. Note that calling your thread's start() method doesn't immediately cause the thread to run; it just makes the thread *eligible* to run. The thread must still contend for CPU time with all the other threads. If all is well, then at some point in the future the thread scheduler will permit your thread to execute.

During its lifetime, a thread spends some time executing and some time in any of several non-executing states. In this section, you can ignore (for the moment) the question of how the thread is moved between states. The question at hand is this: When the thread gets to execute, what does it execute?

The simple answer is that it executes a method called run(). But which object's run() method? You have two choices:

- The thread can execute its own run() method.

- The thread can execute the run() method of some other object.

If you want the thread to execute its own run() method, you need to subclass the Thread class and implement the run() method. For example:

```
1. public class CounterThread extends Thread {
2.   public void run() {
3.     for (int i = 1; i <= 10; i++) {
4.       System.out.println("Counting: " + i);
5.     }
6.   }
7. }
```

This run() method prints out the numbers from 1 to 10. To do this in a thread, you first construct an instance of CounterThread and then invoke its start() method:

```
1. CounterThread ct = new CounterThread();
2. ct.start();      // start(), not run()
```

What you *don't* do is call run() directly; that would just count to 10 in the current thread. Instead, you call start(), which the CounterThread class inherits from its parent class, Thread. The start() method registers the thread ct with the thread scheduler; eventually the thread will execute, and at that time its run() method will be called.

If you want your thread to execute the run() method of some object other than itself, you still need to construct an instance of the Thread class. The only difference is that when you call the Thread constructor, you have to specify which object owns the run() method that you want. To do this, you invoke an alternate form of the Thread constructor:

```
public Thread(Runnable target)
```

The Runnable interface describes a single method:

```
public void run();
```

Thus you can pass any object you want into the Thread constructor, provided it implements the Runnable interface (so that it really does have a run() method for the thread scheduler to invoke). The object is called the thread's *target*. Having constructed an instance of Thread, you proceed as before: you invoke the start() method. As before, doing so registers the thread with the scheduler, and eventually the run() method of the target will be called.

For example, the following class has a run() method that counts down from 10 to 1:

```
1. public class DownCounter implements Runnable {
2.    public void run() {
3.      for (int i = 10; i >= 1; i--) {
4.        System.out.println("Counting Down: " + i);
5.      }
6.    }
7. }
```

This class does not extend Thread. However, it has a run() method, and it declares that it implements the Runnable interface. Thus any instance of the DownCounter class is eligible to be passed into the alternative (nondefault) constructor for Thread:

```
1. DownCounter dc = new DownCounter();
2. Thread t = new Thread(dc);
3. t.start();
```

This section has presented two strategies for constructing threads: extending Thread and implementing Runnable. Superficially, the only difference between these two strategies is the location of the run() method. The second strategy, where a runnable target is passed into the constructor, is perhaps a bit more complicated in the case of the simple examples we have considered. However, there are good reasons why you might choose to make this extra effort. The run() method, like any other member method, is allowed to access the private data, and call the private methods, of the class of which it is a member. Putting run() in a subclass of Thread may mean that the method cannot access the features it needs (or cannot access those features in a clean, reasonable manner).

Another reason that might persuade you to implement your threads using runnables rather than subclassing Thread is the single-implementation inheritance rule. If you write a subclass of Thread, it cannot be a subclass of anything else; but using Runnable, you can subclass whatever other parent class you choose.

Finally, from an object-oriented point of view, a subclass of Thread combines two unrelated functionalities: support for multithreading inherited from the Thread superclass and execution behavior provided by the run() method. These functionalities are not closely related, so good object-oriented discipline suggests that they exist in two separate classes. In the jargon of object-oriented analysis, if you create a class that extends Thread, you're saying that your class "is a" thread. If you create a class that implements Runnable, you're saying that your class "is associated with" a thread.

To summarize, you can use two approaches to specify which run() method will be executed by a thread:

- Subclass Thread. Define your run() method in the subclass.

- Write a class that implements Runnable. Define your run() method in that class. Pass an instance of that class into your call to the Thread constructor.

When Execution Ends

When the run() method returns, the thread has finished its task and is considered *dead*. There is no way out of this state. Once a thread is dead, it cannot be started again; if you want the thread's task to be performed again, you have to construct and start a new thread instance. The dead thread continues to exist; it is an object like any other object, and you can still access its data and call its methods. You just can't make it run again. In other words,

- You *can't* restart a dead thread by calling its start() or run() methods.

- You *can* call other methods (besides start() and run()) of a dead thread.

The Thread methods include a method called stop(), which forcibly terminates a thread, putting it into the dead state. This method is deprecated since JDK 1.2, because it can cause data corruption or deadlock if you kill a thread that is in a critical section of code. Therefore, if a thread might need to be killed from another thread, you should call interrupt() on it from the killing method.

Although you can't restart a dead thread, if you use runnables, you can submit the old Runnable instance to a new thread. However, it is generally poor design to constantly create, use, and discard threads, because constructing a Thread is a relatively heavyweight operation, involving significant kernel resources. It is better to create a pool of reusable worker threads that can be assigned chores as needed.

Thread States

When you call start() on a thread, the thread does not run immediately. It goes into a "ready-to-run" state and stays there until the scheduler moves it to the "running" state. Then the run() method is called. In the course of executing run(), the thread may temporarily give up the CPU and enter some other state for a while. It is important to be aware of the possible states a thread might be in and of the triggers that can cause the thread's state to change.

The thread states are as follows:

Running A running thread gets the full attention of the JVM's processor, which executes the thread's run() method.

Various non-running states The basic non-running states are Suspended, Sleeping, and Blocked. There are also some non-running states that relate to monitors, which are explained later in this chapter.

Ready   A ready thread can enter the Running state as soon as the JVM's processor is assigned to it.

Dead   A dead thread has completed execution of its run() method.

Figure 7.1 shows only the living states.

At the top of Figure 7.1 is the Running state. At the bottom is the Ready state. In between are the various non-running states. A thread in one of these intermediate states is waiting for something to happen; when that something eventually happens, the thread moves to the Ready state, and eventually the thread scheduler will permit it to run again.

Note that the methods associated with the Suspended state are now deprecated; you will not be tested on this state or its associated methods in the exam. For this reason, we will not discuss them in any detail in this book.

The arrows between the bubbles in Figure 7.1 represent state transitions. Be aware that only the thread scheduler can move a ready thread into the CPU.

Later in this chapter, you will examine in detail the various waiting states. For now, the important thing to observe in Figure 7.1 is the general flow: a running thread enters an intermediate non-running state; later, whatever the thread was waiting for comes to pass, and the thread enters the Ready state; later still, the scheduler grants the CPU to the thread. The exceptions to this general flow involve synchronized code and the wait()...notify() sequence—the corresponding portion of Figure 7.1 is depicted as a bubble labeled "Monitor States."

These monitor states are discussed later in this chapter, in the section "Monitors, Waiting, and Notifying."

FIGURE 7.1   Living thread states

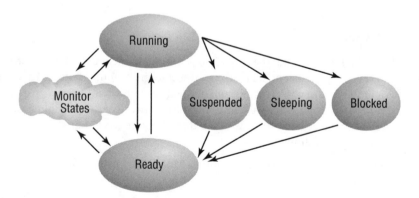

Thread Priorities

Every thread has a *priority*, which is an integer from 1 to 10; threads with higher priority should get preference over threads with lower priority. The thread scheduler considers the priority when it decides which ready thread should execute. The scheduler generally chooses the highest-priority waiting thread. If more than one thread is waiting, the scheduler chooses one of them. There is no guarantee that the thread chosen will be the one that has been waiting the longest.

The default priority is 5, but all newly created threads have their priority set to that of the creating thread. To set a thread's priority, call the setPriority() method, passing in the desired new priority. The getPriority() method returns a thread's priority. The following code fragment increments the priority of thread theThread, provided the priority is less than 10. Instead of hard-coding the value 10, the fragment uses the constant MAX_PRIORITY. The Thread class also defines constants for MIN_PRIORITY (which is 1) and NORM_PRIORITY (which is 5).

```
1. int oldPriority = theThread.getPriority();
2. int newPriority = Math.min(oldPriority+1,
3.    Thread.MAX_PRIORITY);
4. theThread.setPriority(newPriority);
```

The specifics of how thread priorities affect scheduling are platform dependent. The Java specification states that threads must have priorities, but it does not dictate precisely what the scheduler should do about priorities. This vagueness is a problem: algorithms that rely on manipulating thread priorities might not run consistently on all platforms.

Daemon Threads

Some threads are daemon threads. (Pronounced like "demon," the name comes from the rich folklore of the early days of Unix.) Daemon threads are infrastructure threads, created automatically by the JVM. The garbage collector is a daemon thread, and so is the GUI event-processing thread.

When an application begins to run, there is only one non-daemon thread in existence: the main thread, which runs your main() method. Any threads created by daemon threads are initially daemon threads. Threads created by non-daemon threads are initially non-daemon threads. Before a thread begins execution, you can change its daemon status by calling its setDaemon() method, which takes a boolean argument. The JVM runs until the only live threads are daemons. In other words, the JVM considers its work to be done when the only remaining threads are its own infrastructure threads.

Controlling Threads

Thread control is the art of moving threads from state to state. You control threads by triggering state transitions. This section examines the various pathways out of the Running state. These pathways are

- Yielding
- Suspending and then resuming
- Sleeping and then waking up
- Blocking and then continuing
- Waiting and then being notified

The first four of these pathways are presented below. The fifth concerns monitors, and is discussed in the major section "Monitors, Waiting, and Notifying."

Yielding

A thread can offer to move out of the virtual CPU by *yielding*. A call to the `yield()` method causes the currently executing thread to move to the Ready state if the scheduler is willing to run any other thread in place of the yielding thread. The Yield state is shown in Figure 7.2.

A thread that has yielded goes into the Ready state. There are two possible scenarios. If any other threads are in the Ready state, then the thread that just yielded might have to wait a while before it gets to execute again. However, if no other threads are waiting, then the thread that just yielded will get to continue executing immediately. Note that most schedulers do not stop the yielding thread from running in favor of a thread of lower priority.

The `yield()` method is a static method of the `Thread` class. It always causes the currently executing thread to yield.

FIGURE 7.2   Yield

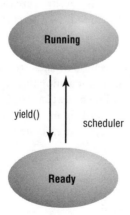

Yielding allows a time-consuming thread to permit other threads to execute. For example, consider an applet that computes a 300 × 300 pixel image using a ray-tracing algorithm. The applet might have a Compute button and an Interrupt button. The action event handler for the Compute button would create and start a separate thread, which would call a `traceRays()` method. A first cut at this method might look like this:

```
1. private void traceRays() {
2.   for (int j = 0; j < 300; j++) {
3.     for (int i = 0; i < 300; i++) {
4.       computeOnePixel(i, j);
5.     }
6.   }
7. }
```

There are 90,000 pixel color values to compute. If it takes 0.1 second to compute the color value of one pixel, then it will take two and a half hours to compute the complete image.

Suppose after half an hour the user looks at the partial image and realizes that something is wrong (perhaps the viewpoint or zoom factor is incorrect). The user will then click the Interrupt button, because there is no sense in continuing to compute the useless image. Unfortunately, the thread that handles GUI input might not get a chance to execute until the thread that is executing `traceRays()` gives up the CPU. Thus the Interrupt button will not have any effect for another two hours.

If priorities are implemented meaningfully in the scheduler, then lowering the priority of the ray-tracing thread will have the desired effect, ensuring that the GUI thread will run when it has something useful to do. However, this mechanism is not reliable between platforms (although it is a good course of action anyway, because it will do no harm). The reliable approach is to have the ray-tracing thread periodically yield. If no input is pending when the yield is executed, then the ray-tracing thread will not be moved off the CPU. If, on the other hand, there is input to be processed, the input-listening thread will get a chance to execute.

The ray-tracing thread can have its priority set like this:

```
rayTraceThread.setPriority(Thread.NORM_PRIORITY-1);
```

The `traceRays()` method listed earlier can yield after each pixel value is computed, after line 4. The revised version looks like this:

```
1. private void traceRays() {
2.   for (int j = 0; j < 300; j++) {
3.     for (int i = 0; i < 300; i++) {
4.       computeOnePixel(i, j);
5.       Thread.yield();
6.     }
7.   }
8. }
```

Suspending

Suspending a thread is a mechanism that allows any arbitrary thread to make another thread unready for an indefinite period of time. The suspended thread becomes ready when some other thread resumes it. This might feel like a useful technique, but it is very easy to cause deadlock in a program using these methods—a thread has no control over when it is suspended (the control comes from outside the thread) and it might be in a critical section, holding an object lock at the time. The exact effect of `suspend()` and `resume()` is much better implemented using `wait()` and `notify()`.

> The `suspend()` and `resume()` methods are deprecated as of the Java 2 release and do not appear in the Certification Exam, so we will not discuss them any further.

Sleeping

A *sleeping* thread passes time without doing anything and without using the CPU. A call to the `sleep()` method requests the currently executing thread to cease executing for (approximately) a specified amount of time. You can call this method two ways, depending on whether you want to specify the sleep period to millisecond precision or to nanosecond precision:

```
public static void sleep(long milliseconds) throws InterruptedException
```

or

```
public static void sleep(long milliseconds, int nanoseconds) throws
InterruptedException
```

> `sleep()`, like `yield()`, is static. Both methods operate on the currently executing thread.

The state diagram for the Sleeping state is shown in Figure 7.3. Notice that when the thread has finished sleeping, it does not continue execution. As you would expect, it enters the Ready state and will execute only when the thread scheduler allows it to do so. For this reason, you should expect that a `sleep()` call will block a thread for at least the requested time, but it might block for much longer. This behavior suggests that you should give very careful thought to your design before you expect any meaning from the nanosecond-accuracy version of the `sleep()` method.

The `Thread` class has a method called `interrupt()`. A sleeping thread that receives an `interrupt()` call moves immediately into the Ready state; when it gets to run, it will execute its `InterruptedException` handler.

FIGURE 7.3   The Sleeping state

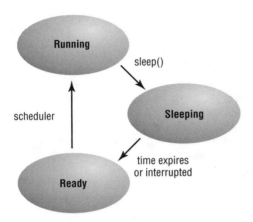

Blocking

Many methods that perform input or output have to wait for some occurrence in the outside world before they can proceed; this behavior is known as *blocking*. A good example is reading from a socket:

```
1. try {
2.    Socket sock = new Socket("magnesium", 5505);
3.    InputStream istr = sock.getInputStream();
4.    int b = istr.read();
5. }
6. catch (IOException ex) {
7.    // Handle the exception
8. }
```

It looks like line 4 reads a byte from an input stream that is connected to port 5505 on a machine called magnesium. Actually, line 4 *tries* to read a byte. If a byte is available (that is, if magnesium has previously written a byte), then line 4 can return immediately and execution can continue. If magnesium has not yet written anything, however, the read() call has to wait. If magnesium is busy doing other things and takes half an hour to get around to writing a byte, then the read() call has to wait for half an hour.

Clearly, it would be a serious problem if the thread executing the read() call on line 4 remained in the Running state for the entire half hour. Nothing else could get done. In general, if a method needs to wait an indeterminable amount of time until some I/O occurrence takes place, then a thread executing that method should graciously step out of the Running state. All Java I/O methods behave this way. A thread that has graciously stepped out in this fashion is said to be *blocked*. Figure 7.4 shows the transitions of the Blocked state.

FIGURE 7.4   The Blocked state

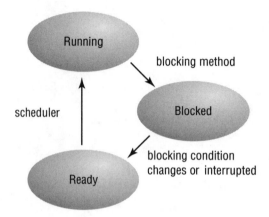

In general, if you see a method with a name that suggests that it might do nothing until something becomes ready—for example, waitForInput() or waitForImages()—you should expect that the caller thread might be blocked, thus losing the CPU, when the method is called. You do not need to know about all APIs to make this assumption; this is a general principle of APIs, both core and third party, in a Java environment.

A thread can also become blocked if it fails to acquire the lock for a monitor or if it issues a wait() call. Locks and monitors are explained in detail later in the remainder of this chapter. Internally, most blocking for I/O, like the read() calls just discussed, is implemented using wait() and notify() calls.

Monitor States

Recall that Figure 7.1 showed all the thread-state transitions. The intermediate states on the right side of the figure (Suspended, Sleeping, and Blocked) have been discussed in previous sections. The monitor states are drawn all alone on the left side of the figure to emphasize that they are very different from the other intermediate states.

The wait() method puts an executing thread into the *Waiting* state, and the notify() and notifyAll() methods move waiting threads out of the Waiting state. However, these methods are very different from suspend(), resume(), and yield(). For one thing, they are implemented in the Object class, not in Thread. For another, they can be called only in synchronized code. The Waiting state and its associated issues and subtleties are discussed in the final sections of this chapter. But first, let's look at one more topic concerning thread control.

Monitors, Waiting, and Notifying

You have seen that various conditions can cause a running thread to lose the JVM processor, entering a non-running state. These non-running states were shown in Figure 7.1, which is repeated here:

FIGURE 7.5   Thread states (reprise)

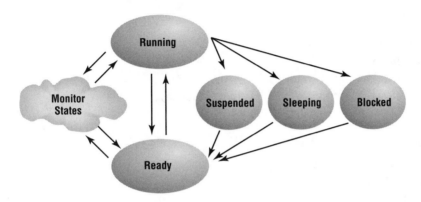

In the remainder of this chapter, you'll look at the Monitor States represented by the cloud at the left of the figure.

A *monitor* is an object that can block and revive threads. The concept is simple, but it takes a bit to understand what monitors are good for and how to use them effectively.

The reason for having monitors is that sometimes a thread cannot perform its job until an object reaches a certain state. For example, consider a class that handles requests to write to standard output:

```
1. class Mailbox {
2.    public boolean     request;
3.    public String      message;
4. }
```

The intention of this class is that a client can set `message` to some value and then set `request` to `true`:

```
1. myMailbox.message = "Hello everybody.";
2. myMailbox.request = true;
```

There must be a thread that checks `request`; on finding it `true`, the thread should write `message` to `System.out` and then set `request` to `false`. (Setting `request` to `false` indicates that the mailbox object is ready to handle another request.) It is tempting to implement the thread like this:

```
1. public class Consumer extends Thread {
2.    private Mailbox myMailbox;
3.
4.    public Consumer(Mailbox box) {
5.      this.myMailbox = box;
6.    }
7.
8.    public void run() {
9.      while (true) {
10.       if (myMailbox.request) {
11.         System.out.println(myMailbox.message);
12.         myMailbox.request = false;
13.       }
14.
15.       try {
16.         sleep(50);
17.       }
18.       catch (InterruptedException e) { }
19.     }
20.  }
```

The consumer thread loops forever, checking for requests every 50 milliseconds. If there is a request (line 10), the consumer thread writes the message to standard output (line 11) and then sets request to false to show that it is ready for more requests.

The Consumer class may look fine at first glance, but it has two serious problems:

- The Consumer class accesses data internal to the Mailbox class, introducing the possibility of corruption. On a time-sliced system, the consumer thread could just possibly be interrupted between lines 10 and 11. The interrupting thread could just possibly be a client that sets message to its own message (ignoring the convention of checking request to see if the handler is available). The consumer thread would send the wrong message.

- The choice of 50 milliseconds for the delay can never be ideal. Sometimes 50 milliseconds will be too long, and clients will receive slow service; sometimes 50 milliseconds will be too frequent, and cycles will be wasted. A thread that wants to send a message has a similar dilemma if it finds the request flag set: the thread should back off for a while, but for how long? There is no good answer to this question.

Ideally, these problems would be solved by making some modifications to the Mailbox class:

- The mailbox should be able to protect its data from irresponsible clients.

- If the mailbox is not available—that is, if the `request` flag is already set—then a client consumer should not have to guess how long to wait before checking the flag again. The handler should tell the client when the time is right.

Java's monitor support addresses these issues by providing the following resources:

- A lock for each object
- The `synchronized` keyword for accessing an object's lock
- The `wait()`, `notify()`, and `notifyAll()` methods, which allow the object to control client threads

The following sections describe locks (including class locks and deadlocking), synchronized code, and the `wait()`, `notify()`, and `notifyAll()` methods, and show how these can be used to make thread code more robust.

The Object Lock and Synchronization

Every object has a *lock*. At any moment, that lock is controlled by, at most, one single thread. The lock controls access to the object's *synchronized code*. A thread that wants to execute an object's synchronized code must first attempt to acquire that object's lock. If the lock is available—that is, if it is not already controlled by another thread—then all is well. If the lock is under another thread's control, then the attempting thread goes into the Seeking Lock state and becomes ready only when the lock becomes available. When a thread that owns a lock passes out of the synchronized code, the thread automatically gives up the lock. All this lock-checking and state-changing is done behind the scenes; the only explicit programming you need to do is to declare code to be synchronized.

Figure 7.6 shows the Seeking Lock state. This figure is the first state in our expansion of the monitor states, as depicted in Figure 7.1.

FIGURE 7.6   The Seeking Lock state

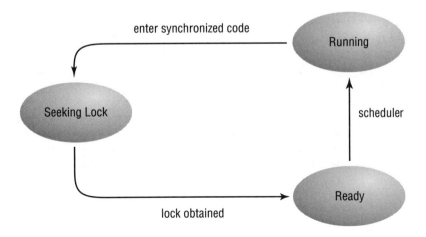

You can mark code as synchronized two ways:

- Synchronize an entire method by putting the `synchronized` modifier in the method's declaration. To execute the method, a thread must acquire the lock of the object that owns the method.

- Synchronize a subset of a method by surrounding the desired lines of code with curly brackets ({}) and inserting the expression `synchronized(someObject)` before the opening curly. This technique allows you to synchronize the block on the lock of any object at all, not necessarily the object that owns the code.

The first technique is by far the more common; synchronizing on any object other than the object that owns the synchronized code can be extremely dangerous.

 The Certification Exam requires you to know how to apply the second technique, but the exam does not make you think through complicated scenarios of synchronizing on external objects. The second technique is discussed at the end of this chapter.

Synchronization makes it easy to clean up some of the problems with the `Mailbox` class:

```
1. class Mailbox {
2.    private boolean    request;
3.    private String     message;
4.
5.    public synchronized void
6.    storeMessage(String message) {
7.      request = true;
8.      this.message = message;
9.    }
10.
11.    public synchronized String retrieveMessage() {
12.      request = false;
13.      return message;
14.    }
15. }
```

Now the `request` flag and the message string are private, so they can be modified only via the public methods of the class. Because `storeMessage()` and `retrieveMessage()` are synchronized, there is no danger of a message-producing thread corrupting the flag and spoiling things for a message-consuming thread, or vice versa.

The Mailbox class is now safe from its clients, but the clients still have problems. A message-producing client should call storeMessage() only when the request flag is false; a message-consuming client should call retrieveMessage() only when the request flag is true. In the Consumer class of the previous section, the consuming thread's main loop polled the request flag every 50 milliseconds. (Presumably a message-producing thread would do something similar.) Now the request flag is private, so you must find another way.

It is possible to come up with any number of clever ways for the client threads to poll the mailbox, but the whole approach is backward. The mailbox becomes available or unavailable based on changes of its own state. The mailbox should be in charge of the progress of the clients. Java's wait() and notify() methods provide the necessary controls, as you will see in the next section.

wait() and notify()

The wait() and notify() methods provide a way for a shared object to pause a thread when it becomes unavailable to that thread and to allow the thread to continue when appropriate. The threads themselves never have to check the state of the shared object.

An object that controls its client threads in this manner is known as a monitor. In strict Java terminology, a *monitor* is any object that has some synchronized code. Any such object has the infrastructure needed to allow it to block and revive threads. To be really useful, most monitors make use of wait() and notify() methods. So, the Mailbox class is already a monitor; it just is not quite useful yet.

Figure 7.7 shows the state transitions of wait() and notify().

FIGURE 7.7   The monitor states

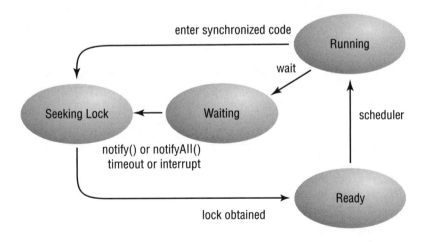

Both wait() and notify() must be called in synchronized code. A thread that calls wait() releases the virtual CPU; at the same time, it releases the lock. It enters a pool of waiting threads, which is managed by the object whose wait() method got called. Every object has such a pool. The following code shows how the Mailbox class's retrieveMessage() method could be modified to begin taking advantage of calling wait():

```
1. public synchronized String retrieveMessage() {
2.    while (request == false) {
3.      try {
4.        wait();
5.      } catch (InterruptedException e) { }
6.    }
7.    request = false;
8.    return message;
9. }
```

Now consider what happens when a message-consuming thread calls this method. The call might look like this:

```
myMailbox.retrieveMessage();
```

When a message-consuming thread calls this method, the thread must first acquire the lock for myMailbox. Acquiring the lock could happen immediately, or it could incur a delay if some other thread is executing any of the synchronized code of myMailbox. One way or another, eventually the consumer thread has the lock and begins to execute at line 2. The code first checks the request flag. If the flag is not set, then myMailbox has no message for the thread to retrieve. In this case the wait() method is called at line 4 (it can throw an InterruptedException, so the try/catch code is required, and the while will retest the condition). When line 4 executes, the consumer thread ceases execution; it also releases the lock for myMailbox and enters the pool of waiting threads managed by myMailbox.

The consumer thread has been successfully prevented from corrupting the myMailbox monitor. Unfortunately, it is stuck in the monitor's pool of waiting threads. When the monitor changes to a state where it can provide the consumer with something to do, then something will have to be done to get the consumer out of the Waiting state. This is done by calling notify() when the monitor's request flag becomes true, which happens only in the storeMessage() method. The revised storeMessage() looks like this:

```
1. public synchronized void
2. storeMessage(String message) {
3.    this.message = message;
4.    request = true;
5.    notify();
6. }
```

On line 5, the code calls notify() just after changing the monitor's state. The notify() method arbitrarily selects one of the threads in the monitor's waiting pool and moves it to the Seeking Lock state. Eventually that thread will acquire the mailbox's lock and can proceed with execution.

Now imagine a complete scenario. A consumer thread calls retrieveMessage() on a mailbox that has no message. It acquires the lock and begins executing the method. It sees that the request flag is false, so it calls wait() and joins the mailbox's waiting pool. (In this simple example, no other threads are in the pool.) Because the consumer has called wait(), it has given up the lock. Later, a message-producing thread calls storeMessage() on the same mailbox. It acquires the lock, stores its message in the monitor's instance variable, and sets the request flag to true. The producer then calls notify(). At this moment, only one thread is in the monitor's waiting pool: the consumer. So the consumer gets moved out of the waiting pool and into the Seeking Lock state. Now the producer returns from storeMessage(); because the producer has exited from synchronized code, it gives up the monitor's lock. Later the patient consumer reacquires the lock and gets to execute; once this happens, it checks the request flag and (finally!) sees that a message is available for consumption. The consumer returns the message; upon return it automatically releases the lock.

To briefly summarize this scenario: a consumer tried to consume something, but there was nothing to consume, so the consumer waited. Later a producer produced something. At that point there was something for the consumer to consume, so the consumer was notified; once the producer was done with the monitor, the consumer consumed a message.

As Figure 7.7 shows, a waiting thread has ways to get out of the Waiting state that do not require being notified. One version of the wait() call takes an argument that specifies a timeout in milliseconds; if the timeout expires, the thread moves to the Seeking Lock state, even if it has not been notified. No matter what version of wait() is invoked, if the waiting thread receives an interrupt() call, it moves immediately to the Seeking Lock state.

This example protected the consumer against the possibility that the monitor might be empty; the protection was implemented with a wait() call in retrieveMessage() and a notify() call in storeMessage(). A similar precaution must be taken in case a producer thread wants to produce into a monitor that already contains a message. To be robust, storeMessage() needs to call wait(), and retrieveMessage() needs to call notify(). The complete Mailbox class looks like this:

```
1.  class Mailbox {
2.      private boolean   request;
3.      private String    message;
4.
5.      public synchronized void
6.      storeMessage(String message) {
7.        while(request == true) {
```

```
 8.        // No room for another message
 9.      try {
10.        wait();
11.      } catch (InterruptedException e) { }
12.    }
13.    request = true;
14.    this.message = message;
15.    notify();
16.  }
17.
18.  public synchronized String retrieveMessage() {
19.    while(request == false) {
20.      // No message to retrieve
21.      try {
22.        wait();
23.      } catch (InterruptedException e) { }
24.    }
25.    request = false;
26.    notify();
27.    return message;
28.  }
29. }
```

By synchronizing code and judiciously calling wait() and notify(), monitors such as the Mailbox class can ensure the proper interaction of client threads and protect shared data from corruption.

Here are the main points to remember about wait():

- The calling thread gives up the CPU.
- The calling thread gives up the lock.
- The calling thread goes into the monitor's waiting pool.

Here are the main points to remember about notify():

- One arbitrarily chosen thread gets moved out of the monitor's waiting pool and into the Seeking Lock state.
- The thread that was notified must reacquire the monitor's lock before it can proceed.

🌐 Real World Scenario

Order of Notification

If an object has multiple threads waiting for it, there is no guarantee about the order in which those threads will be revived when the object receives a notifyAll() call. In this exercise, you'll observe the order of notification on your own JVM.

Begin with a class called Rendezvous, which has a single method called hurryUpAndWait(). The method increments a counter and then calls wait(). Does the method need to be synchronized?

Next create a class called Waiter, which extends Thread. Its constructor should take an argument of type Rendezvous. Its run() method calls hurryUpAndWait() on the instance of Rendezvous and then prints out a message to report that notification has happened. (Getting notified is the only way to return from hurryUpAndWait().) Each instance of Waiter should have a unique serial number, assigned at creation time and printed out after notification, so that you will be able to know the order in which threads were notified.

Your main class should create one instance of Rendezvous and multiple instances of Waiter. The number of Waiter instances should be specified on the command line. After each Waiter is created, call its hurryUpAndWait() method. Eventually all the Waiter instances will be waiting on the Rendezvous object. Then call notifyAll() on Rendezvous. Observe the order in which threads report that they have been notified.

One possible solution appears on the CD-ROM in the file solutions\Chapter_07\NotifyLab.java. Here is a sample of its output:

```
>java NotifyLab 5
Thread #0 just got notified.
Thread #2 just got notified.
Thread #3 just got notified.
Thread #4 just got notified.
Thread #1 just got notified.
```

Your own results could be different, depending on the maker and revision of your JVM. You also might observe different results from one execution to the next. There are three possible results:

- Threads always get notified in serial-number order.

- Threads get notified in a scrambled order that is always the same.

- Threads get notified in a scrambled order that changes from one execution to the next.

> Be careful about drawing the wrong conclusions from your observations. It you see a repeated order (serial or scrambled), that doesn't prove that your JVM's notifier has predictable behavior. It might have random behavior that just happened to come out the same every time you ran your application. Of course, if you see the same order 100 or 1000 times in a row, that's probably not a coincidence. But any conclusion you draw is just an educated speculation about the inner workings of one rev of one JVM. Never rely on observed notification behavior, for the simple reason that other JVMs that could want to run your software might have other notification behavior patterns.

The Class Lock

It is clear by now that every object (that is, every instance of every class) has a lock. Every class also has a lock. The class lock controls access to all synchronized static code in the class. Consider the following example:

```java
class X {
  static int x, y;
  static synchronized void foo() {
    x++;
    y++;
  }
}
```

When the foo() method is called (for example, with the code X.foo()), the invoking thread must acquire the class lock for the X class. Ordinarily, when a thread attempts to call a nonstatic synchronized method, the thread must acquire the lock of the current object; the current object is referenced by this in the scope of the method. However, there is no this reference in a static method because there is no current object.

If Java did not provide class locks, there would be no built-in way to synchronize static code and no way to protect shared static data such as x and y in the previous example.

notifyAll()

The mailbox example above is a very simple example of a situation involving one producer and one consumer. In real life, things are not always so simple. You might have a monitor that has several methods that do not purely produce or purely consume. All you can say in general about such methods is that they cannot proceed unless the monitor is in a certain state, and they themselves can change the monitor's state in ways that could be of vital interest to the other methods.

The notify() method is not precise: You cannot specify which thread is to be notified. In a mixed-up scenario such as the one just described, a thread might alter the monitor's state in a way that is useless to the particular thread that gets notified. In such a case, the monitor's methods should take two precautions:

- Always check the monitor's state in a `while` loop rather than an `if` statement.
- After changing the monitor's state, call `notifyAll()` rather than `notify()`.

The first precaution means that you should *not* do the following:

```
1. public synchronized void mixedUpMethod() {
2.     if (i<16 || f>4.3f || message.equals("UH-OH") {
3.         try { wait(); } catch (InterruptedException e) { }
4.     }
5.
6.     // Proceed in a way that changes state, and then...
7.     notify();
8. }
```

The danger is that sometimes a thread might execute the test on line 2 and then notice that i is (for example) 15 and have to wait. Later, another thread might change the monitor's state by setting i to –23444 and then call `notify()`. If the original thread is the one that gets notified, it will pick up where it left off, even though the monitor is not in a state where it is ready for `mixedUpMethod()`.

The solution is to change `mixedUpMethod()` as follows:

```
1. public synchronized void mixedUpMethod() {
2.     while (i<16 || f>4.3f || message.equals("UH-OH") {
3.         try { wait(); } catch (InterruptedException e) { }
4.     }
5.
6.     // Proceed in a way that changes state, and then...
7.     notifyAll();
8. }
```

The monitor's other synchronized methods should be modified in a similar manner. Now when a waiting thread gets notified, it does not assume that the monitor's state is acceptable. It checks again, in the `while`-loop check on line 2. If the state is still not conducive, the thread waits again.

On line 7, having made its own modifications to the monitor's state, the code calls `notifyAll()`; this call is like `notify()`, but it moves *every* thread in the monitor's waiting pool to the Seeking Lock state. Presumably every thread's `wait()` call happened in a loop like the one on lines 2–4, so every thread will once again check the monitor's state and either wait or proceed. Note that if a monitor has a large number of waiting threads, calling `notifyAll()` can cost a lot of time.

Using a while loop to check the monitor's state is a good idea even if you are coding a pure model of one producer and one consumer. After all, you can never be sure that somebody won't try to add an extra producer or an extra consumer.

Deadlock

The term *deadlock* describes another class of situations that might prevent a thread from executing. In general terms, if a thread blocks because it is waiting for a condition, and something else in the program makes it impossible for that condition to arise, then the thread is said to be deadlocked.

Deadlock conditions can arise for many reasons, but there is one classic example of the situation that is easy to understand. Because it is used as the standard example, this situation has a special name of its own: "deadly embrace."

Imagine a thread is trying to obtain exclusive use of two locks that are encapsulated in objects a and b. First the thread gets the lock on object a, and then it proceeds to try to get the lock on object b. This process sounds innocent enough, but now imagine that another thread already holds the lock on object b. Clearly, the first thread cannot proceed until the second thread releases the lock on object b.

Now for the nasty part: imagine that the other thread, while holding the lock on object b, is trying to get the lock on object a. This situation is now hopeless. The first thread holds the lock on object a and cannot proceed without the lock on object b. Further, the first thread cannot release the lock on object a until it has obtained the lock on object b. At the same time, the second thread holds the lock on object b and cannot release it until it obtains the lock on object a.

Let's have a look at code that could cause this situation:

```
1. public class Deadlock implements Runnable {
2.    public static void main(String [] args)  {
3.       Object a = "Resource A";
4.       Object b = "Resource B";
5.       Thread t1 = new Thread(new Deadlock(a, b));
6.       Thread t2 = new Thread(new Deadlock(b, a));
7.       t1.start();
8.       t2.start();
9.    }
10.
11.   private Object firstResource;
12.   private Object secondResource;
13.
14.   public Deadlock(Object first, Object second) {
```

```
15.     firstResource = first;
16.     secondResource = second;
17.   }
18.
19.   public void run() {
20.     while (true) {
21.       System.out.println(
22.         Thread.currentThread().getName() +
23.         " Looking for lock on " + firstResource);
24.
25.       synchronized (firstResource) {
26.         System.out.println(
27.           Thread.currentThread().getName() +
28.           " Obtained lock on " + firstResource);
29.
30.         System.out.println(
31.           Thread.currentThread().getName() +
32.           " Looking for lock on " + secondResource);
33.
34.         synchronized (secondResource) {
35.           System.out.println(
36.             Thread.currentThread().getName() +
37.             " Obtained lock on " + secondResource);
38.           // simulate some time consuming activity
39.           try { Thread.sleep(100); }
40.           catch (InterruptedException ex) {}
41.         }
42.       }
43.     }
44.   }
45. }
```

In this code, the resources are locked at lines 25 and 34. Notice that, although the same code executes in both threads, the references firstResource and secondResource actually refer to different objects in both threads. This is the case because of the way the two Deadlock instances are constructed on lines 5 and 6.

When you run the code, the exact behavior is nondeterministic, because of differences in thread scheduling between executions. Commonly, however, the output will look something like this:

```
Thread-0 Looking for lock on Resource A
Thread-0 Obtained lock on Resource A
```

```
Thread-1 Looking for lock on Resource B
Thread-0 Looking for lock on Resource B
Thread-1 Obtained lock on Resource B
Thread-1 Looking for lock on Resource A
```

If you study this output, you will see that the first thread (Thread-1) holds the lock on Resource A and is trying to obtain the lock on Resource B. Meanwhile, the second thread (Thread-2) holds the lock on Resource B—which prevents the first thread from ever executing. Further, the second thread is waiting for Resource A and can never proceed because that object will never be released by the first thread.

It is useful to realize that if both threads were looking for the locks in the same order, then the deadly embrace situation would never occur. However, it can be very difficult to arrange for this ordering solution in situations where the threads are disparate parts of the program. Indeed, looking at the variables used in this example, you will see that it can sometimes be difficult to recognize an ordering problem like this even if the code is all in one place.

Synchronizing Part of a Method

There is an additional way to synchronize code. It is hardly common and generally should not be used without a compelling reason. This approach is to synchronize on the lock of a different object.

We briefly mentioned in the section "The Object Lock and Synchronization" that you can synchronize on the lock of any object. Suppose, for example, that you have the following class, which is admittedly a bit contrived:

```
1. class StrangeSync {
2.    Rectangle rect = new Rectangle(11, 13, 1100, 1300);
3.    void doit() {
4.      int x = 504;
5.      int y = x / 3;
6.      rect.width -= x;
7.      rect.height -= y;
8.    }
9. }
```

If you add the synchronized keyword at line 3, then a thread that wants to execute the doit() method of some instance of StrangeSync must first acquire the lock for that instance. That may be exactly what you want. However, perhaps you want to synchronize only lines 6 and 7, and perhaps you want a thread attempting to execute those lines to synchronize on the lock of rect, rather than on the lock of the current executing object. The way to do this is shown here:

```
1. class StrangeSync {
2.    Rectangle rect = new Rectangle(11, 13, 1100, 1300);
3.    void doit() {
```

```
 4.        int x = 504;
 5.        int y = x / 3;
 6.        synchronized(rect) {
 7.          rect.width -= x;
 8.          rect.height -= y;
 9.        }
10.     }
11.   }
```

This code synchronizes on the lock of some arbitrary object (specified in parentheses after the synchronized keyword on line 6), rather than synchronizing on the lock of the current object. Also, the code synchronizes just two lines, rather than an entire method.

It is difficult to find a good reason for synchronizing on an arbitrary object. However, synchronizing only a subset of a method can be useful; sometimes you want to hold the lock as briefly as possible, so that other threads can get their turn as soon as possible. The Java compiler insists that when you synchronize a portion of a method (rather than the entire method), you have to specify an object in parentheses after the synchronized keyword. If you put this in the parentheses, then the goal is achieved: you have synchronized a portion of a method, with the lock using the lock of the object that owns the method.

To summarize, your options are

- To synchronize an entire method, using the lock of the object that owns the method. To do this, put the synchronized keyword in the method's declaration.

- To synchronize part of a method, using the lock of an arbitrary object. Put curly brackets around the code to be synchronized, preceded by synchronized(theArbitraryObject).

- To synchronize part of a method, using the lock of the object that owns the method. Put curly brackets around the code to be synchronized, preceded by synchronized(this).

Summary

A Java thread scheduler can be preemptive or time-sliced, depending on the design of the JVM. No matter which design is used, a thread becomes eligible for execution (ready) when its start() method is invoked. When a thread begins execution, the scheduler calls the run() method of the thread's target (if there is a target) or the run() method of the thread itself (if there is no target). The target must be an instance of a class that implements the Runnable interface.

In the course of execution, a thread can become ineligible for execution for a number of reasons: A thread can suspend, sleep, block, or wait. In due time (we hope!), conditions will change so that the thread once more becomes eligible for execution; then the thread enters the Ready state and eventually can execute.

When a thread returns from its run() method, it enters the Dead state and cannot be restarted.

You might find the following lists to be a useful summary of Java's threads.

- Scheduler implementations:
  - Preemptive
  - Time-sliced
- Constructing a thread:
  - `new Thread()`: no target; thread's own `run()` method is executed
  - `new Thread(Runnable target)`: target's `run()` method is executed
- Nonrunnable thread states:
  - Suspended: caused by `suspend()`, waits for `resume()`
  - Sleeping: caused by `sleep()`, waits for timeout
  - Blocked: caused by various I/O calls or by failing to get a monitor's lock, waits for I/O or for the monitor's lock
  - Waiting: caused by `wait()`, waits for `notify()` or `notifyAll()`
  - Dead: caused by `stop()` or returning from `run()`, no way out

Exam Essentials

Know how to write and run code for a thread by extending `java.lang.Thread`. Extend the Thread class, overriding the `run()` method. Create an instance of the subclass and call its `start()` method to launch the new thread.

Know how to write and run code for a thread by implementing the interface `java.lang.Runnable`. Create a class that implements `Runnable`. Construct the thread with the `Thread(Runnable)` constructor and call its `start()` method.

Know the mechanisms that suspend a thread's execution. These mechanisms include entering any synchronized code or calling `wait()`, `yield()`, or `sleep()`.

Recognize code that might cause deadly embrace. Deadlock conditions cause permanent suspension of threads, and deadly embrace is the classic example of this.

Understand the functionality of the `wait()`, `notify()`, and `notifyAll()` methods. The `wait()` method puts the current thread in the current object's Waiting state. The `notify()` method arbitrarily moves one thread out of the current object's Waiting state. The `notifyAll()` method moves all threadd out of the current object's Waiting state.

Know that the resumption order of threads that execute `wait()` on an object is not specified. The Java specification states that the resumption order for threads waiting on an object is unspecified.

Review Questions

1. Which one statement is true concerning the following code?

```
1. class Greebo extends java.util.Vector
2.    implements Runnable {
3.      public void run(String message) {
4.        System.out.println("in run() method: " +
5.        message);
6.    }
7. }
8.
9. class GreeboTest {
10.    public static void main(String args[]) {
12.      Greebo g = new Greebo();
13.      Thread t = new Thread(g);
14.      t.start();
15.    }
16. }
```

A. There will be a compiler error, because class **Greebo** does not correctly implement the Runnable interface.

B. There will be a compiler error at line 13, because you cannot pass a parameter to the constructor of a **Thread**.

C. The code will compile correctly but will crash with an exception at line 13.

D. The code will compile correctly but will crash with an exception at line 14.

E. The code will compile correctly and will execute without throwing any exceptions.

2. Which one statement is always true about the following application?

```
1. class HiPri extends Thread {
2.    HiPri() {
3.      setPriority(10);
4.    }
5.
6.    public void run() {
7.      System.out.println(
8.        "Another thread starting up.");
9.      while (true) { }
10.    }
11.
12.    public static void main(String args[]) {
```

```
13.    HiPri hp1 = new HiPri();
14.    HiPri hp2 = new HiPri();
15.    HiPri hp3 = new HiPri();
16.    hp1.start();
17.    hp2.start();
18.    hp3.start();
19.  }
20. }
```

   A. When the application is run, thread hp1 will execute; threads hp2 and hp3 will never get the CPU.

   B. When the application is run, thread hp1 will execute to completion, thread hp2 will execute to completion, then thread hp3 will execute to completion.

   C. When the application is run, all three threads (hp1, hp2, and hp3) will execute concurrently, taking time-sliced turns in the CPU.

   D. None of the above scenarios can be guaranteed to happen in all cases.

3. A thread wants to make a second thread ineligible for execution. To do this, the first thread can call the yield() method on the second thread.

   A. True

   B. False

4. A thread's run() method includes the following lines:

```
1. try {
2.    sleep(100);
3. } catch (InterruptedException e) { }
```

Assuming the thread is not interrupted, which one of the following statements is correct?

   A. The code will not compile, because exceptions cannot be caught in a thread's run() method.

   B. At line 2, the thread will stop running. Execution will resume in, at most, 100 milliseconds.

   C. At line 2, the thread will stop running. It will resume running in exactly 100 milliseconds.

   D. At line 2, the thread will stop running. It will resume running some time after 100 milliseconds have elapsed.

5. A monitor called mon has 10 threads in its waiting pool; all these waiting threads have the same priority. One of the threads is thr1. How can you notify thr1 so that it alone moves from the Waiting state to the Ready state?

   A. Execute notify(thr1); from within synchronized code of mon.

   B. Execute mon.notify(thr1); from synchronized code of any object.

   C. Execute thr1.notify(); from synchronized code of any object.

   D. Execute thr1.notify(); from any code (synchronized or not) of any object.

   E. You cannot specify which thread will get notified.

6. If you attempt to compile and execute the following application, will it ever print out the message In xxx?

```
1. class TestThread3 extends Thread {
2.   public void run() {
3.     System.out.println("Running");
4.     System.out.println("Done");
5.   }
6.
7.   private void xxx() {
8.     System.out.println("In xxx");
9.   }
10.
11.   public static void main(String args[]) {
12.     TestThread3 ttt = new TestThread3();
13.     ttt.xxx();
14.     ttt.start();
12.   }
13. }
```

    A. Yes

    B. No

7. A Java monitor must either extend Thread or implement Runnable.

    A. True

    B. False

8. Which of the following methods in the Thread class are deprecated?

    A. suspend() and resume()

    B. wait() and notify()

    C. start() and stop()

    D. sleep() and yield()

9. Which of the following statements about threads is true?

    A. Every thread starts executing with a priority of 5.

    B. Threads inherit their priority from their parent thread.

    C. Threads are guaranteed to run with the priority that you set using the setPriority() method.

    D. Thread priority is an integer ranging from 1 to 100.

10. Which of the following statements about the wait() and notify() methods is true?

   A. The wait() and notify() methods can be called outside synchronized code.

   B. The programmer can specify which thread should be notified in a notify() method call.

   C. The thread that calls wait() goes into the monitor's pool of waiting threads.

   D. The thread that calls notify() gives up the lock.

11. Which of the following may not be synchronized?

   A. Blocks within methods

   B. Static methods

   C. Blocks within static methods

   D. Classes

12. Which of the following calls may be made from a non-static synchronized method?

   A. A call to the same method of the current object.

   B. A call to the same method of a different instance of the current class.

   C. A call to a different synchronized method of the current object.

   D. A call to a static synchronized method of the current class.

13. How many locks does an object have?

   A. One

   B. One for each method

   C. One for each synchronized method

   D. One for each non-static synchronized method

14. Is it possible to write code that can execute only if the current thread owns multiple locks?

   A. Yes.

   B. No.

15. Which of the following are true? (Choose all that apply.)

   A. When an application begins running, there is one daemon thread, whose job is to execute main().

   B. When an application begins running, there is one non-daemon thread, whose job is to execute main().

   C. A thread created by a daemon thread is initially also a daemon thread.

   D. A thread created by a non-daemon thread is initially also a non-daemon thread.

16. Which of the following are true?

   A. The JVM runs until there is only one daemon thread.

   B. The JVM runs until there are no daemon threads.

   C. The JVM runs until there is only one non-daemon thread.

   D. The JVM runs until there are no non-daemon threads.

17. How do you prevent shared data from being corrupted in a multithreaded environment?

    A. Mark all variables as synchronized.

    B. Mark all variables as volatile.

    C. Use only static variables.

    D. Access the variables only via synchronized methods.

18. How can you ensure that multithreaded code does not deadlock?

    A. Synchronize access to all shared variables.

    B. Make sure all threads yield from time to time.

    C. Vary the priorities of your threads.

    D. A, B, and C do not ensure that multithreaded code does not deadlock.

19. Which of the following are true? (Choose all that apply.)

    A. When you declare a method to be synchronized, the method always synchronizes on the lock of the current object.

    B. When you declare a method to be synchronized, you can specify the object on whose lock the method should synchronize.

    C. When you declare a block of code inside a method to be synchronized, the block always synchronizes on the lock of the current object.

    D. When you declare a block of code inside a method to be synchronized, you can specify the object on whose lock the block should synchronize.

20. Suppose you want to create a custom thread class by extending `java.lang.Thread` in order to provide some special functionality. Which of the following must you do?

    A. Declare that your class implements `java.lang.Runnable`.

    B. Override `run()`.

    C. Override `start()`.

    D. Make sure that all access to all data is via synchronized methods.

Answers to Review Questions

1. A. The `Runnable` interface defines a `run()` method with `void` return type and no parameters. The method given in the problem has a `String` parameter, so the compiler will complain that class `Greebo` does not define `void run()` from interface `Runnable`. B is wrong, because you can definitely pass a parameter to a thread's constructor; the parameter becomes the thread's target. C, D, and E are nonsense.

2. C. There is no way to predict how thread priority manipulation will affect the specific performance of individual threads. Priority manipulation only affects overall statistical behavior.

3. B. The `yield()` method is static and always causes the current thread to yield. In this case, ironically, the first thread will yield.

4. D. The thread will sleep for 100 milliseconds (more or less, given the resolution of the JVM being used). Then the thread will enter the Ready state; it will not actually run until the scheduler permits it to run.

5. E. When you call `notify()` on a monitor, you have no control over which waiting thread gets notified.

6. A. The call to `xxx()` occurs before the thread is registered with the thread scheduler, so the object executes the method in the main thread.

7. B. A monitor is an instance of any class that has synchronized code.

8. A. The `suspend()` and `resume()` methods were deprecated in the Java 2 release. They still appear on the API page for `Thread` but should not be used.

9. B. Threads inherit their priority from their parent thread. A is incorrect because, although the default priority for a thread is 5, it may be changed by the parent thread. C is incorrect because Java does not make any promises about priority at runtime. Finally, D is incorrect because thread priorities range from 1 to 10.

10. C. The thread that calls `wait()` goes into the monitor's pool of waiting threads. Option A is incorrect because `wait()` and `notify()` must be called from within synchronized code. Option B is incorrect because the `notify()` call arbitrarily selects a thread to notify from the pool of waiting threads. Option D is incorrect because the thread that calls `wait()` is the thread that gives up the lock.

11. D. You can synchronize a block inside a method by preceding the block with `synchronized`. You can declare a static method to be synchronized; since there is no object, the thread that executes the method will synchronize on a lock belonging to the class. You can synchronize a block inside a static method just as you would a block within a non-static method; again, synchronization will occur on a lock belonging to the class.

12. A, B, C, D. All four situations are legal. Java has no restrictions regarding which methods may call which methods, with respect to synchronization.

13. A. An object has only one lock, which controls access to all synchronized code.

14. A. On way to do this is to have a synchronized method call a synchronized method of a different object.

15. B, C, D. A is wrong because `main()` is executed by a non-daemon thread. B is correct because daemon threads are for the JVM's infrastructure. Non-daemon threads are for programmers. The JVM initially creates a non-daemon thread to run `main()`. C and D are both correct because a thread's daemon state is the same as that of its creating thread.

16. D. The JVM runs until the only threads are its own infrastructure-supporting daemon threads, that is, until there are no more non-daemon threads.

17. D. Variables may not be synchronized. Making the variables volatile or static doesn't address the problem. Shared data in a multithreaded environment should be protected from corruption by ensuring that all access to the data is via synchronized methods. Moreover, all methods should synchronize on the same lock.

18. D. The only way to ensure that multithreaded code won't deadlock is to be careful. There is no single technique that can guarantee non-deadlocking code.

19. A, D. A method may synchronize only on the lock of the current object. A block may synchronize on any object's lock.

20. B. Your class should provide a `run()` method to implement the desired functionality. There is no need to declare that it implements `Runnable`. Overriding `start()` is almost never a good idea. You need to provide synchronized access to data only if that data might be corrupted by other threads.

Chapter 8

The *java.lang* and *java.util* Packages

JAVA CERTIFICATION EXAM OBJECTIVES COVERED IN THIS CHAPTER:

✓ **3.1 Develop code that uses the primitive wrapper classes (such as Boolean, Character, Double, Integer, etc.) and/or autoboxing and unboxing. Discuss the differences between the String, StringBuilder, and StringBuffer classes.**

✓ **3.4 Use standard J2SE APIs in the java.text package to correctly format or parse dates, numbers, and currency values for a specific locale, and, given a scenario, determine the appropriate methods to use if you want to use the default locale or a specific locale. Describe the purpose and use of the java.util.Locale class.**

✓ **3.5 Write code that uses standard J2SE APIs in the java.util and java.util.regex packages to format or parse strings or streams. For strings, write code that uses the Pattern and Matcher classes and the String.split method. Recognize and use regular expression patterns for matching (limited to . (dot), * (star), + (plus), ?, \d, \s, \w, [], ()). The use of *, +, and ? will be limited to greedy quantifiers, and the parenthesis operator will be used only as a grouping mechanism, not for capturing content during matching. For streams, write code using the Formatter and Scanner classes and the PrintWriter.format/printf methods. Recognize and use formatting parameters (limited to %b, %c, %d, %f, %s) in format strings.**

✓ **6.1 Given a design scenario, determine which collection classes and/or interfaces should be used to properly implement that design, including the use of the Comparable interface.**

✓ **6.2 Distinguish between correct and incorrect overrides of corresponding hashCode and equals methods, and explain the difference between == and the equals method.**

✓ **6.3 Write code that uses the generic versions of the Collections API, in particular, the Set<E>, List<E>, Queue<E>, and Map<K,V> interfaces and implementation classes. Recognize the limitations of the non-generic Collections API and how to refactor code to use the generic versions.**

✓ **6.4 Develop code that makes proper use of type parameters in class/interface declarations, instance variables, method arguments, and return types. Write generic methods or methods that make use of wildcard types, and understand the similarities and differences between these two approaches.**

✓ **6.5 Use capabilities in the java.util package to write code to manipulate a list by sorting, performing a binary search, or converting the list to an array. Use capabilities in the java.util package to write code to manipulate an array by sorting, performing a binary search, or converting the array to a list. Use the java.util.Comparator and java.lang.Comparable interfaces to affect the sorting of lists and arrays. Furthermore, recognize the effect of the "natural ordering" of primitive wrapper classes and java.lang.String on sorting.**

The `java.lang` package contains classes that are central to the operation of the Java language and environment. Very little can be done without the `String` class, for example, and the `Object` class is completely indispensable. The Java compiler automatically imports all the classes in the `java.lang` package into every source file.

This chapter examines some of the most important pieces of the `java.lang` package:

- The `Object` class
- The `Math` class
- Strings
- The wrapper classes

The wrapper classes, which were almost trivial through Java 1.4, got a bit more interesting in 5.0 with the introduction of autoboxing and auto-unboxing.

This chapter also covers the collection classes of the `java.util` package. Collections also became more interesting in 5.0, thanks to a significant change to the language: generics. Collections, including generic collections, will be covered in detail.

The chapter finishes with a look at how to scan and format text, using some of the more sophisticated features of the `lang` and `util` packages.

The *Object* Class

The `Object` class is the ultimate ancestor of all Java classes. If a class does not contain the `extends` keyword in its declaration, the compiler builds a class that extends directly from `Object`.

All the methods of `Object` are inherited by every class. Three of these methods (`wait()`, `notify()`, and `notifyAll()`) support thread control, and they are discussed in detail in Chapter 7, "Threads." Two other methods, `equals()` and `toString()`, provide little functionality on their own. The intention is that programmers who develop reusable classes can override `equals()` and `toString()` in order to provide useful class-specific functionality.

The signature of `equals()` is

```
public boolean equals(Object object)
```

The method is supposed to provide "deep" comparison, in contrast to the "shallow" comparison provided by the == operator. To see the difference between the two types of comparisons, consider the `java.util.Date` class, which represents a moment in time. Suppose you have two references of type `Date`: d1 and d2. One way to compare them is with the following line of code:

```
if (d1 == d2)
```

The comparison will be `true` if the *reference* in d1 is equal to the *reference* in d2. Of course, this is the case only when both variables refer to the same object.

Sometimes you want a different kind of comparison. Sometimes you don't care whether d1 and d2 refer to the same `Date` object. Sometimes you *know* they are different objects. What you care about is whether the two objects, which encapsulate day and time information, represent the same moment in time. In this case, you don't want the shallow reference-level comparison of ==; you need to look deeply into the objects themselves. The way to do that is with the `equals()` method:

```
if (d1.equals(d2))
```

The version of `equals()` provided by the `Object` class is not very useful because it just does an == comparison. All classes should override `equals()` so that it performs a useful comparison. That is just what most of the standard Java classes do: they compare the relevant instance variables of two objects.

The purpose of the `toString()` method is to provide a string representation of an object's state. This method is especially useful for debugging.

The `toString()` method is similar to `equals()` in that the version provided by the `Object` class is not especially useful—it just prints out the object's class name, followed by a hash code. Many JDK classes override `toString()` to provide more useful information. Java's string-concatenation facility makes use of this method, as you will see later in this chapter, in the "String Concatenation the Easy Way" section.

The `Object` class provides a `clone()` method, which returns a copy of the current object. In other words, the clone has the same class as the original, and all its data values are identical. Thus all references in the clone point to the same objects as those pointed to in the original.

`Object`'s version of `clone()` is protected, so a class' `clone()` may not be called by any code anywhere. If you want a class' `clone()` to be public, you need to insert something like the following:

```
public Object clone()
             throws CloneNotSupportedException {
  return super.clone();
}
```

Notice the `CloneNotSupportedException`. It is not a runtime exception, so it must be dealt with. Classes that override `clone()` generally declare that they implement `java.lang.Cloneable`, which defines the single `clone()` method.

The *Math* Class

Java's Math class contains a collection of methods and two constants that support mathematical computation. The class is declared final, so you cannot extend it. The constructor is private, so you cannot create an instance. Fortunately, the methods and constants are static, so they can be accessed through the class name without having to construct a Math object. (See Chapter 3, "Modifiers," for an explanation of Java's modifiers, including final, static, and private.)

The two constants of the Math class are Math.PI and Math.E. They are declared to be public, static, final, and double.

The methods of the Math class cover a broad range of mathematical functionality, including trigonometry, logarithms and exponentiation, and rounding. The intensive number-crunching methods are often written as native methods to take advantage of any math-acceleration hardware that might be present on the underlying machine.

You should know about the methods shown in Table 8.1.

TABLE 8.1 Methods of the *Math* Class

Method	Returns
int abs(int i)	Absolute value of i
long abs(long l)	Absolute value of l
float abs(float f)	Absolute value of f
double abs(double d)	Absolute value of d
double ceil(double d)	The smallest integer that is not less than d (returns as a double)
double exp(double a)	e raised to the a power
double floor(double d)	The largest integer that is not greater than d (returns as a double)
double log(double a)	Logarithm of a
int max(int i1, int i2)	Greater of i1 and i2
long max(long l1, long l2)	Greater of l1 and l2
float max(float f1, float f2)	Greater of f1 and f2

TABLE 8.1   Methods of the *Math* Class *(continued)*

Method	Returns
double max(double d1, double d2)	Greater of d1 and d2
int min(int i1, int i2)	Smaller of i1 and i2
long min(long l1, long l2)	Smaller of l1 and l2
float min(float f1, float f2)	Smaller of f1 and f2
double min(double d1, double d2)	Smaller of d1 and d2
double pow(double a, double b)	a raised to the b power
double random()	Random number >= 0.0and < 1.0
int round(float f)	Closest int to f
long round(double d)	Closest long to d
double sin(double d)	Sine of d
double cos(double d)	Cosine of d
double tan(double d)	Tangent of d
double sqrt(double d)	Square root of d

Strings

Java uses the String, StringBuffer, and StringBuilder classes to encapsulate strings of characters. Java uses 16-bit Unicode characters to support a broader range of international alphabets than would be possible with traditional 8-bit characters. Both strings and string buffers contain sequences of 16-bit Unicode characters. The next several sections examine these two classes, as well as Java's string-concatenation feature.

The *String* Class

The String class contains an immutable string. Once an instance is created, the string it contains cannot be changed. Numerous forms of constructors allow you to build an instance out of an array of bytes or chars, a subset of an array of bytes or chars, another string, or a string buffer. Many of these constructors give you the option of specifying a character encoding, specified as a string. However, the Certification Exam does not require you to know the details of character encodings.

Probably the most common string constructor simply takes another string as its input. This constructor is useful when you want to specify a literal value for the new string:

```
String s1 = new String("immutable");
```

An even easier abbreviation could be

```
String s1 = "immutable";
```

It is important to be aware of what happens when you use a string literal ("immutable" in both examples). Every string literal is represented internally by an instance of String. Java classes may have a pool of such strings. When a literal is compiled, the compiler adds an appropriate string to the pool. However, if the same literal already appeared as a literal elsewhere in the class, then it is already represented in the pool. The compiler does not create a new copy. Instead, it uses the existing one from the pool. This process saves on memory and can do no harm. Because strings are immutable, a piece of code can't harm another piece of code by modifying a shared string.

Earlier in this chapter, you saw how the equals() method can be used to provide a deep equality check of two objects. With strings, the equals() method does what you would expect: it checks the two contained collections of characters. The following code shows how this is done:

```
1. String s1 = "Compare me";
2. String s2 = "Compare me";
3. if (s1.equals(s2)) {
4.    // whatever
5. }
```

Not surprisingly, the test at line 3 succeeds. Given what you know about how string literals work, you can see that if line 3 is modified to use the == comparison, as shown here, the test still succeeds:

```
1. String s1 = "Compare me";
2. String s2 = "Compare me";
3. if (s1 == s2) {
4.    // whatever
5. }
```

The == test is true because s2 refers to the String in the pool that was created in line 1. Figure 8.1 shows this graphically.

You can also construct a String by explicitly calling the constructor, as shown next; however, doing so causes extra memory allocation for no obvious advantage:

```
String s2 = new String("Constructed");
```

When this line is compiled, the string literal "Constructed" is placed into the pool. At runtime, the new String() statement is executed and a fresh instance of String is constructed, duplicating the String in the literal pool. Finally, a reference to the new String is assigned to s2. Figure 8.2 shows the chain of events.

Figure 8.2 shows that explicitly calling new String() results in the existence of two objects, one in the literal pool and the other in the program's space.

You just saw that if you create a new String instance at runtime, it will not be in the pool but will be a new and distinct object. You can arrange for your new String to be placed into the pool for possible re-use, or to re-use an existing identical String from the pool, by using the intern() method of the String class. In programs that use a great many similar strings, this approach can reduce memory requirements. More important, in programs that make a lot of String equality comparisons, ensuring that all strings are in the pool allows you to use the == reference comparison in place of the equals() method. The equals() method runs slower because it must do a character-by-character comparison of the two strings, whereas the == operator compares only the two memory addresses.

The String class includes several convenient methods, some of which transform a string. For example, toUpperCase() converts all the characters of a string to uppercase. It is important to remember that the original string is not modified. That would be impossible, because strings are immutable. What really happens is that a new string is constructed and returned. Generally, this new string will not be in the pool unless you explicitly call intern() to put it there.

FIGURE 8.1   Identical literals

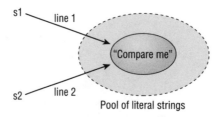

Pool of literal strings

FIGURE 8.2   Explicitly calling the string constructor

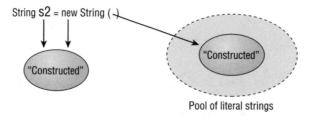

Pool of literal strings

The methods in the following list are just some of the most useful methods of the `String` class. There are more methods than those listed here, and some of those listed have overloaded forms that take different inputs.

This list includes all the methods that you are required to know for the Certification Exam, plus a few additional useful ones.

`char charAt(int index)`   Returns the indexed character of a string, where the index of the initial character is 0.

`String concat(String addThis)`   Returns a new string consisting of the old string followed by `addThis`.

`int compareTo(String otherString)`   Performs a lexical comparison; returns an `int` that is less than 0 if the current string is less than `otherString`, equal to 0 if the strings are identical, and greater than 0 if the current string is greater than `otherString`.

`boolean endsWith(String suffix)`   Returns `true` if the current string ends with `suffix`; otherwise returns `false`.

`boolean equals(Object ob)`   Returns `true` if ob `instanceof String` and the string encapsulated by `ob` matches the string encapsulated by the executing object.

`boolean equalsIgnoreCase(String s)`   Returns `true` if `s` matches the current string, ignoring upper- and lowercase considerations.

`int indexOf(int ch)`   Returns the index within the current string of the first occurrence of `ch`. Alternative forms return the index of a string and begin searching from a specified offset.

`int lastIndexOf(int ch)`   Returns the index within the current string of the last occurrence of `ch`.

`int length()`   Returns the number of characters in the current string.

`String replace(char oldChar, char newChar)`   Returns a new string, generated by replacing every occurrence of `oldChar` with `newChar`.

`boolean startsWith(String prefix)`   Returns `true` if the current string begins with `prefix`; otherwise returns false. Alternate forms begin searching from a specified offset.

`String substring(int startIndex)`   Returns the substring, beginning at `startIndex` of the current string and extending to the end of the current string. An alternate form specifies starting and ending offsets.

`String toLowerCase()`   Converts the executing object to lowercase and returns a new string.

`String toString()`   Returns the executing object (*not* a copy).

`String toUpperCase()`   Converts the executing object to uppercase and returns a new string.

`String trim()`   Returns the string that results from removing whitespace characters from the beginning and ending of the current string.

The following code shows how to use two of these methods to modify a string. The original string is " 5 + 4 = 20". The code first strips off the leading blank space and then converts the addition sign to a multiplication sign:

```
1. String s = " 5 + 4 = 20";
2. s = s.trim();              // "5 + 4 = 20"
3. s = s.replace('+', 'x');   // "5 x 4 = 20"
```

After line 3, s refers to a string whose appearance is shown in the line 3 comment. Of course, the modification has not taken place within the original string. Both the trim() call in line 2 and the replace() call of line 3 construct and return new strings; the address of each new string in turn gets assigned to the reference variable s. Figure 8.3 shows this sequence graphically.

Figure 8.3 shows that the original string seems to be only modified, but it is actually replaced, because strings are immutable. If much modification is required, then this process becomes very inefficient—it stresses the garbage collector cleaning up all the old strings, and it takes time to copy the contents of the old strings into the new ones. The next section discusses two classes that alleviate these problems by representing mutable strings. These are the StringBuffer and StringBuilder classes.

FIGURE 8.3   Trimming and replacing

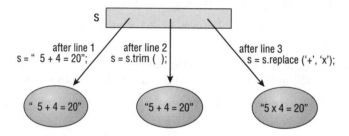

The *StringBuffer* and *StringBuilder* Classes

Java's StringBuffer and StringBuilder classes represent strings that can be dynamically modified.

The most commonly used StringBuffer constructor takes a String instance as input. You can also construct an empty string buffer (probably with the intention of adding characters to it later). An empty string buffer can have its initial capacity specified at construction time. The three constructors are

StringBuffer()   Constructs an empty string buffer.

StringBuffer(int capacity)   Constructs an empty string buffer with the specified initial capacity.

StringBuffer(String initialString)   Constructs a string buffer that initially contains the specified string.

A string buffer has a capacity, which is the longest string it can represent without needing to allocate more memory. A string buffer can grow beyond this capacity as necessary, so usually you do not have to worry about it. However, it is more efficient to declare a large initial capacity when instantiating a string buffer to avoid the system calls required to allocate more memory.

The following list presents some of the methods that modify the contents of a string buffer. All of them return the original string buffer:

StringBuffer append(String str)   Appends `str` to the current string buffer. Alternative forms support appending primitives and character arrays, which are converted to strings before appending.

StringBuffer append(Object obj)   Calls `toString()` on `obj` and appends the result to the current string buffer.

StringBuffer insert(int offset, String str)   Inserts `str` into the current string buffer at position `offset`. There are numerous alternative forms.

StringBuffer reverse()   Reverses the characters of the current string buffer.

StringBuffer setCharAt(int offset, char newChar)   Replaces the character at position `offset` with `newChar`.

StringBuffer setLength(int newLength)   Sets the length of the string buffer to `newLength`. If `newLength` is less than the current length, the string is truncated. If `newLength` is greater than the current length, the string is padded with null characters.

The following code shows the effect of using several of these methods in combination:

```
1. StringBuffer sbuf = new StringBuffer("12345");
2. sbuf.reverse();          // "54321"
3. sbuf.insert(3, "aaa");    // "543aaa21"
4. sbuf.append("zzz");       // "543aaa21zzz"
```

The method calls actually modify the string buffer they operate on (unlike the `String` class example of the previous section). Figure 8.4 graphically shows what this code does.

FIGURE 8.4   Modifying a string buffer

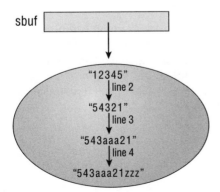

The `StringBuffer` class does not override the version of `equals()` that it inherits from `Object`. Thus the method returns `true` only when comparing references to the same single object. If two distinct instances encapsulate identical strings, `equals()` will return `false`.

One last string buffer method that bears mentioning is `toString()`. You saw earlier in this chapter that every class has one of these methods. Not surprisingly, the string buffer's version just returns the encapsulated string as an instance of class `String`. You will see in the next section that this method plays a crucial role in string concatenation.

String buffers are threadsafe. If multiple threads make concurrent calls on a single string buffer, the string buffer will not become internally corrupt no matter what combination of calls is made. This is achieved through judicious synchronization of the class' code.

The `StringBuilder` class was introduced in 5.0. It is nearly identical to `StringBuffer`, but with one major difference: string builders are not threadsafe. If you want multiple threads to have concurrent access to a mutable string, use a string buffer. If your mutable string will be accessed only by a single thread, there is an advantage to using a string builder, which will generally execute faster than a string buffer.

Both `StringBuffer` and `StringBuilder` implement the `java.lang.Appendable` interface, which specifies several overloaded forms of an `append()` method. Later in this chapter, in the "Formatting Text" section, you'll see how this interface is used.

String Concatenation the Easy Way

The `concat()` method of the `String` class and the `append()` method of the `StringBuffer` class glue two strings together. Another way to concatenate strings is to use Java's overloaded + operator. Similarly, another way to append a string is to use Java's overloaded += operator. However, don't forget that you, the programmer, cannot define additional operator overloads.

String concatenation is useful in many situations—for example, in debugging print statements. So, to print the value of a `double` called `radius`, all you have to do is this:

```
System.out.println("radius = " + radius);
```

This technique also works for object data types. To print the value of a `Dimension` called `dimension`, all you need is

```
System.out.println("dimension = " + dimension);
```

It is important to understand how the technique works. At compile time, if either operand of a + operator (that is, what appears on either side of a + sign) is a `String` object, then the compiler recognizes that it is in a *string context*. In a string context, the + sign is interpreted as calling for string concatenation rather than arithmetic addition.

A string context is simply a run of additions, where one of the operands is a string. For example, if variable `a` is a string, then the following partial line of code is a string context, regardless of the types of the other operands:

```
a + b + c
```

The Java compiler treats the previous code as if it were the following:

```
new
StringBuffer().append(a).append(b).append(c).toString();
```

If any of the variables (a, b, or c) is a primitive, the append() method computes an appropriate string representation. For an object variable, the append() method uses the string returned from calling toString() on the object. The conversion begins with an empty string buffer, then appends each element in turn to the string buffer, and finally calls toString() to convert the string buffer to a string.

The following code implements a class with its own toString() method:

```
1. class Abc {
2.    private int a;
3.    private int b;
4.    private int c;
5.
6.    Abc(int a, int b, int c) {
7.       this.a = a;
8.       this.b = b;
9.       this.c = c;
10.   }
11.
12.   public String toString() {
13.      return "a = " + a + ", b = " + b + ", c = " + c;
14.   }
15. }
```

Now the toString() method (lines 12–14) can be used by any code that wants to take advantage of string concatenation. For example:

```
Abc theAbc = new Abc(11, 13, 48);
System.out.println("Here it is: " + theAbc);
```

The output is

```
Here it is: a = 11, b = 13, c = 48
```

To summarize the sequence of events for a string context:

1. An empty string buffer is constructed.

2. Each argument in turn is concatenated to the string buffer, using the append() method.

3. The string buffer is converted to a string with a call to toString().

That is all you need to know about string manipulation for the Certification Exam, and it's probably all you need to know to write effective and efficient code, too.

The Wrapper Classes

Each Java primitive data type has a corresponding *wrapper class*. A wrapper class is simply a class that encapsulates a single, immutable value. For example, the Integer class wraps up an int value, and the Float class wraps up a float value. The wrapper class names do not perfectly match the corresponding primitive data type names. Table 8.2 lists the primitives and wrappers.

TABLE 8.2   Primitives and Wrappers

Primitive Data Type	Wrapper Class
boolean	Boolean
byte	Byte
char	Character
short	Short
int	Integer
long	Long
float	Float
double	Double

All the wrapper classes can be constructed by passing the value to be wrapped into the appropriate constructor. The following code fragment shows how to construct an instance of each wrapper type:

```
1. boolean   primitiveBoolean = true;
2. Boolean   wrappedBoolean =
3.               new Boolean(primitiveBoolean);
4.
5. byte      primitiveByte = 41;
6. Byte      wrappedByte = new Byte(primitiveByte);
7.
8. char      primitiveChar = 'M';
9. Character wrappedChar = new Character(primitiveChar);
10.
```

```
11. short     primitiveShort = 31313;
12. Short     wrappedShort = new Short(primitiveShort);
13.
14. int       primitiveInt = 12345678;
15. Integer   wrappedInt = new Integer(primitiveInt);
16.
17. long      primitiveLong = 12345678987654321L;
18. Long      wrappedLong = new Long(primitiveLong);
19.
20. float     primitiveFloat = 1.11f;
21. Float     wrappedFloat = new Float(primitiveFloat);
22.
23. double    primitiveDouble = 1.11111111;
24. Double    wrappedDouble =
25.               new Double(primitiveDouble);
```

There is another way to construct any of these classes, with the exception of Character: You can pass into the constructor a String that represents the value to be wrapped. Most of these constructors throw NumberFormatException, because there is always the possibility that the string will not represent a valid value. Only Boolean does not throw this exception; the constructor accepts any String input and wraps a true value if the string (ignoring case) is true. The following code fragment shows how to construct wrappers from strings:

```
 1. Boolean wrappedBoolean = new Boolean("True");
 2. try {
 3.     Byte wrappedByte = new Byte("41");
 4.     Short wrappedShort = new Short("31313");
 5.     Integer wrappedInt = new Integer("12345678");
 6.     Long wrappedLong = new Long("12345678987654321");
 7.     Float wrappedFloat = new Float("1.11f");
 8.     Double wrappedDouble = new Double("1.11111111");
 9. }
10. catch (NumberFormatException e) {
11.     System.out.println("Bad Number Format");
12. }
```

The values wrapped inside two wrappers of the same type can be checked for equality by using the equals() method discussed previously. For example, the following code fragment checks two instances of Double:

```
1. Double d1 = new Double(1.01055);
2. Double d2 = new Double("1.11348");
```

```
3. if (d1.equals(d2)) {
4.    // Do something.
5. }
```

After a value has been wrapped, you may eventually need to extract it. For an instance of `Boolean`, you can call `booleanValue()`. For an instance of `Character`, you can call `charValue()`. The other six classes extend from the abstract superclass `Number`, which provides methods to retrieve the wrapped value as a `byte`, a `short`, an `int`, a `long`, a `float`, or a `double`. In other words, the value of any wrapped number can be retrieved as any numeric type. The retrieval methods are

- `public byte byteValue()`
- `public short shortValue()`
- `public int intValue()`
- `public long longValue()`
- `public float floatValue()`
- `public double doubleValue()`

The wrapper classes are useful whenever it would be convenient to treat a piece of primitive data as if it were an object. A good example is the `Vector` class, which is a dynamically growing collection of objects of arbitrary type. The method for adding an object to a vector is

```
public boolean add(Object ob)
```

Using this method, you can add any object of any type to a vector; you can even add an array (you saw why in Chapter 4, "Converting and Casting"). You cannot, however, add an `int`, a `long`, or any other primitive to a vector. No special methods exist for doing so, and `add(Object ob)` will not work because there is no automatic conversion from a primitive to an object. Thus, the following code will not compile:

```
1. Vector vec = new Vector();
2. boolean boo = false;
3. vec.add(boo);  // Illegal
```

The solution is to wrap the `boolean` primitive, as shown here:

```
1. Vector vec = new Vector();
2. boolean boo = false;
3. Boolean wrapper = new Boolean(boo);
4. vec.add(wrapper);  // Legal
```

The wrapper classes are useful in another way: They provide a variety of utility methods, most of which are static. For example, the static method `Character.isDigit(char ch)` returns a `boolean` that tells whether the character represents a base-10 digit. All the wrapper classes except

Character have a static method called valueOf(String s), which parses a string and constructs and returns a wrapper instance of the same type as the class whose method was called. So, for example, Long.valueOf("23") constructs and returns an instance of the Long class that wraps the value 23.

One set of static wrapper methods is the parse*XXX*() methods. These are Byte.parseByte(), Short.parseShort(), Integer.parseInt(), Long.parseLong(), Float.parseFloat(), and Double.parseDouble(). Each of these takes a String argument and returns the corresponding primitive type. They all throw NumberFormatException.

Other static methods that are mentioned in the exam objectives are the get*XXX*() methods. These are Boolean.getBoolean(), Integer.getInteger(), and Long.getLong(). Each of these takes a String argument that is the name of a system property and returns the value of the property. The return value is a primitive boolean or a wrapper Integer or Long that encapsulates the property value, provided the property is defined, is not empty, and is compatible with the respective type. Integer.getInteger() and Long.getLong() have overloaded forms that take a second argument, which is a primitive of the respective type. The second argument is a default value that is wrapped and returned in case the property is not defined, is empty, or is not compatible with the respective type.

All the wrapper classes provide toString() methods. In addition, the Integer and Long classes provide toBinaryString(), toOctalString(), and toHexString(), which return strings in base 2, 8, and 16.

All wrapper classes have an inconvenient feature: The values they wrap are immutable. After an instance is constructed, the encapsulated value cannot be changed. It is tempting to try to subclass the wrappers, so that the subclasses inherit all the useful functionality of the original classes while offering mutable contents. Unfortunately, this strategy doesn't work because the wrapper classes are final.

To summarize the major facts about the primitive wrapper classes:

- Every primitive type has a corresponding wrapper class type.

- All wrapper types can be constructed from primitives. All except Character can also be constructed from strings.

- Wrapped values can be tested for equality with the equals() method.

- Wrapped values can be extracted with various *XXX*Value() methods. All six numeric wrapper types support all six numeric *XXX*Value() methods.

- Wrapper classes provide various utility methods, including the static valueOf() and parse*XXX*() methods, which parse an input string.

- Wrapped values cannot be modified.

Java's wrapper classes are useful in situations where a primitive must act like an object: as an element in a vector, for example, or as key or value in a Map. Unfortunately, dealing with the wrapped value has historically been inconvenient.

Suppose, for instance, you want to add 10 to the Long referenced by wrappedWeight. There is no way to modify the contents of the object, because wrapped values are final. Prior to release 5.0 2xs, if you wanted to perform calculations on wrapped values you had to do something like this:

```
Double area(Double radius) {
  double r = radius.doubleValue();
  double a = Math.PI * r * r;
  return new Double(a);
}
```

This method is supposed to calculate the area of a circle, but two-thirds of its body is dedicated to unwrapping the argument and wrapping up the return value. Java 5.0 introduces two very simple but convenient functions that unwrap wrapper objects and wrap up primitives. These functions are called *autoboxing* and *auto-unboxing* (or, more briefly, *boxing* and *unboxing*). These are compiler modifications that permit previously illegal combinations of wrappers and primitives in operations, assignments, and method returns.

Boxing is the automatic assignment of a primitive value to a compatible wrapper type. You can think of the primitive value as being stored in a box (the wrapper object). For example, as of release 5.0 2xs you can make the following assignment:

```
Integer wrappedInt = 25;
```

You can think of the line above as an abbreviation for

```
Integer wrappedInt = new Integer(25);
```

The wrapper on the left-hand side of the equals sign must correspond exactly to the primitive type on the right-hand side. Thus all of the following assignments are legal:

```
Boolean wboo = false;
Character wc = 'L';
Byte wb = 1;
Short ws = 1000;
Integer wi = 123456;
Long wl = 12345678L;
Float wf = 123.45f;
Double wd = 123.45;
```

However, the following assignment is illegal:

```
Double wd = 123;
```

The primitive value 123 is an `int`. It doesn't matter that `ints` can be assigned to `doubles` (in accordance with the primitive assignment conversion rules discussed in Chapter 4), because boxing requires an exact match between the wrapper class and the primitive type. The line of code above can be fixed by changing it to

```
Double wd = 123d;
```

which boxes a double into a Double. The following change, which boxes an int into an Integer, also works:

```
Integer wi = 123;
```

Boxing also occurs when a method's return type is a wrapper. You do not need to explicitly construct a returned wrapper object. For example, you can now get away with the following:

```
Double area(double radius) {
  return Math.PI * radius * radius;
}
```

The Java 5.0 compiler also allows you to unbox a wrapped value. Unboxing is the automatic extraction of a wrapped value. Unboxing happens when a wrapper object appears as an operand in a boolean or numerical operation, as shown in the example below:

```
1. Integer wi = 234;
2. int times9 = wi * 9;
```

Line 1 uses boxing to construct a wrapper object. Line 2 multiplies the wrapper by a (primitive) int. Prior to 5.0, line 2 would not have compiled, but in 5.0 the compiler emits code that extracts (unboxes) the primitive value wrapped in wi and multiplies that value by 9.

We can now rewrite the area() method as follows:

```
Double area(Double radius) {
  return Math.PI * radius * radius;
}
```

This version of the method shows the power and convenience of boxing and unboxing. However, you should always be aware that the boxing and unboxing syntaxes are just abbreviations. They do not eliminate the creation of wrapper objects or the extraction of wrapped values; they just hide these operations from the untrained eye. Consider the following code:

```
Double rad;
for (rad=0d; rad<=1d; rad+=1.0e-9)
  System.out.println(area(rad));
```

This code calls area() one billion times. The loop's increment step constructs (via the boxing mechanism) one billion wrapper objects, which later are garbage collected; it also extracts one billion wrapped values (via the unboxing mechanism). The radius() method unboxes and boxes once during each of its one billion calls. The innocent-looking loop and the innocent-looking method have phenomenally more overhead than equivalent code that uses double primitives, but the overhead is visible only to people who understand the underlying mechanisms.

The Collections Framework

Many programs need to keep track of groups of related data items. The most basic mechanism for doing this is the array. Although they are useful for many purposes, arrays have some limitations. For example, they provide only a very simple mechanism for storing and accessing data. Moreover, their capacity must be known at construction time because there is no way to make an array bigger or smaller. Java's collections classes and interfaces support much more generalized data management.

> Collections are a mechanism for manipulating object references. Although arrays are capable of storing primitives or references, collections are not. If you need to take advantage of collection functionality to manipulate primitives, you have to wrap the primitives in the wrapper classes that were presented earlier in this chapter.

Java's Collections API is often referred to as a *framework*, which consists of several interfaces and a number of classes that implement those interfaces. The central interfaces are

- `java.util.Collection`
- `java.util.List` (which extends `Collection`)
- `java.util.Set` (which also extends `Collection`)
- `java.util.Map` (which doesn't extend `Collection`)

There is more to the framework than just interfaces and classes. The framework also defines semantics. In nontechnical speech, "semantics" means "meaning." (When people argue about the precise definition of a word, we say they are "quibbling about semantics.") In technical speech, the semantics of a method is an agreement about what the method is supposed to do.

For example, the Set interface has a method called addAll(). If you look up that method in the API page for Set, you'll see that the return type is boolean and the argument sequence is a single Set. That's not semantics, it's just syntax: it tells you that any addAll() method in any implementing class takes a `Set` and returns a boolean; but it doesn't tell you what the method *does*. To learn what the method does, you have to read the API's explanatory comment: "Adds all of the elements in the specified collection to this set if they're not already present." It's the comment that defines the semantics, by explaining what it means to call the method. *All* classes that implement the interface will take the described action when the method is called. So now you know the semantics of "semantics."

Since the semantics of all the implementing classes are well defined (and easily found in the API pages), if you think you might want to use a collection in a particular situation, your decision process is straightforward. First you figure out which interface (List, Set, or Map) is appropriate to your situation. Then you decide which implementing class to use. The class description in the API page for each implementing class explains what makes the class different from the other implementing classes. Since all implementers have pretty much the same functionality, they differ mostly in their performance profiles. Some collections might execute very quickly, at the cost of using lots of memory; in that case you have to decide whether time or memory is more important. Other collections might execute quickly under certain conditions but not under other conditions. In that case you need to think about which conditions are more likely to apply to your code.

A class or group of classes is considered *threadsafe* if any thread can call any method of any instance at any time. The collections framework as a whole is not threadsafe. If you use collections in a multithreaded environment, you are responsible for protecting the integrity of the encapsulated data, using the techniques that were presented in Chapter 7.

Now let's look at the individual interfaces.

The *Collection* Superinterface and Iteration

The Set and List interfaces extend java.util.Collection. The Collection interface contains about a dozen methods that describe common operations on groups of objects. These are summarized in Table 8.3.

TABLE 8.3   Commonly Used Methods of *java.util.Collection*

Method	Description
add(Object x)	Adds x to this collection
addAll(Collection c)	Adds every element of c to this collection
clear()	Removes every element from this collection
contains(Object x)	Returns true if this collection contains x
containsAll(Collection c)	Returns true if this collection contains every element of c
isEmpty()	Returns true if this collection contains no elements
iterator()	Returns an Iterator over this collection (see below)
remove(Object x)	Removes x from this collection
removeAll(Collection c)	Removes every element in c from this collection
retainAll(Collection c)	Removes from this collection every element that is not in c
size()	Returns the number of elements in this collection
toArray()	Returns an array containing the elements in this collection

If you look up the API page for `java.util.Collection`, you'll see some strange things in the method summaries. For example, the summary for `addAll()` is not exactly as it appears in Table 8.3. It actually is

```
addAll(Collection<? Extends E> c)
```

In fact, the interface declaration itself is strange. At the top of the API page you won't see the expected

```
Interface Collection
```

You'll actually see

```
Interface Collection<E>
```

The angle-bracket notation supports generic collections, which were introduced in Java 1.5. Generics, including the new notation, are explained in detail below in their own section. For now, you can ignore anything you see in the API pages that is enclosed in angle brackets.

The only method in Table 8.3 that isn't straightforward is `iterator()`. This method returns an extremely useful object called an Iterator, which helps you traverse the elements of a collection. Iterators implement the `java.util.Iterator` interface, which has only three methods:

boolean hasNext()   Returns `true` if there are more elements.

Object next()   Returns the next element.

void remove()   Removes the last element returned by `next()`.

The `remove()` method is rarely used. The most common way to use Iterators (and it is *very* common when you use collections) is to call `hasNext()` in the control statement of a `while` loop and to call `next()` in the body of the loop. Here's a simple example:

```
1. public void dumpCollection(Collection c) {
2.    System.out.println("Collection has " + c.size() +
3.                          " elements.");
4.    Iterator iter = c.iterator();
5.    while (iter.hasNext())
6.      System.out.println("Next element is " +
7.                          iter.next());
8. }
```

An Iterator's `next()` method returns its collection's elements in a predictable order that is dictated by the collection class. (We'll look at iteration order in detail when we examine individual implementing classes.) So the loop in lines 5–8 processes each element in order, whatever that order might be.

Now let's look in detail at the Java's collection types: Lists, Sets, and Maps. We'll also look at two useful support classes: `Collections` and `Arrays`.

Lists

Lists are the most straightforward of Java's collections. A List keeps it elements in the order in which they were added. Each element of a List has an index, starting from 0. So you can think of a List as something like an array that grows as needed (and can't contain primitives).

The java.util.List interface contains a few methods in addition to those inherited from the java.util.Collection superinterface. These include

void add(int index, Object x)   Inserts x at index. The index of each subsequent element is increased by 1, so indices remain sequential.

Object get(int index)   Returns the element at index.

int indexOf(Object x)   Returns the index of the first occurrence of x, or -1 if the List does not contain x.

Object remove(int index)   Removes the element at index. The index of each subsequent element is reduced by 1, so indices remain sequential.

The most common class that implements List is Vector, which provides a straightforward implementation of the interface. The methods of Vector are synchronized so that multiple threads accessing a single instance don't have to worry about corrupting the vector's contents. The following code stores the wrapped integers 101 through 110 in a Vector and then uses an Iterator to retrieve and print them:

```
1. for (int i=101; i<=110; i++)
2. vec.add(i);
3.
4. Iterator iter = vec.iterator();
5. while (iter.hasNext())
6.     System.out.println(iter.next());
```

Line 2 looks like it adds an int to the Vector, but don't be deceived by appearances. Vectors and other collections can't store primitives; they store only object references. Line 2 takes advantage of boxing to convert the int to the corresponding Integer. The code is equivalent to

```
vec.add(new Integer(i));
```

In addition to Vector, three other classes in java.util implement List. These are Stack, ArrayList, and LinkedList. The first two are simple. Stack extends Vector, adding push(), pop(), and peek() methods to support classic stack behavior. ArrayList is nearly identical to Vector, but its methods are not synchronized.

LinkedList is an implementation that is intended to support the operations of classic linked list and double-ended queue data structures. In addition to the methods of the List interface, LinkedList has methods called addFirst(), addLast(), getFirst(), getLast(), removeFirst(), and removeLast(). These let you append, retrieve, and remove at either end of the List.

Sets

You've seen that Lists are based on an ordering of their members. Sets have no concept of order. A Set is just a cluster of references to objects.

Sets may not contain duplicate elements. If you try to add an object to a Set that already contains that object, the add() call will return false and the Set will not be changed. A true return value from add() means the Set did not formerly contain the object, but now it does.

Sets use the equals() method, not the == operator, to check for duplication of elements. So you might be surprised by the following code:

```
1. void addTwice(Set set) {
2.    set.clear();
3.    Point p1 = new Point(10, 20);
4.    Point p2 = new Point(10, 20);
5.    set.add(p1);
6.    set.add(p2);
7.    System.out.println(set.size());
8. }
```

The Point class (in the java.awt package) is a very simple class that contains ints called x and y. The class' equals() method returns true if the two points being compared have identical x values and identical y values. The two Point instances created in lines 2 and 3 are distinct but equal, so p1.equals(p2) is true. Since Sets use equals() to check for membership duplication, line 6 will not affect the Set, and line 7 will print out 1, not 2.

The java.util.Set interface extends java.util.Collection but does not add any additional methods. The two most commonly used implementing classes are java.util.HashSet and java.util.TreeSet. The class names are unfortunate, since they refer to the classes' underlying technologies (hash tables and red-black trees) and aren't very descriptive to the majority of programmers. It's important to understand the difference between the two, and for that you need to understand what it means to iterate over a Set.

When you use a List's Iterator, the Iterator presents elements in their order of appearance in the List. A List has an inherent sense of natural order, and it would make no sense to present the elements in any other order. But a Set has no inherent order, so how should an Iterator perform? We can imagine three possibilities:

1.   An Iterator could present elements in the order in which they were added to the Set.

2.   An Iterator could present elements in an unpredictable random order.

3.   An Iterator could present elements in some kind of sorted order.

Option 1 isn't very useful, since Lists already present elements in the order in which they were added. Option 2 is implemented by the HashSet class, and option 3 is implemented by the TreeSet class.

When you iterate over a Hash Set, you can't predict the order in which elements will be presented. This means that Hash Sets are appropriate only in situations where you don't care about the order. The API page for the HashSet class explains that no matter how many elements a Hash Set contains, its basic operations (that is, its add(), remove(), and contains() methods) will always execute in constant time.

When you iterate over a Tree Set, elements will always be presented in sorted order. (Whatever *that* might mean! See below.) You might expect that there is a performance cost to be paid for maintaining order. In fact, as you can read in the TreeSet API page, the amount of time required to perform a basic operation on a Tree Set is proportional to the logarithm of the number of elements in the set.

 Don't worry if you've forgotten your high school math. You don't need to remember what a logarithm is. All you have to know is that as a Tree Set's population grows, the time to perform basic operations increases, but not drastically.

The TreeSet class implements the java.util.SortedSet interface, which extends java.util.Set. The SortedSet interface provides several useful methods that support dealing with sorted data. These include:

Object first()   Returns this set's first element.

Object last()   Returns this set's last element.

SortedSet headSet(Object thru)   Returns a sorted set containing this set's elements through the specified element.

SortedSet tailSet(Object from)   Returns a sorted set containing this set's elements from the specified element through the end.

SortedSet subSet(Object from, Object to)   Returns a sorted set containing this set's elements from from through to.

So how do you choose which set to use? If you care about iteration order, use a Tree Set and pay the time penalty. If iteration order doesn't matter, use the higher-performance Hash Set.

But what exactly does iteration order mean? If a Tree Set contains only instances of Integer or String, you would hope that elements would be presented in numerical or alphabetical order, and indeed that's what would happen. There is nothing magic about this result. Tree Sets rely on all their elements implementing the java.lang.Comparable interface, which defines a single method:

```
public int compareTo(Object x)
```

The method returns a positive number if the current object is "greater than" x, by whatever definition of "greater than" the class itself wants to use. The method returns a negative number if the current object is "less than" x, and 0 if the current object is "equal to" x. When you add an object to a Tree Set, the Tree Set maintains ordering by calling compareTo() on its elements and on the object being added.

There's something strange going on here. Did you spot it? TreeSet implements Collection, and Collection's add() method has an argument of type Object. But the internals of TreeSet require that you add a `Comparable`, not an `Object`. This requirement isn't enforced by the compiler. You just have to *know* that you can store only `Comparable`s, and if you forget, you'll get into trouble at runtime. You're fine as long as your Tree Set contains only one element. When you try to add a second element, the Tree Set needs to determine how the second element compares to the first. The second element is cast to `Comparable`, and if the cast is illegal, a `ClassCastException` is thrown. If that makes you uneasy about using Tree Sets, don't worry. The problem can be completely eliminated by using generics, which are discussed a little later in this chapter.

Many of the core Java classes can reasonably be thought of as having an inherent order. These all implement `Comparable`. So, for example, if you want to store some strings or wrapper instances in a Tree Set, you don't need to worry about getting that `ClassCastException` at runtime.

The following method generates random numbers, wraps them, and stores them in a Tree Set. Then the Tree Set's contents are printed out in their natural order.

```
1. static void sortRandoms(int nRandoms)
2. {
3.    TreeSet set = new TreeSet();
4.    for (int i=0; i<nRandoms; i++)
5.       set.add(Math.random());
6.
7.    Iterator iter = set.iterator();
8.    while (iter.hasNext())
9.       System.out.println(iter.next());
10. }
```

Once again, we have used boxing as a convenience for avoiding typing. Line 5 is equivalent to

```
set.add(new Double(Math.random()));
```

Here is a sample of output from the method:

```
0.09753894845505195
0.14214429064845446
0.2406814471249824
0.3746330333848745
0.4430642976950666
```

Notice how the numbers appear in ascending order. The only effort we spent on ordering the numbers was the thought process that went into deciding to use a Tree Set. If you've ever studied sorting algorithms, you'll understand how enormously useful it is to have a class that specializes in sorting, leaving you free to think about other issues.

Maps

Maps are an important part of Java's collections framework, but the java.util.Map class doesn't implement the java.util.Collection interface. So in one sense Maps are collections, and in another sense they aren't.

A Map combines *two* collections, called keys and values. The Map's job is to associate exactly one value with each key. You never add a single object to a Map; you add a key and the corresponding value. When you retrieve data from a Map, a key is used to get to the value. A good analogy for this process is a dictionary, where the keys are the words being defined and the values are the definitions. Dictionaries aren't perfect analogies, because a word might have several dictionary definitions. But in a Map, every key appears exactly once and is associated with exactly one value.

Here are the important methods of the Map interface:

Object put(Object key, Object value)   Associates key and value. If the Map already associates a value with key, the old value is removed and returned; otherwise it returns null.

Object get(Object key)   Returns the value associated with key, or null if no value is associated with key.

boolean containsKey(Object key)   Returns true if the Map associates some value with key.

void clear()   Empties the Map.

Set keySet()   Returns a Set containing the Map's keys. Changes to the Map will be reflected in the Set, and changes to the Set will affect the Map, so it's not a good idea to modify the Set.

Collection values()   Returns a collection containing the Map's values. Changes to the Map will be reflected in the collection, and changes to the collection will affect the Map, so it's not a good idea to modify the collection.

Suppose you are writing a software system for a hospital. Each patient has a unique medical record ID, which is a string. Associated with each patient is an object that contains information about the patient's prescriptions; this object's class is called Prescriptions. It would be natural to store the Prescriptions objects as values in a Map, using the medical record IDs as the keys. Suppose the Map is called idToPrescriptions. Then to add Prescriptions object scrips for patient id, you would call

```
idToPrescriptions.put(id, scrips);
```

To retrieve the prescriptions for the patient, you would do something like the following:

```
Prescriptions pres;
pres = (Prescriptions)idToPrescriptions.get(id);
```

The cast is necessary because the get() method's return type is Object. If it seems tedious to cast every time you retrieve something from a Map, read on. Generics will soon make life easier.

> In our example, the name of the Map (idToPrescriptions) explains both the keys and the values of the Map. It's always a good idea to use names that are as descriptive as possible. Partially descriptive names, such as idMap or prescriptionsMap, are especially irritating to people who have to figure out your code. The Programmer Exam doesn't test your skill at choosing names, but it's an essential skill in the professional world, and you can lose points on the Developer Exam for poor naming.

Now suppose the hospital system has a billForMeds() method, whose arguments are a patient ID and a Prescriptions object. To call this method for every patient, you would do the following:

```
1. String id;
2. Prescriptions scrips;
3. Iterator iter;
4. iter = idToPrescriptions.keySet().iterator();
5. while (iter.hasNext()) {
6.   id = (String)iter.next();
7.   scrips = (Prescriptions)idToPrescriptions.get(id);
8.   billForMeds(id, scrips);
9. }
```

Line 4 retrieves the Map's key set (containing patient IDs) and then extracts an Iterator for the key set. The loop retrieves each ID in turn (line 6), uses the ID to look up the Prescriptions object (line 7), and then calls billForMeds() (line 8).

If the billForMeds() method didn't require you to pass in the patient ID, you could ignore the Map's keys and iterate over the values instead:

```
1. Prescriptions scrips;
2. Iterator iter;
3. iter = idToPrescriptions.values().iterator();
4. while (iter.hasNext()) {
5.   scrips = (Prescriptions)iter.next(id);
6.   billForMeds(scrips);
7. }
```

Java's two most important Map classes are java.util.HashMap and java.util.TreeMap. In our discussion of Sets, you saw that "Hash" meant "unpredictable order" and "Tree" meant "natural order." This applies to Maps as well: specifically, to Map keys. A Hash Map's keys (as delivered by the keySet() method) are iterated in unpredictable order. A Tree Map's keys are iterated in natural order. Recall from the previous section that natural order is determined by the Comparable interface; when you use a Tree Map, all keys must implement Comparable. In our example, if it's important for prescriptions to be processed in alphabetical order of patient ID, then idToPrescriptions should be a Tree Map. If processing order isn't important, the Map should be a less-costly Hash Map.

The TreeMap class implements the java.util.SortedMap interface, which extends java.util.Map. The SortedMap interface provides several useful methods that support dealing with sorted data. These include:

Object first()   Returns this set's first key.

Object lastKey()   Returns this set's last key.

SortedMap headMap(Object toKey)   Returns a sorted Map containing this Map's mappings with keys up through the specified key.

SortedMap tailMap(Object fromKey)   Returns a sorted Map containing this Map's mappings from the specified key through the last key.

SortedMap subMap(Object fromKey, Object toKey)   Returns a sorted Map containing this Map's mappings from fromKey through toKey.

Maps check for key uniqueness the same way that Sets check for element uniqueness: they use the equals() method, not the == operator. Let's look at an example to see how this works. Recall that the java.awt.Point class contains just an x and a y value. Suppose the Map pointToText associates Strings with Points. How many entries does the Map contain after the following code executes?

```
1. pointToText.clear();
2. Point p1 = new Point(1, 2);
3. pointToText.put(p1, "First");
4. Point p2 = new Point(1, 2);
5. pointToText.put(p2, "Second");
```

The Point objects created in lines 2 and 4 are unique but identical. That is, p1 == p2 is false, but p1.equals(p2) is true. So the put() call on line 5 *replaces* the single entry that was added on line 3, and at the end the Map contains only one entry.

Support Classes

The java.util package contains two support classes, called Collections and Arrays. These provide static methods that operate on collections and arrays.

The methods of Collections tend to be advanced, beyond the scope of the Programmer's Exam. The simpler ones include

static boolean disjoint(Collection c1, Collection c2)   Returns true if the two collections have no elements in common.

static int frequency(Collection c, Object ob)   Returns the number of elements in c that are equal to ob.

🌐 Real World Scenario

A Sortable, Reversible Vector

Here's a scenario in which you will write a class that implements a Vector of Characters, with additional properties.

The class should have a constructor that populates the Vector with a specified number of instances of the Character class. These Characters should be random and unique. Provide methods called sort() and reverse(), which should respectively sort and reverse the contents of the Vector. Provide a main() method that demonstrates the functionality of the constructor and of the sort() and reverse() methods. Remember to use generics! Here is a sample:

```
>java CleverVector
Initial State: CZqnWSNMyu
       Sorted: CMNSWZnquy
     Reversed: yuqnZWSNMC
```

A second run produces different output because the Vector is initialized with different random Characters:

```
>java CleverVector
Initial State: DZBpUlPMbI
       Sorted: BDIMPUZblp
     Reversed: plbZUPMIDB
```

Without collections, initializing, sorting, and reversing would require a lot of original code. With the proper use of the classes in the java.util package, these operations require only a few lines each. One possible solution appears on your CD-ROM in the file solutions\Chapter_08\CleverVector.java.

---

static Object max(Collection c)   Returns the maximum element of c according to the natural ordering of the elements.

static Object min(Collection c)   Returns the maximum element of c according to the natural ordering of the elements.

static void reverse(List list)   Reverses the order of the elements in the specified List.

static void shuffle(List list)   Randomly rearranges the List's elements.

static void sort(List list)   Rearranges the List's elements into their natural order.

The methods of Arrays support sorting and searching of arrays. There is also a method that converts an array to a list. The important methods of this class are

static void asList(Object[] arr)   Returns a list representing array arr. Changing an element in the List also changes the corresponding element of the array.

static void sort(byte[] arr)   Rearranges the List's elements into their natural order. This method is extensively overloaded, with versions that take arrays of each primitive type, as well as a version that takes an array of Object.

static int binarySearch(byte[] arr, byte key)   Efficiently searches the array and returns the index of key. The array's elements must be sorted before the method is called. This method is extensively overloaded, with versions that take arrays and keys of each primitive type, as well as a version that takes an array of Object and an Object key.

static boolean equals(Object[] a1, Object[] a2)   Returns true if the arrays have the same length, and each element in a1 is equal to the corresponding element in a2.

Collections and Code Maintenance

There is no such thing as the "best implementation" of a collection. Using any kind of collection involves several kinds of overhead penalty: memory usage, storage time, and retrieval time. No implementation can optimize all three of these features. So, instead of looking for the best List or the best hash table or the best Set, it is more reasonable to look for the most appropriate List, Set, or hash table implementation for a particular programming situation.

As a program evolves, its data collections tend to grow. A collection that was created to hold a little bit of data may later be required to hold a large amount of data, while still providing reasonable response time. It is prudent from the outset to design code in such a way that it is easy to substitute one collection implementation type for another. Java's collections framework makes this easy because of its emphasis on interfaces. This section presents a typical scenario.

Imagine a program that maintains data about shoppers who are uniquely identified by their e-mail addresses. Such a program might use a Shopper class, with instances of this class stored in some kind of Map, keyed by e-mail address. Suppose that when the program is first written, it is known that there are and always will be only three shoppers. The following code fragment constructs one instance for each shopper and stores the data in a hash map; then the Map is passed to various methods for processing:

```
1.  private void getShoppers() {
2.    Shopper sh1 = getNextShopper();
3.    String email1 = getNextEmail();
4.    Shopper sh2 = getNextShopper();
5.    String email2 = getNextEmail();
6.    Shopper sh3 = getNextShopper();
7.    String email3 = getNextEmail();
8.
9.    Map map = new HashMap();  // Very important!
10.   map.put(email1, sh1);
11.   map.put(email2, sh2);
12.   map.put(email3, sh3);
13.
```

```
14.    findDesiredProducts(map);
15.    shipProducts(map);
16.    printInvoices(map);
17.    collectMoney(map);
18. }
```

Note the declaration of map on line 9. The reference type on the left-hand side of the = sign is Map, not HashMap (the interface, rather than the class). This is a very important difference whose value will become clear later on. The four processing methods do not much concern us here. Just consider their declarations:

```
private void findDesiredProducts(Map map) { ... }
private void shipProducts (Map map) { ... }
private void printInvoices (Map map) { ... }
private void collectMoney (Map map) { ... }
```

Imagine that each of these methods passes the hash map to other subordinate methods, which pass it to still other methods; our program has a large number of processing methods. Throughout the code, the argument types will be Map, not HashMap (again, the interface, rather than the class).

As development proceeds, suppose it becomes clear that the getShoppers() method should return the Map's keys (which are the shoppers' e-mail addresses) in a sorted array. Because there are and always will be only three shoppers, there are and always will be only three keys to sort; the easiest implementation is therefore as follows:

```
1. private String[] getShoppers() {  // New return type
2.    Shopper sh1 = getNextShopper();
3.    String email1 = getNextEmail();
4.    Shopper sh2 = getNextShopper();
5.    String email2 = getNextEmail();
6.    Shopper sh3 = getNextShopper();
7.    String email3 = getNextEmail();
8.
9.    Map map = new HashMap();
10.   map.put(email1, sh1);
11.   map.put(email2, sh2);
12.   map.put(email3, sh3);
13.
14.   findDesiredProducts(map);
15.   shipProducts(map);
16.   printInvoices(map);
17.   collectMoney(map);
18.
```

```
19.   // New sorting code.
20.   String[] sortedKeys = new String[3];
21.   if (email1.compareTo(email2) < 0  &&
22.        email1.compareTo(email3) < 0) {
23.      sortedKeys[0] = email1;
24.      if (email2.compareTo(email3) < 0)
25.         sortedKeys[1] = email2;
26.      else
27.         sortedKeys[2] = email3;
28.   }
29.   else if (email2.compareTo(email3) < 0) {
30.      sortedKeys[0] = email2;
31.      if (email1.compareTo(email3) < 0)
32.         sortedKeys[1] = email1;
33.      else
34.         sortedKeys[2] = email3;
35.   }
36.   else {
37.      sortedKeys[0] = email3;
38.      if (email1.compareTo(email2) < 0)
39.         sortedKeys[1] = email1;
40.      else
41.      sortedKeys[2] = email2;
42.   }
43.   return sortedKeys;
44. }
```

The added code is fairly lengthy: 26 lines.

Beware of specs claiming that the size of anything is and always will be small.

Predictably, as soon as the code is developed and debugged, someone will decide that the program needs to be expanded to accommodate 20 shoppers instead of the original three. The new requirement suggests the need for a separate sorting algorithm, in its own separate method. The new method will be called sortStringArray(). We won't list it here, but you can imagine that it involves a couple of loops and a lot of comparison and quite a bit of swapping of array members. The next evolution of getShoppers() looks like this:

```
1. private String[] getShoppers() {
2.   String[] keys = new String[20];
3.   Map map = new HashMap()
```

```
4.    for (int i=0; i<20; i++) {
5.      Shopper s = getNextShopper();
6.      keys[i] = getNextEmail();
7.      map.put(keys[i], s);
8.    }
9.
10.   findDesiredProducts(map);
11.   shipProducts(map);
12.   printInvoices(map);
13.   collectMoney(map);
14.
15.   sortStringArray(keys);
16.   return keys;
17. }
```

This code is much more modular and compact. However, it is still not mature. The next requirement is that it has to be able to handle any number of shoppers, even a very large number. At first glance, the solution seems very simple: just pass the number of shoppers into the method, as shown here:

```
1. private String[] getShoppers(int nShoppers) {
2.    String[] keys = new String[nShoppers];
3.    Map map = new HashMap()
4.    for (int i = 0; i < nShoppers; i++) {
5.      Shopper s = getNextShopper();
6.      keys[i] = getNextEmail();
7.      map.put(keys[i], s);
8.    }
9.
10.   findDesiredProducts(map);
11.   shipProducts(map);
12.   printInvoices(map);
13.   collectMoney(map);
14.
15.   sortStringArray(keys);
16.   return keys;
17. }
```

This code seems fine until the number of shoppers crosses some threshold. Then the amount of time spent sorting the keys (in the method sortStringArray(), called on line 15) becomes prohibitive. Now is the time when the collections framework shows its true value. In particular, you are about to see the value of referencing the Map with variables of type Map, rather than HashMap (the interface, rather than the class).

Because the sorting method is now the bottleneck, it is reasonable to wonder whether a different kind of Map could solve the performance problem. It is time for a quick look at the API pages for the classes that implement the Map interface. You'll find a suitable alternative: the TreeMap class. This implementation maintains its keys in sorted order and has a method for returning them in sorted order. Because the keys are always sorted, there seems to be zero overhead for sorting. Actually, the situation is not quite so good—there must be some extra overhead (which you can hope will be slight) in the put() method, when the tree map stores a new key. Before deciding that TreeMap is the right class to use, it is important to ascertain that storing and retrieving data in the new collection will not cost an unreasonable amount of time, even if the Map is very large.

First, what is the current cost of storing and retrieving in a hash map? The API page for HashMap says that storage and retrieval take constant time, no matter what the size of the Map might be. This is ideal; let's hope the performance of a tree map will also be constant. If it is not constant, it must still be acceptable when the data collection is large.

The API page for TreeMap says that the class "provides guaranteed log(n) time cost" for various operations, including storage and retrieval. This means that the time to store and retrieve data grows with the logarithm of the size of the data set. Figure 8.5 shows a graph of the logarithm function.

The graph in the figure rises steadily, but at an ever-decreasing rate. The cost for accessing a large tree map is only slightly greater than the cost for accessing a small one. Logarithmic overhead is almost as good as constant overhead; it is certainly acceptable for the current application.

FIGURE 8.5   The logarithm function

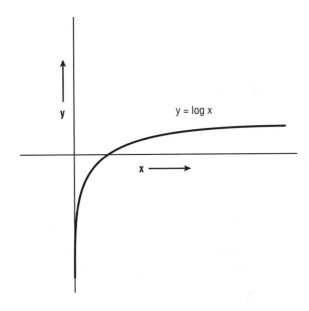

Apparently, the TreeMap class is a very good substitute for the original HashMap class. Now you see how easy it is to replace one collection implementation with another. Because all references to the hash map are of type Map (the interface) rather than type HashMap (the class), only one line of code needs to be modified: the line in which the hash map is constructed. That line originally was

```
Map map = new HashMap();
```

All that is required is to call a different constructor:

```
Map map = new TreeMap();
```

Many data-processing methods pass references to the hash map back and forth among themselves. Not one of these methods needs to be modified at all. In fact, the only major change that needs to be made is to dispense with the **sortStringArray()** method and the call to it, substituting the tree map's intrinsic functionality. This modification is not directly relevant to the main point of this example, which is how easy it is to replace one collection type with another. However, it is instructive to see how the modification is accomplished. The final code looks like this:

```
1. private String[] getShoppers(int nShoppers) {
2.    Map map = new TreeMap();
3.    for (int i=0; i< nShoppers; i++) {
4.      map.put(getNextEmail(), getNextShopper());
5.    }
6.
7.    findDesiredProducts(map);
8.    shipProducts(map);
9.    printInvoices(map);
10.    collectMoney(map);
11.
12.    String[] keys = new String[nShoppers];
13.    Iterator iter = map.keySet().iterator();
14.    int i = 0;
15.    while (iter.hasNext())
16.      keys[i++] = (String)iter.next();
17.    return keys;
18. }
```

Here the Iterator on line 13 returns the elements of the hash map key set. Because the hash map is an instance of TreeMap, the key set is guaranteed to be sorted.

This example shows the importance of referencing collections with variables of the interface rather than the class type. If you do this, replacing one collection type with another type becomes trivially easy.

Generic Collections

If you have spent much time with Java's collection classes, you know that putting an object into a collection is a lot easier than getting it out again. This is because when you store an object you take advantage of conversion, but when you retrieve you are obliged to cast. For example:

```
Vector myVec;
myVec = new Vector();
myVec.add(myDragon);
// … and later …
Dragon myOtherDragon = (Dragon)myVec.get(0);
```

Java Release 1.5 lets you avoid the cast in many situations. *Generic collections* (or just *generics*) are collections whose members are of a single type that is known to the compiler.

 The 5.0 Collections framework is backward compatible with Java 1.4, which did not support generics. This means that you don't need to rewrite all your Java 1.4 code to use generics. Also, new code that you write in 5.0 doesn't *have* to use generics, though it's almost always a good idea.

Generics provide two substantial benefits:

- Objects retrieved from generic collections need not be cast.
- The compiler ensures that objects of the wrong type are not stored in generics.

The first benefit is a convenience, because casting is a nuisance. The second benefit eliminates bugs before they happen, because the wrong object can never be stored in the wrong collection.

To create a generic Vector that contains only dragons, you would use the following syntax:

```
1. Vector<Dragon> myVec;
2. myVec = new Vector<Dragon>();
```

The identifier between the angle brackets may be the name of any class or interface. The declaration on line 1 says that myVec is not merely a Vector, but a Vector of dragons. You can think of the <Dragon> notation as being part of the type, which is not Vector but rather Vector<Dragon>. Notice that this notation also appears on line 2, where the Vector is constructed. If the angle-bracket notation is used in a variable's declaration (as on line 1), then that variable should be used to reference an object whose constructor also used the angle-bracket notation (as on line 2). If you don't follow this rule, you'll get a compiler warning (but your code will still compile).

The Vector of dragons constructed in lines 1 and 2 may contain only objects that are compatible with the Dragon class. The most common way to add to a Vector is to call the add()

method. The compiler insists that the arguments of all `add()` calls made on `myVec` must be of type `Dragon` or subclasses of `Dragon`. Assuming that class `WaterDragon` extends `Dragon`, the following code compiles:

```
1. Vector<Dragon> myVec;
2. myVec = new Vector<Dragon>();
3. Dragon ulaShan = new Dragon();
4. myVec.add(ulaShan);
5. WaterDragon mangJiro = new WaterDragon();
6. myVec.add(mangJiro);
```

However, the following code does not compile:

```
1. Vector<Dragon> myVec;
2. myVec = new Vector<Dragon>();
3. String s = "fireproof";
4. myVec.add(s);
```

Line 4 generates a compiler error.

When you retrieve a member of a generic vector, you may assign the retrieved value to a variable of the vector's type without casting. Thus the following code is legal:

```
1. Vector<Dragon> myVec;
2. myVec = new Vector<Dragon>();
3. Dragon ulaShan = new Dragon();
4. myVec.add(ulaShan);
5. Dragon d = myVec.get(0);
```

The compiler knows that `myVec` contains dragons, so on line 5 the cast that would otherwise be required may be omitted.

Iterators may be generic. To declare a generic Iterator, you use the same angle-bracket notation that you use to declare a generic vector:

```
Iterator<Dragon> driter;
```

When you call a generic Iterator's `next()` method, the returned value may be assigned without casting to a variable of the Iterator's type. For example:

```
1. public void allDragonsSeekTreasure(Vector<Dragon> vec) {
2.   Iterator<Dragon> driter = vec.iterator();
3.   while (driter.hasNext()) {
4.     Dragon d = driter.next();
5.     d.seekTreasure();
6.   }
7. }
```

Notice the absence of casting on line 4. This code can be simplified to

```
1. public void allDragonsSeekTreasure(Vector<Dragon> vec) {
2.   Iterator<Dragon> driter = vec.iterator();
3.   while (driter.hasNext())
4.     driter.next().seekTreasure();
5. }
```

To appreciate the benefits of generic vectors and Iterators, compare the version above to the code that would be required without generics:

```
1. public void allDragonsSeekTreasure(Vector vec) {
2.   Iterator driter = vec.iterator();
3.   while (driter.hasNext())
4.     ((Dragon)driter.next()).seekTreasure();
5. }
```

Now line 4 requires the more complicated casting syntax, and you have to get the parentheses right. Moreover, if vec contains an object that is not dragon-compatible, you will get a ClassCastException at line 4. Then you will have track down the code where the incompatible object got added to the vector. With generics, you never get a ClassCastException, because no incompatible objects can get added to the Vector.

The Vector class of our examples is just one of the classes that implement the List interface. All the principles governing declaration, construction, and iteration of a Vector can also be applied to any other class that implements List.

Sets can be generic. To declare and construct a generic Set, just use the angle-bracket syntax. The following code creates a Set containing Strings:

```
Set<String> stringSet;
stringSet = new TreeSet<String>();
```

Notice that the second line assigns a tree set of strings to a reference whose type is a set of strings. Generics obey the conversion rules that you learned about in Chapter 4. The types declared in the angle brackets (String in this case) must be identical, but the types of the generic collections (Set and TreeSet) may be different.

You can use a generic Iterator to retrieve the members of a generic set. The following method uses a generic Iterator to compute the average length of the Strings in a generic Set:

```
public float meanStringLength(Set<String> stringSet) {
  float totalLengths = 0f;
  Iterator<String> iter = stringSet.iterator();
  while (iter.hasNext())
    totalLengths += iter.next().length();
  return totalLengths / stringSet.size();
}
```

In addition to Lists and Sets, Maps also may be generic. To make a Map generic, you specify a type for the keys and a second type for the values, as shown in the following example:

```
TreeMap<String, Dragon> nameToDragon;
nameToDragon = new TreeMap<String, Dragon>();
```

The code above creates a Tree Map whose keys are strings and whose values are dragons. Note that the angle brackets in the declaration and constructor now contain two type names, separated by a comma. The first type is the key type; the second is the value type.

The Iterators of the Map's keys and values are generic:

```
Iterator<String> nameIter = nameToDragon.keySet().iterator();
Iterator<Dragon> dragonIter = nameToDragon.values().iterator();
```

Generic Lists, Sets, Maps, and Iterators provide a powerful compile-time check on your code, by guaranteeing that only the right type of object can be stored. They also save your typing fingers some effort by eliminating many casting operations. Your code can become even more concise with the use of enhanced for loops, which are discussed two sections down. Before introducing enhanced loops, let's see how generic classes are described in the API pages.

Generics and the API Pages

Learning to use generic collections involves getting used to the angle-bracket notation. Angle brackets show up in the API pages for Java's generic classes and interfaces. In order to understand the APIs, you need to be able to read them!

Let's start with the page for the java.util.Set interface. (If there's a computer nearby, you might want to look at the page at this point.) Up to Java Release 1.4, the page header said

```
Interface Set
```

Now it says

```
Interface Set<E>
```

The E in angle brackets tell you that this interface is generic. That is, you can think of it as a Set *of* something. Of what? Of whatever you like, but we'll call it E. Throughout the API page, E will stand for whatever type a programmer specifies in the declaration of the Set. E will show up in the method summaries in a variety of ways.

Up to Java Release 1.4, the method summary for add() was

```
boolean add(Object o)
```

Now it's

```
boolean add(E o)
```

The new notation says that the argument to add() is no longer any Object but must be compatible with the type of the Set.

The notation for addAll() is even stranger. It used to be

```
boolean addAll(Collection c)
```

Now it's

```
boolean addAll(Collection<? extends E> c)
```

So the argument of addAll() is no longer any collection at all. The ? extends E notation says that the argument must be a *generic* collection whose type is compatible with E. ? refers to the type of the argument collection. Don't be confused by the extends keyword; it *doesn't* mean that the argument Collection's type must extend E. It means the argument Collection's type must be *compatible* with E, as determined by the instanceof operator. So if E is a class, the argument Collection's type might be E or any subclass of E. If E is an interface, the argument Collection's type might be E, or any subinterface of E, or any class that implements E. The big idea is that it must be legal, according to the rules of generics, to add every element of the argument Collection to the current Collection.

One last notation you will encounter on Set's API page is

```
Iterator<E> iterator();
```

Here the angle brackets appear in the return type. This tells you that the method returns a generic Iterator whose type is E.

The angle-bracket notation takes some getting used to, but once you are familiar with it you will be able to fully understand the API pages. If you look at the source code for a generic collection class, you'll see that the notation is actually part of the language. If you want to create your own generic class, you can do so by using the angle-bracket notation.

Generics and Enhanced *For* Loops

In Chapter 5, "Flow Control, Assertions, and Exception Handling," you saw how Java's enhanced for loops can ease iteration over arrays. You have also just seen that generics can improve code that iterates over collections. Here you will learn how enhanced for loops can make collection processing even easier.

Almost all collection iteration is structured like this:

```
Iterator<SomeClass> iter = myCollection.iterator();
while (iter.hasNext())
  iter.next().doSomething();
```

Enhanced for loops let you abbreviate this structure by completely hiding the Iterator. As an example, suppose you have a set containing Dragons:

```
HashSet<Dragon> dragons;
```

If you want to call sitOnGold() on each dragon in the set, you can now do it like this:

```
for (Dragon d:dragons)
  d.sitOnGold();
```

The code above is identical to the following pre-Java 1.5 code:

```
Iterator iter = dragons.iterator();
while (iter.hasNext()) {
  Dragon d = (Dragon)iter.next();
  d.sitOnGold();
}
```

The Java 5.0 version is perfectly understandable (once you get used to the colon notation), but it is shorter by 60 percent and eliminates the Iterator and the cast. The new syntax is

```
for (type varable_name : collection)
```

The type and variable name form a variable declaration whose scope is the statement or block following the for statement. Each pass through the loop, the variable takes on a different value; the values are the contents of the collection, presented in the order that an Iterator would present them. (This is to be expected, since an Iterator is still created and used as the underlying mechanism, even though it can't be seen.)

The Collection that appears after the colon can be anything that implements the Collection interface: a List (of which Vectors are the most common example), a Set, or the keys or values of a Map.

The enhanced for loop, like generic collections, provides a way to write code that is cleaner, less vulnerable to errors, and easier to read.

Scanning and Formatting Text

Java contains extensive facilities for dealing with text. The relevant classes reside in the java.lang and java.util packages. Text can present special problems for programs and programmers. Text contains meaning, which is expressed in language, and both meaning and language are very deep concepts, intimately involved in what makes us human. No wonder computers have trouble dealing with text!

The problems fall into two areas: how to extract meaning from existing text and how to create new grammatically correct text that contains meaning. One way to address these problems is to get a Ph.D. in computational linguistics and dedicate your life to figuring it all out. But if your goal is just to pass the Programmer's Exam, all you need to do is learn about Java's facilities for scanning and formatting text.

Scanning Text

Text scanning is the art of extracting information from text. This can be daunting because human-language text is designed to have its information extracted by human minds. Release 5.0 helps the process by providing a class called `java.util.Scanner`.

The API page for this class calls it "A simple text scanner which can parse primitive types and strings using regular expressions." In this context, *parse* means to extract the types and strings from their natural language context. The term *simple* is subject to debate. It's easy enough to figure out how to use the class, except for one detail: regular expressions.

Regular expressions are an extensive topic in their own right, dating back to the early days of Unix. You can think of a regular expression as a string that encodes a description of a general text pattern. For example, the regular expression `\s+` represents one or more blank spaces. Encoding a representation for a more sophisticated pattern, such as an optional sign followed by five to seven digits that are optionally followed by a period, takes concentration and experience. If you look at the description of regular expressions in the API (it's on the page for `java.util.regex.Pattern`), you'll see that the spec is so extensive that you can't possibly be required to know it by heart. So you can treat this section as an overview to give you just the basic idea. As long as you can recognize a very simple regular expression, you'll do fine on the exam.

 The description of regular expressions in the API is on the page for the `Pattern` class in the `java.util.regex` package. This package also contains a class named `Matcher`. A matcher is an engine that scans input, using a pattern to guide its behavior. You rarely if ever use these classes directly. Instead, you use classes like `Scanner`, which in turn use `Pattern` and `Matcher`.

A scanner breaks up an input string into tokens and delimiters. *Tokens* are parts of a string that have meaning. *Delimiters* are text used to separate tokens. For example, if you're trying to extract the numeric values from the comma-separated string "12, 3.1415, 49", then the tokens are 12, 3.1415, and 49, because those are the parts of the string that convey meaning to you. The commas are the delimiters.

The `Scanner` class has a large number of constructors. The simplest one is

`public Scanner(String source)`

The source is the string to be scanned for tokens. Other constructor versions specify different text sources, such as files or input streams.

After a scanner instance in constructed, it must be told what delimiter or delimiters to use. This is done by calling the scanner's `useDelimiter()` method, passing in a regular expression that represents the desired delimiters. For example, suppose your input string consists of integer numbers, separated by `x` characters. You could set up your scanner as follows:

```
String scanMe = "123x2x3x4";
String delim = "x";
```

```
Scanner scanner = new Scanner(scanMe);
scanner.useDelimiter(delim);
```

Now to extract tokens from scanMe, you can use the methods hasNext() and next(). These methods function just like their counterparts in Iterator, except that here next() returns a string. The lines below extract tokens:

```
while (scanner.hasNext())
  System.out.println(scanner.next());
```

The output is

```
123
2
3
4
```

A regular expression can specify a class or group of characters. This is done by enclosing a specification inside square brackets. The expression "[aeiou]" matches any of the letters a, e, i, o, or u. Here's a piece of code that uses this expression:

```
String scanMe = "abcdefghijkl";
String delim = "[aeoiu]";
Scanner scanner = new Scanner(scanMe);
scanner.useDelimiter(delim);
while (scanner.hasNext())
  System.out.println(scanner.next());
```

The output is:

```
bcd
fgh
jkl
```

You can specify a range of characters to be matched by using a hyphen. For example, "[a-e]" matches any of a, b, c, d, or e.

There are several predefined classes. The ones to be aware of for the exam are

.Matches any character

\dMatches any digit ("0" - "9")

\sMatches any whitespace character, such as space, tab, or newline

\wMatches any letter ("a" - "z" or "A" - "Z") or digit

Note the backslashes, which tell the regular expression-processing code that the next character has special rather than literal meaning. There's a big difference between "d", which recognizes the fourth letter of the alphabet, and "\d", which recognizes any digit.

Backslashes are tricky. Suppose you want to use "\s" as a delimiter-specifying regular expression. The following code won't work:

```
scanner.useDelimiter("\s");
```

In fact, this line won't even compile! The regular expression processor isn't the only kid on the block that uses backslashes in literal strings. The Java compiler also does, and it doesn't recognize "\s" as a legal escape sequence. The line above produces an "illegal escape character" compiler error. The proper code is

```
scanner.useDelimiter("\\s");
```

The first backslash tells the compiler that the second backslash is to be accepted literally and not as an instruction to treat the "s" in a special way. The compiler strips off the first backslash and internally stores "\s". It's unfortunate that regular expression programming requires you to think about this. Whenever a regular expression doesn't do what you thought it would, ask yourself if the literal string in your source code is the same as the string the expression processor uses.

Now suppose you want to scan an input string where the tokens might be separated by groups of one or more "x" character. For example, the input might be "132xxxx555". The scanner as it stands won't work: the output will have several blank lines between "132" and "555". This happens because the scanner sees those consecutive "x"s as delimiters between empty tokens, each of which gets printed on its own line.

We need a delimiter-describing regular expression that represents one or more "x"s. The string that does what we want is "x+". The plus sign means *one or more*, so "x+" means *one or more "x"s*. The "+" sign is called a *quantifier*. A quantifier is a symbol in a regular expression that represents a sequence of input characters. The quantifiers you should know about for the exam are these:

   *Matches zero or more occurrences of the preceding pattern

   +Matches one or more occurrences of the preceding pattern

   ?Matches zero or one occurrences of the preceding pattern

If you look at the regular expression spec (on the API page for `java.util.regex.Pattern`), you'll see that each of these quantifiers can be made to behave in a "greedy," "reluctant," or "possessive" way. The distinction is subtle, and the exam requires you to know only about the default behavior, which is "greedy." A greedy quantifier matches the largest possible character sequence.

You can use parentheses to group characters together and then apply a quantifier to the group as a unit. So, for example, the expression "(ab)*" matches one or more occurrences of "ab", such as "ababab" and "abababababababab".

The `String` class has a new method (since 5.0) called `split()` that uses a regular expression to split a string into an array of substrings. The syntax is

```
public String[] split(String regex)
```

Scanners are a rich and powerful tool for extracting information from human-language text. The information presented here just scratches the surface of what scanners can do for you.

Formatting Text

Text formatting is the art of generating human-language text that presents data in easily readable and grammatically correct ways. Text formatting in the early releases of Java required large amounts of custom coding. Later releases have included classes that relieve programmers of much of the burden of inventing formatting algorithms. This relief comes at a price: some of the classes have significant learning curves. Here we'll look at how to use Java's formatting classes to format text in general and to perform special formatting for numbers, dates, and currency.

Sometimes appropriate formatting varies from place to place. For example, in the U.S. the value of pi to five decimal places is written as 3.14159. But in much of Europe a comma is used instead of a decimal point: 3,14159. Some of Java's formatting classes are sensitive to regional variations of customs.

A cultural or linguistic region is represented in Java by the `java.util.Locale` class. A glance at the API page for `Locale` shows that the class has static instances named CANADA, CHINA, UK, and so on. Thus it's easy to get a locale instance for many regions of the world. To get the locale for the current computer, call the static method `Locale.getDefault()`. (The method doesn't use magic or GPS to figure out where it is—the operating system knows its locale, and the method asks the operating system.)

> If you're playing with locales, it's useful to know about the `getDisplay()` method. This returns the name of the country in human-recognizable form. The `getCountry()` method just returns a two-letter code.

Java's formatting methods generally have versions that use the default locale, with overloaded versions where you can specify a different locale. These overloaded versions are useful for making sure that code produces reasonable text in locales other than the default.

Now let's see how to format text in specific situations.

Formatting General Text

The `java.util.Formatter` class performs general-purpose string formatting. The most common constructor is

```
Formatter(Appendable a)
```

Recall that both `StringBuffer` and `StringBuilder` implement the `Appendable` interface. Remember that string builders are faster than string buffers but are not threadsafe.

An alternate constructor is

```
Formatter(Appendable a, Locale loc)
```

This version uses the specified locale as a guideline when performing region-specific formatting.

The API page for `Formatter` says that the class is "heavily inspired" by the C language's `printf` function. This doesn't help you much if you haven't programmed in C. In case you haven't, here's the big idea: text to be formatted is specified by a string and a number of values.

The string contains invariant text and formatting instructions for the values. Let's look at a simple example:

```
StringBuilder sb = new StringBuilder();
Formatter f = new Formatter(sb);
boolean b = false;
f.format("The value is %b, so there.", b);
System.out.println(sb);
```

The output is

```
The value is false, so there.
```

The `format()` call uses its first argument as a guideline. Any text up to a special character is appended literally to the string builder. The `%` sign is a special code that indicates that the method's second argument is to be formatted and inserted into the text. The argument index is followed by a dollar sign (`$`), which is followed by formatting information. In the simplest cases, the formatting information is a single letter. The format codes you need to know about for the exam are these:

%b Formats a boolean value (wrapper or primitive)

%c Formats a character

%d Formats an integer

%f Formats a floating-point number

%s Formats an object, generally by calling its `toString()` method

Now you can see how our first example worked. The format string was appended verbatim to the string builder until the `%b` code was reached. This meant that the method's second argument was to be formatted as text representing a boolean value and appended to the string builder. After that the remainder of the format string (since it has no more special characters) was to be appended verbatim.

If a format string has more than one special character, the formatter expects the `format()` method to have one argument for each special character. By default, these are formatted in their order of appearance. For example, here's a format string with two format codes and two additional arguments:

```
StringBuilder sb = new StringBuilder();
Formatter f = new Formatter(sb);
boolean b = false;
f.format("Would you like some %f? %b", Math.PI, true);
System.out.println(sb);
```

The output is

```
Would you like some 3.141593? true
```

Actually, the special codes don't need to match up one-for-one with the method arguments. If you want to jumble the order, you can stick a number and then a dollar sign ($) immediately after the % sign, as follows.

```
StringBuilder sb = new StringBuilder();
Formatter f = new Formatter(sb);
boolean b = false;
f.format("Would you like some %2$b? %1$f", Math.PI, true);
System.out.println(sb);
```

The $ notation says to use the specified argument rather than the next one. The output is

```
Would you like some true? 3.141593
```

So far you might not be very impressed with formatters, but that's because you've seen only the basics of what they can do, and if you just stick to the basics you aren't much better off than you are with ordinary string concatenation. After all, out last code example produces the same output as the single line

```
System.out.println("Would you like some " +
                   true + "? " + Math.PI);
```

The real power of formatters comes into play when you make subtle adjustments to make your strings more readable to us quirky humans. A very powerful readability feature of formatters is the field width specification. This is a number (it may be positive or negative) that dictates how many characters wide a value's representation will be. The field width comes right after the % sign (just like the argument specifier but without the dollar sign). If the width is positive, the value will be right-justified in a field of the specified width; if the width is negative, the value will be left-justified. Here's an example:

```
StringBuilder sb = new StringBuilder();
Formatter f = new Formatter(sb);
int a = 1234;
int b = 5;
f.format("a = %7d and b = %-7d!!!", a, b);
System.out.println(sb);
```

The output is

```
a =    1234 and b = 5      !!!
```

Notice that the value of a occupies the right end of its field, with the left end padded with spaces. The value of b occupies the left end of its field, and the right end is padded with spaces.

If the format code is %f, you're formatting a floating-point value, and in addition to the overall width of the value, you can control the number of characters that will appear to the right of the decimal point. The format of the specification is

%w.df

where w is the overall field with and d is the number of digits to the right of the decimal point. The following code prints the value of PI to 18 digits of precision to the right of the decimal point, in a 25-character field:

```
StringBuilder sb = new StringBuilder();
Formatter f = new Formatter(sb);
int a = 1234;
int b = 5;
f.format("PI is %25.18f!", Math.PI);
System.out.println(sb);
```

The output is

```
PI is       3.141592653589793000!
```

Incidentally, we mentioned that formatters are sensitive to locale variations. How would the output of this code differ in, let's say, France? There are two ways to find out. We could all go to a nice Internet café in Paris and just find out. I'd love to do that, but since I'm writing to a deadline I'll propose the following alternative:

```
StringBuilder sb = new StringBuilder();
Formatter f = new Formatter(sb, Locale.FRANCE);
int a = 1234;
int b = 5;
f.format("PI is %25.18f!", Math.PI);
System.out.println(sb);
```

Now the output is

```
PI is       3,141592653589793000!
```

The decimal point has become a comma.

Quite often a formatted string is printed out and then discarded. In release 5.0 the PrintStream class (of which System.out is an instance) has two format() methods, which write out formatted text. One takes a format string, followed by a list of arguments. The other takes a locale, followed by a format string and a list of arguments. The methods use a formatter to do the work. You might find yourself writing something like this:

```
StringBuilder sb = new StringBuilder();
Formatter f = new Formatter(sb, aLocale);
```

```
f.format(formatString, arg1, arg2);
System.out.println(sb);
```

You can simplify this code as

```
System.out.format(aLocale, formatString, arg1, arg2);
```

There is much more to learn about formatters, but this is as much as the exam requires you to know, so we'll move on to the issue of formatting dates and currency.

Formatting Dates

The java.util.Calendar class encapsulates an instant in time. You can obtain an instance that represents the present moment by calling the static getInstance() method.

The java.util.Date class encapsulates an instant in time. To find out what time it is right now, you use an indirect approach: you call the static getInstance() method of java.util.Calendar. The Calendar class contains a Date instance, which can be retrieved by calling the getTime() method. The following code prints out the current time:

```
Calendar cal = Calendar.getInstance();
System.out.println(cal.getTime());
```

The output is (well, *was*)

```
Mon Jan 17 21:09:57 PST 2005
```

That's not bad for two lines of code, but there's no easy way to vary the formatting. There are ways to extract the underlying information from the date object, and if you do that you can use a formatter to do your own formatting, but the java.text.DateFormat class makes life much easier for you. Here is a very simple use of a date formatter:

```
Calendar cal = Calendar.getInstance();
Date date = cal.getTime();
DateFormat df = DateFormat.getDateInstance();
System.out.println(df.format(date));
```

The static getDateInstance() method returns a default formatter that is tuned for the current locale. (The method name is misleading, since the return value is a date format, not a date.) The formatter has a format() method that takes an instance of Date, which in our case is extracted from a calendar.

The output is, or rather was

```
Jan 17, 2005
```

The output is a bit terse. Date formats support four levels of detail: short, medium, long, and full. These styles are represented by the constants SHORT, MEDIUM, LONG, and FULL in the

`DateFormat` class. To obtain a formatter for the current locale that uses a specific style, pass the style into the `getDateInstance()` call. Here's a piece of code that prints out a date in each of the four formats. (The locale is the U.S.)

```
int[] styles = { DateFormat.SHORT, DateFormat.MEDIUM,
                 DateFormat.LONG, DateFormat.FULL };

Calendar cal = Calendar.getInstance();
Date date = cal.getTime();
for (int style:styles) {
  DateFormat df = DateFormat.getDateInstance(style);
  System.out.println(df.format(date));
}
```

Here's the output:

```
1/17/05
Jan 17, 2005
January 17, 2005
Monday, January 17, 2005
```

Another form of `getDateInstance()` accepts a style and a locale. Here's an example that prints out each style for several locales:

```
int[] styles = { DateFormat.SHORT, DateFormat.MEDIUM,
                 DateFormat.LONG, DateFormat.FULL };

Locale[] locales = { Locale.FRANCE,
                     Locale.CHINA,
                     Locale.ITALY };

Calendar cal = Calendar.getInstance();
Date date = cal.getTime();
for (Locale loc:locales) {
  System.out.format("\n%10s:\n", loc.getDisplayCountry());
  for (int style:styles) {
    DateFormat df = DateFormat.getDateInstance(style, loc);
    System.out.println(df.format(date) + "\n");
  }
}
```

The output is

```
   France:
17/01/05
17 janv. 2005
17 janvier 2005
lundi 17 janvier 2005

   China:
05-1-17
2005-1-17
2005?1?17?
2005?1?17? ???

   Italy:
17/01/05
17-gen-2005
17 gennaio 2005
lunedi 17 gennaio 2005
```

Formatting Numbers and Currency

The java.text.NumberFormat class is useful for formatting numbers in general, and especially numbers that represent currency.

Standard number formats vary somewhat from one region to another. The variation is slight compared to variations among date formats, but it needs to be dealt with. Obviously, variations in currency formats are significant. So it is not surprising that the behavior of the NumberFormat class is affected by locale. Once again, a default instance of the formatting class is controlled by the current locale; it is possible to use other instances that use other locales.

NumberFormat is actually an abstract superclass, so you never call its constructors. Instead you call a static factory method. The factory methods you should know about for the exam are these:

public static NumberFormat getInstance()   Returns a number formatter that uses the current locale.

public static NumberFormat getInstance(Locale loc)   Returns a number formatter that uses the specified locale.

public static NumberFormat getCurrencyInstance()   Returns a currency formatter that uses the current locale.

public static NumberFormat getInstance(Locale loc)   Returns a currency formatter that uses the specified locale.

After you obtain an instance, you can call the `format()` method, passing in the value to be formatted. For numbers, the value is an integer or floating-point number. For currency, the value is an amount of money. The return value is a string.

Here's a code example that demonstrates the use of commas and periods in formatting numbers:

```
Locale[] locales = { Locale.US, Locale.ITALY };
for (Locale loc:locales) {
  NumberFormat f = NumberFormat.getInstance(loc);
  String formattedNumber = f.format(111123456.78911);
  System.out.format("%15s: %s\n", loc.getDisplayCountry(),
                    formattedNumber);
}
```

The output is

```
United States: 111,123,456.789
        Italy: 111.123.456,789
```

Notice the Italian format (actually it's standard throughout most of Europe), which uses a "decimal comma" to separate the tens digit from the tenths digit, and separates triples of digits with a period. In most of the Americas the sense of the comma and period are reversed. Notice also how, thanks to formatting, it's easy to create output that lines up vertically in an easily readable way. It would be possible but tedious to achieve the same result using `System.out.println()` and string concatenation.

To format currency, call `NumberFormat.getCurrencyInstance()`. Pass in a locale if you don't want to use the default. Here's an example that expresses 123.45 as an amount of local currency for the U.S. and Taiwan:

```
Locale[] locales = { Locale.US, Locale.TAIWAN };
for (Locale loc:locales) {
  NumberFormat f = NumberFormat.getCurrencyInstance(loc);
  String formattedMoney = f.format(123.45);
  System.out.format("%15s: %s\n",
                    loc.getDisplayCountry(),
                    formattedMoney);
}
```

The output is

```
United States: $123.45
       Taiwan: NT$123.45
```

Summary

The java.lang package contains classes that are indispensable to Java's operation, so all the classes of the package are automatically imported into all source files. Some of the most important classes in the package are

- Object
- Math
- String
- StringBuffer
- The wrapper classes

In a string context, addition operands are appended in turn to a string buffer, which is then converted to a string; primitive operands are converted to strings, and objects are converted by having their toString() methods invoked.

The wrapper classes encapsulate single immutable primitive values. Boxing and unboxing ease the task of accessing the values.

The java.util package contains many utilities, but for the Certification Exam, the Collections framework is of primary interest. Collections provide ways to store and retrieve data in a program. Different types of collections provide different semantics for storage, and different collection implementations optimize different access and update behaviors. The use of collections is simplified by generics and the enhanced for loop.

Exam Essentials

Understand the common methods of the Math class.   These methods perform basic number crunching functions, including rounding, exponentiation, and trigonometry functions. They are summarized in Table 8.1.

Understand the functionality of the wrapper classes.   Each of the eight primitive types has a corresponding wrapper class. Know how to use boxing and unboxing to access the wrapped values.

Understand the functionality of the String class.   The encapsulated text is immutable. Strings are supported by the string literal pool.

Understand the functionality of the StringBuffer class.   The encapsulated text is mutable. String concatenation via the + operator is implemented with behind-the-scenes string buffers.

Know the main characteristics of each kind of Collections API: List, Set, and Map.   Be aware that List maintains order, Set prohibits duplicate members, and Map associates keys with values.

Understand how collections test for duplication and equality.   Collections use the `equals()` method rather than the `==` operator.

Understand that collection classes are not threadsafe.   Most implementation classes are not threadsafe. You should assume that a collection class is not threadsafe unless its API documentation explicitly states otherwise.

Understand why it is preferable for references to collections to have interface type rather than class type.   Be aware of the maintenance benefits when substituting one implementing class for another.

Know how to use generic collections.   Be able to use the angle-bracket notation.

Know how to iterate over collections using enhanced `for` loops.   Be able to use the colon notation.

Know how to scan and format text.   Be able to use an instance of `Scanner` to parse text, using regular expressions to describe delimiters. Know how to use the `DateFormat` and `NumberFormat` classes to format date, number, and currency strings that are appropriate for any locale.

Review Questions

1. Given a string constructed by calling s = new String("xyzzy"), which of the calls modifies the string?

   A. s.append("aaa");

   B. s.trim();

   C. s.substring(3);

   D. s.replace('z', 'a');

   E. s.concat(s);

   F. None of the above

2. Which one statement is true about the following code?

   ```
   1. String s1 = "abc" + "def";
   2. String s2 = new String(s1);
   3. if (s1 == s2)
   4.    System.out.println("== succeeded");
   5. if (s1.equals(s2))
   6.    System.out.println(".equals() succeeded");
   ```

   A. Lines 4 and 6 both execute.

   B. Line 4 executes and line 6 does not.

   C. Line 6 executes and line 4 does not.

   D. Neither line 4 nor line 6 executes.

3. Suppose you want to write a class that offers static methods to compute hyperbolic trigonometric functions. You decide to subclass java.lang.Math and provide the new functionality as a set of static methods. Which one statement is true about this strategy?

   A. The strategy works.

   B. The strategy works, provided the new methods are public.

   C. The strategy works, provided the new methods are not private.

   D. The strategy fails because you cannot subclass java.lang.Math.

   E. The strategy fails because you cannot add static methods to a subclass.

4. Which one statement is true about the following code fragment?

```
1. import java.lang.Math;
2. Math myMath = new Math();
3. System.out.println("cosine of 0.123 = " +
4.    myMath.cos(0.123));
```

    A. Compilation fails at line 2.

    B. Compilation fails at line 3 or 4.

    C. Compilation succeeds, although the import on line 1 is not necessary. During execution, an exception is thrown at line 3 or 4.

    D. Compilation succeeds. The import on line 1 is necessary. During execution, an exception is thrown at line 3 or 4.

    E. Compilation succeeds and no exception is thrown during execution.

5. Which one statement is true about the following code fragment?

```
1. String s = "abcde";
2. StringBuffer s1 = new StringBuffer("abcde");
3. if (s.equals(s1))
4.    s1 = null;
5. if (s1.equals(s))
6.    s = null;
```

    A. Compilation fails at line 1 because the `String` constructor must be called explicitly.

    B. Compilation fails at line 3 because `s` and `s1` have different types.

    C. Compilation succeeds. During execution, an exception is thrown at line 3.

    D. Compilation succeeds. During execution, an exception is thrown at line 5.

    E. Compilation succeeds. No exception is thrown during execution.

6. In the following code fragment, after execution of line 1, `sbuf` references an instance of the `StringBuffer` class. After execution of line 2, `sbuf` still references the same instance.

```
1. StringBuffer sbuf = new StringBuffer("abcde");
2. sbuf.insert(3, "xyz");
```

    A. True

    B. False

7.   In the following code fragment, after execution of line 1, sbuf references an instance of the StringBuffer class. After execution of line 2, sbuf still references the same instance.

```
1. StringBuffer sbuf = new StringBuffer("abcde");
2. sbuf.append("xyz");
```

   A. True

   B. False

8.   In the following code fragment, line 4 is executed.

```
1. String s1 = "xyz";
2. String s2 = "xyz";
3. if (s1 == s2)
4.    System.out.println("Line 4");
```

   A. True

   B. False

9.   In the following code fragment, line 4 is executed.

```
1. String s1 = "xyz";
2. String s2 = new String(s1);
3. if (s1 == s2)
4.    System.out.println("Line 4");
```

   A. True

   B. False

10. Suppose prim is an int and wrapped is an Integer. Which of the following are legal Java statements? (Choose all that apply.)

   A. prim = wrapped;

   B. wrapped = prim;

   C. prim = new Integer(9);

   D. wrapped = 9;

11. Which of the following are legal? (Choose all that apply.)

   A. List<String> theList = new Vector<String>;

   B. List<String> theList = new Vector<String>();

   C. Vector <String> theVec = new Vector<String>;

   D. Vector <String> theVec = new Vector<String>();

12. Given the following,

    ```
    Map<String> names = new HashMap<String>();
    ```

    which of the following are legal? (Choose all that apply.)

    A. `Iterator<String> iter = names.iterator();`

    B. `for (String s:names)`

    C. `while (String s:names)`

13. Which of the following are legal `clone()` methods in a class called Q13 that extends `Object`?

    A. `public Object clone() { return super.clone(); }`

    B. `public Object clone()`
       `        throws CloneNotSupportedException { return super.clone(); }`

    C. `public Q13 clone() { return (Q13)super.clone(); }`

    D. `public Q13 clone()`
       `        throws CloneNotSupportedException { return (Q13)super.clone(); }`

14. Which of the following classes implement `java.util.List`?

    A. `java.util.ArrayList`

    B. `java.util.HashList`

    C. `java.util.StackList`

    D. `java.util.Stack`

15. Which of the following are methods of the `java.util.SortedSet` interface?

    A. `first`

    B. `last`

    C. `headSet`

    D. `tailSet`

    E. `subSet`

16. Which of the following are methods of the `java.util.SortedMap` interface?

    A. `first`

    B. `last`

    C. `headMap`

    D. `tailMap`

    E. `subMap`

17. Which line of code tells a scanner called `sc` to use a single digit as a delimiter?

A. `sc.useDelimiter("d");`

B. `sc.useDelimiter("\d");`

C. `sc.useDelimiter("\\d");`

D. `sc.useDelimiter("d+");`

E. `sc.useDelimiter("\d+");`

F. `sc.useDelimiter("\\d+");`

18. What happens when you try to compile and run this application?

```
1. import java.util.*;
2.
3. public class Apple {
4.    public static void main(String[] a) {
5.       Set<Apple> set = new TreeSet<Apple>();
6.       set.add(new Apple());
7.       set.add(new Apple());
8.       set.add(new Apple());
9.    }
10. }
```

A. Compiler error.

B. An exception is thrown at line 6.

C. An exception is thrown at line 7.

D. An exception is thrown at line 8.

E. No exception is thrown.

19. Given arrays a1 and a2, which call returns `true` if a1 and a2 have the same length, and `a1[i].equals(a2[i])` for every legal index i?

A. `java.util.Arrays.equals(a1, a2);`

B. `java.util.Arrays.compare(a1, a2);`

C. `java.util.List.compare(a1, a2);`

D. `java.util.List.compare(a1, a2);`

20. Which of the following statements are true?

A. `StringBuilder` is generally faster than `StringBuffer`.

B. `StringBuffer` is generally faster than `StringBuilder`.

C. `StringBuilder` is threadsafe; `StringBuffer` is not.

D. `StringBuffer` is threadsafe; `StringBuilder` is not.

Answers to Review Questions

1. F. Strings are immutable.

2. C. Because `s1` and `s2` are references to two different objects, the `==` test fails. However, the strings contained within the two `String` objects are identical, so the `equals()` test passes.

3. D. The `java.lang.Math` class is final, so it cannot be subclassed.

4. A. The constructor for the `Math` class is private, so it cannot be called. The `Math` class methods are static, so it is never necessary to construct an instance. The import at line 1 is not required, because all classes of the `java.lang` package are automatically imported.

5. E. A is wrong because line 1 is a perfectly acceptable way to create a `String` and is actually more efficient than explicitly calling the constructor. B is wrong because the argument to the `equals()` method is of type `Object`; thus any object reference or array variable may be passed. The calls on lines 3 and 5 return `false` without throwing exceptions because s and s1 are objects of different types.

6. A. The `StringBuffer` class is mutable. After execution of line 2, `sbuf` refers to the same object, although the object has been modified.

7. A. The `StringBuffer` class is mutable. After execution of line 2, `sbuf` refers to the same object, although the object has been modified.

8. A. Line 1 constructs a new instance of `String` and stores it in the string pool. In line 2, `"xyz"` is already represented in the pool, so no new instance is constructed.

9. B. Line 1 constructs a new instance of `String` and stores it in the string pool. Line 2 explicitly constructs another instance.

10. A, B, C, D. All four statements are legal, thanks to boxing and unboxing.

11. B, D. A and C are illegal, because a constructor call consists of a class name followed by parentheses. B and D add the parentheses. B assigns a Vector of Strings to a List of Strings, which is a legal assignment conversion.

12. A, B. A is the way to get a generic Iterator over a generic Set. B uses the enhanced `for` loop to iterate the Set's elements. C is illegal because there is no such thing as an enhanced `while` loop.

13. B, D. The `CloneNotSupportedException` must be dealt with, so A and C are wrong. The version being overridden (in `Object`) has return type `Object`, so prior to release 5.0 the return type in D would be illegal; however, now that covariant returns are legal, D is allowed.

14. A, D. The `HashList` and `StackList` classes do not exist.

15. A, B, C, D , E. These methods all exist.

16. C, D , E. The `SortedMap` interface has `firstKey()` and `lastKey()` methods, but not `first()` or `last()`.

17. C. The + sign matches one or more occurrences, so it won't match just a single digit. The correct string is "\d"; the extra escape is consumed by the Java compiler when it builds the literal string.

18. C. The Apple class doesn't implement Comparable, so a tree set doesn't know how to handle it. The problem appears when the second Apple instance is added to the set, requiring the set to perform a comparison between its two members. The add() method throws ClassCastException.

19. A. The Arrays class has a static equals() method that compares arrays member by member.

20. A, D. StringBuffer is threadsafe, StringBuilder is fast.

Chapter

9

I/O and Streams

JAVA CERTIFICATION EXAM OBJECTIVES COVERED IN THIS CHAPTER:

✓ 3.2 Given a scenario involving navigating file systems, reading from files, or writing to files, develop the correct solution using the following classes (sometimes in combination) from java.io: BufferedReader,BufferedWriter, File, FileReader, FileWriter and PrintWriter.

✓ 3.3 Develop code that serializes and/or de-serializes objects using the following APIs from java.io: DataInputStream, DataOutputStream, FileInputStream, FileOutputStream, ObjectInputStream, ObjectOutputStream, and Serializable. In addition, develop Serializable classes that correctly declare and use transient variables and private readObject and writeObject methods. Given a scenario and/or code example, recognize when, if, and which constructors will be called in an object's inheritance chain during deserialization.

Java's Input/Output (I/O) structure is substantially based on the concept of streams, which are classes that help you read and write files and networks. The Programmer's Exam requires you to know about file I/O. This chapter covers all the I/O knowledge you need for the Programmer's Exam and also prepares you for Chapter 13, "Networking and RMI."

This chapter begins with a look at how Java represents text, both inside and outside the Java Virtual Machine (JVM). Then you'll see how to read and write files byte by byte. After that you'll learn about using streams to perform more sophisticated I/O. The chapter ends with a discussion of object streams and serialization.

Text, UTF, and Unicode

Since files often contain text, we'll start by discussing how Java represents text. In the early days of computers, when memory was an expensive commodity, each character was represented by a single byte. A standard called ASCII determined which of the 256 possible bit combinations represented which characters. With only 256 possible values, there was room for all American and English characters but not much else. Some European characters were accommodated (accented vowels and the like), but Asian, African, Middle Eastern, and Slavic alphabets were ignored.

Not surprisingly, many communities developed their own standards for mapping bytes to characters. It became impossible to process a file correctly without knowing which standard it used. For example, the bit pattern 01000001 represented A in the U.S. and Europe. In Armenia it represented a letter that looks like a cursive Q, and in Tibet it represented a letter that looks vaguely like a guillotine.

Clearly, 8 bits are not enough to represent all the characters of all the communities of our planet. The Unicode standard was developed as a way to map characters to 16-bit values. Using 16 bits means that there are 65,536 possible characters that can be represented, so almost all languages can be fully encoded. (Chinese, Japanese, and Korean, which have huge numbers of characters, are not completely represented.)

Unicode is the encoding of the future, but it does not address a problem of the present: there are billions of files in the world that use pre-Unicode 8-bit mappings. Moreover, 8-bit characters are the norm for network communication. No modern programming language can succeed if it ignores all these 8-bit characters, so Java uses a double strategy:

- Programs may use UTF to read and write Unicode.

- Programs may use readers and writers to convert between internal Unicode and external 8-bit encodings.

UTF stands for UCS Transformation Format, and UCS in turn stands for Universal Character Set. (Don't worry: you will not be tested on your knowledge of these abbreviations.) UTF is a standard for compressing strings of Unicode text. As you study certain classes later in this chapter, you will see that they have methods for reading and writing UTF. These methods convert between external UTF and internal Unicode.

Java's various reader and writer classes allow Java applications to take advantage of 8-bit text in files and on the Web. They are presented in the "Streams, Readers, and Writers" section later on in this chapter.

File Input and Output

Java's `java.io.File` and `java.io.RandomAccessFile` classes provide functionality for navigating the local file system, describing files and directories, and accessing files in non-sequential order. (Accessing files sequentially is done with streams, readers, and writers, which are described later in this chapter.) All file access begins with the creation of an instance of one of these classes.

The *File* Class

The `java.io.File` class represents the name of a file or directory that might exist on the host machine's file system. The simplest form of the constructor for this class is

```
File(String pathname);
```

It is important to know that constructing an instance of `File` does not create a file on the local file system. Calling the constructor simply creates an instance that encapsulates the specified string. Of course, if the instance is to be of any use, most likely it should encapsulate a string that represents an existing file or directory, or one that will shortly be created. However, at construction time no checks are made.

It is even possible to create a `File` instance that uses the wrong file-naming semantics. The class accepts both the forward-slash separator used by Unix and the drive-letter-plus-backslash-separator notation used by Windows.

There are two other versions of the `File` constructor:

```
File(String dir, String subpath);
File(File dir, String subpath);
```

Both versions require you to provide a directory and a relative path (the subpath argument) within that directory. In one version, you use a string to specify the directory; in the other, you use an instance of `File`. (Remember that the `File` class can represent a directory as well as a file.) You might, for example, execute the following code on a Unix machine:

```
1. File f1 =
2.    new File("/tmp", "xyz"); // Assume /tmp is a dir
3. File f2 = new File(f1, "Xyz.java");
```

You might execute the following code on a Windows platform:

```
1. File f1 =
2.    new File("C:\\a");    // Assume C:\a is a dir
3. File f2 = new File(f1, "Xyz.java");
```

(In line 2, the first backslash is an escape character that ensures the second backslash is accepted literally.)

Of course, there is no theoretical reason why you could not run the first example on a Windows machine and the second example on a Unix platform. Up to this point, you are doing nothing more than constructing objects that encapsulate strings. In practice, however, nothing is gained from using the wrong pathname semantics. Eventually, if you try to access a file via a `File` instance that uses the wrong semantics, you'll get a `FileNotFoundException`.

After constructing an instance of `File`, you can make several method calls on it. Some of these calls simply do string manipulation on the file's pathname, and others access or modify the local file system.

The major methods that support navigation are as follows:

boolean exists()   Returns `true` if the file or directory exists; otherwise returns `false`.

String getAbsolutePath()   Returns the absolute (that is, not relative) path of the file or directory.

String getCanonicalPath()   Returns the canonical path of the file or directory. This method is similar to `getAbsolutePath()`, but the symbols . and .. are resolved.

String getName()   Returns the name of the file or directory. The name is the last element of the path.

String getParent()   Returns the name of the directory that contains the `File`.

boolean isDirectory()   Returns `true` if the `File` object describes a directory that exists on the file system.

boolean isFile()   Returns `true` if the `File` object describes a file that exists on the file system.

String[] list()   Returns an array containing the names of the files and directories within the `File` instance, which `File` must describe a directory, not a file.

Some non-navigation methods are as follows:

boolean canRead()   Returns `true` if the file or directory may be read.

boolean canWrite()   Returns `true` if the file or directory may be modified.

boolean createNewFile()   Creates a new empty disk file as described by the current object, if such a file does not already exist. Returns `true` if the file was created.

boolean delete()   Attempts to delete the file or directory.

long length()   Returns the length of the file.

boolean mkdir()   Attempts to create a directory whose path is described by the current instance of File.

boolean renameTo(File *newname*)   Renames the file or directory. This method returns true if the renaming succeeded; otherwise it returns false.

The following program uses some of the navigation methods to create a recursive listing of a directory. The application expects the directory to be specified in the command line. The listing appears in a text area within a frame:

```java
1. import java.awt.*;
2. import java.io.File;
3.
4. public class Lister extends Frame {
5.   TextArea      ta;
6.
7.   public static void main(String args[]) {
8.     // Get path or dir to be listed.
9.     // Default to cwd if no command line arg.
10.     String path = ".";
11.     if (args.length >= 1)
12.       path = args[0];
13.
14.     // Make sure path exists and is a directory.
15.     File f = new File(path);
16.     if (!f.isDirectory()) {
17.       System.out.println(path +
18.         " doesn't exist or not dir");
19.       System.exit(0);
20.     }
21.
22.     // Recursively list contents.
23.     Lister lister = new Lister(f);
24.     lister.setVisible(true);
25.   }
26.
27.   Lister(File f) {
28.     setSize(300, 450);
29.     ta = new TextArea();
30.     ta.setFont(new Font(
31.             "Monospaced", Font.PLAIN, 14));
32.     add(ta, BorderLayout.CENTER);
```

```
33.     recurse(f, 0);
34.   }
35.
36.   // Recursively list the contents of dirfile.
37.   // Indent 5 spaces for each level of depth.
38.
39.   void recurse(File dirfile, int depth) {
40.     String contents[] = dirfile.list();
41.     // For each child ...
42.     for (int i=0; i<contents.length; i++) {
43.       // Indent
44.       for (int spaces=0; spaces<depth; spaces++)
45.         ta.append("     ");
46.       // Print name
47.       ta.append(contents[i] + "\n");
48.       File child = new File(dirfile, contents[i]);
49.       if (child.isDirectory())
50.         // Recurse if dir
51.         recurse(child, depth+1);
52.     }
53.   }
54. }
```

Figure 9.1 shows a sample of this program's output.

The program first checks for a command-line argument (lines 10–12). If one is supplied, it is assumed to be the name of the directory to be listed; if there is no argument, the current working directory will be listed. Note the call to isDirectory() on line 16. This call returns true only if path represents an existing directory.

After establishing that the thing to be listed really is a directory, the code constructs an instance of Lister, which makes a call to recurse(), passing in the File to be listed in the parameter dirfile.

The recurse() method makes a call to list() (line 40) to get a listing of the contents of the directory. Each file or subdirectory is printed (line 47) after appropriate indentation (five spaces per level, lines 44 and 45). If the child is a directory (tested on line 49), its contents are listed recursively.

The Lister program shows one way to use the methods of the File class to navigate the local file system. These methods do not modify the contents of files in any way; to modify a file, you must use either the RandomAccessFile class or Java's stream, reader, and writer facilities. All these topics are covered in the sections that follow, but first, here is a summary of the key points concerning the File class:

- An instance of File describes a file or directory.

- The file or directory might or might not exist.

- Constructing/garbage collecting an instance of File has no effect on the local file system.

FIGURE 9.1　　Sample listing

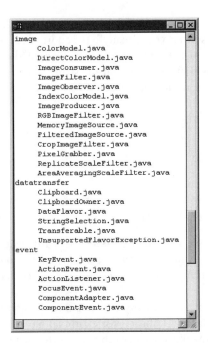

The *RandomAccessFile* Class

One way to read or modify a file is to use the `java.io.RandomAccessFile` class. This class presents a model of files that is incompatible with the stream/reader/writer model described later in this chapter. The stream/reader/writer model was developed for general I/O, whereas the `RandomAccessFile` class takes advantage of a particular behavior of files that is not found in general I/O devices.

With a random-access file, you can seek to a desired position within a file and then read or write a desired amount of data. The `RandomAccessFile` class provides methods that support seeking, reading, and writing.

The constructors for the class are as follows:

```
RandomAccessFile(String file, String mode)
RandomAccessFile(File file, String mode)
```

The *mode* string should be either `"r"` or `"rw"`. Use `"r"` to open the file for reading only, and use `"rw"` to open for both reading and writing. In revision 5.0 two more modes were introduced: `"rws"` and `"rwd."` With a mode of `"rws"` the file is opened for reading and writing, and any changes to the file's content or metadata take place immediately. (Metadata is all the data that describes a file: its permission modes, ownership, last-modified time, etc.) With the `"rwd"` mode, the file is opened for reading and writing, and changes to the files content, but not its metadata, take place immediately.

The second form of the constructor is useful when you want to use some of the methods of the File class before opening a random-access file, so that you already have an instance of File at hand when it comes time to call the RandomAccessFile constructor. For example, the following code fragment constructs an instance of File in order to verify that the string path represents a file that exists and may be written. If this is the case, the RandomAccessFile constructor is called; otherwise an exception is thrown:

```
1. File file = new File(path);
2. if (!file.isFile()    ||
3.      !file.canRead()  ||
4.      !file.canWrite())
5.    throw new IOException();
6. RandomAccessFile raf = new RandomAccessFile(file, "rw");
```

When the named file does not exist, constructing a RandomAccessFile is different from constructing an ordinary File. In this situation, if the random-access file is constructed in read-only mode, a FileNotFoundException is thrown. If the random-access file is constructed in read-write mode, then a zero-length file is created.

After a random-access file is constructed, you can seek to any byte position within the file and then read or write. Pre-Java systems (the C standard I/O library, for example) have supported seeking to a position relative to the beginning of the file, the end of the file, or the current position within the file. Java's random-access files support only seeking relative to the beginning of the file; but methods exist that report the current position and the length of the file, so you can effectively perform the other kinds of seeking as long as you are willing to do the arithmetic.

The methods that support seeking are as follows:

long getFilePointer() throws IOException   Returns the current position within the file, in bytes. Subsequent reading and writing will take place starting at this position.

long length() throws IOException   Returns the length of the file, in bytes.

void seek(long *position*) throws IOException   Sets the current position within the file, in bytes. Subsequent reading and writing will take place starting at this position. Files start at position 0.

The following code is a subclass of RandomAccessFile that adds two new methods to support seeking from the current position or the end of the file. The code illustrates the use of the methods just listed:

```
import java.io.*;

class GeneralRAF extends RandomAccessFile {
    public GeneralRAF(File path, String mode)
```

```
    throws IOException {
      super(path, mode);
    }
  }

  public GeneralRAF(String path, String mode)
    throws IOException {
      super(path, mode);
    }
  }

  public void seekFromEnd(long offset)
    throws IOException {
      seek(length() - offset);
  }

  public void seekFromCurrent(long offset)
    throws IOException {
      seek(getFilePointer() + offset);
  }
}
```

The whole point of seeking, of course, is to read from or write to a desired position within a file. All the reading and writing methods advance the current file position. Files are ordered collections of bytes, and the RandomAccessFile class has several methods that support reading and writing of bytes. However, the bytes in a file often combine to represent richer data formats. For example, two bytes could represent a Unicode character; four bytes could represent a float or an int.

The more common methods that support byte reading and writing are as follows:

int read() throws IOException   Returns the next byte from the file (stored in the low-order eight bits of an int) or -1 if at the end of the file.

int read(byte *dest*[]) throws IOException   Attempts to read enough bytes to fill array *dest*[]. It returns the number of bytes read, or -1 if at the end of the file.

int read(byte *dest*[], int *offset*, int *len*) throws IOException   Attempts to read *len* bytes into array *dest*[], starting at *offset*. It returns the number of bytes read, or -1 if at the end of the file.

void write(int *b*) throws IOException   Writes the low-order byte of *b*.

void write(byte *b*[]) throws IOException   Writes all of byte array *b*[].

void write(byte *b*[], int *offset*, int *len*) throws IOException   Writes *len* bytes from byte array *b*[], starting at *offset*.

Random-access files support reading and writing of all primitive data types. Each read or write operation advances the current file position by the number of bytes read or written. Table 9.1 presents the various primitive-oriented methods, all of which throw IOException.

When a random-access file is no longer needed, it should be closed:

```
void close() throws IOException
```

The close() method releases non-memory system resources associated with the file.

To summarize, random-access files offer the following functionality:

- Seeking to any position within a file
- Reading and writing single or multiple bytes
- Reading and writing groups of bytes, treated as higher-level data types
- Closing

TABLE 9.1   Random-Access File Methods for Primitive Data Types

Read Method	Write Method
boolean readBoolean()	void writeBoolean(boolean b)
byte readByte()	void writeByte(int b)
short readShort()	void writeShort(int s)
char readChar()	void writeChar(int c)
int readInt()	void writeInt(int i)
long readLong()	void writeLong(long l)
float readFloat()	void writeFloat(float f)
double readDouble()	void writeDouble(double d)
int readUnsignedByte()	None
int readUnsignedShort()	None
String readLine()	None
String readUTF()	void writeUTF(String s)

Streams, Readers, and Writers

Java's stream, reader, and writer classes view input and output as ordered sequences of bytes. Of course, dealing strictly with bytes would be tremendously bothersome, because data appears sometimes as bytes, sometimes as ints, sometimes as floats, and so on. You have already seen how the RandomAccessFile class allows you to read and write all of Java's primitive data types. The readInt() method, for example, reads four bytes from a file, pieces them together, and returns an int. Java's general I/O classes provide a similar structured approach:

- A low-level output stream receives bytes and writes bytes to an output device.

- A high-level filter output stream receives general-format data, such as primitives, and writes bytes to a low-level output stream or to another filter output stream.

- A writer is similar to a filter output stream but is specialized for writing Java strings in units of Unicode characters.

- A low-level input stream reads bytes from an input device and returns bytes to its caller.

- A high-level filter input stream reads bytes from a low-level input stream, or from another filter input stream, and returns general-format data to its caller.

- A reader is similar to a filter input stream but is specialized for reading UTF strings in units of Unicode characters.

The stream, reader, and writer classes are not very complicated. The easiest way to review them is to begin with the low-level streams.

Low-Level Streams

Low-level input streams have methods that read input and return the input as bytes. *Low-level output streams* have methods that are passed bytes and write the bytes as output. The FileInputStream and FileOutputStream classes are excellent examples.

The two most common file input stream constructors are

- FileInputStream(String *pathname*)

- FileInputStream(File *file*)

After a file input stream has been constructed, you can call methods to read a single byte, an array of bytes, or a portion of an array of bytes. The functionality is similar to the byte-input methods you have already seen in the RandomAccessFile class:

int read() throws IOException   Returns the next byte from the file (stored in the low-order eight bits of an int) or –1 if at the end of the file.

int read(byte *dest*[]) throws IOException   Attempts to read enough bytes to fill array *dest*[]. It returns the number of bytes read or –1 if at the end of the file.

int read(byte *dest*[], int *offset*, int *len*) throws IOException   Attempts to read *len* bytes into array *dest*[], starting at *offset*. It returns the number of bytes read or –1 if at the end of the file.

The following code fragment illustrates the use of these methods by reading a single byte into byte b, then enough bytes to fill byte array bytes[], and finally 20 bytes into the first 20 locations of byte array morebytes[]:

```
byte b;
byte bytes[] = new byte[100];
byte morebytes[] = new byte[50];
try {
  FileInputStream fis = new FileInputStream("fname");
  b = (byte) fis.read();          // Single byte
  fis.read(bytes);                // Fill the array
  fis.read(morebytes, 0, 20);     // 1st 20 elements
  fis.close();
}
catch (IOException e) { }
```

The FileInputStream class has a few very useful utility methods:

int available() throws IOException   Returns the number of bytes that can be read without blocking.

void close() throws IOException   Releases non-memory system resources associated with the file. A file input stream should always be closed when no longer needed.

long skip(long *nbytes*) throws IOException   Attempts to read and discard *nbytes* bytes. Returns the number of bytes actually skipped.

It is not surprising that file output streams are almost identical to file input streams. The commonly used constructors are

- FileOutputStream(String *pathname*)
- FileOutputStream(File *file*)

There are methods to support writing a single byte, an array of bytes, or a subset of an array of bytes:

void write(int *b*) throws IOException   Writes the low-order byte of *b*.

void write(byte *bytes*[]) throws IOException   Writes all members of byte array *bytes*[].

void write(byte *bytes*[], int *offset*, int *len*) throws IOException   Writes *len* bytes from array *bytes*[], starting at *offset*.

The FileOutputStream class also has a close() method, which should always be called when a file output stream is no longer needed.

In addition to the two classes described earlier, the `java.io` package has other low-level input and output stream classes:

InputStream and **OutputStream**   These are the superclasses of the other low-level stream classes. They can be used for reading and writing network sockets.

ByteArrayInputStream and **ByteArrayOutputStream**   These classes read and write arrays of bytes. `Byte` arrays are certainly not hardware I/O devices, but the classes are useful when you want to process or create sequences of bytes.

PipedInputStream and **PipedOutputStream**   These classes provide a mechanism for synchronized communication between threads.

High-Level Streams

It is all very well to read bytes from input devices and write bytes to output devices, if bytes are the unit of information you are interested in. However, more often than not the bytes to be read or written constitute higher-level information such as an `int` or a `String`.

Java supports high-level I/O with high-level streams. The most common of these (and the ones covered in this chapter) extend from the superclasses `FilterInputStream` and `FilterOutputStream`. *High-level input streams* do not read from input devices such as files or sockets; rather, they read from other streams. *High-level output streams* do not write to output devices but to other streams.

A good example of a high-level input stream is the data input stream. This class has only one constructor:

- `DataInputStream(InputStream instream)`

The constructor requires you to pass in an input stream. This instance might be a file input stream (because `FileInputStream` extends `InputStream`), an input stream from a socket, or any other kind of input stream. When the instance of `DataInputStream` is called on to deliver data, it will make some number of `read()` calls on *instream*, process the bytes, and return an appropriate value. The commonly used input methods of the `DataInputStream` class are as follows:

```
boolean readBoolean() throws IOException
byte readByte() throws IOException
char readChar () throws IOException
double readDouble () throws IOException
float readFloat () throws IOException
int readInt() throws IOException
long readLong() throws IOException
short readShort() throws IOException
String readUTF() throws IOException
```

There is, of course, a `close()` method.

When creating chains of streams, it is recommended that you close all streams when you no longer need them, making sure to close the streams in the reverse of the order in which they were constructed.

The following code fragment illustrates a small input chain:

```
try {
  // Construct the chain
  FileInputStream fis = new FileInputStream("fname");
  DataInputStream dis = new DataInputStream(fis);

  // Read
  double d = dis.readDouble();
  int i = dis.readInt();
  String s = dis.readUTF();

  // Close the chain
  dis.close();          // Close dis first, because it
  fis.close();          // was created last
}
catch (IOException e) { }
```

Figure 9.2 shows the hierarchy of the input chain.

The code expects that the first 8 bytes in the file represent a **double**, the next 4 bytes represent an **int**, and the next who-knows-how-many bytes represent a UTF string. This means that the code that originally created the file must have been writing a **double**, an **int**, and a UTF string. The file need not have been created by a Java program, but if it was, the easiest approach would be to use a data output stream.

The **DataOutputStream** class is the mirror image of the **DataInputStream** class. The constructor is **DataOutputStream(OutputStream *ostream*)**.

The constructor requires you to pass in an output stream. When you write to the data output stream, it converts the parameters of the write methods to bytes and writes them to *ostream*. The commonly used output methods of the **DataOutputStream** class are as follows:

```
void writeBoolean(boolean b) throws IOException
void writeByte(int b) throws IOException
void writeBytes(String s) throws IOException
void writeChar(int c) throws IOException
void writeDouble(double d) throws IOException
```

```
void writeFloat(float b) throws IOException
void writeInt(int i) throws IOException
void writeLong(long l) throws IOException
void writeShort(int s) throws IOException
void writeUTF(String s) throws IOException
```

All these methods convert their input to bytes in the obvious way, with the exception of `writeBytes()`, which writes out only the low-order byte of each character in its string. As usual, there is a `close()` method. Again, chains of output streams should be closed in reverse order from their order of creation.

FIGURE 9.2   A chain of input streams

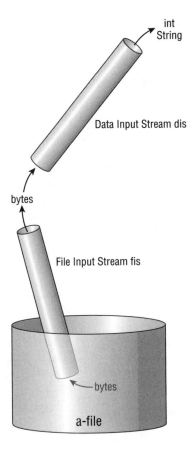

int
String

Data Input Stream dis

bytes

File Input Stream fis

bytes

a-file

With these methods in mind, you can now write code that creates a file like the one read in the previous example. In that example, the file contained a `double`, an `int`, and a `String`. The file might be created as follows:

Real World Scenario

Creating a Custom Input Stream

In this exercise, you will create your own input stream and use it in a chain. You will create a class called CborksumInputStream, which reads and delivers bytes while maintaining a checksum of all bytes read since the instance was created. The checksum is a long; every time a byte is read into the stream, its value is added to the checksum.

The class you create should extend the InputStream abstract class. The constructor for your class should take a single argument of type InputStream; this will be the source of data for the new class. Provide the byte-reading method that is abstract in the superclass; it should return just the data read by making the corresponding call on the data source stream while maintaining the checksum. Also provide a getChecksum() method.

The class you create should be able to function in a chain of input streams. Your main() method should test this functionality by creating a chain of three streams, with your new class in the middle. Use the following code in main() to create the chain of streams:

```
FileInputStream fis = new FileInputStream("Ch12.data");
ChecksumInputStream cis = new ChecksumInputStream(fis);
DataInputStream dis = new DataInputStream(cis);
```

A sample solution appears on your CD-ROM in the solutions\Chapter_9 directory, which also contains a data file, Ch9.data, for testing your solution. To use the data file, first read 300 doubles from the data input stream dis. Then read 300 ints from dis. Print out the checksum found in dis, in hexadecimal (base-16) format. (This is easy: the java.lang.Long class has a method called toHexString().) The result will tell you what the ChecksumInputStream just did.

```
try {
  // Create the chain
  FileOutputStream fos = new FileOutputStream("txt");
  DataOutputStream dos = new DataOutputStream(fos);

  // Write
  dos.writeDouble(123.456);
  dos.writeInt(55);
  dos.writeUTF("The moving finger writes");
```

```
  // Close the chain
  dos.close();
  fos.close();
}
catch (IOException e) { }
```

In addition to data input streams and output streams, the java.io package offers several other high-level stream classes. The constructors for all high-level input streams require you to pass in the next-lower input stream in the chain; it will be the source of data read by the new object. Similarly, the constructors for the high-level output streams require you to pass in the next-lower output stream in the chain; the new object will write data to this stream. Some of the high-level streams are listed here:

BufferedInputStream and BufferedOutputStream   These classes have internal buffers so that bytes can be read or written in large blocks, thus minimizing I/O overhead.

PrintStream   This class can be asked to write text or primitives. Primitives are converted to character representations. The System.out and System.err objects are examples of this class. The class has a println() method that outputs a string followed by a newline character. It also has a format() method that prints formatted text. Text formatting is covered in Chapter 8, "The java.lang and java.util packages."

PushbackInputStream   This class allows the most recently read byte to be put back into the stream, as if it had not yet been read. This functionality is very useful for certain kinds of parsers.

It is possible to create stream chains of arbitrary length. For example, the following code fragment implements a data input stream that reads from a buffered input stream, which in turn reads from a file input stream:

```
FileInputStream f = new FileInputStream("text");
BufferedInputStream b = new BufferedInputStream(f);
DataInputStream d = new DataInputStream(b);
```

The chain that this code creates is shown in Figure 9.3.

Readers and Writers

Readers and *writers* are like input and output streams: The low-level varieties communicate with I/O devices, and the high-level varieties communicate with low-level varieties. What makes readers and writers different is that they are exclusively oriented to Unicode characters.

FIGURE 9.3   A longer chain

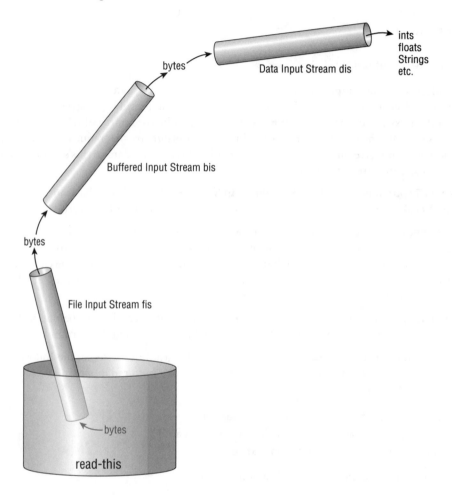

A good example of a low-level reader is the `FileReader` class. Its commonly used constructors are

- `FileReader(String `*`pathname`*`)`
- `FileReader(File `*`file`*`)`

Of course, any file passed into these constructors must genuinely contain UTF strings.

The corresponding writer is the `FileWriter` class:

- `FileWriter(String `*`pathname`*`)`
- `FileWriter(File `*`file`*`)`

The other low-level reader and writer classes are as follows:

CharArrayReader and **CharArrayWriter**   Read and write char arrays.

PipedReader and **PipedWriter**   Provide a mechanism for thread communication.

StringReader and **StringWriter**   Read and write strings.

The low-level readers all extend from the abstract Reader superclass. This class offers the now-familiar trio of read() methods for reading a single char, an array of chars, or a subset of an array of chars. Note, however, that the unit of information is now the char, not the byte. The three methods are

int read() throws IOException   Returns the next char (stored in the low-order 16 bits of the int return value) or -1 if at the end of input.

int read(char *dest*[]) throws IOException   Attempts to read enough chars to fill array *dest*[]. It returns the number of chars read or -1 if at the end of input.

int read(char *dest*[], int *offset*, int *len*) throws IOException   Attempts to read *len* chars into array *dest*[], starting at *offset*. It returns the number of chars read or -1 if at the end of input.

The low-level writers all extend from the abstract Writer superclass. This class provides methods that are a bit different from the standard trio of write() methods:

void write(int *ch*) throws IOException   Writes the char that appears in the low-order 16 bits of *ch*.

void write(String *str*) throws IOException   Writes the string called *str*.

void write(String *str*, int *offset*, int *len*) throws IOException   Writes the substring of *str* that begins at *offset* and has length *len*.

void write(char *chars*[]) throws IOException   Writes the char array *chars*[].

void write(char *chars*[], int *offset*, int *len*) throws IOException   Writes *len* chars from array *chars*[], beginning at *offset*.

The high-level readers and writers all inherit from the Reader or Writer superclass, so they also support the methods just listed. As with high-level streams, when you construct a high-level reader or writer, you pass in the next-lower object in the chain. The high-level classes are as follows:

BufferedReader and **BufferedWriter**   These classes have internal buffers so that data can be read or written in large blocks, thus minimizing I/O overhead. They are similar to buffered input streams and buffered output streams.

InputStreamReader and **OutputStreamWriter**   These classes convert between streams of bytes and sequences of Unicode characters. By default, the classes assume that the streams use the platform's default character encoding; alternative constructors provide any desired encoding.

LineNumberReader   This class views its input as a sequence of lines of text. A method called `readLine()` returns the next line, and the class keeps track of the current line number.

PrintWriter   This class is similar to `PrintStream`, but it writes `chars` rather than `bytes`.

PushbackReader   This class is similar to `PushbackInputStream`, but it reads `chars` rather than `bytes`.

The following code fragment chains a line number reader onto a file reader. The code prints each line of the file, preceded by a line number:

```
1. try {
2.    FileReader fr = new FileReader("data");
3.    LineNumberReader lnr = new LineNumberReader(fr);
4.    String s;
5.
6.    while ((s = lnr.readLine()) != null) {
7.       System.out.println(lnr.getLineNumber() +
8.       " : " + s);
9.    }
10.   lnr.close();
11.   fr.close();
12. }
13. catch (IOException x) { }
```

Figure 9.4 shows the reader chain implemented by this code.

Encodings

The preceding discussion has carefully avoided a crucial point. Consider a file reader, which reads bytes from a file and returns strings of Unicode. How does the reader know how to translate an 8-bit character on the disk into a 16-bit character inside the JVM? Similarly, how does a file writer know how to translate a 16-bit Unicode character into an 8-bit byte?

The whole idea of readers and writers is that they connect the world inside the JVM, where characters are strictly 16-bit Unicode, to the external world, where text is historically presented as ordered sequences of bytes. Bytes represent different characters depending on where they appear in the world. Only 256 bit combinations are available in a byte; different languages and cultures map these combinations to different characters, and thus to different Unicode values. Readers and writers are sensitive to these linguistic and cultural differences.

An *encoding* is a mapping between 8-bit characters and Unicode. Figure 9.5 shows a few of the encodings that have been established by the Unicode Consortium. The figure is not drawn to scale. Note that some encodings are quite small (Greek requires only 144 Unicode values), whereas others are huge (more than 50,000 values for various Chinese, Japanese, and Korean characters; in the 8-bit world, such a character is represented by a sequence of multiple bytes).

FIGURE 9.4   A chain of readers

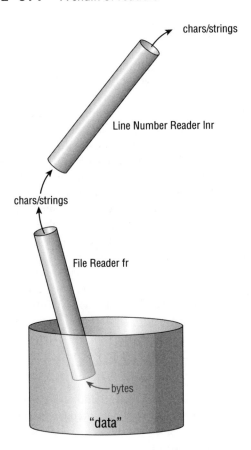

chars/strings

Line Number Reader lnr

chars/strings

File Reader fr

bytes

"data"

FIGURE 9.5   Selected character encodings

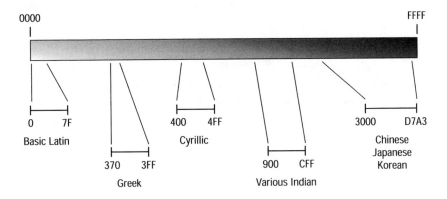

0000

FFFF

0   7F

Basic Latin

370   3FF

Greek

400   4FF

Cyrillic

900   CFF

Various Indian

3000   D7A3

Chinese
Japanese
Korean

For an informative look at all Unicode mappings, see http://www.unicode.org. This is an outstanding website, with a minimum of extraneous graphic design and a maximum of well-organized, clearly presented information.

Most modern operating systems know what part of the world they are operating in—they are given this information when they are installed. The machine's locale is accessible to the JVM. By default, the encoding used by a reader or writer is the one appropriate to the machine's locale. However, readers and writers have forms of constructors that allow you to specify any desired locale. (You specify a locale by providing a string that identifies it.)

When the data written by a writer is to be read within the same locale, you don't need to consider what encoding to use; the default encoding will be appropriate. On the other hand, it may be that the data will cross a locale boundary. The writer might be connected to a socket, which communicates with a machine in a different locale. Or perhaps the writer is writing to a file on a floppy disk that will be carried across a boundary. In such cases, the people involved must agree on an encoding; the common practice is to use the U.S. ASCII encoding. For programmers in the United States, this is conveniently the default. Others must specify this encoding when constructing readers and writers. The strings that denote encoding names are determined by standards committees, so they are not especially obvious or informative. For example, the U.S. ASCII encoding name is not USASCII as you might expect, but rather ISO8859-1.

Object Streams and Serialization

As you have seen, data input and output streams allow you to read and write primitives and strings, rather than individual bytes. Object streams go one step beyond data streams by allowing you to read and write entire objects.

The process of writing an object is called *serialization*. To serialize an object, first create an instance of java.io.ObjectOutputStream. This class, like DataOutputStream, expects to be chained onto a lower-level byte-oriented stream such as a file output stream or a socket's output stream. The method below uses an object stream to store a string buffer in a file named sbuf.ser.

```
void writeStringBuffer(StringBuffer writeMe)
                       throws IOException {
  FileOutputStream fos = new FileOutputStrem("sbuf.ser");
  ObjectOutputStream oos = new ObjectOutputStream(fos);
  oos.writeObject(writeMe);
  oos.close();
  fos.close();
}
```

The `.ser` filename suffix is conventional for files containing serialized objects. To read the stored object back into a program, you can do the following:

```
StringBuffer readStringBuffer()
            throws IOException, ClassNotFoundException {
  FileInputStream fis = new FileInputStream ("sbuf.ser");
  ObjectInputStream ois = new ObjectInputStream(fis);
  StringBuffer sb = (StringBuffer)ois.readObject();
  ois.close();
  fis.close();
  return sb;
}
```

Notice that the value returned by `readObject()` is of type `Object`, so it must be cast. The object read in is identical to the one that was written out in the previous code example.

The `ObjectOutputStream` class has a `writeUTF()` method, as well as `writeByte()`, `writeShort()`, and all other write-primitive methods that also appear in data output streams. The `ObjectInputStream` class has corresponding reading methods. So if you want to create a file that contains serialized primitives and strings as well as serialized objects, you can do it with a single output stream.

When you use object streams, it's important to know what information gets serialized and what does not. It is only an object's data that is serialized, not its class definition. Moreover, not all data is written. Static fields are not, because it would not be appropriate to change a static variable, which is shared by all instances of a class, just because one instance of the class got deserialized. (To *deserialize* is to convert a serialized representation into a replica of the original object.) Transient fields are also not serialized. This provides a level of security in situations where you are concerned that sensitive variable values, serialized onto the network or into a file, might be read by hostile parties. By declaring a variable to be transient, you tell the JVM not to serialize that variable.

You might expect that private data would not be serialized, but in fact object streams pay no attention to access modes. All non-static non-transient fields are written to object output streams, regardless of whether they are public, private, default, or protected.

When an object is serialized, it will probably be deserialized by a different JVM. Any JVM that tries to deserialize an object must have access to that object's class definition. In other words, if the class is not already loaded, its class file must appear in the new JVM's classpath. If this is not the case, `readObject()` will throw an exception.

When an object output stream serializes an object that contains references to other object, every referenced object is serialized along with the original object. For example, consider a Vector that contains Bytes:

```
Vector<Byte> vec = new Vector<Byte>();
vec.add(new Byte(11));
vec.add(new Byte(22));
vec.add(new Byte(33));
```

FIGURE 9.6 A Vector and its references

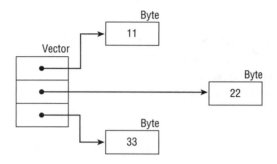

The Vector contains three references and can be diagrammed as shown in Figure 9.6.

When an object output stream writes the Vector of Figure 9.6, the three Bytes are also serialized. If instead of Bytes the Vector contains objects that have references to still other objects, those other objects would also be serialized. In the terminology of serialization, when an object is serialized, its entire *graph* is serialized. An object's graph is the object itself, plus all the objects it references, plus all the objects those objects reference, and so on. When an object input stream deserializes an object, the entire graph is deserialized.

Not all objects may be serialized, though this is not obvious from a casual glance at the API page for ObjectOutputStream. The method summary entry for writeObject() says

```
public void writeObject(Object obj)
```

However, if you look at the method detail section for writeObject(), you'll see that it throws NotSerializableException if "some object to be serialized does not implement the java.io.Serializable interface." So even though the method declares that its argument is an object, it contains code that checks for the precondition that the argument must be an instanceof Serializable, and it throws the exception if the precondition is not met. Even if the object being passed into the method implements Serializable, the exception might still be thrown. Since the object's entire graph is serialized, all objects referenced by the object must implement Serializable, and all objects referenced by *those* objects must do the same, and so on.

Recall from Chapter 5, "Flow Control, Assertions, and Exception Handling," in the discussion on assertions, that assertions should not be used to check preconditions in public methods. Fortunately, writeObject() respects this rule.

You probably recognize the Serializable interface from your reading of the API pages. Most of the core Java classes implement it. All the wrapper classes do so, and so do the collection classes. In fact, the only core Java classes that do *not* implement Serializable are ones that should not be serialized. For example, it would make no sense to try to serialize a thread, because a thread's state is tightly bound to the current JVM's thread scheduler. So it wouldn't really be helpful or meaningful to serialize a thread. Likewise, the low-level output and input streams of the java.io package don't implement Serializable because they interact with the underlying hardware.

When you create a class that might be serialized, the class should implement Serializable. This is easy, because the interface doesn't define any methods at all. All you need to do is type implements java.io.Serializable in your class declaration, and you're finished. Empty interfaces such as Serializable are known as *tagging interfaces*. They identify implementing classes as having certain properties, without requiring those classes to actually implement any methods. Arrays of primitives or serializable objects are themselves serializable.

Deserializing involves a lot of tricky business behind the scenes. The object input stream creates a blank instance of the object being deserialized and then sets its field values. In order for this to happen, a bizarre condition must apply. Think about the class hierarchy of the object being deserialized. The object itself implements Serializable; the object's parent class might or might not implement Serializable. As you work your way up the inheritance hierarchy, you eventually get to the first superclass that is not itself serializable. That superclass must have a no-args constructor. Often the first non-serializable superclass is Object, which does have the right kind of constructor. If the condition isn't met, readObject() throws java.io.InvalidClassException. The exception message says, "no valid constructor."

A serializable class may dictate how it is serialized and deserialized by implementing the following two methods:

```
private void writeObject(ObjectOutputStream oos)
    throws IOException
private void readObject(ObjectInputStream ois)
    throws IOException, ClassNotFoundException
```

Notice the private access. When an object output stream executes its writeObject() method, it checks to see if the object has a writeObject() method matching the above signature. If this is the case, the stream bypasses its default behavior (which is to serialize the object's non-static non-transient fields) and just calls the object's writeObject() method. Similarly, when an object input stream executes its readObject() method, it checks to see if the object has a readObject() method matching the above signature, and if so the ordinary deserialization process is bypassed in favor of a call to the readObject() method.

If a class wants its writeObject() method to take special action *in addition to*, rather than *instead of*, the default serialization behavior, it can call the output stream's defaultWriteObject() method, which serializes the object's non-static non-transient fields. As you might expect, the ObjectInputStream class has a defaultReadObject() method, which deserializes the current object from the object input stream. Here's an example of a serializable class that provides its own serialization code:

```
Import java.io.*;

class DoItMyself implements Serializable {
```

```
   private String    id;
   protected int     n;
   transient byte    notMe;

   private void writeObject(ObjectOutputStream oos)
                                 throws IOException {
     oos.writeUTF("The password is swordfish");
     oos.defaultWriteObject();
   }

   private void readObject(ObjectInputStream ois)
       throws IOException, ClassNotFoundException {
     String password = ois.readUTF();
     if (!password.equals("The password is swordfish"))
       throw new SecurityException("Bad password");
     ois.defaultReadObject();
   }
 }
```

When an instance of this class is serialized, the object output stream notices that the instance has a writeObject() method with the appropriate signature. This method is called. A password string is serialized. Then the output stream's defaultWriteObject() is called, and default serialization is performed.

When object input stream tries to deserialize an instance of DoItMyself, the stream detects the existence of a readObject() method with the appropriate signature, so the method is called. The serialized password is checked. If it's not the expected value, a security exception is thrown. (SecurityException is runtime, so it doesn't need to be declared.) If the password is okay, a call to defaultReadObject() causes normal deserialization of the object's fields.

This class could avoid calling defaultWriteObject() and defaultReadObject() by explicitly serializing and deserializing the variables id and n. That would require only a slight extra effort, compared to the code actually shown in the example. However, if the class had a large number of fields, the benefit of calling the default behavior would be obvious.

Another way to provide custom serialization and deserialization is to implement a subinterface of Serializable, called Externalizable. (Notice that since Externalizable extends Serializable, the implements Serializable precondition in writeObject() is met by any object that implements Externalizable.

Externalizable contains two method signatures:

```
void writeExternal(ObjectOutput out)
  throws IOException
void readExternal(ObjectInput in)
  throws IOException, ClassNotFoundException
```

ObjectOutput and ObjectInput are interfaces that are implemented by ObjectOutputStream and ObjectInputStream. They define, respectively, writeObject() and readObject() methods. Here is an example of a class that performs its own serialization, protecting the password field by reversing it before writing it out:

```
import java.io.*;

public class Account implements Externalizable {
  private String  ownerName;
  private String  password;
  private float   balance;

  private String reverse(String reverseMe) {
    String reversed = "";
    for (int i=reverseMe.length()-1; i>=0; i--)
      reversed += reverseMe.charAt(i);
    return reversed;
  }

  public void writeExternal(ObjectOutput outStream)
            throws IOException {
    outStream.writeObject(ownerName);
    outStream.writeObject(reverse(password));
    outStream.writeObject(new Float(balance));
  }

  public void readExternal(ObjectInput inStream)
            throws IOException, ClassNotFoundException {
    ownerName = (String)inStream.readObject();
    String reversedPassword =
     (String)inStream.readObject();
    password = reverse(reversedPassword);
    balance = ((Float)inStream.readObject()).floatValue();
  }
}
```

When an instance of this class is passed to an object output stream, the default serialization procedure is bypassed; instead, the stream calls the instance's writeExternal() method. When an object input stream reads a serialized instance of **Account**, a call is made to the no-args constructor for the **Account** class; this constructor must be public. Then the newly constructed object receives a readExternal() call so that it can reconstitute its serialized values.

Notice that the readObject() mechanism of ObjectInputStream relies on the existence of a no-args constructor for any class that implements Externalizable. If an externalizable class has no no-args constructor, the readObject() method will throw java.io.InvalidClassException.

Summary

This chapter has covered the following concepts of Java's I/Of support:

- Inside the JVM, text is represented by 16-bit Unicode. In files, some text is represented by UTF, which translates directly to Unicode. Other text is represented by old-style 8-bit encodings; Readers and Writers translate between these encodings and 16-bit Unicode.

- The File class is useful for navigating the local file system.

- The RandomAccessFile class lets you read and write at arbitrary places within a file.

- Input streams, output streams, readers, and writers provide a mechanism for creating input and output chains. Streams operate on bytes, readers and writers operate on chars.

- Object input and output streams support serialization and deserialization of objects.

Exam Essentials

Know the methods of the File class that provide navigation tools. The most useful navigation methods are exists(), isDirectory(), isFile(), and list(). Others are described at the beginning of this chapter.

Know how to use a RandomAccessFile for reading and writing and how to seek to a given point in the file. Understand and recognize the methods that read various kinds of data and the methods that position the file.

Understand that FilterInputStream classes need an InputStream object as a constructor argument, whereas FilterOutputStream classes need an OutputStream object as a constructor argument. Because filter streams are subclasses of the basic streams, filters can be joined in sequences.

Know how the various write methods encode data when writing with either a FileOutputStream or a RandomAccessFile. FileOutputStream writes bytes, or arrays of bytes, only. The RandomAccessFile can write the primitive data types directly. It does so using the JVM's standard data format: 1 byte for byte and boolean, 2 bytes for char and short, 4 bytes for int and float, and 8 bytes for long and double.

Understand the relationship between platform encoding standards, Unicode, streams, readers, writers, and the Unicode standard used in the JVM. Underlying platforms generally use 8-bit formats for keyboard, screen, and file I/O. This behavior is most closely represented by streams. By contrast, readers and writers use 16-bit Unicode. Unicode is also used in the JVM, so it makes sense that the JVM should read from readers and write to writers.

Review Questions

1. Which of the statements below are true? (Choose all that apply.)

   A. UTF characters are all 8 bits.

   B. UTF characters are all 16 bits.

   C. UTF characters are all 24 bits.

   D. Unicode characters are all 16 bits.

   E. Bytecode characters are all 16 bits.

   F. None of the above.

2. Which of the statements below are true? (Choose all that apply.)

   A. When you construct an instance of `File`, if you do not use the file-naming semantics of the local machine, the constructor will throw an `IOException`.

   B. When you construct an instance of `File`, if the corresponding file does not exist on the local file system, one will be created.

   C. When an instance of `File` is garbage collected, the corresponding file on the local file system is deleted.

   D. None of the above.

3. Which of the statements below are true? (Choose all that apply.)

   A. To change the current working directory, call the `setWorkingDirectory()` method of the `File` class.

   B. To change the current working directory, call the `cd()` method of the `File` class.

   C. To change the current working directory, call the `changeWorkingDirectory()` method of the `File` class.

   D. None of the above.

4. How do you use the `File` class to list the contents of a directory?

   A. `String[] contents = myFile.list();`

   B. `File[] contents = myFile.list();`

   C. `StringBuilder[] contents = myFile.list();`

   D. The `File` class does not provide a way to list the contents of a directory.

5. How many bytes does the following code write to file `dest`?

```
1. try {
2.    FileOutputStream fos = newFileOutputStream("dest");
3.    DataOutputStream dos = new DataOutputStream(fos);
4.    dos.writeInt(3);
5.    dos.writeDouble(0.0001);
```

```
6.    dos.close();
7.    fos.close();
8. }
9. catch (IOException e) { }
```

   A. 2

   B. 8

   C. 12

   D. 16

   E. The number of bytes depends on the underlying system.

6. What does the following code fragment print out at line 9?

```
1. FileOutputStream fos = new FileOutputStream("xx");
2. for (byte b=10; b<50; b++)
3.    fos.write(b);
4. fos.close();
5. RandomAccessFile raf = new RandomAccessFile("xx", "r");
6. raf.seek(10);
7. int i = raf.read();
8. raf.close()
9. System.out.println("i = " + i);
```

   A. The output is i = 30.

   B. The output is i = 20.

   C. The output is i = 10.

   D. There is no output because the code throws an exception at line 1.

   E. There is no output because the code throws an exception at line 5.

7. A file is created with the following code:

```
1. FileOutputStream fos = new FileOutputStream("datafile");
2. DataOutputStream dos = new DataOutputStream(fos);
3. for (int i=0; i<500; i++)
4.    dos.writeInt(i);
```

You would like to write code to read back the data from this file. Which solutions will work? (Choose all that apply.)

A. Construct a `FileInputStream`, passing the name of the file. Onto the `FileInputStream`, chain a `DataInputStream`, and call its `readInt()` method.

B. Construct a `FileReader`, passing the name of the file. Call the file reader's `readInt()` method.

C. Construct a `PipedInputStream`, passing the name of the file. Call the piped input stream's `readInt()` method.

D. Construct a `RandomAccessFile`, passing the name of the file. Call the random access file's `readInt()` method.

E. Construct a `FileReader`, passing the name of the file. Onto the `FileReader`, chain a `DataInputStream`, and call its `readInt()` method.

8. Which of the following is true?

A. Readers have methods that can read and return `float`s and `double`s.

B. Readers have methods that can read and return `float`s.

C. Readers have methods that can read and return `double`s.

D. Readers have methods that can read and return `int`s.

E. None of the above.

9. You execute the following code in an empty directory. What is the result?

```
1. File f1 = new File("dirname");
2. File f2 = new File(f1, "filename");
```

A. A new directory called `dirname` is created in the current working directory.

B. A new directory called `dirname` is created in the current working directory. A new file called `filename` is created in directory `dirname`.

C. A new directory called `dirname` and a new file called `filename` are created, both in the current working directory.

D. A new file called `filename` is created in the current working directory.

E. No directory is created, and no file is created.

10. What is the result of attempting to compile and execute the following code fragment? Assume that the code fragment is part of an application that has write permission in the current working directory. Also assume that before execution, the current working directory does not contain a file called `datafile`.

```
1. try {
2.    RandomAccessFile raf = new
3.       RandomAccessFile("datafile" ,"rw");
4.    BufferedOutputStream bos = new
```

```
 5.     BufferedOutputStream(raf);
 6.   DataOutputStream dos = new
 7.     DataOutputStream(bos);
 8.   dos.writeDouble(Math.PI);
 9.   dos.close();
10.   bos.close();
11.   raf.close();
12. }
13. catch (IOException e) { }
```

A. The code fails to compile.

B. The code compiles but throws an exception at line 4.

C. The code compiles and executes but has no effect on the local file system.

D. The code compiles and executes; afterward, the current working directory contains a file called datafile.

11. Suppose you are writing a class that will provide custom serialization. The class implements java.io.Serializable (not java.io.Externalizable). What access mode should the writeObject() method have?

A. public

B. protected

C. default

D. private

12. Suppose you are writing a class that will provide custom deserialization. The class implements java.io.Serializable (not java.io.Externalizable). What access mode should the readObject() method have?

A. public

B. protected

C. default

D. private

13. Suppose class A extends Object; class B extends A; and class C extends B. Of these, only class C implements java.io.Serializable. Which of the following must be true in order to avoid an exception during deserialization of an instance of C?

A. A must have a no-args constructor.

B. B must have a no-args constructor.

C. C must have a no-args constructor.

D. There are no restrictions regarding no-args constructors.

14. Suppose class A extends `Object`; Class B extends A; and class C extends B. Of these, only class C implements `java.io.Externalizable`. Which of the following must be true in order to avoid an exception during deserialization of an instance of C?

   A. A must have a no-args constructor.

   B. B must have a no-args constructor.

   C. C must have a no-args constructor.

   D. There are no restrictions regarding no-args constructors.

15. Given the following class:

```
public class Xyz implements java.io.Serializable {
    public int      iAmPublic;
    private int     iAmPrivate;
    static int      iAmStatic;
    transient int   iAmTransient;
    volatile int    iAmVolatile;

    . . .

}
```

   Assuming the class does not perform custom serialization, which fields are written when an instance of Xyz is serialized? (Choose all that apply.)

   A. `iAmPublic`

   B. `iAmPrivate`

   C. `iAmStatic`

   D. `iAmTransient`

   E. `iAmVolatile`

16. What method of the `java.io.File` class can create a file on the hard drive?

   A. `newFile()`

   B. `makeFile()`

   C. `makeNewFile()`

   D. `createFile()`

   E. `createNewFile()`

17. Which of the following are true? (Choose all that apply.)

   A. `System.out` has a `println()` method.

   B. `System.out` has a `format()` method.

   C. `System.err` has a `println()` method.

   D. `System.err` has a `format ()` method.

18. What happens when you try to compile and run the following application?

```
1. import java.io.*;
2.
3. public class Xxx {
4.    public static void main(String[] args) {
5.       try {
6.          File f = new File("xxx.ser");
7.          FileOutputStream fos = new FileOutputStream(f);
8.          ObjectOutputStream oos = new ObjectOutputStream(fos);
9.          oos.writeObject(new Object());
10.         oos.close();
11.         fos.close();
12.      }
13.      catch (Exception x) { }
14.   }
15. }
```

   A. Compiler error at line 9.

   B. An exception is thrown at line 9.

   C. An exception is thrown at line 10.

   D. No compiler error and no exception.

19. Which of the following are valid mode strings for the `RandomAccessFile` constructor? (Choose all that apply.)

   A. `"r"`

   B. `"ro"`

   C. `"rw"`

   D. `"rws"`

   E. `"rwd"`

20. Which of the following are valid arguments to the `DataInputStream` constructor?

   A. `File`

   B. `FileReader`

   C. `FileInputStream`

   D. `RandomAccessFile`

Answers to Review Questions

1. D. UTF characters are as big as they need to be. Unicode characters are all 16 bits. There is no such thing as a bytecode character; bytecode is the format generated by the Java compiler.

2. D. A, B, and C are all false. The `File` constructor doesn't check the file-naming semantics. Construction and garbage collection of a `File` have no effect on the local file system.

3. D. The `File` class does not provide a way to change the current working directory.

4. A. The `list()` method returns an array of strings.

5. C. The `writeInt()` call writes out an `int`, which is 4 bytes long; the `writeDouble()` call writes out a `double`, which is 8 bytes long. The total is 12 bytes.

6. B. All the code is perfectly legal, so no exceptions are thrown. The first byte in the file is 10, the next byte is 11, the next is 12, and so on. The byte at file position 10 is 20, so the output is i = 20.

7. A, D. Option A chains a data input stream onto a file input stream. D simply uses the `RandomAccessFile` class. B fails because the `FileReader` class has no `readInt()` method; readers and writers handle only text. C fails because the `PipedInputStream` class has nothing to do with file I/O. (Piped input and output streams are used in inter-thread communication.) E fails because you cannot chain a data input stream onto a file reader. Readers read `chars`, and input streams handle `bytes`.

8. E. Readers and writers deal only with character I/O.

9. E. Constructing an instance of the `File` class has no effect on the local file system.

10. A. Compilation fails at lines 4 and 5, because there is no constructor for `BufferedOutputStream` that takes a `RandomAccessFile` object as a parameter. You can be sure of this even if you are not familiar with buffered output streams, because random-access files are completely incompatible with the stream/reader/writer model.

11. D. Default serialization is bypassed only if the `writeObject()` method has private access.

12. D. Default deserialization is bypassed only if the `readObject()` method has private access.

13. B. The lowest-level non-serializable superclass of the object being deserialized must have a no-args constructor.

14. C. An externalizable object must have a no-args constructor.

15. A, B, E. Default serialization writes all non-static non-transient fields.

16. E. The `createNewFile()` method creates a new empty file.

17. A, B, C, D. Both `System.out` and `System.err` are instances of `PrintStream`, which has a `println()` method and (as of version 5.0) a `format()` method.

18. B. The writeObject() method is declared to take an Object argument. At runtime, there is a precondition check to make sure the argument implements Serializable, which Object doesn't do.

19. A, C, D, E. Only "ro" is not valid. "r" opens for reading only. "rw" opens for reading and writing. "rws" opens for reading and writing, with immediate updating of data and metadata changes. "rwd" opens for reading and writing, with immediate updating of data (but not metadata) changes.

20. C. A DataInputStream reads bytes from its data source, which must be an InputStream. The only valid option is C, FileInputStream.

The Sun Certified Developer's Exam

Chapter

10

About the Developer's Exam

The Sun Certified Java Developer's (SCJD) exam is the most difficult of the Java certification exams. It is a performance test, meaning that candidates perform realistic tasks, rather than answering simple objective questions. When you sign up for the exam, you will be given a specification for a Java application that you are to implement. Most of your grade depends on how well you implement the spec.

This chapter explains the mechanics of taking the exam and gives an overview of the Java technologies you need to know in order to pass. The chapters that follow review those technologies.

To discourage collaboration and cheating, there are a large number of project specs. Individual candidates are assigned individual specs by a random process. The specs are treated as highly confidential information, and very few people have access to them. The good news is that all of them were developed by your two authors, and one of your authors is also the lead assessor for the exam. So you can be sure of two things:

1. No other author has seen all the specs, so the best they can do is guess at what's important. You've come to the right book!

2. Everything you read in the following chapters will be important, because we're the only authors who *don't* need to guess.

Of course, we can't get too specific. Our goal here isn't to give away any answers. Our goal is help you become competent in the necessary skills.

The Developer exam is a performance exam. This means that instead of answering clear-cut questions, you will be given a programming assignment. In the remainder of this book, our approach will be different from the one used in the chapters that covered the Sun Certified Java Programmer (SCJP) exam material. There won't be any more review questions. Instead, at the end of each chapter you'll find a Chapter Review Lab. These labs are programming exercises designed to give you experience in the techniques presented in the chapter. As with the Real World Scenarios of the earlier chapters, suggested solutions appear on your CD-ROM, in the `solutions` directory, in subdirectories whose names correspond to the chapter names.

Are You Ready?

The Developer exam has one prerequisite: you must already be a Sun Certified Java Programmer. If you have already passed the Programmer exam, or if you are confident that you can pass when the time comes, read on. If not…read on anyway! There's no bad time for learning.

The exam tests your ability to create an application, given a spec. If you have done that kind of thing before, you know that a finished product is much more than a program that works. In order to pass the exam, you need to write code that can be understood by other people; you need to create a program that can be easily used by other people; and you need to create Javadoc pages for all your classes. A theoretical knowledge of the Java language won't be enough; you can pass only if you have experience at putting that knowledge to use. We can imagine a profile for a candidate with ideal experience. You match the profile if

- You write Java code at least three days a week.

- Your code includes Javadoc comments.

- You have written classes and applications based only on written instructions.

- You have created simple GUIs and have thought about GUI ease-of-use issues.

- You have written multithreaded applications.

- You frequently use collections.

- You have written a client/server application.

If you match this profile, you are definitely ready to take the exam. If you don't match the profile very closely, rest assured that this book will cover all the topics you need to know about; however, it would be a good idea to practice what you learn before you take the exam.

 Sun offers a five-day course called Java Programming Language Workshop that is well suited to preparing students for this certification. The course is numbered SL-285; you can view the course description by pointing your browser to http://suned.sun.com. Sun also offers courses specific to major areas of the exam, but these are not defined as certification courses. You may also wish to browse SL-320, GUI Construction with Java Foundation Classes, and SL-301, Distributed Programming with Java Technology, which treats RMI in detail.

Formalities of the Exam

Taking the Developer exam is a process. Here's what you do:

1. Register. You can do this on the Web at www.sun.com/training/certification/java. Be prepared to pay $250. You'll be given instructions on how to do the other steps.

2. Download the assignment. This consists of an HTML file and a data file. The HTML file describes an application that you are to write. The application reads and writes the data file.

3. Write the application. No rush. You have a year.

4. Submit your work.

5. Take an essay exam. This happens at a testing center, like the Programmer exam. The cost was included in your fee.

6. Wait for your results. Be patient. All work is assessed in detail, and sometimes there are backlogs. You'll get your results within 30 days of taking the exam.

Of course, from your point of view the most important part is developing the application. Most of the rest of this chapter is devoted to telling you about the assignment...in as much detail as Sun will allow us.

The Project Assignment

The most important thing for you to know is that there are lots of ways to fail the Developer exam. One way, of course, is to submit poor work so that your total score is below the minimum passing grade. The other ways are easily avoidable, though for some reason some people tragically don't avoid them. These can be summed up by the saying, "Must means must." There are numerous places in the assignment specs that say, "You must...." Your spec will explain that if you don't do exactly whatever it is you're told you must do, you will fail. For example, you will receive specific instructions regarding the directory tree that you submit, including the location and name of the directory containing your source code. If your source code isn't exactly where it's supposed to be, you'll fail. It won't matter if your application is so great that it glows in the dark, because the assessor won't run your application. Assessment of your project ends the moment any violation of any "must" specifications is detected. So remember...must means must.

The next most important thing for you to know about the assignment is that your spec comes from a large pool of documents. Sun created this pool of specs in order to ensure that collaboration is likely to lower your grade. If you borrow code from someone else, that code probably implements the wrong assignment. Since you are graded on how well you implement your own spec, collaboration most likely will have a disastrous effect on your score. Resist the temptation to use someone else's work; instead, get good enough that you can pass all on your own.

There is a common structure to all the specs in the pool. No matter which assignment you get, your project will consist of three parts:

-   A GUI front end, called the "client"
-   A server back end, accessing a data file that is provided to you
-   Communication between the client and the server

Your finished project will look like Figure 10.1.

The client must be built from Swing components. Chapter 11, "Swing Components," and Chapter 12, "Layout Managers," discuss what you need to know to create your front end. Earlier in this book Chapter 9, "I/O and Streams," discussed file access, which will be at the heart of your server. Your client and server will communicate via your choice of object streams or RMI. You read about object streams in Chapter 9; Chapter 13, "Networking," explains using object streams for your network communication and introduces RMI. Be aware that RMI is a huge topic, and it would take a thick book to cover it fully.

FIGURE 10.1   The assignment

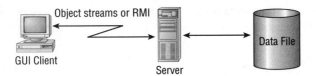

Object streams or RMI

GUI Client

Server

Data File

In addition to all the programming you have to do, you will be required to submit API pages for your classes, created using Javadoc. Chapter 14, "Putting It All Together," covers several miscellaneous topics, including the Javadoc tool.

Before we dive into the technical information of the next four chapters, let's look at the follow-up essay exam and the grading process.

The Essay Exam

The follow-up essay exam requires you to do something you might not have done for a very long time: write essays. Like the assignment specs, the essay topics are selected from a pool, so you'll probably get different essay questions from the ones your colleagues get.

Did you hate writing essays in high school? Do you believe that one of the benefits of graduating from high school is a lifetime of freedom from writing any more of them? Don't panic! And if English isn't your native language, please don't worry. You won't be graded on spelling or grammar style. You don't have to worry about organization, because the essay topics are very narrow, and there won't be very much information for you to organize. You can't go wrong if you keep in mind what it is that the assessors want to see in your essays.

The assessors want to see two things. First, of course, they want to make sure you know the information you are being asked about. Second, they want confirmation that you, having walked into a testing center and shown a photo ID, are really the person who submitted a project under your name. (Remember, you take the follow-up exam *after* submitting your project.) There is no way to prevent you from paying someone else to write your project, but people who do so are likely to be unfamiliar with the details of the project. Some of the essays questions ask you to briefly describe certain design choices that you made. For example, you know that for your client/server communication, you may choose either object streams or RMI. In the follow-up exam, you might be asked to write an essay describing which protocol you chose and why. Of course, the "why" part is a test of your technical knowledge. The "which" part is an honesty test. Nobody in their right mind could possibly implement RMI communication and then accidentally say they used object streams. Equally, nobody would use object streams and then say they used RMI. If your answer to any "describe how your project does such-and-such" question doesn't match your actual project, you automatically fail.

The essay questions don't require you to do any unreasonable memorization. For example, you won't be asked to list the names of all the custom exception classes you created. You'll only be asked to write about implementations details that would stick in your mind because you took the time to implement them. To be safe, consider reviewing your source code the day before you take the follow-up exam.

Grading

Grading of your exam begins when you complete the essay exam. Your essays and your project submission are sent to an assessor, along with information about which project spec was assigned to you.

Your project is to be submitted as a single jar file archive. The examiner begins by extracting this archive and making sure that you have provided the required files (source, class, data, and documentation) and that these files are in the required directory locations within the archive. If anything is missing or in the wrong place, your project fails. As with any automatic failure criterion (these are the "must means must" criteria in your project spec), if you fail, then the assessor immediately stops assessing your project. Misplaced files are the most tragic way to fail the Developer exam.

Next, the assessor reads the essays that you wrote for the follow-up exam. If your project doesn't match the description in the essays, you get a failing grade.

Now the deduction phase of grading begins. You are initially given a perfect score of 400 points. As the assessors find problems with your project, they deduct points according to some very extensive and specific guidelines. Sun recognizes that grading the Developer exam requires assessors to make judgments about the quality of various parts of your work. Every effort has been made to make the deductions as objective as possible.

During the deduction phase, the assessor executes your application, reads your source code, and inspects your Javadoc API pages. This happens in no particular order. When it's done, if your score is 320 or better you pass.

We can't tell you what the deductions are; Sun rightly keeps that information proprietary. However, we can tell you that the deductions fall into seven broad categories, which in turn have sub- and sub-sub-categories:

General Considerations   Covers miscellaneous factors such as readability and maintainability of your source code. These are reviewed in Chapter 14.

Documentation   Covers your source-code comments and your Javadoc pages. You'll get some guidelines in Chapter 14.

Object-Oriented Design   Covers your knowledge of Java's object-oriented facilities, as well as your ability to use them well. The object-oriented facilities were presented in Chapter 6. You'll get some general programming suggestions in Chapter 14.

GUI   Covers the appearance, behavior, and ease-of-use of your GUI. We look at GUIs in Chapters 10 and 11.

Locking   This refers to the safety and efficiency of your multithreaded code. Your server must be capable of handling multiple client connections, so you will be using the thread concepts you learned in Chapter 7, "Threads." Chapter 14 will provide some advanced information about threads.

Data Store   Data Store and Network Server together refer to your server code. Data Store is the code that interacts with the data file. File issues were covered in Chapter 9.

Network Server   This is the code that interacts with the client, and it is discussed in Chapter 13.

The deduction system has an interesting consequence. It doesn't provide a way to account for extra credit. This is deliberate on Sun's part. It's important in any performance exam to keep grading as uniform as possible. Extra credit work is, by its nature, work that goes beyond the restrictions of the assignment. It's impossible to anticipate all the different creative ways people can do this, so it's impossible to develop fair scoring criteria for extra credit work.

So you can't gain points for extra work. However, and this is very important, you can *lose* points for extra work. For example, you might create a class that sends the user an e-mail message every time the server executes a transaction. That sort of thing is definitely above and beyond the requirements of any of the specs in the pool. If you neglect to create a Javadoc page for the extra class, or if the source is difficult to understand, you'll lose points just as you would for a required class. If you do extra credit work, the best you can do is break even.

Since the details of the scoring sub-categories and sub-sub-categories are a secret, you don't get much information with your score. If you pass, you are told your total score, plus a breakdown of your score in each of the seven categories (general considerations, documentation, object-oriented design, GUI, locking, data store, and network server). If you don't pass, you'll also receive a brief note that explains in general terms the area in which you lost the most points. This explanation will be more specific than just the name of the category…you could figure that out from the category score breakdown. Hopefully the explanation will be enough to direct you to the part of your code that needs attention, so that you can do some fixing and then resubmit your project. However, Sun obviously can't be too specific about what you need to do, since that would be telling you how to pass.

Rather than worry about what happens if you fail, assume you have what it takes to learn all you need in order to pass. Read on!

Chapter

11

Swing Components

 Two topics on the Developer's Exam are so extensive that they cannot possibly be fully explained in a single chapter, or even several chapters. These topics are Swing, which is discussed in this chapter and in Chapter 12, "Layout Managers," and RMI, which is discussed in Chapter 13, "Object Streams and RMI." The goal of this book is to give you a solid conceptual foundation in Swing and RMI, without exhaustively presenting those topics. Later, perhaps when you have downloaded your assignment, you will probably find it useful to read some single-topic books to help you develop your GUI and your network communication.

Our Swing foundation takes up two chapters. In this chapter you'll look at the most common Swing components, one by one. In the next chapter, you'll learn about using layout managers to create a unified GUI whose components have appropriate sizes and locations.

This chapter begins with a strategy for approaching your GUI design. Then you'll learn about some methods that are common to all Swing component classes. After that we'll examine container, button, text, and menu components. We'll finish with the two most complex Swing component types: `JTable` and `JTree`.

A Strategy for Designing the GUI

There's no need to worry if you don't have much experience in creating GUIs. The Developer's Exam recognizes that there are lots of ways to put together a graphical interface. There is no one "correct" GUI. You will not be graded on your talents as a graphics designer. Moreover, you are not expected to have mastered all the conventions and principles that are second nature to an experienced, full-time GUI programmer. Even if you have no GUI development experience at all, you can't go very wrong by applying common sense. The worst that can happen is that you might lose some points. A submission with a poor GUI that does well in other areas is very likely to pass.

The next four sections present a simple four-step approach to help you organize your GUI thinking. The four steps are

1. Identify needed components.

2. Isolate regions of behavior.

3. Sketch the GUI.

4. Choose layout managers.

Let's look at these steps in detail.

Step 1: Identify Needed Components

Before you think about what your GUI will *look like*, it's important to think about what it will *do*. Swing's various component classes are designed to support a range of functionality, and there is little functional overlap. Usually there is exactly one component that is the appropriate choice for providing any desired behavior; any other component would be not just less convenient, but wildly inappropriate.

For example, suppose you want to create a GUI that lets users specify a flavor of ice cream. The flavor can be chocolate, vanilla, or strawberry. Swing's combo box component (supported by the `javax.swing.JComboBox` class) is ideal. Of course, you could use a text field instead and require users to type in the desired flavor, but that approach would have two huge disadvantages. First, your users would have no way of knowing which flavors were available; they would just have to remember them. Second, users would have to spell each flavor correctly. So the choice of a text field rather than a combo box isn't just inferior, it's spectacularly bad.

This chapter presents most of Swing's component classes. As you read their descriptions, think about the situations for which each class would be appropriate.

Step 2: Isolate Regions of Behavior

Often it takes several components to support a single task. For example, consider the components of a text-processing GUI that support selection of a font. A font is determined by a family, a style, and a size. So a GUI for choosing a font would require three combo boxes, as well as some kind of "make it so" button.

After you decide which components to use, you need to group those components into regions of behavior. A good rule of thumb is that if components are functionally related, they should also be visually related (that is, close to one another). So the combo boxes and the "make it so" button of our font example should be close to one another. (Other rules of thumb are presented in Chapter 14, "Putting It All Together.")

Some regions of behavior might contain only a single component; others might contain many. When you figure out which components should be visually related (and not before!), you are ready to sketch your GUI.

Step 3: Sketch the GUI

At this point you know what components will appear in your GUI, and you know which of those components should appear near one another to form functional groups. You are now ready to make a preliminary sketch. There is more to this than meets the eye.

Figure 11.1 shows a sketch for a simple mail-reader GUI. The interface requires an area where you can review your directory tree of sorted mail in folders; this has been placed to the left. An area at the bottom of the frame will display status messages on the current attempt to send or retrieve mail. A dynamic display area for the list of pending incoming mail is located to the right of the tree structure and on top of another dynamic area that displays the current mail item.

FIGURE 11.1 Mail client window

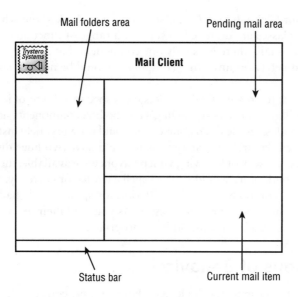

Figure 11.1 is incomplete. A GUI sketch must do more than show the sizes and locations of components. The sketch must also show how component geometry changes when the GUI is resized. This is very important, because some components or regions should be allowed to grow horizontally but prevented from growing vertically. Others should be allowed to grow vertically but prevented from growing horizontally. Still others should be allowed to grow freely both horizontally and vertically, and some components should never change size. And no matter how a GUI's components change size, their spatial relationships with one another should always make sense.

Fortunately, Java's layout managers take care of most of the tedium of enforcing resizing policies. Layout managers are essential to building a useful GUI, and they are a broad enough topic that they deserve their own chapter (Chapter 12). For now, be aware that it's not enough to sketch a static picture of your intended GUI; you have to think about how the GUI should react to resizing.

To continue our example, let's think about what should happen to the components of Figure 11.1, when a user resizes the main window as shown in Figure 11.2.

We need to consider the fate of each of the four screen regions: the folders area along the left edge, the status bar along the bottom, and the unread-mail and current-mail regions.

We can assume that the folders area is just as wide as it needs to be. When the window resizes, the folders area should not become wider or narrower. However, it should always grow vertically.

The status bar, on the other hand, is just as tall as it needs to be (that is, tall enough to display a few lines of text). When the window resizes, the status bar should not become taller or shorter. However, it should always grow horizontally, so as to fill the entire width of the window.

The unread-mail and current-mail regions are stacked one on top of the other. When the window becomes wider or narrower, these regions should grow or shrink horizontally. (Remember, the folders area does *not* become wider or narrower, and that horizontal space has to go somewhere.) What about vertical resizing? There are several ways to go. One simple approach is to assume that the (upper) unread-mail region is just as tall as it needs to be, so when the window resizes vertically the extra space should be allocated to the (lower) current-mail region.

Of course, there are other ways to allocate growth. The important thing is to consider your users' intentions or desires when they resize a window. Which functional region do they want to cause to grow or shrink? Usually there is one work area on which the user's attention will be concentrated. In our example we assumed this would be the current-mail region. This region should grow or shrink in both directions.

The next chapter will explain how to implement resizing behavior. For now, let's look at the Swing components.

FIGURE 11.2   Mail client window resized

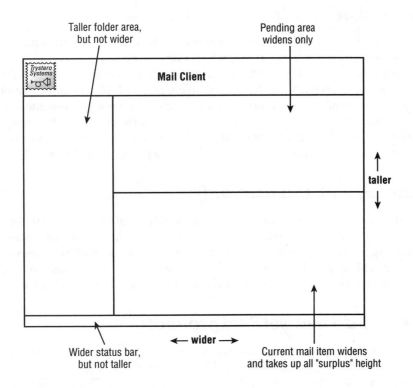

Step 4: Choose Layout Managers

Layout managers are objects that manage the size and location of components. In Java you don't directly program component geometry; you choose a layout manager and let it take care of the details.

Layout managers are discussed in detail in Chapter 12, so for now let's just say that the work of designing a GUI includes deciding how to use layout managers.

Common Swing Methods

Some properties are common to nearly all component types. These include size, location, foreground and background color, font, and enabled state. The methods that support these properties are described in the following sections. AWT programmers will recognize these methods from the `java.awt.Component` class, because the Swing components inherit from `java.awt.Component`.

getSize() and setSize()

The `getSize()` method returns the size of a component. The return type is `Dimension`, which has public data members `height` and `width`, whose units are pixels.

The `setSize()` method takes two `int` arguments: `width` and `height`; an overloaded form takes a single `Dimension` object. If you have tried calling this method, you know that doing so is usually futile. A layout manager generally overrides the size and position you attempt to give a component. In fact, the `setSize()` method exists mostly for the use of layout managers. The major exceptions to this rule are the `JFrame` and `JDialog` classes, which are not under the thumb of a layout manager and are perfectly willing to have you set their size or bounds.

getLocation() and setLocation()

These methods access and set the location of a component in pixel units relative to the top-left corner of the component. The return type of `getLocation()` is `Point`. The `setLocation()` method's argument list requires either width and height `int`s or a single `Point` object.

Calling `setLocation()` is like calling `setSize()`: usually a layout manager overrides the location you try to set, but you can always set the location of a `JFrame` or `JDialog`.

setForeground() and setBackground()

These methods set a component's foreground and background color. The argument is an instance of `java.awt.Color`. The foreground color is used for rendering the component's decorations and text label (if the component uses any text). The background color is used for rendering the component's background.

setFont()

The setFont() method dictates which font a component will use for rendering any text it might display. The setFont() method takes one argument of type Font whose constructor takes three arguments: a font family, a style, and a size. The family is a string. Different platforms offer different fonts, but you can always count on "Serif", "SansSerif", and "Monospaced" a fixed-width font such as Courier). The style may be Font.PLAIN, Font.BOLD, Font.ITALIC, or the bitwise combination Font.BOLD|Font.ITALIC. The size argument defines the point size of the font.

setEnabled()

The setEnabled() method determines whether a component may respond to user input. The method takes a single **boolean** argument. A disabled component changes its appearance to a slightly grayed-out look. A component should be disabled if the application is in a state that cannot accept input from the component.

Disabling is preferable to the two commonly seen alternatives:

- Leave the component enabled. When the user uses the component, display some sort of "unavailable" message.

- Remove unusable components from the screen until they become usable, thus creating a visually unstable control area.

Judicious use of setEnabled() calls helps create a GUI that clearly reflects the application's state to the user.

Basic Swing Components

The Swing component classes can be found in the javax.swing package. The component class names all begin with the letter J. The remainder of the class name is the name of the component, with each word starting with a capital letter. For example, a scroll bar is represented by the javax.swing.JScrollBar class.

Swing components cannot be combined with AWT components. However, certain non-component AWT classes are essential to Swing. All Swing components are subclasses of java.awt.Container, and most of them emit events from the java.awt.event package. In addition, all the AWT layout managers work perfectly well with Swing components.

One way to approach the daunting number of components is to divide them into three categories:

- Container components

- Ordinary components

- Menu components

Let's begin by looking at the container components.

Container Components

Container components are components that can contain other components (including other containers). Containers use layout managers to determine the size and position of their child components. The code examples in this chapter all use the very basic FlowLayout manager. If you are unfamiliar with this class, for now just be aware that it arranges contained components in an evenly spaced row.

The container components that we will cover here are

- JFrame
- JPanel

JFrame

A JFrame is an independent window that can be moved around on the screen independently of any other GUI windows. Any application that requires a GUI must use one or more frames to contain the desired components. The following code displays an empty JFrame:

```
1. import javax.swing.*;
2.
3. public class FrameDemo {
4.   public static void main(String[] args) {
5.     JFrame f = new JFrame("Frame Demo");
6.     f.setSize(350, 250);
7.     f.setVisible(true);
8.   }
9. }
```

Line 5 demonstrates a constructor whose argument is a string that is to appear in the frame's banner. Line 6 is necessary because a newly constructed JFrame has zero width and zero height and must be given a nonzero size before it can be seen. You can set the size explicitly, as in line 6, or you can call the pack() method, which sizes the frame to fit the preferred sizes and layouts of its contained components. Line 7 is necessary because a newly constructed JFrame is not visible on the screen. If, at some point, you want to remove a visible frame from the screen, you can call setVisible(false).

Figure 11.3 shows the frame created by this application.

Of course, an empty frame is not very useful. Frames are intended to be populated with child components. Readers familiar with Java's AWT know that the AWT frame implementation (the java.awt.Frame class) is a container to which child components can be directly added. The JFrame class is different in that it is not a container. You access the container portion of the frame by calling the JFrame's getContentPane() method. The following application displays a frame whose content pane contains three buttons. (In order to demonstrate the content pane, we have to get a bit ahead of ourselves by using a layout manager and the JButton class. We will explain these soon.)

```
1.  import java.awt.*;
2.  import javax.swing.*;
3.
4.  public class ContentDemo {
5.    public static void main(String[] args) {
6.      JFrame f = new JFrame("Content Pane Demo");
7.      f.setSize(350, 250);
8.      Container cont = f.getContentPane();
9.      cont.setLayout(new FlowLayout());
10.     for (int i=1; i<=3; i++)
11.       cont.add(new JButton("Button #" + i));
12.     f.setVisible(true);
13.   }
14. }
```

FIGURE 11.3   An empty *JFrame*

FIGURE 11.4   Using a *JFrame's* content pane

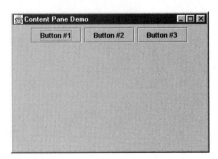

Note line 9, which sets a layout manager for the content pane rather than for the frame, and line 11, which adds buttons to the content pane rather than to the frame. Figure 11.4 shows the result of running this application.

JFrame emits Window events to notify listeners when the frame iconifies, de-iconifies, is first displayed, and so on. Clicking a frame's "close" button (the X button in the upper-right corner on a Windows platform) does not automatically cause the frame to close. Instead, the click invokes the windowClosing() method to all of the frame's Window listeners. One listener must explicitly remove the frame from the screen; otherwise the user's click will have no effect.

JPanel

A JPanel is a blank rectangular component that can contain other components. Each panel uses a layout manager to determine the position and size of its child components. The following application adds two panels to a frame. Each panel contains three buttons. For better visibility, the upper panel is light gray and the lower panel is white. The application uses a Grid layout manager, which is covered in detail in the next chapter:

```
import java.awt.*;
import javax.swing.*;
public class PanelDemo {
  public static void main(String[] args) {
    JFrame f = new JFrame("Content Pane Demo");
    f.setSize(350, 250);
    Container cont = f.getContentPane();
    cont.setLayout(new GridLayout(2,1));
    for (int i=0; i<2; i++) {
      JPanel pan = new JPanel();
      pan.setBackground(i==0 ? Color.lightGray : Color.white);
      for (int j=0; j<3; j++)
        pan.add(new JButton("Button"));
      cont.add(pan);
    }
    f.setVisible(true);
  }
}
```

Figure 11.5 shows this application's frame.

FIGURE 11.5   *JPanel* example

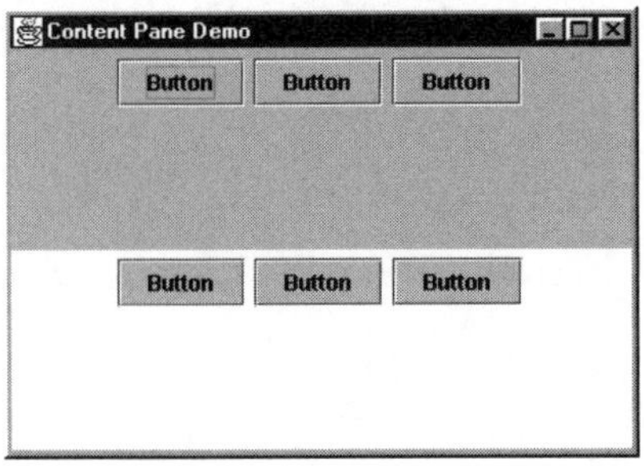

JPanels do not emit any important events.

Ordinary Components

In this section, we'll discuss eight *ordinary components*. They are ordinary in the sense that they are the components in which the user directly inputs data, in contrast to containers. We will review the following component types:

- JLabel
- JButton
- JCheckBox
- JRadioButton
- JScrollBar
- JTextField
- JTextArea
- JComboBox

JLabel

The simplest component type is the JLabel, which displays a single line of text and/or an image. JLabels do not respond to user input and do not emit events. The following application displays a label in a frame, as shown in Figure 11.6.

```
import java.awt.*;
import javax.swing.*;
```

```java
public class LabelDemo {
  public static void main(String[] args) {
    JFrame f = new JFrame("Label Demo");
    f.setSize(350, 250);
    Container cont = f.getContentPane();
    cont.setLayout(new FlowLayout());
    cont.add(new Label("This is a JLabel"));
    f.setVisible(true);
  }
}
```

FIGURE 11.6   *JLabel* example

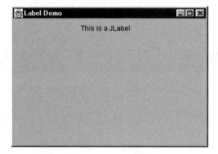

JButton

The JButton class implements a simple pushbutton. The button can display a text label, an icon, or both. When the user clicks the button, Action events are sent to all registered Action listeners.

The following application builds a frame that contains two buttons:

```java
import java.awt.*;
import java.awt.event.*;
import javax.swing.*;

public class ButtonDemo extends JFrame {
  private JButton helloBtn, goodbyeBtn;

  public static void main(String[] args) {
    (new ButtonDemo()).setVisible(true);
  }

  ButtonDemo() {
    super("Button Demo");
```

```
    setSize(350, 250);
    Container cont = getContentPane();
    cont.setLayout(new FlowLayout());
    helloBtn = new JButton("Hello");
    goodbyeBtn = new JButton("Goodbye");
    cont.add(helloBtn);
    cont.add(goodbyeBtn);
    ButtonListener listener = new ButtonListener();
    helloBtn.addActionListener(listener);
    goodbyeBtn.addActionListener(listener);
  }

  class ButtonListener implements ActionListener {
    public void actionPerformed(ActionEvent e) {
        if (e.getSource() == helloBtn)      // Which
          System.out.println("Hello");      // button
        else                                // was
          System.out.println("Goodbye");    // pushed?
    }
  }
}
```

JButtons send Action events. The ActionListener interface contains only one method:
public void actionPerformed(ActionEvent). This example creates a single Action listener
and registers it with each of two buttons. Note the convenience of defining ButtonListener as
an inner class. Its functionality is isolated, but it can still access the helloBtn private variable
of the creating instance of the enclosing class. This makes it easy for the listener to determine
which button was pressed.

Figure 11.7 shows the output of this application.

FIGURE 11.7   *JButton* example

JCheckBox

The JCheckBox class implements a check box that can be selected and deselected. The following code creates a frame that contains two check boxes:

```java
import java.awt.*;
import javax.swing.*;

public class CheckBoxDemo {
  public static void main(String[] args) {
    JFrame frame = new JFrame("CheckBox Demo");
    frame.setSize(350, 250);
    Container cont = frame.getContentPane();
    cont.setLayout(new FlowLayout());
    cont.add(new JCheckBox("Charge my acct"));
    cont.add(new JCheckBox("Gift wrap"));
    cont.add(new JButton("Submit"));
    frame.setVisible(true);
  }
}
```

This application does not register any listeners with the check boxes, even though the JCheckBox class emits Action and Item events; it is usually unnecessary or inappropriate to catch check-box events. Usually check boxes are used to input a number of binary options, which are later submitted to the application using a button. The example application shows two check boxes that might appear in the GUI for any online shopping application. The user decides whether to charge the order to an account and whether the order should be gift-wrapped. After these decisions have been made, the user clicks the Submit button to indicate that the application should process the order. In general, the actionPerformed() method of some button will read the state of a GUI's check boxes.

Figure 11.8 shows the GUI built by this application.

FIGURE 11.8   *JCheckBox* example

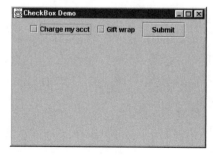

JRadioButton

Radio buttons are typically used in groups to present exclusive selection. The name comes from the station buttons of older car radios: at any moment, exactly one button is pushed in, and pushing in a new button causes the old button to pop out. The JRadioButton class is generally used with the ButtonGroup class, which has an add(AbstractButton) method. When a radio button is selected, any other button in the same button group is automatically deselected.

The following application creates three radio buttons:

```
1.  import java.awt.*;
2.  import javax.swing.*;
3.
4.  public class RadioDemo {
5.
6.    public static void main(String[] args) {
7.        JFrame frame = new JFrame("Radio Demo");
8.        frame.setSize(350, 250);
9.        Container cont = frame.getContentPane();
10.       cont.setLayout(new FlowLayout());
11.       ButtonGroup btnGroup = new ButtonGroup();
12.       JRadioButton rbtn = new JRadioButton("Rare", true);
13.       btnGroup.add(rbtn);
14.       cont.add(rbtn);
15.       rbtn = new JRadioButton("Medium");
16.       btnGroup.add(rbtn);
17.       cont.add(rbtn);
18.       rbtn = new JRadioButton("Well Done");
19.       btnGroup.add(rbtn);
20.       cont.add(rbtn);
21.       frame.setVisible(true);
22.    }
23. }
```

Figure 11.9 shows this application's GUI. Because the three radio buttons are added to a button group (lines 13, 16, and 19), they exhibit radio behavior: Selecting one of them causes the previously selected one to become deselected.

Radio buttons, like check boxes, can send Action and Item events. However, as with check boxes, listening for these events is generally not appropriate. A group of radio buttons is often found near an Apply button; the appropriate approach is to read the state of the radio buttons when the user clicks Apply.

FIGURE 11.9   *JRadioButton* example

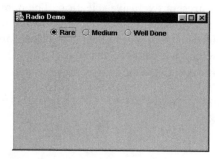

JScrollBar

A `JScrollBar` is a component that lets the user enter an adjustable pseudo-analog value. Scroll bars can be oriented horizontally or vertically; the constants `JScrollBar.HORIZONTAL` and `JScrollBar.VERTICAL` can be passed into various constructor forms to determine orientation.

The following application creates one horizontal scroll bar. The simple Flow layout manager that we have used so far in this chapter does not do a very good job of displaying scroll bars, so we will use the more sophisticated Border layout manager. If you are not familiar with it, stay tuned until Chapter 12:

```java
import java.awt.*;
import java.awt.event.*;
import javax.swing.*;

public class ScrollBarDemo extends JFrame {
  public static void main(String[] args) {
    (new ScrollBarDemo()).setVisible(true);
  }
  ScrollBarDemo() {
    super("Scroll Bar Demo");
    setSize(350, 250);
    Container cont = getContentPane();
    JScrollBar sbar = new JScrollBar(JScrollBar.HORIZONTAL);
    cont.add(sbar, BorderLayout.NORTH);
    BarListener listener = new BarListener();
    sbar.addAdjustmentListener(listener);
  }
```

```
class BarListener implements AdjustmentListener {
    public void adjustmentValueChanged(AdjustmentEvent e) {
        System.out.println("Val = " + e.getValue());
    }
  }
}
```

Scroll bars send `Adjustment` events to registered `Adjustment` listeners. In this example, the listener is an instance of the `BarListener` inner class.

The `ScrollBarDemo` application produces the GUI shown in Figure 11.10.

FIGURE 11.10   *JScrollBar* example

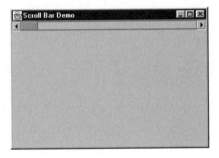

JTextField and JTextArea

The `JTextField` and `JTextArea` components support single-line and multiline text entry. Both classes extend `javax.swing.text.JTextComponent`, which provides methods for accessing and modifying the component's text. The API page for `JTextComponent` includes a good description of text functionality.

Both `JTextField` and `JTextArea` send `Key` events when they receive keyboard input. In addition, `JTextField` sends `Action` events when the user presses Enter. The following application contains one of each component; the `JTextArea` displays information about events in the `JTextField`. Once again, the Flow layout manager is inappropriate for the components we want to demonstrate, so we use a Border layout manager:

```
import java.awt.*;
import java.awt.event.*;
import javax.swing.*;

public class TextDemo extends JFrame
    implements ActionListener, KeyListener {
    private JTextField    field;
```

```
private JTextArea     area;
public static void main(String[] args) {
  (new TextDemo()).setVisible(true);
}

TextDemo() {
  super("TextDemo");
  setSize(350, 250);
  Container cont = getContentPane();
  field = new JTextField("Type here");
  field.addKeyListener(this);
  field.addActionListener(this);
  cont.add(field, BorderLayout.NORTH);
  area = new JTextArea();
  cont.add(area, BorderLayout.CENTER);
}

public void keyPressed(KeyEvent e)  { }
public void keyReleased(KeyEvent e) { }
public void keyTyped(KeyEvent e) {
  area.append("KEY: " + e.getKeyChar() + '
}

public void actionPerformed(ActionEvent e) {
  area.append("ACTION: " + field.getText() + '
  }
}
```

Figure 11.11 shows this application's frame after several keystrokes have been typed into the JTextField.

FIGURE 11.11   *JTextField and JTextArea example*

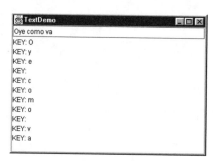

JComboBox

The JComboBox component combines the functionality of a text field and a drop-down list. With a JComboBox, you can present users with a preset list of options while giving them the alternative of entering an option that does not appear on the list. This component emits Action events when the user presses the Enter key and Item events when the user selects a preset item.

The following application displays a simple JComboBox:

```
1.  import java.awt.*;
2.  import javax.swing.*;
3.
4.  public class ComboDemo extends JFrame {
5.    public static void main(String[] args) {
6.      (new ComboDemo()).setVisible(true);
7.    }
8.
9.    ComboDemo() {
10.     super("ComboDemo");
11.     setSize(350, 250);
12.     Container cont = getContentPane();
13.     cont.setLayout(new FlowLayout());
14.     String[] initialVals = {"Dragon", "Ghost", "Unicorn"};
15.     JComboBox combo = new JComboBox(initialVals);
16.     combo.setEditable(true);
17.     cont.add(combo);
18.   }
19. }
```

Note line 16, which calls setEditable() on the combo box. Without this call, the component does not support typing but just implements a simple drop-down list. Figure 11.12 shows this application's GUI. Note that the figure shows the value "Centaur," which has been typed in by the user.

FIGURE 11.12   *JComboBox example*

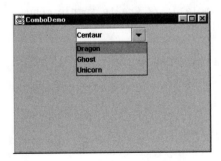

Menu Components

Menu components allow the programmer to organize Swing components in menus instead of placing all the components in the user's view. The JMenuBar component implements a menu bar that occupies the top portion of a JFrame and can contain drop-down menus. To insert a JMenuBar into a JFrame, call setJMenuBar(theMenuBar) on the JFrame.

To populate a menu bar, construct a number of instances of JMenu and install them in the menu bar by calling theMenuBar.add(theMenu). The JMenu constructor takes as an argument the string that will appear on the menu bar.

The menus in a menu bar must themselves be populated with menu items. The most common type of menu item is the JMenuItem, which is a simple text item. You can also add separators, check boxes, radio buttons, and submenus to a menu. If you want check boxes or radio buttons, however, don't use JCheckBox or JRadioButton—instead use the JCheckBoxMenuItem and JRadioButtonMenuItem classes.

The following application creates two menus, populates them, and installs them into a menu bar. The second menu contains a plain menu item, a separator, a check box item, two radio items, and a submenu:

```
1. import java.awt.*;
2. import javax.swing.*;
3.
4. public class MenuDemo {
5.
6.   public static void main(String[] args) {
7.     JFrame frame = new JFrame("Menu");
8.
9.     JMenuBar mbar = new JMenuBar();          // Create menu bar
10.
11.    JMenu fileMenu = new JMenu("File");       // Create file menu
12.    fileMenu.add(new JMenuItem("New"));
13.    fileMenu.add(new JMenuItem("Exit"));
14.    mbar.add(fileMenu);
15.
16.    JMenu sampleMenu = new JMenu("Sample"); // Create sample menu
17.    sampleMenu.add(new JMenuItem("Plain"));
18.    sampleMenu.insertSeparator(1);
19.    sampleMenu.add(new JCheckBoxMenuItem("Check"));
20.    ButtonGroup group = new ButtonGroup();
21.    JRadioButtonMenuItem radioMI;
22.    for (int i=0; i<2; i++) {
23.      radioMI = new JRadioButtonMenuItem("Radio" + i);
24.      group.add(radioMI);
```

```
25.        sampleMenu.add(radioMI);
26.      }
27.      JMenu subMenu = new JMenu("SubOptions");
28.      subMenu.add(new JMenuItem("AAA"));
29.      subMenu.add(new JMenuItem("BBB"));
30.      subMenu.add(new JMenuItem("CCC"));
31.      sampleMenu.add(subMenu);
32.      mbar.add(sampleMenu);
33.
34.      frame.setJMenuBar(mbar);                // Install menu bar
35.      frame.setSize(350, 250);
36.      frame.setVisible(true);
37.    }
38. }
```

Note the ButtonGroup that is created at line 20. This class can accommodate both radio buttons and radio button menu items.

Figure 11.13 shows this application's GUI.

FIGURE 11.13   Menu example

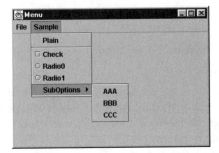

JTable

A first glance at javax.swing.JTable is overwhelming: the description is *huge*. A second glance is worse: numerous obscure event classes and listener interfaces are involved in ways that are not clear at all from reading the API page.

Fortunately, most of the methods never need to be called, and most of the events are just for the class' internal parts to communicate with one another. Still, you need a way to understand which parts of the class can sensibly be manipulated. The way to really understand JTable is to understand the *Model-View-Controller* design pattern.

You may already have come across the term Model-View-Controller (MVC) in other contexts: it's a standard pattern and has been around for a long time. Unfortunately, its exact meaning depends on whose book you're reading. For the purpose of understanding JTable, it's important to know what MVC means to the designers of Swing.

In Swing, a component's *model* is the data that the component presents to a user. A text field's model is the text it contains. A combo box's model is the list of values it displays when pulled down. The Swing components we have studied so far have all had simple models, so it hasn't been necessary to discuss them. (But if you check the APIs, you'll see that some of these components have methods called getModel(), indicating the presence of a model lurking somewhere inside the class.)

In Swing, a component's *view* is the region of the screen dedicated to displaying the current state of the model, plus the software that supports displaying the model. So a view consists of code and pixels. A component's *controller* is the region of the screen dedicated to modifying the state of the model, along with the software that supports this activity. So a controller also consists of code and pixels. Sometimes a view and a controller share pixels. For example, in any text component, the screen region where the component displays its model's text is the same region where the user enters new text.

This book isn't going to tell you everything about JTable—there's too much to tell. Here you'll get enough of the basics to get you through your exam project. We'll start by saying that when you use a JTable, you get to choose the level of complexity on which you will operate. Broadly speaking, the levels available to you are these:

1. Use only the methods of the JTable class. Use the standard table model.
2. Create your own table model class by extending AbstractTableModel.
3. Create your own table model class by implementing TableModel.
4. Create your own renderer and editor classes.

Level 1 is the simplest way to use a JTable. You don't get a lot of control. The table's appearance is standard. You can change the model by calling the table's setValueAt() method, whose arguments are a row number, a column number, and a value. Operating at this level is fine for many applications that just need to display data, but many programmers prefer the additional flexibility (with small additional cost) of level 2.

At level 2, you control the table's contents by extending the javax.swing.table.AbstractTableModel class. The abstract class provides all the glue that connects the model to its view and controller; all you need to do is implement a few simple methods to control the model's data. We'll look at how to do this in a moment, but first let's look at levels 3 and 4.

Most people use the level 3 approach by mistake. They see that JTable has a number of methods (as well as a constructor) that require a TableModel, so they go ahead and implement that interface. This is usually unnecessary work. TableModel defines methods for maintaining the model's data and for communicating with the table's other parts. The javax.swing.table.AbstractTableModel class implements TableModel, providing perfectly good methods for handling the internal communication. If you stick to level 2, you don't have to reinvent code; you just have to implement the functionality that is unique to your application. Occasionally situations may call for the level 3 approach, but the Developer's Exam isn't one of those situations.

On level 4 you modify the table's view and controller. Swing uses the term *renderer* to refer to code that implements view functionality and the term *editor* to refer to code that implements controller functionality. If you check out the API page for the javax.swing.table package, you'll find interfaces called TableCellEditor and TableCellRenderer. Level 4 is beyond the scope of this book and beyond what you'll need for your exam assignment.

Let's get back to level 2, where you subclass AbstractTableModel. This class contains three abstract methods, so to create your own model class you need only implement three methods:

- public int getRowCount()
- public int getColumnCount()
- public Object getValueAt(int rowNum, int colNum)

The first two methods return the number of rows and columns in the table. The getValueAt() method does the real work of supplying data. Simple model classes use two-dimensional arrays of strings to store values. Note, however, that the method's return type is Object, not String. In general, returned values will really be strings, but if they aren't then the table's view code will usually call their toString() method. Thus if it's more convenient to store data as instances of Integer or StringBuffer or some other class, you don't need to worry about converting to a string.

There are a few methods that the AbstractTableModel implements that you can easily override. These are

- public String getColumnName(int colNum)
- public boolean isCellEditable(int rowNum, int colNum)
- public void setValueAt(Object value, int rowNum, int colNum)

If you override getColumnName(), you can provide custom names for your table's columns. These names appear as column headers. Conveniently, column names stay in place when a table scrolls vertically. (We'll see how to make a scrolling table a little later on.)

By default, a table's cells are not editable. That is, if a uses clicks on a cell and starts typing, nothing happens. The table determines which cells may be editable by calling the model's isCellEditable() method. The version in AbstractTableModel always returns false. If you provide your own implementation, you can make editable any cells you like. Usually, an entire column is monolithically editable or not editable.

If you want to be able to change the model's data programmatically (versus by user typing), you can override setValueAt(). Doing this is very slightly fraught with danger. It is clear that your implementation of this method should modify the class' data. It isn't obvious that the method needs to do something extra. When the data changes, a model's obligation is to notify other parts of the component (certainly the view needs to know, and possibly the controller as well). JTable has a complicated mechanism for communication among its various parts. Fortunately, the complexity is handled by the AbstractTableModel class. (Another good reason for operating on level 2 and staying away from level 3!) All you need to do, after your setValueAt() code stores the new value, is to call fireTableCellUpdated(), passing in the row and column numbers of the changed cell. If you look at JTable's API page, you'll see that there are seven methods whose names begin with fire. Throughout Swing, such methods are used to support a component's internal communication. Usually you should stay away from them.

If a cell is editable, the model's `setValueAt()` method is called by when the user hits the Enter key (with keyboard input focused on the editable cell).

That's really all there is to creating your own model class. To create a table that uses a custom model, create an instance of the model class and pass it into the `JTable` constructor. Let's look at an example.

The following model class has a constructor whose argument is a set containing strings. The corresponding table has two columns. The first column contains the strings, sorted in alphabetical order. The second column contains the string lengths.

```
1. import java.util.*;
2. import javax.swing.*;
3. import javax.swing.table.*;
4.
5. public class StringLengthTableModel extends AbstractTableModel {
6.    private String[]    strings;
7.
8.    public StringLengthTableModel(String[] strings) {
9.      this.strings = strings;
10.   }
11.
12.   public int getRowCount() {
13.     return strings.length;
14.   }
15.
16.   public int getColumnCount() {
17.     return 2;
18.   }
19.
20.   public Object getValueAt(int row, int col) {
21.     if (col == 0)
22.       return strings[row];
23.     else
24.       return strings[row].length();
25.   }
26.
27.   public String getColumnName(int col) {
28.     return (col == 0)  ?  "String" : "Length";
29.   }
30.
```

```
31.    public static void main(String[] args) {
32.      JFrame frame = new JFrame();
33.      String[] strings = { "January", "February", "March",
34.                           "April", May", "June",
35.                           "July", "August", September",
36.                           "October", "November", "December" };
37.      StringLengthTableModel model =
38.        new StringLengthTableModel(strings);
39.      JTable table = new JTable(model);
40.      frame.getContentPane().add(table);
41.      frame.setSize(500, 250);
42.      frame.setVisible(true);
43.    }
44. }
```

On line 24, in getValueAt(), the return value is an int, which at first glance is not compatible with the return type, which is Object. Line 24 relies on boxing to convert the int to an instance of Integer.

Lines 37 and 38 construct an instance of the model. Line 39 constructs an instance of JTable that uses the new model. Figure 11.14 shows the result.

You can see that the model works, but the table's size and location in the window are a bit clumsy. That's okay. Chapter 12 will explain how to use layout managers to control the position and location of components.

Often a table contains more data than can fit in the available screen space. In these situations you can put the table inside a JScrollPane, which provides intelligent scrolling for the components it contains. Scrolling a table requires a bit of intelligence because when the user scrolls vertically, you want only the table's body to move; the column headers should stay put. Fortunately, JScrollPane knows what should and what should not scroll.

FIGURE 11.14   A *JTable* with a custom model

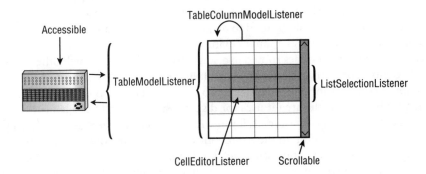

The JScrollPane constructor takes a single argument, which is the component to be scrolled. To change our code example to use a JScrollPane, just replace line 40 with the following:

```
JScrollPane sp = new JScrollPane(table);
getContentPane().add(sp);
```

Figure 11.15 shows the result, with the frame made sufficiently short to require insertion of a vertical scrollbar.

Figure 11.16 shows the same GUI, but scrolled to the bottom of the table.

FIGURE 11.15   A scrolling *JTable*

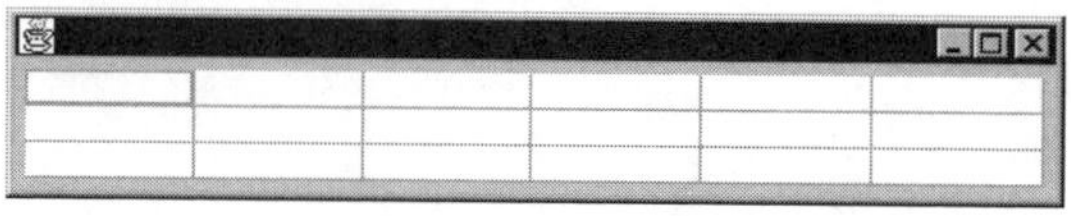

FIGURE 11.16   A scrolling *JTable*, scrolled to the bottom

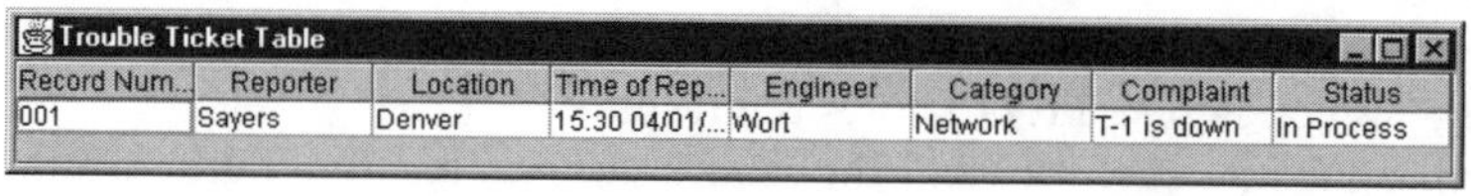

JTree

Like a JTable, a JTree is complex enough to warrant its own library of support classes. It is becoming more widely used in GUI designs, typically as a drill-down or focus-oriented controller, or as an indexing tool for things like e-mail messages and, of course, files.

But JTree is not as well-defined a listener as JTable, because it implements only the Scrollable and Accessible interfaces. The primary use for a JTree is outlining any data structure that lends itself to hierarchical order. It could be used to diagram, say, the operations of a recursive descent parser, but it is more readily useful as an indexing tool.

Trees consist of a series of nodes rooted in a single *root node*, from which other nodes called *child nodes* extend. A node that cannot have children is called a *leaf node*; otherwise it is called a *branch node*. A node is principally identified two ways: by its path, the route that links it back to the root; and by its row, the area it uses for display (similar to a List element).

Aside from defining user actions for adding and removing nodes, the most common event type associated with a tree is selection. In the trouble-ticket system, for example, you might want to associate a different display or action with each kind of node you present. If a user clicks a child of the Reporter node, you might want to display contact information for that person, or perhaps limit the table display to the trouble items reported by that person. To get the visual effect first, you can mock up a tree using the DefaultMutableTreeNode class.

FIGURE 11.17   Updating a tree outline with table data

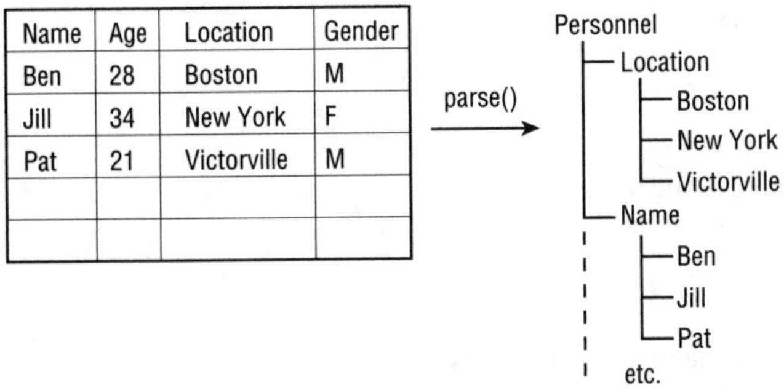

It might also make sense for the table model to alter the node population of the tree using the data it receives to update the tabular view. A tree model could listen to property changes issued by the table model. The table model could filter the data before firing it, or the tree model could filter the table data. Or, instead of adding this work to either class, where the fit is arbitrary, you could instead perform the translation work through an event adapter, whose only job is creating tree data out of table data. Keeping the two models separated this way makes it possible to keep changes in the bootstrap code and out of the component code. Figure 11.17 is a logical diagram of this interaction.

Creating a reusable mock-up of a tree display can take a little doing. Rather than embed some static data in a demo class that makes a JTree, we decided to take an extra step and write one that could accept input in the form of a property file. Property files present data in the form of key-value pairs, where the key is always a String (and in the example, so are the values). Our file sample looks like this:

```
Location=Chicago New York Parkersburg
Reporter=Padula Hunter Gant Anonymous
Engineer=Wort Brown Carrigan None
Category=Network Office Workstation
```

You treat the key as a parent node and the values as children, once the file contents are read in. To do that, we created (in the following code) a class called TreeSetup to take any file that's written as a "bundle" of properties and convert it to a series of parent and children elements:

```
import java.io.*;
import java.util.*;
import javax.swing.tree.*;


/**
 * TreeSetup converts a properties file into a set
 * of parent and child nodes. Each key in the file
 * becomes a parent, and each value is a child to its
```

```
 * key.
 *
 * @author The CJ2CSG Guys
 */
public class TreeSetup
{
  private PropertyResourceBundle prb;
  private String filename;

  /**
    * Accepts a String filename and converts it to a
    * PropertyResourceBundle.
    *
    * @see java.util.PropertyResourceBundle
    */
  public TreeSetup(String filename) {
    this.filename = filename;
    FileInputStream fis = null;
    try {
      fis = new FileInputStream(filename);
      prb = new PropertyResourceBundle(fis);
    }
    catch (FileNotFoundException fnfe) {
      System.err.println(filename + " was not found");
      System.exit(1);
    }
    catch (IOException ioe) {
      ioe.printStackTrace();
      System.err.println(
        "Error trying to open input stream");
      System.exit(1);
    }
  }

  /**
    * Returns a Vector of String values, given
    * a String key as a parameter.
    */
  public Vector getChildren(String node) {
```

```
    StringTokenizer st = null;
    Vector vec = new Vector();
    String children = prb.getString(node);
    st = new StringTokenizer(children);
    while (st.hasMoreTokens()) {
      vec.addElement(st.nextToken());
    }
    return vec;
  }

  /**
   * Returns a Vector of Strings representing
   * each key found.
   */
  public Vector getParents() {
    Enumeration enum = null;
    Vector vec = new Vector();
    enum = prb.getKeys();
    while (enum.hasMoreElements()) {
      Object key = (String)enum.nextElement();
      vec.addElement(key);
    }
    return vec;
  }
}
```

The Vector returned by getParents() contains all the keys in the file. Passing each element of that Vector, as a String, into getChildren() will then return a Vector containing the key's values. Finally, we write (in the next code sample) a SampleTree class to create a DefaultTreeModel by passing the property filename as a parameter to the TreeSetup constructor and using that object to create DefaultMutableTreeNode instances:

```
import java.util.*;
import javax.swing.*;
import javax.swing.tree.*;

public class SampleTree
{
  private DefaultMutableTreeNode[] nodes;
  private TreeSetup tsu;
```

```java
private DefaultMutableTreeNode root;
private DefaultTreeModel dtm;

public SampleTree(String schema) {
  root = new DefaultMutableTreeNode("Trouble Fields");
  tsu = new TreeSetup(schema);
  Enumeration enum = tsu.getParents().elements();

  while (enum.hasMoreElements()) {
    String category = (String)enum.nextElement();
    DefaultMutableTreeNode parent;
    parent = new DefaultMutableTreeNode(category);
    root.add(parent);
    Enumeration enum2;
    enum2 = tsu.getChildren(category).elements();

    while (enum2.hasMoreElements()) {
      String child = (String)enum2.nextElement();
      parent.add(new DefaultMutableTreeNode(child));
    }
  }

  dtm = new DefaultTreeModel(root, false);
}

public DefaultTreeModel getSampleTreeModel() {
  return dtm;
}

public static void main(String args[]) {
  if (args.length == 0) {
    System.out.println("Provide a valid property " +
      "file name and try again");
    System.exit(1);
  }
  SampleTree st = new SampleTree(args[0]);
  DefaultTreeModel tm = st.getSampleTreeModel();
  JTree jt = new JTree(tm);
  JScrollPane jsp = new JScrollPane(jt);
```

```
    JFrame jf = new JFrame("Sample Tree");
    jf.getContentPane().add(jsp);
    jf.setDefaultCloseOperation(JFrame.EXIT_ON_CLOSE);
    jf.pack();
    jf.setVisible(true);
  }
}
```

The resulting work takes the sample file listed earlier and displays it in a JTree like the one in Figure 11.18.

The work here was neither trivial nor difficult, but the result is a tool for creating any two-tier tree display quickly from a file—well worth the effort for a prototype tool.

FIGURE 11.18   A *JTree* that displays the contents of the file sample

JMenus and *Actions*

The Swing library seems particularly thoughtful when it comes to providing conveniences for common GUI-based tasks. It's easy to create a single action as an object and bind its behavior to a ready-made Swing widget. Action objects encapsulate their behavior so that multiple widgets can reference them. An icon on a toolbar, a menu choice, or even a KeyStroke can all use the same object for processing. Using KeyStroke objects goes beyond the requirements of the Developer's Exam, but they can make the GUI friendlier for users who favor keyboard input over the mouse.

Classes must meet the same requirements as ActionListener in order to implement Action (or subclass AbstractAction). Action implementations are different in that they allow for direct containment by a JComponent, although only JMenu, JToolBar, and JPopupMenu know how to contain, display, and listen to them. Here's a simple look at creating an Action and binding it to a menu (the result of the following code is shown in Figure 11.19):

```
import java.awt.event.*;
import javax.swing.*;
```

```java
/**
 * This subclass of AbstractAction serves as a prototype
 * for creating simple Action objects. No provision is
 * made for icons - just a String value so the containing
 * component has something to display.
 *
 * @author The CJ2CSG Guys
 */
public class SampleAction extends AbstractAction
{
  private String message;

  /**
   * Passes the supplied String to the parent class;
   * also maintains a copy locally.
   */
  public SampleAction(String output) {
    super(output);
    message = output;
  }

  /**
   * Sends the Action message to stdout.
   */
  public void actionPerformed(ActionEvent ae) {
    System.out.println(message);
  }

  /**
   * A bootstrap test. Adds the object to a JMenu.
   */
  public static void main(String args[]) {
    SampleAction sa = new SampleAction(args[0]);
    JFrame jf = new JFrame("Action Test");
    JMenuBar jmb = new JMenuBar();
    jf.setJMenuBar(jmb);
    JMenu jm = new JMenu("Sample");
    jmb.add(jm);
    jm.add(sa);
```

```
        jf.setSize(100,100);
        jf.setVisible(true);
        jf.setDefaultCloseOperation(JFrame.EXIT_ON_CLOSE);
    }
}
```

Take another look at the `TreeSetup` class from the last section. This same code could be used to create a quick menu prototype, using a file that lists `Menus` as keys and `MenuItems` as values. It wouldn't have much interesting functionality, but it would provide a quick means for choosing how to visually arrange menu items.

It makes sense to rename `TreeSetup` to something more general, such as `WidgetSetup`, to suggest wider usage. As practice, write a `SampleMenu` class that reads from a menu property file and builds a GUI menu for you.

FIGURE 11.19   Adding an Action to a *JMenu*

Panes

Swing panes all provide some form of containment service. The services they provide vary widely, from delegated layout managers (`content pane`) to specialized layout managers (`JSplitPane`, `JScrollPane`) and dialog boxes (`JOptionPane`, `JTabbedPane`, `JFileChooser`) to embedded layers that have no class of their own (the "glass pane" in the `JFrame`). The `content pane` is something everyone who writes a Swing application must use, and `JFileChooser` is a straightforward class, so we briefly discuss here two of the panes you might not think to use: `JSplitPane` and `JOptionPane`.

JSplitPane

As the name suggests, a `JSplitPane` holds two other components and provides an adjustable divider service. A `JSplitPane` is not a layout manager subclass, but it contains layout behavior just the same: it has its own rules regarding `minimumSize` and `preferredSize` requests from the components it contains. `JSplitPane` looks at `minimumSize` on a resize request, ensuring that one component does not encroach on the other's needed space. The range of the divider's location is normally fixed by the minimum sizes of the components in the pane, but it is adjustable.

Other properties of JSplitPane include

orientation   HORIZONTAL_SPLIT or VERTICAL_SPLIT

dividerSize   In pixels

dividerLocation   Current position

minimumDividerLocation   Left/bottom minimum size

maximumDividerLocation   Right/top minimum size

Now you're ready to put the tree, table, and simple menu together for a first look, which you can create with the following code:

```java
import java.awt.*;
import java.awt.event.*;
import javax.swing.*;
import javax.swing.tree.*;

/** A bootstrap class that combines our table and tree,
 * in a split pane, along with a trivial menu that is
 * backed by an Action.
 *
 * @author The CJ2CSG Guys
 */
public class Prototype
{
  public static void main(String args[]) {
    JFrame jf = new JFrame("SplitPane Test");

    TroubleTicketModel ttm = new TroubleTicketModel();
    JTable jta = new JTable(ttm);

    SampleTree st = new SampleTree("sample");
    DefaultTreeModel tm = st.getSampleTreeModel();
    JTree jtr = new JTree(tm);

    SampleAction sa = new SampleAction("PROTOTYPE");
    JMenuBar jmb = new JMenuBar();
    jf.setJMenuBar(jmb);
    JMenu jm = new JMenu("Sample");
    jmb.add(jm);
    jm.add(sa);
```

```
    JSplitPane jsp = new
      JSplitPane(JSplitPane.HORIZONTAL_SPLIT, jtr, jta);

    jf.getContentPane().add(jsp, BorderLayout.WEST);
    jf.setDefaultCloseOperation(JFrame.EXIT_ON_CLOSE);
    jf.setSize(650,200);
    jf.setVisible(true);
  }
}
```

The result is shown in Figure 11.20. You didn't spend time refining appearances in this first round, but now you have a quick look at your elements. Most of the adjustments to appearance can be made in the bootstrap code, amounting to less focus on changing class behavior and more on experimenting with it.

FIGURE 11.20   Menu, table, and tree together in one *JFrame*

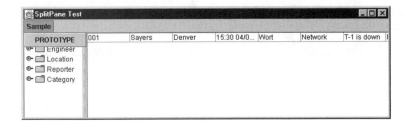

JOptionPane

The JOptionPane class encapsulates several conventional dialog-box formats, but with one clear advantage: You don't need to declare a Frame and bind to it (more on that in a moment).

JOptionPane defines five message types:

- ERROR_MESSAGE

- INFORMATION_MESSAGE

- WARNING_MESSAGE

- QUESTION_MESSAGE

- PLAIN_MESSAGE

Each of these types maps to a prepared display format. These formats can be associated one of two ways: using a confirmation request that locks the underlying frame (a modal dialog) or using a dismiss-on-demand style that does not interfere with the application (a nonmodal dialog). These behaviors are respectively enabled by the static methods showConfirmDialog() and showMessageDialog().

Add the following code snippets to the `Prototype` class as a way to experiment, and compare your perception of speed before and after these changes. The dialogs that pop up are depicted in Figure 11.21:

```
...
JOptionPane.showMessageDialog(null, "Tree created",
     "Program Note", JOptionPane.INFORMATION_MESSAGE);
...
JOptionPane.showConfirmDialog(null, "Load the GUI?",
     "Roll Call!", JOptionPane.YES_NO_CANCEL_OPTION,
     JOptionPane.QUESTION_MESSAGE);
...
```

FIGURE 11.21 *JOptionPane's* information (a) and question (b) dialogs

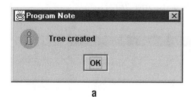
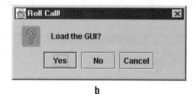

a   b

Summary

A simple, four-step plan to design a GUI includes identifying the needed components, isolating regions of behavior, sketching the GUI, and choosing layout managers.

Some properties are common to nearly all Swing components. These include size, location, foreground and background color, font, and enabled state. There are public methods for each component to set and get each of these properties.

The categories of Swing components are container components, ordinary components, and menu components. Containers include `JFrame`, `JPanel`, and `JPane`. Ordinary components include `JLabel`, `JButton`, `JCheckBox`, `JRadioButton`, `JScrollBar`, `JTextField`, `JTextArea`, and `JComboBox`. The menu components include `JMenu`, `JMenuBar`, `JMenuItem`, `JCheckBoxMenuItem`, and `JRadioButtonMenuItem`.

`JTables` have three core internal models, including `TableModel`, `TableColumnModel`, and `ListenerSelectionModel`. It's also possible (and simpler) to subclass `AbstractTableModel` and use it as a `JTable` constructor argument.

The primary use for a `JTree` is implementing any data structure that lends itself to a hierarchy. Trees consist of a root node and child nodes (leaf nodes and branch nodes).

Chapter Review Lab

A Custom Table Model Class

In this exercise you will create your own table model class. The model should support a table with 10 rows and 10 columns. The cell at row r and column c should display the value r × c. In other words, it's a multiplication table for 0 times 0 through 9 times 9. The column headers should be the values 0 through 9. A good size for your frame is 800 × 200 pixels.

The cells in the rightmost column and the bottom row should be blank and editable. The user should type in the correct values for these cells.

The GUI should display the table and a button labeled Check. When the user clicks the button, the application should print out the number of cells that the user correctly filled in.

If you're not familiar with layout managers, you might run into a problem. If you just create a table and a button and add them to a frame's content pane, you'll see only one of the components. To work around this, insert the following line of code immediately after you create the frame (*before* you add the components):

```
frame.getContentPane().setLayout(new java.awt.FlowLayout());
```

Your model class should extend `AbstractTableModel`. It should also implement `ActionListener`, so that it can receive notification from the Check button. One possible solution appears on your CD-ROM, in the file `solutions\Chapter11\MultiplicationTableModel.java`.

When you test your application, be sure to hit the Enter key after you type the last value into the last cell. Otherwise, the table will not send a `setValueAt()` call to the model, and the model will not detect the value you typed in.

Chapter

12

Layout Managers

In Chapter 11, "Swing Components," we covered the basic look and feel of some of the basic Swing components. A sophisticated GUI, such as the one you will be required to create for your Developer's Exam project, consists of a number of interrelated components positioned so as to make the application easy to understand and use.

Java practically insists that you use layout managers to control the size and position of your GUI components. This requirement can be irritating, but it has the benefit of forcing programmers to think about the dynamic resizing behavior of their user interfaces. In this chapter we will examine the standard layout managers of the `java.awt` package: Flow, Grid, Border, Card, and GridBag. Note that these classes can lay out Swing components as well as AWT components.

Layout Manager Theory

The AWT toolkit includes five main layout manager classes:

- Flow
- Grid
- Border
- Card
- GridBag

You might expect that there would be a common abstract superclass, called something like `LayoutManager`, from which these five layout managers would inherit common functionality. In fact, the common ancestor is `java.awt .LayoutManager`. However, it is an interface, not a class, because the layout managers are so different from one another that they have nothing in common except a handful of method names. (There is also a `java.awt .LayoutManager2` subinterface, which the GridBag, Border, and Card layout managers implement.)

Layout managers work in partnership with containers. To understand layout managers, it is important to understand what a container is and what happens when a component gets inserted into a container. The next two sections explore these topics.

Swing GUIs reside in `JFrames` or in `JApplets`. For simple applications, you just add your components to your frame; for simple applets, you just put your components into your applet. (In both cases, you might wonder how the components end up where they do; layout managers are lurking in the background, taking care of details.) For more complicated GUIs, it is convenient to divide the frame or applet into smaller regions. These regions might constitute, for example, a toolbar or a matrix of radio buttons. In Java, GUI subregions are implemented most commonly with the `JPanel` container. Panels, like frames and applets, can contain other components: buttons, check boxes, scroll bars, text areas, text fields, and of course other panels. Complicated GUIs sometimes have very complicated containment hierarchies of panels within panels within panels, and so on, down through many layers of containment.

> In most object-oriented windowing systems, including Java, the term *hierarchy* is ambiguous. When discussing classes, hierarchy refers to the structure of inheritance from superclass to subclass. When discussing GUIs, hierarchy can refer to the containment structure of GUI components, such as applets, frames, panels, buttons, and so on.

The GUI in Figure 12.1 is a moderate-size frame for specifying a color. You can see at a glance that the panel contains labels, scroll bars, text fields, and buttons. You have probably guessed that the frame also contains some panels, even though they cannot be seen. In fact, the frame contains five panels, not counting the frame's content pane. Each of the six containers (the five panels, plus the content pane) has its own layout manager: There are four instances of Grid layout managers, one Flow layout manager, and one Border layout manager.

Figure 12.2 schematically shows the frame's containment hierarchy. A Java GUI programmer must master the art of transforming a proposed GUI into a workable and efficient containment hierarchy. This skill comes with experience, once the fundamentals are understood. The Java Developer's Certification Exam does not require you to develop any complicated containments, but it does require you to understand the fundamentals.

FIGURE 12.1   A GUI with several levels of containment

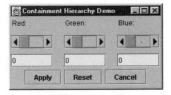

The code that implements the color chooser in Figure 12.1 is listed here:

```
1.  import java.awt.*;
2.  import javax.swing.*;
3.
4.  public class Hier extends JFrame {
5.    Hier() {
6.      super("Containment Hierarchy Demo");
7.      Container cont = getContentPane();
8.      // Build upper panel with 3 horizontal "strips".
9.      String strings[] = {"Red:", "Green:", "Blue:"};
10.     JPanel upperPan = new JPanel();
11.     upperPan.setLayout(new GridLayout(1, 3, 20, 0));
```

```
12.      for (int i=0; i<3; i++) {
13.        // Add strips.
14.        // Each strip is a panel within upperPan.
15.        JPanel levelPan = new JPanel();
16.        levelPan.setLayout(new GridLayout(3, 1, 0, 10));
17.        levelPan.add(new Label(strings[i]));
18.        levelPan.add(new
             JScrollBar(JScrollBar.HORIZONTAL));
19.        levelPan.add(new JTextField("0"));
20.        upperPan.add(levelPan);
21.      }
22.      cont.add(upperPan, BorderLayout.CENTER);
23.      // Build lower panel containing 3 buttons.
24.      JPanel lowerPan = new JPanel();
25.      lowerPan.add(new JButton("Apply"));
26.      lowerPan.add(new JButton("Reset"));
27.      lowerPan.add(new JButton("Cancel"));
28.      cont.add(lowerPan, BorderLayout.SOUTH);
29.      pack();
30.    }
31.
32.    public static void main(String[] args) {
33.      (new Hier()).setVisible(true);
34.    }
35. }
```

FIGURE 12.2   Containment hierarchy

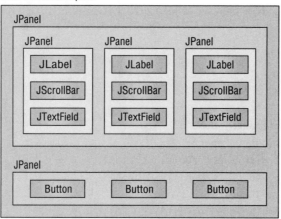

As you can see from the listing, no code specifies exactly where the labels, scroll bars, text fields, buttons, or panels should go or what size they should be. Instead, each container (the content pane of the JFrame, as well as the various JPanels) uses its default layout manager or is specifically assigned a non-default layout manager.

After each container is constructed and possibly assigned a new layout manager, the container is populated with the components it is to contain. For example, the lower JPanel, constructed in line 24, is populated with JButtons in lines 25, 26, and 27 (using its default layout manager).

Finally, the now-populated panel is added to the container that is to hold it (line 28).

Each panel in the sample code is built in four steps:

1. Construct the panel.

2. Give the panel a layout manager.

3. Populate the panel.

4. Add the panel to its own container.

When a container is constructed (step 1), it is given a default layout manager. For panels, the default is a Flow layout manager, and step 2 can be skipped if this is the desired manager. In step 3, populating the panel involves constructing components and adding them to the panel; if any of these components is itself a panel, steps 1–4 must be executed recursively.

There is a version of the JPanel constructor whose single argument is a layout manager, which of course is assigned to the panel. So lines 15 and 16 above could be abbreviated as

```
JPanel levelPan = new JPanel(new GridLayout(3, 1, 0, 10));
```

A container delegates to its layout manager the job of determining where components will be placed and (optionally) how they will be resized. If the container is subsequently resized, the layout manager again lays out the container's components (probably with different results, because it has a different area to work with). This "conference" between the container and the layout manager is the subject of the next section.

Component Size and Position

Components know where they are and how big they are. That is to say, the java.awt.Component class, which is a superclass of all AWT and Swing components, has instance variables called x, y, width, and height. The x and y variables specify the position of the component's upper-left corner (as measured from the upper-left corner of the container that contains the component), and width and height are in pixels. Figure 12.3 illustrates the x, y, width, and height of a text area inside a panel inside a frame.

A component's position and size can be changed by calling the component's setSize() method. It seems reasonable to expect that the following code, which calls setSize() on a button, would create two fairly big buttons:

```
1. import java.awt.*;
2. import javax.swing.*;
3.
```

```
4. public class Disa extends JFrame {
5.    public static void main(String[] args) {
6.        JFrame frame = new JFrame();
7.        JPanel panel = new JPanel();
8.        for (int i=0; i<2; i++) {
9.            JButton btn = new JButton("We're enormous!");
10.           btn.setSize(300, 300);
11.           panel.add(btn);
12.       }
13.       frame.getContentPane().add(panel);
14.       frame.setSize(450, 70);
15.       frame.setVisible(true);
16.   }
17. }
```

If you have tried something like this, you know that the result is disappointing. A screen shot appears in Figure 12.4.

FIGURE 12.3   Position and size

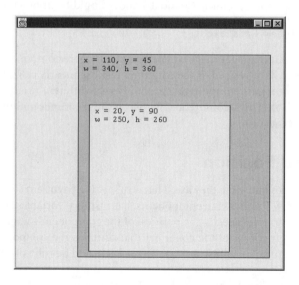

FIGURE 12.4   Disappointing buttons: too large

It seems that line 10 should force the buttons to be 300 pixels wide by 300 pixels tall. In fact, the buttons are just the size they would be if line 10 were omitted or commented out.

Line 10 has no effect because after it executes, the button is added to a panel (line 11). Eventually (after a fairly complicated sequence of events), the panel calls on its layout manager to enforce its layout policy on the button. The layout manager decides where and how big the button should be; in this case, the layout manager wants the button to be just large enough to accommodate its label. When this size has been calculated, the layout manager calls `setBounds()` on the button, clobbering the work you did in line 10.

In general, it is futile to call `setBounds()` on a component, because layout managers always get the last word; that is, their call to `setBounds()` happens after yours. There are ways to defeat this functionality, but they tend to be complicated, difficult to maintain, and not in the spirit of Java. Java's GUI system wants you to let the layout managers do the layout work. In order to build a sophisticated GUI, you have to be familiar with the layout policies of the available layout managers. These policies are covered in the next several sections.

Layout Policies

Every Java component has a *preferred size* that expresses how big the component would like to be, barring conflict with a layout manager. Preferred size is generally the smallest size necessary to render the component in a visually meaningful way. For example, a button's preferred size is the size of its label text, plus a little border of empty space around the text, plus the shadowed decorations that mark the boundary of the button. Thus a button's preferred size is "just big enough."

When a layout manager lays out its container's child components, it has to balance two considerations: the layout policy and each component's preferred size. First priority goes to enforcing layout policy. If honoring a component's preferred size would mean violating the layout policy, then the layout manager overrules the component's preferred size.

Understanding a layout manager means understanding where it will place a component and also how it will treat a component's preferred size. The next several sections discuss the layout managers: Flow, Grid, Border, Card, and GridBag.

The Flow Layout Manager

The Flow layout manager arranges components in horizontal rows. It is the default manager type for panels and applets, so it is usually the first layout manager that programmers encounter. It is a common experience for new Java developers to add a few components to an applet and wonder how they came to be arranged so neatly. The following code is a good example:

```
1. import java.awt.*;
2. import javax.swing.*;
3.
4. public class Flow extends JFrame {
5.   public static void main(String[] args) {
```

```
6.      JFrame frame = new JFrame();
7.      Container cont = frame.getContentPane();
8.      cont.setLayout(new FlowLayout());
9.      cont.add(new JLabel("Name: "));
10.     cont.add(new JTextField("Beowulf   "));
11.     cont.add(new JButton("OK"));
12.     frame.setSize(450, 90);
13.     frame.setVisible(true);
14.   }
15. }
```

The resulting frame is shown in Figure 12.5.

If the same three components appear in a narrower frame, as shown in Figure 12.6, there is not enough space for all three to fit in a single row.

The Flow layout manager fits as many components as possible into the top row and spills the remainder into a second row. The components always appear, left to right, in the order they were added to their container.

If the frame is thinner still, as in Figure 12.7, then the Flow layout manager creates still another row.

FIGURE 12.5   Simple frame using the Flow layout manager

FIGURE 12.6   A narrower frame using the Flow layout manager

FIGURE 12.7   A very narrow frame using the Flow layout manager

Within every row the components are evenly spaced, and the cluster of components is centered. The alignment (sometimes called *justification*) of the clustering can be controlled by passing a parameter to the FlowLayout constructor. The possible values are FlowLayout.LEFT, FlowLayout.CENTER, and FlowLayout.RIGHT. The code that follows explicitly constructs a Flow layout manager to right-justify four buttons:

```
1. import java.awt.*;
2. import javax.swing.*;
3.
4. public class FlowRight extends JFrame {
5.   public static void main(String[] args) {
6.     JFrame frame = new JFrame();
7.     Container cont = frame.getContentPane();
8.     cont.setLayout(new FlowLayout(FlowLayout.RIGHT));
9.     for (int i=1; i<=4; i++)
10.       cont.add(new JButton("Button #" + i));
11.     frame.setSize(470, 90);
12.     frame.setVisible(true);
13.   }
14. }
```

Figure 12.8 shows the resulting frame.

Figure 12.9 shows the frame of the previous figure, resized to be somewhat narrower.

By default, the Flow layout manager leaves a gap of five pixels between components in both the horizontal and vertical directions. You can change this default by calling an overloaded version of the FlowLayout constructor, passing in the desired horizontal and vertical gaps. All layout managers have this capability.

FIGURE 12.8   A right-justifying Flow layout manager

FIGURE 12.9   A narrow right-justifying Flow layout manager

The Grid Layout Manager

The Flow layout manager always honors a component's preferred size. The Grid layout manager takes the opposite extreme: when it performs a layout in a given space, it ignores a component's preferred size.

The Grid layout manager subdivides its territory into a matrix of rows and columns. The number of rows and number of columns are specified as parameters to the manager's constructor:

```
public GridLayout(int nRows, int nColumns)
```

Each row and each column in a Grid layout will be the same size; the overall area available to the layout is divided equally among the number of rows and among the number of columns.

The following code uses a Grid layout manager to divide a frame into five rows and three columns and then puts a component in each grid cell:

```
1. import java.awt.*;
2. import javax.swing.*;
3.
4. public class Grid extends JFrame {
5.   public static void main(String[] args) {
6.     JFrame frame = new JFrame();
7.     Container cont = frame.getContentPane();
8.     cont.setLayout(new GridLayout(5, 3));
9.     for (int row=0; row<5; row++) {
10.       cont.add(new JLabel("Label " + row));
11.       cont.add(new JButton("Button " + row));
12.       cont.add(new JTextField("Text Field " + row));
13.     }
14.     frame.setSize(470, 140);
15.     frame.setVisible(true);
16.   }
17. }
```

Note that the constructor in line 8 creates five rows and three columns, not the other way around. After so many years of programming with Cartesian coordinates, it is probably second nature for most programmers to specify horizontal sorts of information before the comma and vertical sorts of information after the comma. The GridLayout constructor uses "row-major" notation, which sometimes confuses people.

If you specify zero for either rows or columns, then the grid will size itself based on the number of components and the other dimension.

As you can see in Figure 12.10, every component is exactly the same size. Components appear in the order in which they were added, from left to right, row by row.

If the same components are laid out in a taller, narrower frame, then every component is proportionally taller and narrower, as shown in Figure 12.11.

FIGURE 12.10 Grid layout

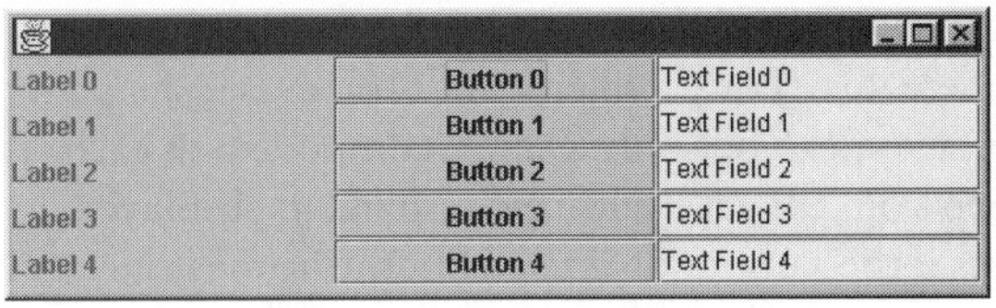

FIGURE 12.11 Tall, narrow Grid layout

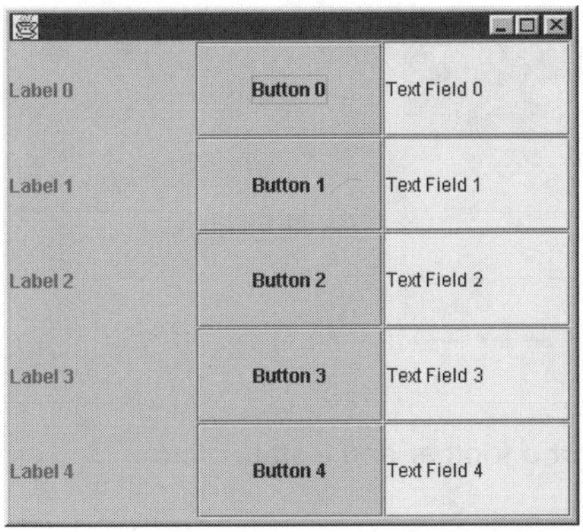

Grid layout managers behave strangely when they manage very few components (that is, significantly fewer than the number of rows times the number of columns) or very many components (that is, more than the number of rows times the number of columns).

The Border Layout Manager

The Border layout manager is the default manager for a JFrame's content pane, so sooner or later you must come to grips with it. It enforces a very useful layout policy, but it is less intuitive than either the Flow or Grid manager.

The Flow layout manager always honors a component's preferred size; the Grid layout manager never does. The Border layout manager does something in between. The Border layout manager divides its territory into five regions: North, South, East, West, and Center. Each region may be empty or may contain one component (that is, no region is *required* to contain a component, but the regions can contain only one component).

The component at North gets positioned at the top of the container, and the component at South gets positioned at the bottom. The layout manager honors the preferred height of the North and South components and forces them to be exactly as wide as the container.

The North and South regions are useful for toolbars, status lines, and any other controls that ought to be as wide as possible but no higher than necessary. Figure 12.12 shows a frame that uses a Border layout manager to position a toolbar at North and a status line at South. The font of the status line is very large to illustrate that the height of each region is dictated by the preferred height of the component in the region. The panel that contains the toolbar buttons has its background set to black so you can see where it is. (For simplicity, the toolbar is just a panel containing a few buttons. Remember we said that you can put only a single component in each region? Well, if that component is a container, then you can get multiple components displayed.)

Figure 12.13 shows what happens if the same code is used but the frame is larger. Notice that the toolbar is still at the top and the status line is still at the bottom. The toolbar and the status line are as tall as they were in Figure 11.12, and they are automatically as wide as the frame.

FIGURE 12.12 Border layout for a toolbar and a status line

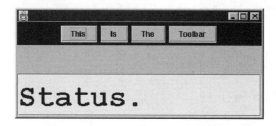

FIGURE 12.13 Larger Border layout for a toolbar and a status line

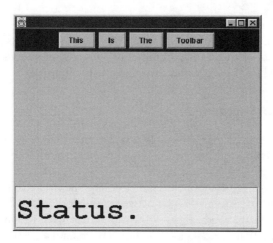

The code that produced these screen shots is as follows:

```
1. import java.awt.*;
2. import javax.swing.*;
3.
4. public class Border extends JFrame {
```

```
5.    public static void main(String[] args) {
6.       JFrame frame = new JFrame();
7.       Container cont = frame.getContentPane();
8.
9.       // Build, populate, and add toolbar.
10.      JPanel toolbar = new JPanel();
11.      toolbar.setBackground(Color.black);
12.      toolbar.add(new JButton("This"));
13.      toolbar.add(new JButton("Is"));
14.      toolbar.add(new JButton("The"));
15.      toolbar.add(new JButton("Toolbar"));
16.      cont.add(toolbar, BorderLayout.NORTH);
17.
18.      // Add status line.
19.      JTextField status = new JTextField("Status.");
20.      Font font = new Font("Monospaced", Font.BOLD, 48);
21.      status.setFont(font);
22.      cont.add(status, BorderLayout.SOUTH);
23.
24.      frame.setSize(400, 375);
25.      frame.setVisible(true);
26.   }
27. }
```

Notice that in lines 16 and 22, an overloaded form of the add() method is used. The Border layout manager is not affected by the order in which you add components. Instead, you must specify which of the five regions will receive the component you are adding. The overloaded version of add() takes two parameters: first the component being added and second an Object. Proper use of the Border layout manager requires that the second parameter be a constant defined in the BorderLayout class itself. The five constants that you should know about are these:

- BorderLayout.NORTH

- BorderLayout.SOUTH

- BorderLayout.EAST

- BorderLayout.WEST

- BorderLayout.CENTER

These constants are of type String. You can use the string values rather than the constants, simply by passing in one of the literal strings North, South, East, West, or Center. However, this approach is less robust than using the constants, because it does not protect you against spelling errors. For example, if you accidentally type BorderLayout.SUOTH, the compiler will flag your error at compile time. If you use the literal value and make the corresponding typo, the compiler sees Suoth, which is a valid string, and does not produce a compiler error.

The East and West regions are almost the opposite of North and South: in East and West, a component gets to be its preferred width but has its height constrained. Here a component extends vertically up to the bottom of the North component (if there is one) or to the top of the container (if there is no North component). A component extends down to the top of the South component (if there is one) or to the bottom of the container (if there is no South component). Figures 12.14 through 12.17 show frames that use a Border layout manager to lay out two scroll bars, one at East and one at West. In Figure 12.14, there are no components at North or South to contend with.

In Figure 12.15 there is a label at North.

FIGURE 12.14   East and West

FIGURE 12.15   East and West, with North

FIGURE 12.16   East and West, with South

FIGURE 12.17   East and West, with both North and South

In Figure 12.16 there is a label at South. The label has white text on a black background so that you can see exactly where the South region is.

In Figure 12.17, there are labels at both North and South. The labels have white text on a black background so that you can see exactly where the North and South regions are.

The code that generated these four images is listed here. There is only one application. The code, as shown, generates Figure 12.17 (both North and South); lines 17 and 24 were judiciously commented out to generate the other figures:

```
1. import java.awt.*;
2. import javax.swing.*;
```

```
3.
4. public class EastWest extends JFrame {
5.   public static void main(String[] args) {
6.     JFrame frame = new JFrame();
7.     Container cont = frame.getContentPane();
8.
9.     cont.add(new JScrollBar(), BorderLayout.WEST);
10.    cont.add(new JScrollBar(), BorderLayout.EAST);
11.
12.    JLabel topLabel = new JLabel("This is North");
13.    topLabel.setOpaque(true);
14.    topLabel.setFont(new Font("Serif", Font.PLAIN, 36));
15.    topLabel.setForeground(Color.white);
16.    topLabel.setBackground(Color.black);
17.    cont.add(topLabel, BorderLayout.NORTH);
18.
19.    JLabel bottomLabel = new JLabel("This is South");
20.    bottomLabel.setOpaque(true);
21.    bottomLabel.setFont(new Font("Monospaced",
         Font.PLAIN, 18));
22.    bottomLabel.setForeground(Color.white);
23.    bottomLabel.setBackground(Color.black);
24.    cont.add(bottomLabel, BorderLayout.SOUTH);
25.
26.    frame.setSize(400, 375);
27.    frame.setVisible(true);
28.  }
29. }
```

The fifth region that a Border layout manager controls is called Center. Center is simply the part of a container that remains after North, South, East, and West have been allocated. Figure 12.18 shows a frame with buttons at North, South, East, and West and a text area at Center.

The code that generated Figure 12.18 is as follows:

```
1. import java.awt.*;
2. import javax.swing.*;
3.
4. public class Center extends JFrame {
5.   public static void main(String[] args) {
6.     JFrame frame = new JFrame();
7.     Container cont = frame.getContentPane();
```

```
8.
9.        cont.add(new JButton("N"), BorderLayout.NORTH);
10.       cont.add(new JButton("S"), BorderLayout.SOUTH);
11.       cont.add(new JButton("E"), BorderLayout.EAST);
12.       cont.add(new JButton("W"), BorderLayout.WEST);
13.
14.       JTextArea ta = new JTextArea();
15.       for (int i=0; i<10; i++)
16.         ta.append("Center Text Area Line " + i + "
17.       cont.add(ta, BorderLayout.CENTER);
18.
19.       frame.setSize(400, 375);
20.       frame.setVisible(true);
21.     }
22.   }
```

In line 17, the text area is added to the Center region. When adding a component to Center, it is legal, although unwise, to omit the second parameter to the **add( )** call. In the Java 2 platform, the Border layout manager will assume that you mean Center; however, in older versions, the behavior was unpredictable and typically resulted in the component's being entirely invisible. Generally, it is easier for other people to understand your code if you explicitly specify the region, as in line 17.

Figures 12.19 and 12.20 show what happens to the Center region in the absence of various regions. The frames are generated by commenting out line 9 (for Figure 12.19) and lines 10–12 (for Figure 12.20). The figures show that Center (the text area) is simply the area that is left over after space has been given to the other regions.

FIGURE 12.18   The Center region

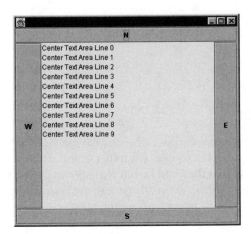

FIGURE 12.19   Center, no North

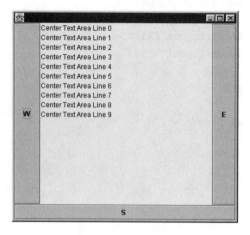

FIGURE 12.20   Center, no South, East, or West

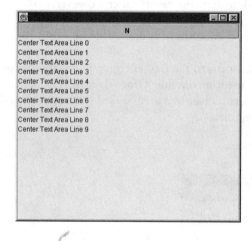

The Card Layout Manager

The Card layout manager lays out its components in time rather than in space. At any moment, a container using a Card layout manager is displaying one or another of its components; all the other components are unseen. A method call to the Card layout manager can tell it to display a different component. All the components (which are usually panels) are resized to occupy the entire container. The result is similar to a tabbed panel without the tabs.

When you use a Card layout, you have a couple of options for controlling which component is displayed and when. The Card layout gives the components that it manages a sequence, and you can ask it to display the first or last component in that sequence explicitly. In addition, you can ask for the next or previous component in the sequence. In this way, you can cycle through the components easily.

The second way to control component display is to give each component a name. If you take this approach, the Card layout allows you to select the component to be displayed using that name. This approach is much like an API equivalent of selecting a pane from a tabbed pane based on the label that it displays.

Adding Components to a Card Layout

To add components to a Card layout, you simply add them to the appropriate container. This process is like any other layout. You need to be aware of two things that influence the exact way that you add your components. First, the order in which you add the components determines the order in which they will be cycled by the Card layout manager, should you choose to use this feature. Second, if you want to select particular components for display using the "by name" feature mentioned in the previous paragraph, then you must supply a name when adding the component. (Obviously, the name should not be shared by any other component in the same container.)

To add a named component , simply use the String object that represents that name in the second argument of the add method, like this:

```
JPanel p = new JPanel();
p.setLayout(new CardLayout());
JButton b = new JButton("A Component");
p.add(b, "Button-B");
```

If you examine the API for the Container class, you'll see that there is another add method that takes a string as the first argument and the Component as the second. You can use this method, and it works. However, the API says that the add(*Component, Object)* version is "strongly preferred."

Selecting the Displayed Component

The Card layout manager provides five methods that can be used to select the component that is to be displayed:

- void first(Container)
- void last(Container)
- void next(Container)
- void previous(Container)
- void show(Container, String)

The first four of these methods are straightforward; first and last cause the display to select the first or last added component, respectively. Similarly, the methods next and previous cause the displayed component to be cycled based on the order in which the components were originally added to the container.

The final method, show(), selects a particular component based on the textual name that was given to the component when the component was added to the container. To use this method, naturally, you must provide a name for the component. You do so by using the method

```
add(Component, Object)
```

to add the component to its container and ensuring that the names given to the components are unique for that container.

Let's look at an example. Note especially the underlined lines, where components are added and displayed:

```
import java.awt.*;
import java.awt.event.*;
import javax.swing.*;


public class CardDemo extends JPanel {
  private JPanel cardPanel = new JPanel();
  private CardLayout cardLayout = new CardLayout();

  private JPanel controlPanel = new JPanel();

  private JButton firstButton = new JButton("First");
  private JButton lastButton = new JButton("Last");
  private JButton nextButton = new JButton("Next");
  private JButton prevButton = new JButton("Prev");
  private JTextField selectText = new JTextField(" ");

  public CardDemo() {
    setLayout(new BorderLayout());

    cardPanel.setLayout(cardLayout);

    JPanel p = new JPanel();
    p.setLayout(new BorderLayout());
    p.add(new Label("This is panel One"),
        BorderLayout.CENTER);
    p.add(new Button("dummy button one"),
```

```
            BorderLayout.WEST);
      cardPanel.add(p, "1");


      p = new JPanel();
      p.setLayout(new BorderLayout());
      p.add(new Label("This is panel Two"),
            BorderLayout.CENTER);
      p.add(new Button("dummy button two"),
            BorderLayout.NORTH);
      cardPanel.add(p, "2");


      p = new JPanel();
      p.setLayout(new BorderLayout());
      p.add(new Label("This is panel Three"),
            BorderLayout.CENTER);
      p.add(new Button("dummy button three"),
            BorderLayout.SOUTH);
      cardPanel.add(p, "3");


      p = new JPanel();
      p.setLayout(new BorderLayout());
      p.add(new Label("This is panel Four"),
            BorderLayout.CENTER);
      p.add(new Button("dummy button four"),
            BorderLayout.EAST);
      cardPanel.add(p, "4");


      add(cardPanel, BorderLayout.CENTER);

      firstButton.addActionListener(
        new ActionListener() {
          public void actionPerformed(ActionEvent e){
            cardLayout.first(cardPanel);
          }
        }
      );

      lastButton.addActionListener(
        new ActionListener() {
          public void actionPerformed(ActionEvent e){
            cardLayout.last(cardPanel);
```

```
        }
      }
    );

    nextButton.addActionListener(
      new ActionListener() {
        public void actionPerformed(ActionEvent e){
          cardLayout.next(cardPanel);
        }
      }
    );

    prevButton.addActionListener(
      new ActionListener() {
        public void actionPerformed(ActionEvent e){
          cardLayout.previous(cardPanel);
        }
      }
    );

    selectText.addActionListener(
      new ActionListener() {
        public void actionPerformed(ActionEvent e) {
          cardLayout.show(cardPanel,
                          selectText.getText().trim());
        }
      }
    );

    JPanel cp1 = new JPanel();
    JPanel cp2 = new JPanel();
    cp1.add(firstButton);
    cp1.add(prevButton);
    cp1.add(nextButton);
    cp1.add(lastButton);

    cp2.add(new Label("Enter Panel Number: "));
    cp2.add(selectText);
```

```
        controlPanel.setLayout(new BorderLayout());
        controlPanel.add(cp1, BorderLayout.NORTH);
        controlPanel.add(cp2, BorderLayout.SOUTH);

        add(controlPanel, BorderLayout.SOUTH);
    }

    public static void main(String args[]) {
        JFrame f = new JFrame("CardLayout Example");
        CardDemo card = new CardDemo();
        f.getContentPane().add(card, BorderLayout.CENTER);
        f.pack();
        f.setVisible(true);
    }
}
```

The GridBag Layout Manager

The GridBag layout manager is by far the most powerful layout manager. It can perform the work of the Flow, Grid, and Border layout managers if appropriately programmed and is capable of much more, often without the need for nesting multiple panels as is so often required with the other layout managers.

The GridBag layout manager divides its container into an array of cells, but (unlike the cells of a Grid layout manager) different cell rows can have different heights, and different cell columns can have different widths. A component can occupy part or all of a region that is based on either a single cell or a rectangle made up of multiple cells. A GridBag layout manager requires a lot of information to know where to put a component. A helper class called GridBagConstraints is used to hold all the layout position information. When you add a component, you use the add(*Component, Object*) version of the add() method, passing an instance of GridBagConstraints as the *Object* parameter.

Designing a Layout with GridBag

Although the GridBag layout manager is powerful, it is sometimes considered hard to use. This perception stems mostly from two things. First, the supplied documentation, although precise and complete from a technical point of view, does not describe much more than the API. An explanation of the principles of operation is noticeably missing. Second, some aspects of the control of the GridBag layout manager are confusing. Specifically, you will notice that the row and column sizing controls are typically mixed in with the individual component controls. To use the GridBag layout manager easily and confidently, you need to first understand the principles that drive it and then worry about the API that you must use.

Three levels of control are applied to a GridBag layout to make up the final layout in the container. The sizes of the various rows and columns, along with the way they stretch when the container is resized, must be considered. Also, the cell (or cells) that provides the target space for each component is determined. The final control determines how each component is stretched to fit or, if it isn't, how the component is positioned within the target space.

The API governing each of these aspects is built into a single mechanism based around the `GridBagConstraints` class. This class can be confusing, so we will discuss each of the principles of control separately as much as possible. As we do so, we will describe how the API controls this behavior. Finally, we will look at the interactions between these various controls and distill some generalizations that will be useful to you both when designing layouts and when answering examination questions.

Controlling the Rows and Columns

The row and column behavior of a GridBag layout has three aspects. The first is the number of rows and columns present. Typically, this total is determined by the number of rows and columns you ask to add components into. So, for example, if you place components at X coordinates 0, 1, 2, and 3, then you will find four columns in the container.

There is another way to specify that you want a particular number of rows or columns. The GridBag layout manager has two public variables called `columnWidths` and `rowHeights`. These are arrays of `int` values. If the `columnWidths` array contains four elements, then there will be (at least) four columns in the layout. The `rowHeights` array affects the row count similarly. If you use these arrays, then the layout will contain at least as many rows as the size of the `rowHeights` array, and similarly the column count will be influenced by the size of the `columnWidths` array.

The second aspect is the default size of a row or column. The default height of a row is normally the preferred height of the tallest component in the row. Similarly, the default width of a column is the width of the widest component in the column. If you provided either or both of the `columnWidths` and `rowHeights` arrays, and if the value specified in the array for that particular row or column is greater than that calculated from the components, the array value will be used instead. That's easy enough, isn't it?

The final aspect of rows and columns is the stretchiness that occurs when the container is resized. It is governed by a property called *weight*. The rest of this section discusses row and column count, size, and weight.

Let's look at a trivial example that demonstrates controlling both the number of columns and the default size of those columns (it's hard to avoid having both at the same time, of course). The following example code creates a GridBag layout of three rows and three columns:

```
1. import java.awt.*;
2. import javax.swing.*;
3.
4. public class GB1 extends JPanel {
5.   private JPanel tallPanel = new JPanel();
6.   private JPanel tallPanel2 = new JPanel();
7.
```

```
8.   public GB1() {
9.     tallPanel.setLayout(new GridLayout(3, 1));
10.    tallPanel.add(new Button("Press"));
11.    tallPanel.add(new Button("Any"));
12.    tallPanel.add(new Button("One"));
13.
14.    tallPanel2.setLayout(new GridLayout(3, 1));
15.    tallPanel2.add(new Button("Don't"));
16.    tallPanel2.add(new Button("Press"));
17.    tallPanel2.add(new Button("These"));
18.
19.    setLayout(new GridBagLayout());
20.
21.    GridBagConstraints c = new GridBagConstraints();
22.    c.gridx = 0; c.gridy = 0;
23.    add(new JButton("topleft"), c);
24.    c.gridx = 1;
25.    add(new JButton("topmiddle"), c);
26.    c.gridx = 2;
27.    add(new JButton("topright"), c);
28.
29.    c.gridx = 0; c.gridy = 1;
30.    add(new JButton("lefthandsidemiddle"), c);
31.    c.gridx = 1;
32.    add(tallPanel, c);
33.
34.    c.gridy = 2; // note, sets _y_
35.    add(new JButton("bottomcenter"), c);
36.    c.gridx = 2;
37.    add(tallPanel2, c);
38.  }
39.
40.  public static void main(String args[]) {
41.    JFrame f = new JFrame("GridBag 1 example");
42.    f.getContentPane().add(new GB1());
43.    f.pack();
44.    f.setVisible(true);
45.  }
46. }
```

This code results in a display like the one in Figure 12.21.

Notice how each component that is added is positioned using a `GridBagConstraints` object—actually the same object but with different values. The `GridBagConstraints` object is used to specify all the controlling parameters for a GridBag layout and is provided each time a component is added. The GridBag layout itself copies the values, so it's quite all right to reuse the constraints object for each component you add.

Let's look at the behavior for a moment. We've said that this example produces three rows and three columns, and yet it might not be obvious where those row and column boundaries are. The diagram in Figure 12.22 shows these boundaries.

You will see that two cells of the layout are unused, at 0, 2 (the bottom-left corner) and 2, 1 (right side, halfway down). This is not a problem, because the GridBag layout manager calculates the number of rows and columns required.

Each component in this layout was positioned explicitly using the `gridx` and `gridy` elements of the `GridBagConstraints` object. You do not always have to work quite this hard, but for now, it is easier to understand what is happening if you do. Therefore, we will continue to use this approach for a while longer.

Notice that each row has a height, determined by the tallest component that it contains; similarly, the width of each row is based on the widest component. For components that are smaller in one dimension or the other than the space available to them, you'll see that the component is left at its natural size and is placed in the middle of the available space. Although this behavior is the default, you will see later how to change it, too.

So, the remaining question to address is, what happens if the container is resized? We didn't specify any stretchiness for these rows and columns, so all that happens is that the space is wasted—actually, it is distributed evenly around the whole layout, as shown in Figure 12.23.

FIGURE 12.21 GridBag layout example

FIGURE 12.22 Row and column boundaries in the GridBag layout example

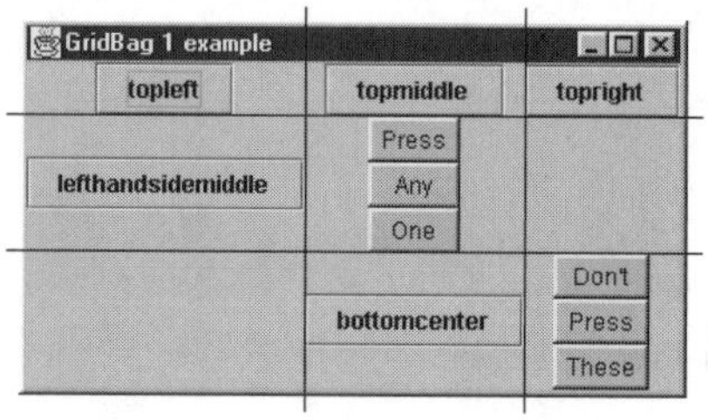

FIGURE 12.23   GridBag layout example with an enlarged window

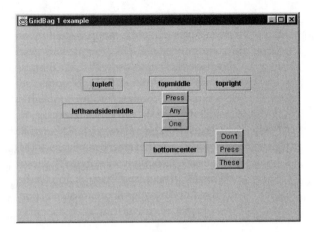

Often you will want to use this extra space, and doing so involves two steps. As we just said, components that are smaller than the available cell sit in the middle of the available space. If we enlarge the space, we must also change that behavior. We'll look at that technique shortly; for now, let's see how to enlarge the space. We will modify the program so that the center row and center column are allocated all the available space when the container is enlarged. To do this, we specify a nonzero value for the weight applied to the row and column.

The curious thing about weight is that it is specified using the members `weightx` and `weighty` in the `GridBagConstraints` object, so a value is specified for every component. This is odd because the value applies to the *row* or *column*, not to the individual component. To deal with this approach, be careful to specify a `weightx` in only one component in each column (`weightx` controls horizontal stretchiness) and a `weighty` in only one component in each row. We will modify our earlier example so that the right column and bottom row stretch to use up the available space. Rather than reprint the entire program to show the two areas of modification, we'll just show you the parts that relate to adding components to the layout:

```
21.     GridBagConstraints c = new GridBagConstraints();
22.     c.gridx = 0; c.gridy = 0;
23.     add(new JButton("topleft"), c);
24.     c.gridx = 1;
25.     add(new JButton("topmiddle"), c);
26.     c.gridx = 2;
27.     c.weightx = 1.0;  // This col is stretchy
28.     add(new JButton("topright"), c);
29.     c.weightx = 0.0;  // No other col stretches
30.
31.     c.gridx = 0; c.gridy = 1;
32.     add(new JButton("lefthandsidemiddle"), c);
```

```
33.       c.gridx = 1;
34.       add(tallPanel, c);
35.
36.       c.gridy = 2; // sets _y_
37.       add(new JButton("bottomcenter"), c);
38.       c.gridx = 2;
39.       c.weighty = 1.0;  // This row is stretchy
40.       add(tallPanel2, c);
41.       c.weighty = 0.0;  // No other row stretches
```

You'll see that the components added at lines 28 and 40 have had weight applied to them. Don't forget: although this weight is carried on the back of a component, it applies to the row or column being added to and *not* to the component. So, at line 28, we're really setting a weightx value of 1 on *column* 2 (the last column), and similarly at line 40, we're setting a weighty value on *row* 2.

The effect of this change, after enlarging the window and adding the grid boundary lines, is shown in Figure 12.24.

Two questions remain. First, what is the significance of the value "1.0" that was set as the weight—what would be the effect of other values? Second, how can you make more than one row or column stretch? It turns out that these two questions are related. If you apply weight values to more than one row or column, then the available space is divided among those rows or columns. Exactly how it is divided is determined by the weight values.

The weight values you specify represent a *proportion* of the whole space; the width (in the case of columns) gained is the ratio of a column's weight to the total of all column weights. If you have three columns with weights of 9, 9, and 18, respectively, then the first two will each get one-fourth of the total width gain: $9 / (9 + 9 + 18)$. The third column will get one-half of the extra space for itself. Similarly, if you specify the same weight for each (7, 7, and 7, for instance), then each column will gain one-third of the total space gained. The same calculations hold true for vertical stretch by rows.

Weights can be any number. They do not have to add to 1.0 or 100, but it is generally reasonable to use weights that add to 100 (or thereabouts) so that you can consider the values to be percentages. Just bear in mind that doing so is not required.

Although it is usual to set weights for rows and columns by using a GridBagConstraints object when a component is added, this is neither the only nor perhaps the best way to do so. Instead, you can use the public variables rowWeights and columnWeights. These variables are both arrays of double values and will act as minimum weights for each row or column. It makes little sense from a style point of view to specify weights for a row or column by means of data passed when adding a component to a cell.

Using the rowWeights and columnWeights arrays has two advantages. First, it makes much more sense to set the weights this way. Second, and more important, it lets you set a weight on a row or column that might not have any one component uniquely in that row or column. Using these arrays in conjunction with the rowHeights and columnWidths arrays allows you to simplify the code of many layouts and to avoid the use of dummy components (a technique you sometimes see used in complex GridBag layouts).

FIGURE 12.24   GridBag layout example with weights applied and an enlarged window

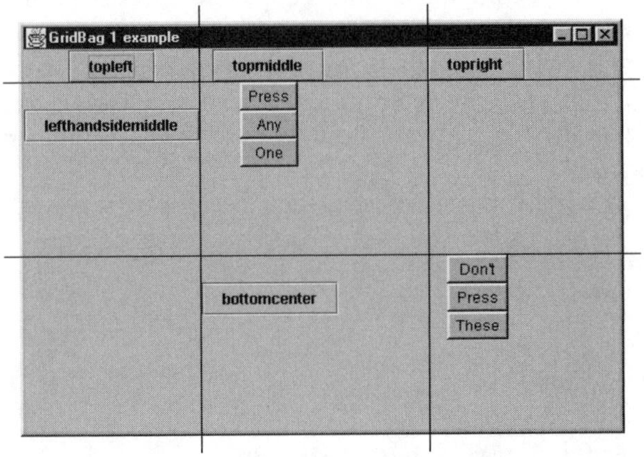

We have spent a long time on this discussion, so let's summarize what you've learned so far:

- The number of rows and columns in a GridBag layout is the greater of the number of cells that are used or the size of the `rowHeights` and `columnWidths` arrays if these exist.

- The default size of each row and column is the size of its tallest or widest component, respectively, or the value in the relevant entry in the `rowHeights` or `columnWidths` array if the array exists and specifies a larger size than the default would otherwise be.

- Stretchiness of rows and columns is controlled by weight.

- Stretchiness is applied using the `weightx` (for a column) and `weighty` (for a row) values of the `GridBagConstraints` object or by using the `rowWeights` and `columnWeights` arrays.

- Although `weightx` and `weighty` values exist for every component that is added, the values are meant for the row or column to which the component is added, not for the component itself. You should set a nonzero value for *at most* one component per row and one per column. (Note that you might have a component with both `weightx` and `weighty` set; rows and columns are independent things.) Using the `rowWeights` and `columnWeights` arrays can simplify this process considerably.

- The amount of stretch in a row or column is calculated as the total stretch divided in the same ratio as the individual weight values relative to the total weight for that axis. In math terms, if the weights are $w1$, $w2$, and $w3$, and the total stretch available is s, then the stretch applied to each column will be $s1$, $s2$, and $s3$ where s1 = s $\therefore$ w1 / (w1 + w2 + w3) and s2 = s $\therefore$ w2 / (w1 + w2 + w3) and s3 = s $\therefore$ w3 / (w1 + w2 + w3).

The next aspect we will look at is how a component is positioned when the target region in which it is located is larger than the component itself.

Controlling Component Position and Stretch in a Cell

You saw in the previous example that a component that occupies an oversized cell is normally placed in the center of the space, at its preferred size. Both of these features are controllable. Using a feature called anchor, you can control where the component is placed within its available space. Using a feature called fill, you can determine whether a component stretches to fill the available space, either horizontally, vertically, or both. Let's look at several examples. We will start with this code:

```
1. import java.awt.*;
2. import java.awt.event.*;
3. import javax.swing.*;
4.
5. public class GB2 extends JPanel {
6.   public GB2() {
7.     Font bigfont = new Font("Serif", Font.PLAIN, 36);
8.     setLayout(new GridBagLayout());
9.     GridBagConstraints c = new GridBagConstraints();
10.
11.     c.gridx = 0; c.gridy = 0;
12.     addButton("TL", bigfont, c);
13.     c.gridx = 1;
14.     addButton("Top Middle", bigfont, c);
15.     c.gridx = 2;
16.     addButton("TR", bigfont, c);
17.
18.     c.gridx = 0; c.gridy = 1;
19.     addButton("ML", bigfont, c);
20.     c.gridx = 2;  // note skipped over x=1, y=1
21.     addButton("MR", bigfont, c);
22.
23.     c.gridx = 0; c.gridy = 2;
24.     addButton("BL", bigfont, c);
25.     c.gridx = 1;
26.     addButton("Bottom Middle", bigfont, c);
27.     c.gridx = 2;
28.     addButton("BR", bigfont, c);
29.
30.     Font smallfont = new Font("SansSerif", Font.PLAIN, 10);
31.     c.gridx = 1; c.gridy = 1;
32.     addButton("x", smallfont, c);
```

```
33.    }
34.
35.    private void addButton(String label, Font font,
36.                        GridBagConstraints gbc)
37.    {
38.      JButton btn = new JButton(label);
39.      btn.setFont(font);
40.      add(btn, gbc);
41.    }
42.
43.    public static void main(String args[]) {
44.      JFrame f = new JFrame("GridBag Example 2");
45.      f.getContentPane().add(new GB2(),
           BorderLayout.CENTER);
46.      f.pack();
47.      f.setVisible(true);
48.    }
49. }
```

When run, this code produces the output shown in Figure 12.25. Notice that the little button in the middle simply lies in the center of the space available to it.

Let's look at the positions this component can occupy if we set different anchor values for it. The names of the anchor values are based on compass point names and are defined in the GridBagConstraints class as: NORTH, SOUTH, EAST, WEST, NORTHWEST, SOUTHWEST, NORTHEAST, SOUTHEAST, and CENTER. The default value for anchor, and the one exemplified in Figure 12.25, is CENTER. Now we'll make a small modification to the example program to see what happens if we change this anchor value. The modified programs are almost identical to the previous one, except that an additional constraint value is set on the small button to define the anchor. Figures 12.26, 12.27, and 12.28 show anchor values of NORTHWEST, SOUTHEAST, and EAST respectively. The effect of the anchor will be clear from these three examples without showing all the possible values.

FIGURE 12.25   GridBag layout example showing an unfilled, centered component

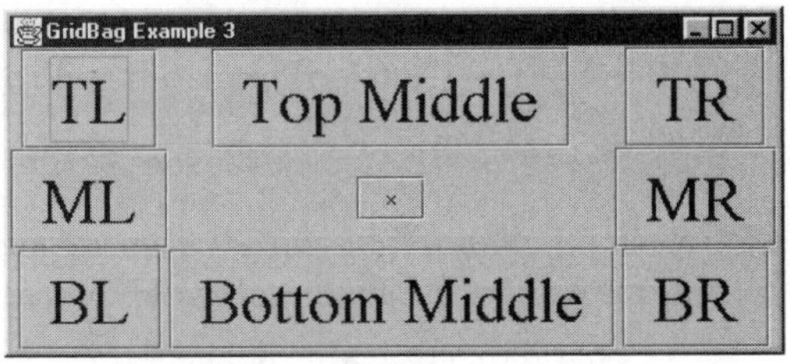

FIGURE 12.26   GridBag layout example showing an unfilled component with a NORTHWEST anchor

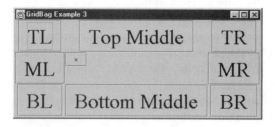

FIGURE 12.27   GridBag layout example showing an unfilled component with a SOUTHEAST anchor

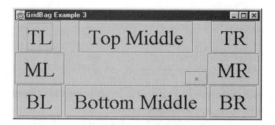

FIGURE 12.28   GridBag layout example showing an unfilled component with an EAST anchor

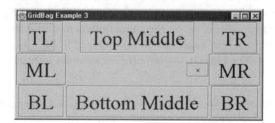

Now let's examine the fill feature. We'll start with the same code we used before, but instead of setting anchor values for the small button, we will set fill values. There are four fill values to choose from, and as with anchor values, they are defined in the GridBagConstraints class. The values are NONE (the default), HORIZONTAL, VERTICAL, and BOTH. In the current example, we can give the button's anchor a default value and its fill a value of GridBagConstraints.HORIZONTAL to get the effect shown in Figure 12.29.

Figures 12.30 and 12.31 respectively show what happens if we change the fill value to VERTICAL and BOTH.

FIGURE 12.29   GridBag layout example showing a component with HORIZONTAL fill

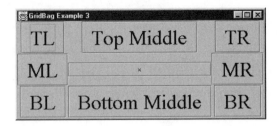

FIGURE 12.30   GridBag layout example showing a component with VERTICAL fill

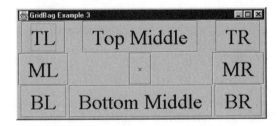

FIGURE 12.31   GridBag layout example showing a component with BOTH fill

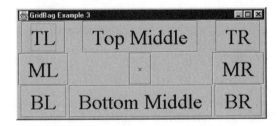

You can see that the effects of fill somewhat nullify the effects of anchor. That is, if a component is stretched to fill its cell horizontally, then the anchor cannot move it left, right, or center. Similarly, if the component fills its cell vertically, then trying to anchor it to the top, middle, or bottom is meaningless. So, if you have a fill value of HORIZONTAL, then anchor values of WEST, CENTER, and EAST would all produce the same effect. If fill is BOTH, the anchor value has no effect and should most sensibly be left at its default (CENTER).

Controlling the Cell Size for a Component

When you design a GUI using a GridBag layout manager, you sometimes find that components do not fit neatly into a simple grid, but the layout still presents the general idea of rows and columns. Consider the layout in Figure 12.32.

FIGURE 12.32   GridBag layout example showing components overlapping multiple rows and columns

FIGURE 12.33   GridBag layout example showing boundaries of rows and columns

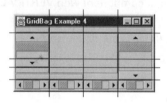

This example has five rows and four columns, although several of the components extend over more than one of each. Figure 12.33 has been modified to show the boundaries of the rows and columns more clearly.

To achieve this effect of component cells that span multiple rows and/or columns, the `GridBagConstraints` object provides fields called `gridwidth` and `gridheight`. Let's look at the code that produced this example, and you will see these fields in action:

```
1. import java.awt.*;
2. import javax.swing.*;
3.
4.
5. public class CellSize extends JPanel {
6.    public CellSize () {
7.       setLayout(new GridBagLayout());
8.       GridBagConstraints c = new GridBagConstraints();
9.
10.      // show entire cell region for all components
11.      c.fill = GridBagConstraints.BOTH;
12.      c.gridx = 0; c.gridy = 0;
13.      c.gridwidth = 1;
14.      c.gridheight = 1;
15.      add(new JButton(), c);
16.
17.      c.gridx = 1; c.gridy = 0;
```

```
18.     c.gridwidth = 3;
19.     c.gridheight = 1;
20.     add(new JButton(), c);
21.
22.     c.gridx = 0; c.gridy = 1;
23.     c.gridwidth = 1;
24.     c.gridheight = 1;
25.     add(new JScrollBar(JScrollBar.VERTICAL,
26.             0, 10, 0, 100), c);
27.
28.     c.gridx = 1; c.gridy = 1;
29.     c.gridwidth = 2;
30.     c.gridheight = 2;
31.     add(new JButton(), c);
32.
33.     c.gridx = 3; c.gridy = 1;
34.     c.gridwidth = 1;
35.     c.gridheight = 3;
36.     add(new JScrollBar(JScrollBar.VERTICAL,
37.             0, 10, 0, 250), c);
38.
39.     c.gridx = 0; c.gridy = 2;
40.     c.gridwidth = 1;
41.     c.gridheight = 1;
42.     add(new JButton(), c);
43.
44.     c.gridx = 0; c.gridy = 3;
45.     c.gridwidth = 2;
46.     c.gridheight = 1;
47.     add(new JButton(), c);
48.
49.     c.gridx = 0; c.gridy = 4;
50.     c.gridwidth = 1;
51.     c.gridheight = 1;
52.     add(new JScrollBar(JScrollBar.HORIZONTAL,
53.             0, 10, 0, 100), c);
54.
55.     c.gridx = 1; c.gridy = 4;
56.     c.gridwidth = 1;
57.     c.gridheight = 1;
58.     add(new JScrollBar(JScrollBar.HORIZONTAL,
```

```
59.              0, 10, 0, 100), c);
60.
61.       c.gridx = 2; c.gridy = 4;
62.       c.gridwidth = 1;
63.       c.gridheight = 1;
64.       add(new JScrollBar(JScrollBar.HORIZONTAL,
65.              0, 10, 0, 100), c);
66.
67.       c.gridx = 3; c.gridy = 4;
68.       c.gridwidth = 1;
69.       c.gridheight = 1;
70.       add(new JScrollBar(JScrollBar.HORIZONTAL,
71.              0, 10, 0, 100), c);
72.
73.    }
74.
75.    public static void main(String args[]) {
76.       JFrame f = new JFrame("GridBag Example 4");
77.       f.getContentPane().add(new CellSize(),
             BorderLayout.CENTER);
78.       f.pack();
79.       f.setVisible(true);
80.    }
81. }
```

Notice that at line 11 the fill value has been set to BOTH and is left at this setting for all uses of the GridBagConstraints object. As a result, all components will be stretched to fill their cells; this is the case even if the cell extends over multiple rows or columns. This way, you can see more easily where the boundaries of the cells are.

The next point about this code is that it is considerably longer than it needs to be. For every component that is added, the settings of gridx, gridy, gridwidth, and gridheight are explicitly set just before the add() method is called. You do so even when a value is not being changed, simply to make it easier to see how each value is set without having to scan up and down too far.

Compare the code with the screen shot in Figure 12.33. You will see the correspondence between gridwidth and the number of columns a component spans, and between gridheight and the number of rows a component spans. For example, the right button at the top of the layout is created by lines 17–20 of the code. At line 18, gridwidth is set to 3, and Figure 12.33 shows that the button extends across three columns.

Similarly, the large central button is set up by lines 28–31. Notice that the gridwidth and gridheight values are set to 2. Figure 12.33 shows that the button is two columns wide and two rows high.

One aspect warrants further mention. At row 3, column 2, there is a blank space. This is perfectly acceptable, although it is unlikely to happen in a real GUI layout. If you work through all the positions, `gridwidth` values, and `gridheight` values, you will see that no component has been placed in, or overlaps, that region.

That's about it for spanning multiple rows and columns. It's not really difficult, although it may have seemed that way before. Now, let's look at a convenient shorthand mechanism that the GridBag layout offers.

GridBag's Shorthand

You have undoubtedly seen two features used in GridBag layout examples: RELATIVE and REMAINDER. These settings provide a shorthand mechanism designed to reduce typing when you're coding a GridBag layout. They can also simplify maintenance of some types of layout.

If you think back to the earlier examples, you will recall seeing many lines setting values for `gridx` and `gridy`. Very often, the value being set was greater by one than the current value; this is often the case in real layouts, too. If you add your components in an orderly fashion, then you will probably set up the component in row zero, column zero first; then do column one, column two; and so on. You could do so by using code like this:

```
c.gridx++;
```

instead of the explicit numeric assignment used earlier.

In many cases, if you are filling a layout completely, from top-left to bottom-right, one row at a time, then the shorthand mechanism of RELATIVE and REMAINDER will help. Let's look at a simple example:

```
import java.awt.*;
import javax.swing.*;

public class Shorthand extends JPanel {

  public Shorthand () {
    setLayout(new GridBagLayout());
    GridBagConstraints c = new GridBagConstraints();
    c.fill = GridBagConstraints.BOTH;
    c.weightx = 1;

    add(new JButton("1"), c);
    add(new JButton("2"), c);
    add(new JButton("3"), c);
    add(new JButton("4"), c);
    c.gridwidth = GridBagConstraints.REMAINDER;
    add(new JButton("5"), c);
    c.gridwidth = 1;
    c.weightx = 0;

    add(new JButton("A"), c);
    add(new JButton("B"), c);
```

```
      add(new JButton("C"), c);
      c.gridwidth = GridBagConstraints.REMAINDER;
      add(new JButton("D"), c);
      c.gridwidth = 1;

      add(new JButton("a"), c);
      c.gridwidth = GridBagConstraints.RELATIVE;
      add(new JButton("b"), c);
      c.gridwidth = GridBagConstraints.REMAINDER;
      add(new JButton("c"), c);
      c.gridwidth = 1;
    }

  public static void main(String args[]) {
    JFrame f = new JFrame("GridBag Example 5");
    Shorthand sh = new Shorthand();
    f.getContentPane().add(sh, BorderLayout.CENTER);
    f.pack();
    f.setVisible(true);
  }
}
```

The output of this program is shown in Figure 12.34.

Notice that when the GridBagConstraints object is constructed, its values are mostly left constant. Notably, we never set any value for gridx or gridy; in fact, these values remain at their default—RELATIVE—throughout the program. It's important to realize that the X and Y control in this example is done entirely with the gridwidth value.

We use the value REMAINDER in the gridwidth field to indicate the last component on each line. After each line end, we set gridwidth back to 1, because failing to do so would cause every component to be on a line of its own for the rest of the layout.

The button labeled b is interesting, too. You will see that we set a value for gridwidth of RELATIVE for this button. As a result, it fills the space from its own starting point to the start of the last column. The documentation describes the component as being the "last but one." This effect can be useful when you are creating a workspace area and want to have a row of buttons either under it or down the right side, as you might for a toolbar.

FIGURE 12.34   GridBag layout example using the RELATIVE and REMAINDER shorthands

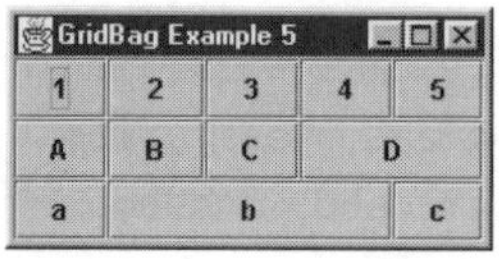

Clearly, this way of using the GridBag layout can make the code much simpler, although in some layouts it might still be easier to read the code if you explicitly state the X and Y coordinate values for each component as you add it. You will have to use your own judgment on this point.

This concludes our discussion of the GridBag layout and of the AWT suite of five layout managers.

Other Layout Options

The five layout managers of the AWT package will support most layout schemes you might want to implement. However, it is useful to know a little about the other options. If you are in a situation where Flow, Grid, Border, Card, and GridBag will not create the layout you need, your choices are

- To find a layout manager from another source

- To create your own layout manager

- To use no layout manager

Finding a third-party layout manager might be simple or hard, depending on the particular behavior you want. Several have been described in books, and more are available as freeware, as shareware, or in commercial graphics libraries for Java.

It is beyond the scope of this book to show you how to concoct your own layout manager, but for simple layout policies it is not especially difficult to do so. The advantage of creating a custom layout manager over setting a container's layout manager to `null` is that you no longer have to write code to detect resizing of the container; you just write code to implement the layout policy, and the system will make the right calls at the right time. Writing your own layout manager class involves implementing the `LayoutManager` interface (or possibly the `LayoutManager2` interface).

You always have the option of using no layout manager at all. To do this, just call

```
myContainer.setLayout(null);
```

If a container has no layout manager, it honors each component's `x`, `y`, `width`, and `height` values. Thus, you can call `setBounds()` on a component, `add()` it to a container that has no layout manager, and have the component end up where you expect it to be. This approach is tempting, but we hope the first part of this chapter has convinced you that layout managers are simple and efficient to work with. Moreover, if your container resides in a larger container (a frame, for example) that gets resized, your layout may need to be redone to save components from being overlaid or clipped away. People who set a container's layout manager to `null` find that they have to write code to detect when the container resizes, and more code to do the right thing when resizing occurs. Doing so ends up being more complicated than creating your own layout manager.

Summary

Layout managers provide a layer of geometrical support that relieves you of having to specify the size and position of each GUI component you create. The trade-off is that you must be aware of the layout policy implemented by each of the various layout managers. You are forced to think in terms of layout policy, rather than in terms of size and position.

This chapter has discussed the five AWT layout managers: Flow, Grid, Border, Card, and Grid-Bag. Each implements a distinct layout policy that dictates size, position, and resizing behavior of components. Alternatives to using the layout managers presented here include using a different manager, creating your own, and setting the layout manager to null.

 Real World Scenario

Not Quite a Border Layout

In this lab you will create and test a subclass of JFrame whose appearance is slightly different from an ordinary frame that uses a Border layout manager.

In an ordinary frame, the components at the top and bottom edges extend the entire width of the frame. Any components along the left and right edges do not extend all the way to the top or all the way to the bottom of the frame, since they yield to the top and bottom components. In other words, the top and bottom components get the corners.

Your subclass will reverse this geometry: the left and right components will extend all the way to the top and all the way to the bottom of the frame. In other words, the left and right components will get the corners, while the top and bottom components will have to be slightly narrower than the entire width of the frame.

There are some sophisticated ways to solve the problem, such as using a GridBag layout manager or creating your own layout manager class, but there is also a very simple approach that appears on your CD-ROM in the directory solutions\Chapter_12.

You will use enums to specify the locations of the components to be contained by your frame subclass. Create an enum called Side with four constants, named TOP, BOTTOM, LEFT, and RIGHT.

Your JFrame subclass' constructor should take a single argument: a generic map from Side to java.awt.Component. (Recall that java.awt.Component is the superclass of all Swing component classes.) So your constructor will look something like this:

```
public SidePriorityFrame(Map <Edge, Component> edgeToComponent)
```

The map may contain up to four elements, since the enum contains four constants. If, for example, the map contains the key Side.TOP, then the value associated with that key will be the component that should go at the top of your frame.

Chapter
13

Object Streams and RMI

In Chapter 10, "About the Developer's Exam," and Chapter 11, "Swing Components," you learned about using Swing to create a GUI. In Chapter 12, "Layout Managers," you learned how to read and write files. Now it's time to learn how to connect these two seemingly unrelated tasks.

Your Developer's Exam project requires you to create a GUI that displays and modifies the contents of a file. To complicate matters, the GUI and the file are running on separate machines that are connected by a network. Your spec calls the file-management program the "server," and the GUI program is called the "client." There might be multiple clients, all simultaneously trying to get the server's attention.

Clearly, some kind of networking code must be written for the server and client programs. The assignment lets you use object streams or Remote Method Invocation (RMI). This chapter presents both technologies. We'll begin with some concepts that are common to both: sockets and object serialization.

RMI is a huge topic, requiring an entire book for full coverage. Our goal here is not to present it in its entirety, but rather to give you a solid conceptual foundation.

Sockets and Streams

Most networking Java programs communicate using sockets and TCP. These technologies have been around for several decades, so by now they are dependable. Through the 1980s, networking was an arcane field; there was a lot to know, it was easy to make mistakes, and bugs were very hard to fix. Fortunately, Java has encapsulated the arcane functionality in the `java.net.Socket` and `java.net.ServerSocket` classes, which are quite easy to use.

If you decide to use object streams for your project's network communication, you will be constructing instances of `Socket` and `ServerSocket`. RMI uses sockets, so if you choose RMI, the `Socket` and `ServerSocket` instances will be created and used invisibly. In either case, it's important to know how these classes work.

TCP: A Reliable Protocol

Computers communicate with one another by transmitting sequences of 0s and 1s. A *protocol* is an agreement among programmers concerning the meanings of different bit sequences and the appropriate responses to bit sequences. For example, HTTP describes the bit sequences that web clients should send to web servers in order to request web pages and other services; the protocol also describes the formats of all the various responses that web servers might issue.

TCP is a low-level protocol with a single goal: reliability. A *reliable protocol* is one in which every message sent from one computer to another is eventually received without any distortion or omission. Reliable protocols are necessary because most computer communication takes place over telephone lines, which are vulnerable to the environment in many ways. With TCP, the receiver of a message is given a lot of information regarding the message's structure. If the message does not match the expected structure, the receiver can request that part or all of the message be retransmitted. Of course, reliability has its price: verifying the structure of each message takes time.

Many higher-level protocols use TCP for transferring data. SMTP, HTTP, and FTP all use TCP. If you choose to implement your exam project using object streams, you will concoct your own higher-level protocol over TCP. If you decide to use RMI, your RMI calls will use TCP in a way that will be invisible to you.

Sockets and Ports

TCP uses two abstractions called *sockets* and *ports*. They are called abstractions because there are no actual physical sockets or ports involved. The names are just metaphors that do a moderately good job of describing how to use TCP.

From the point of view of writing Java code, you can think of a socket as being an object that knows how to exchange data with another computer, using TCP.

Servers are capable of offering a variety of services. For example, the two most commonly used services are e-mail and the World Wide Web. Servers keep track of the services they offer by associating each service with a number, known as the *port number*. A client that wants to make use of a server needs to know the desired port number, as well as the hostname or IP address of the server. For example, when you point your browser to www.sybex.com, your computer connects to port 80 on server sybex.com (because 80 is the standard port number for web servers). Servers that exchange e-mail with sybex.com will connect to a different port (one that supports e-mail exchange) on the same server.

Now let's see how to write Java code that connects to a server.

Client Sockets in Java

The java.net.Socket class contains code that knows how to find and communicate with a server. The communication uses TCP, so it is reliable. To create a socket instance, use one of the constructors described on the API page. By far the most useful form is

```
public Socket(String servername, int portNumber)
```

The constructor throws IOException if the connection cannot be made.

Once the constructor returns, the socket is ready to communicate. You do not directly read from or write to a socket. Instead, the socket provides you with an input stream and an output stream, which can be used for reading and writing bytes, as shown in Figure 13.1.

FIGURE 13.1 A socket and its streams

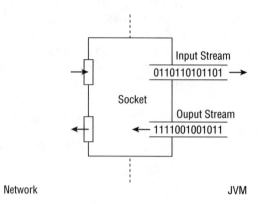

The following code constructs a socket connected to port 1234 on a server named mangfalo, then reads and prints out a byte sent by the server, and then sends a byte to the server:

```
try {
  // Make the socket.
  Socket sock = new Socket("mangfalo", 1234);

  // Get the streams.
  OutputStream ostr = sock.getOutputStream();
  InputStream istr = sock.getInputStream();

  // Read & print.
  System.out.println(istr.read());

  // Transmit.
  ostr.write(7);

  // Clean up.
  istr.close();
  ostr.close();
  sock.close();
}
catch (IOException x) {
  System.out.println("Stress: " + x.getMessage());
}
```

The code assumes that when server `mangfalo` receives a connection from a client on port 1234, it sends a single byte and then gets ready to receive a single byte. All communication code assumes a willing participant at the other end of the connection.

Notice the clean-up code, which closes the streams and then the socket.

WARNING   In this code example, and in the others that follow in this chapter, you will always see the output stream accessed before the input stream. The order shouldn't make a difference, but some versions of Java have a bug that makes communication fail if you call a socket's `getInputStream()` method before you call `getOutputStream()`.

Actually, people hardly ever write code that directly reads and writes a socket's streams. The streams deal with very low-level data: their methods can handle only single bytes, arrays of bytes, or pieces of arrays of bytes.

Does this situation remind you of anything? Recall from Chapter 12 that disk files are sequences of bytes. The bytes can be accessed (one by one, or as arrays, or as pieces of arrays) with the `FileInputStream` and `FileOutputStream` classes, but this is hardly ever done. Instead, more sophisticated streams are chained onto the raw streams. For example, a DataOutputStream can be chained onto a FileOutputStream, so that `ints`, `floats`, other primitives, and UTF strings can be written.

Fortunately, the higher-level input and output streams that you learned about in Chapter 12 can be chained onto the input and output streams of a socket, as shown in Figure 13.2.

FIGURE 13.2   A socket with chained streams

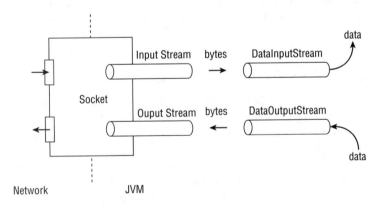

The following code reads a UTF string from the server and then writes a `double`:

```
try {
  // Make the socket.
  Socket sock = new Socket("mangfalo", 1234);
```

```
    // Get the streams.
    OutputStream ostr = sock.getOutputStream();
    DataOutputStream dostr = new DataOutputStream(ostr);
    InputStream istr = sock.getInputStream();
    DataInputStream distr = new DataInputStream(istr);

    // Read & print.
    System.out.println(distr.readUTF());

    // Transmit.
    dostr.writeDouble(Math.PI);

    // Clean up.
    dostr.close();
    ostr.close();
    distr.close();
    istr.close();
    sock.close();
}
catch (IOException x) {
    System.out.println("Stress: " + x.getMessage());
}
```

Of course, this code works only if server `mangfalo` cooperates by transmitting a UTF string and then preparing to receive a `double`. Writing server code in Java is easy, as you'll see in the next section.

Server Sockets in Java

From a programmer's point of view, the main difference between a client and a server has to do with initiation. A client always gets to assume that a server is available. You can see this assumption at work when you construct a `Socket` instance: the constructor automatically connects to the specified server's specified port.

A server, on the other hand, makes itself available and then waits for clients to initiate connections. This is done with an abstraction called a *server socket*, which in Java is represented by the java.net.ServerSocket class. The most useful form of the ServerSocket constructor is

```
public ServerSocket(int portNumber)
```

The constructor throws IOException if it gets into trouble. To make the new object available for client connections, call its accept() method, which returns an instance of Socket, as shown below:

```
try {
  ServerSocket ss = new ServerSocket(1234);
  Socket sock = ss.accept();
  . . .
}
catch (IOException x) {
  System.out.println("Stress: " + x.getMessage());
}
```

There is no way to know how long the accept() call will take. It depends on how promptly a client wants to take advantage of the service that the code just made available on port 1234 of server mangfalo. Once a client connects, the accept() method constructs and returns an instance of Socket. The subsequent server code can use the socket's input and output streams directly for byte communication, or higher-level streams can be chained to support communication of higher-level data. Thus, once a client has connected to the server, writing server code is just like writing client code.

Using sockets is a bit like using telephones in the following sense. At first the situation is asymmetrical. One person (analogous to the server) is hanging out at home, willing to communicate but not paying much attention to the phone. Another person (corresponding to the client), initiates a dialog by dialing their phone. The "server's" phone rings. The moment the "server" picks up the ringing phone, the two people are in identical situations, communicating with identical equipment. Similarly, server and client code starts out looking different: the server constructs a ServerSocket and calls accept(), while the client constructs a Socket. However, once the connection is established, both sides use identical equipment (a socket and its streams) to communicate.

When a ServerSocket instance executes an accept() call, the method blocks until a client connects. Blocking is an extremely important concept. A method *blocks* if, when realizing that a necessary resource is unavailable, the method gives up the processor until the resource becomes available. In the case of accept(), the necessary resource is the client. Clearly the method can't proceed until a client appears. In Java, methods block by calling wait(), which puts the current thread in a waiting state as you saw in Chapter 7, "Threads." In a properly designed program, another thread will eventually detect the presence of the desired resource; that thread will notify the waiting thread.

TCP allows multiple clients to be connected to a single port on a server. (On a popular web or mail server, the number of clients on a port at any moment can be quite large.) Often the most sensible thing for a server to do after accept() returns is to create a new thread to deal with the new client, leaving the current thread free to accept more client connections. For example, a server might rely on a class called `ServiceGiver`, which implements `java.lang.Runnable`. The class' constructor can store a socket on which communication is to take place, for which the `run()` method provides the communication:

```java
import java.net.*;
import java.io.*;

class ServiceGiver implements Runnable {
  private Socket sock;

  ServiceGiver(Socket sock) {
    this.sock = sock;
  }

  public void run() {
    try {
      OutputStream ostr = sock.getOutputStream();
      InputStream istr = sock.getInputStream();
      // Do something with the streams.
      . . .
    }
    catch (IOException x) {
      System.out.println("Stress: " + x.getMessage());
    }
  }
}
```

A server can use the `ServiceGiver` class like this:

```java
try {
  ServerSocket ss = new ServerSocket(1234);
  while (true) {
    Socket sock = ss.accept();
    ServiceGiver sg = new ServiceGiver(sock);
    (new Thread(sg)).start();
  }
}
catch (IOException x) {
  System.out.println("Stress: " + x.getMessage());
}
```

The thread that calls `accept()` is almost always waiting for new client connections; it is unavailable only for the brief time required to pass a newly connected socket to a `ServiceGiver` instance.

Object Streams and Serialization

As you have seen, data streams allow you to read and write primitives and strings, rather than individual bytes. Object streams go one step beyond data streams by allowing you to read and write entire objects.

The process of writing an object is called *serialization*. To serialize an object, first create an instance of `java.io.ObjectOutputStream`. This class, like `DataOutputStream`, expects to be chained onto a lower-level byte-oriented stream such as a file output stream or a socket's output stream. The method below uses an object stream to store a string buffer in a file named `sbuf.ser`.

```
void writeStringBuffer(StringBuffer writeMe)
                    throws IOException {
  FileOutputStream fos = new FileOutputStream("sbuf.ser");
  ObjectOutputStream oos = new ObjectOutputStream(fos);
  oos.writeObject(writeMe);
  oos.close();
  fos.close();
}
```

The `.ser` filename extension is conventional for files containing serialized objects.

To read the stored object back into a program, you can do the following:

```
StringBuffer readStringBuffer()
          throws IOException, ClassNotFoundException {
  FileInputStream fis = new FileInputStream ("sbuf.ser");
  ObjectInputStream ois = new ObjectInputStream(fis);
  StringBuffer sb = (StringBuffer)ois.readObject();
  ois.close();
  fis.close();
  return sb;
}
```

Notice that the value returned by `readObject()` is of type `Object`, so it must be cast. The object read in is identical to the one that was written out in the previous code example.

The `ObjectOutputStream` class has a `writeUTF()` method, as well as `writeByte()`, `writeShort()`, and all other write-primitive methods that also appear in data output streams. The `ObjectInputStream` class has corresponding reading methods. So if you want to create a file that contains serialized primitives and strings as well as serialized objects, you can do it with a single output stream.

When you use object streams, it's important to know what information gets serialized and what does not. It is only an object's data that is serialized, not its class definition. Moreover, not all data is written. Static fields are not, because it would not be appropriate to change a static variable, which is shared by all instances of a class, just because one instance of the class got reserialized. Transient fields are also not serialized. This provides a level of security in situations where you are concerned that sensitive variable values, serialized onto the network or into a file, might be read by hostile parties. By declaring a variable to be transient, you tell the JVM not to serialize that variable.

You might expect that private data would not be serialized, but in fact object streams pay no attention to access modes. All non-static non-transient fields are written to object output streams, regardless of whether they are public, private, default, or protected.

When an object is serialized, it will probably be deserialized by a different JVM. Any JVM that tries to deserialize an object must have access to that object's class definition. In other words, if the class is not already loaded, its class file must appear in the new JVM's classpath. If this is not the case, readObject() will throw an exception.

When an Object Output Stream serializes an object that contains references to another object, every referenced object is serialized along with the original object. For example, consider a Vector that contains bytes:

```
Vector<Byte> vec = new Vector<Byte>();
vec.add(new Byte("11"));
vec.add(new Byte("22"));
vec.add(new Byte("33"));
```

The Vector contains three references, and it can be diagrammed as shown in Figure 13.3.

When an Object Output Stream writes the Vector of Figure 13.3, the three bytes are also serialized. If instead of bytes the Vector contained objects that had references to still other objects, those other objects would also be serialized. In the terminology of serialization, when an object is serialized, its entire *graph* is serialized. An object's graph is the object itself, plus all the objects it references, plus all the objects those objects reference, and so on. When an object input stream deserializes an object, the entire graph is deserialized.

FIGURE 13.3   A Vector and its references

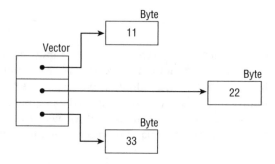

Serializable Objects

Not all objects may be serialized, though this is not obvious from a casual glance at the API page for `ObjectOutputStream`. The method summary entry for `writeObject()` says

```
public void writeObject(Object obj)
```

However, if you look at the method detail section for `writeObject()`, you'll see that it throws `NotSerializableException` if "some object to be serialized does not implement the `java.io.Serializable` interface." So even though the method declares that its argument is an object, it contains code that checks for the precondition that the argument must be an `instanceof Serializable` and throws the exception if the precondition is not met. Even if the object being passed into the method implements `Serializable`, the exception might still be thrown. Since the object's entire graph is serialized, all objects referenced by the object must implement `Serializable`, and all objects referenced by *those* objects must do the same, and so on.

 Recall from Chapter 5, "Flow Control, Assertions, and Exception Handling," in the discussion on assertions, that assertions should not be used to check preconditions in public methods. Fortunately, `writeObject()` respects this rule.

You probably recognize the `Serializable` interface from your reading of the API pages. Most of the core Java classes implement it. All the wrapper classes do so, and so do the collection classes. In fact, the only core Java classes that do *not* implement `Serializable` are ones that should not be serialized. For example, it would make no sense to try to serialize a thread, because a thread's state is tightly bound to the current JVM's thread scheduler. So it wouldn't really be helpful or meaningful to serialize a thread. Likewise, the low-level output and input streams of the `java.io` package don't implement `Serializable` because they interact with the underlying hardware.

When you create a class that might be serialized, the class should implement `Serializable`. This is easy, because the interface doesn't define any methods at all. All you need to do is type **implements java.io.Serializable** in your class declaration, and you're finished. Empty interfaces such as `Serializable` are known as *tagging interfaces*. They identify implementing classes as having certain properties, without requiring those classes to actually implement any methods. Arrays of primitives or serializable objects are themselves serializable.

`Serializable` has a subinterface called `Externalizable`, which you can implement if you want to customize the way a class is serialized. Notice that since `Externalizable` extends `Serializable`, the `implements Serializable` precondition in `writeObject()` is met by any object that implements `Externalizable`.

`Externalizable` contains two method signatures:

```
void writeExternal(ObjectOutput out)
   throws IOException
void readExternal(ObjectInput in)
   throws IOException, ClassNotFoundException
```

ObjectOutput and ObjectInput are interfaces that are implemented by ObjectOutputStream and ObjectInputStream. They define, respectively, writeObject() and readObject() methods.

Implementing Externalizable is useful when you don't trust the environment in which serialized instances of your class will be stored. If you're concerned that hostile parties might be able to read sensitive fields of your class, you have the option of encrypting those fields. (You also can choose not to serialize sensitive fields at all, but that is more easily accomplished by declaring them to be transient.) For example, the following class performs its own serialization, protecting the password field by reversing it before writing it out.

```
import java.io.*;

public class Account implements Externalizable {
  private String  ownerName;
  private String  password;
  private float   balance;

  private String reverse(String reverseMe) {
    String reversed = "";
    for (int i=reverseMe.length()-1; i>=0; i--)
      reversed += reverseMe.charAt(i);
    return reversed;
  }

  public void writeExternal(ObjectOutput outStream)
            throws IOException {
    outStream.writeObject(ownerName);
    outStream.writeObject(reverse(password));
    outStream.writeObject(new Float(balance));
  }

  public void readExternal(ObjectInput inStream)
            throws IOException, ClassNotFoundException {
    ownerName = (String)inStream.readObject();
    String reversedPassword =
     (String)inStream.readObject();
    password = reverse(reversedPassword);
    balance = ((Float)inStream.readObject()).floatValue();
  }
}
```

When an instance of this class is passed to an Object Output Stream, the default serialization procedure is bypassed; instead, the stream calls the instance's `writeExternal()` method. When an Object Input Stream reads a serialized instance of `Account`, a call is made to the no-args constructor for the `Account` class. Then the newly constructed object receives a `readExternal()` call so that it can reconstitute its serialized values.

Notice that the `readObject()` mechanism of `ObjectInputStream` relies on the existence of a no-args constructor for any class that implements `Externalizable`. If an externalizable class has no no-args constructor, the `readObject()` method will throw `java.io.InvalidClassException`.

Remote Control Using Object Streams

If you decide to use object streams for your project, you need to build a mechanism for one JVM to tell another JVM what to do. Your client JVM will be displaying the Swing GUI, which will capture commands from the user. The commands will involve retrieving or modifying the contents of the database file, which is under the control of the server JVM.

The straightforward way to build a remote-control system is to create a class that represents a command. The client can issue commands to the server by writing an instance of a command object to an Object Output Stream that is connected to the server. The server can interpret the command object, take appropriate action, and if necessary send some kind of response object back to the client.

In this section we'll develop the code for a very simple remote-control system. We'll create a server that can add and subtract floats on behalf of a client. Of course, the client is perfectly capable of doing its own arithmetic; the goal here is to provide an example that's simple enough that the communication between client and server is clear.

Let's start by developing an object that can encapsulate a request from the client. We'll call the class `Command`. It should contain the `floats` to be added or subtracted, as well as a field that specifies what operation should be performed. Without enums, it would probably make sense to use an `int` to encode the desired operation. But since enums are available, we should make use of them. Here is an enum that describes the server's various services:

```
enum Operation {
   ADD, SUBTRACT, DONE;
}
```

In addition to `ADD` and `SUBTRACT`, the enum has a `DONE` value that tells the server that the client is done. On receiving this value, the server can close its streams.

The `Command` class is straightforward:

```
import java.io.*;
```

```java
class Command implements Serializable {
  private Operation  operation;
  private float[]    operands;

  Command(Operation operation) {
    this.operation = operation;
  }

  Command(Operation operation, float[] operands) {
    this.operation = operation;
    this.operands = operands;
  }

  Operation getOperation() {
    return operation;
  }

  float[] getOperands() {
    return operands;
  }
}
```

Fortunately, enums are serializable, so the Command class' entire graph is serializable.

The Server class is an application that creates a server socket on port 7654. (The port number was assigned arbitrarily. Numbers through 1024 are reserved for assignment by a standards committee. Numbers greater than 1024 are uncontrolled and may be used freely.) The server waits for a client connection, then spawns a thread to service the connection, and then goes back to waiting for connections. We'll look first at the Server class and then at the service-providing thread class.

Here's the Server class:

```java
import java.io.*;
import java.net.*;

public class Server {
  public static void main(String[] args) {
    try {
      ServerSocket ss = new ServerSocket(7654);
      while (true) {
        Socket sock = ss.accept();
        ServiceGiver sg = new ServiceGiver(sock);
        sg.start();
      }
```

```
      }
    catch (IOException x) {
      System.out.println("Server Stress: " +
                              x.getMessage());
    }
  }
}
```

There is nothing difficult about the Server class. Its main() is structured just like the example in the Server Socket discussion earlier in this chapter, in the "Server Sockets in Java" section. There is nothing in the code to indicate what kind of service is performed, and that's a good sign: it indicates that functionality has been nicely partitioned. The Server class takes care of establishing connections, while the ServiceGiver class provides service on those connections.

Here is the ServiceGiver code:

```
import java.io.*;
import java.net.*;

class ServiceGiver extends Thread {
  private Socket sock;

  ServiceGiver(Socket sock) {
    this.sock = sock;
  }

  public void run() {
    try {
      // Build object streams.
      OutputStream os = sock.getOutputStream();
      ObjectOutputStream oos = new ObjectOutputStream(os);
      InputStream is = sock.getInputStream();
      ObjectInputStream ois = new ObjectInputStream(is);

      // Provide service.
      while (true) {
        Command command = (Command)ois.readObject();
        float[] operands = command.getOperands();
        switch (command.getOperation()) {
          case ADD:
            Float result = operands[0] + operands[1];
            oos.writeObject(result);
            break;
```

```
              case SUBTRACT:
                result = operands[0] - operands[1];
                oos.writeObject(result);
                break;
              case DONE:
                oos.close();
                ois.close();
                os.close();
                is.close();
                sock.close();
                return;
            }
          }
        }
        catch (IOException x) {
          System.out.println("IO Stress: " + x.getMessage());
        }
        catch (ClassNotFoundException x) {
          System.out.println("Class Stress: " +
                              x.getMessage());
        }
      }
    }
```

This class follows the structure of the example given earlier in this chapter, in the "Server Sockets in Java" section. There it was suggested that a service-providing class should implement Runnable. In the example here the code is quite simple, so it's sufficient to extend Thread.

The constructor caches the socket that is to receive service. All service takes place in the run() method, which loops on reading a Command object from the input stream, extracting the Operation from the Command object, and taking appropriate action. Recall that Operation is an enum, so here you see an example of switching on an enum value.

Let's finish this example by looking at simple client that connects to a server and then commands the server to perform each of its operations:

```
import java.io.*;
import java.net.*;

public class Client {
  public static void main(String[] args) {
    try {
      test(args[0]);    // args[0] is server name
```

```
      }
      catch (IOException x) {
        System.out.println("IO Stress: " + x.getMessage());
      }
      catch (ClassNotFoundException x) {
        System.out.println("Class Stress: " +
                           x.getMessage());
      }
    }
  }

  private static void test(String serverName)
                   throws IOException, ClassNotFoundException {
    // Connect to server.
    Socket sock = new Socket(serverName, 7654);

    // Build object streams.
    OutputStream os = sock.getOutputStream();
    ObjectOutputStream oos = new ObjectOutputStream(os);
    InputStream is = sock.getInputStream();
    ObjectInputStream ois = new ObjectInputStream(is);

    // Test addition.
    float[] addUs = {12.3f, 56.7f};
    Command command = new Command(Operation.ADD, addUs);
    oos.writeObject(command);
    Float result = (Float)ois.readObject();
    System.out.println("Addition result: " + result);

    // Test subtraction.
    float[] subtractUs = {3.14159f, 1.11111f};
    command = new Command(Operation.SUBTRACT, subtractUs);
    oos.writeObject(command);
    result = (Float)ois.readObject();
    System.out.println("Subtraction result: " + result);

    // Done.
    command = new Command(Operation.DONE);
    oos.writeObject(command);
    oos.close();
    ois.close();
```

```
    os.close();
    is.close();
    sock.close();
  }
}
```

The `Client` application assumes that the server's hostname is supplied on the command line. The `main()` method calls `test()`, which commands the server to add, then subtract, and then be done.

The server and client are able to function together because each is aware of the other's requirements and behavior. These define a little protocol, which can be summarized as follows:

1. The client initiates all communication, by sending a `Command` instance to the server.

2. When the server receives an `ADD` or `SUBTRACT` command, it responds with a `float`.

3. When the server receives a `DONE` command, it closes the connection without responding.

If you decide to use object streams for your project, your protocol will be much more intricate than the one shown here, but its structure will be similar: the client will initiate communication by sending something to the server, which will do something with the database and then send a response.

So far in this chapter you've seen how object streams are a good foundation for a system in which a client giver orders to a server. The drawback is that your code has to take care of a sizable number of implementation details. In particular

- Your client has to know the port number on the server.

- Your server and client have to deal with sockets, low-level streams, and object streams.

- Your client cannot directly issue commands to the server. You have to create a class to represent a command and its parameters.

Now we can turn our attention to your alternative to object streams: RMI.

Remote Method Invocation

Java's *Remote Method Invocation (RMI)* facility lets you make method calls on objects that exist outside your JVM. RMI hides many of the details that you have to take care of when you use object streams, including knowledge of the server port number, socket and stream maintenance, and the need for a command class.

RMI is extensive, and this chapter can't go into full detail. Our goal is to give you an overview. Let's start by looking at the main idea of RMI: remote references.

Remote References

The goal of RMI is to support remote calls in a way that resembles as much as possible the experience of making local calls.

When you make a call on a local object—that is, on an object in the same JVM as the code making the call—you use a reference to the local object. RMI provides *remote references*, which act as references to remote objects. Remote references don't really point to remote objects, though they do a good job of sustaining that illusion. They really point to local objects called *stubs*. A stub is a local object that supports RMI by communicating with a remote object.

You make an RMI call by making a call on a stub. The stub is in communication with the host that owns the remote object. The stub sends the method arguments to the remote object and tells it to execute the appropriate method. The remote object executes the method; if there is a return value or if an exception is thrown, the remote object transmits the return value or exception back to the stub. Figure 13.4 shows the relationship between the stub and the remote object.

Using RMI is easy: you just use a remote reference to make calls on a stub, and the stub takes care of the work. You don't even have to write the stub code; it's written for you by the `rmic` (RMI compiler) tool, as you'll see shortly. The difficulty of RMI lies not in using it but in setting it up. You need to do meticulous work on both the server and client sides. In the next section you'll learn the details of writing and running an RMI application.

FIGURE 13.4   A stub and a remote object

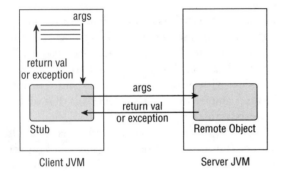

RMI Step by Step

An RMI application is a partner dance between a client and a server. When it's done right it looks easy, because both partners are well prepared. In this section, we'll describe a six-step plan for creating and executing client and server code.

The steps are

1. Create the remote interface.
2. Create the remote class.
3. Create the stub.
4. Create the remote server.
5. Create the client.
6. Start the programs.

Each step is described below in its own section. We'll develop a simple example that mimics the object-stream example you saw earlier in the chapter.

Step 1: Create the Remote Interface

A *remote interface* is an interface that describes the remotely accessible methods of a remote object. A remote object and the stub that communicates with it both implement the remote interface.

Recall that RMI clients use remote references, which point to stubs. The type of a remote reference is a remote interface. So a client makes RMI calls by calling the remote interface's methods on the remote reference. Later on you'll see how that's done. For now, be aware that the first step is to create an interface that lists the remote object's remotely accessible methods.

All remote interfaces must extend `java.rmi.Remote`, which is a tagging interface. Recall that a tagging interface has an empty method list, so a class can implement `Remote` without actually providing any method implementations.

All methods in a remote interface must throw `java.rmi.RemoteException`, in addition to any other specified exceptions. The stub throws `RemoteException` if something goes wrong with the connection to the server. This means that in all client code, all RMI calls must catch `RemoteException` or deal with it by some other means.

RMI uses serialized objects to send method arguments from a client to a server and to send return values and exceptions back to a client from a server. Thus all arguments, return values, and exceptions must be serializable. You don't need to worry about exceptions, because `java.lang.Exception` implements `Serializable`, but you do have to pay attention to all arguments and return values. RMI can deal with primitive arguments and return values, so what you really need to remember about a remote interface's methods is that all object-type arguments and return values must be serializable.

In our discussion of object streams, you saw example code in which a server could add or subtract two floats, returning a float value. The argument floats were passed to the server in an array. Here we begin converting that example to RMI. Following is a remote interface that describes the remote services:

```
import java.rmi.*;

public interface MathServices extends Remote {
  public float add(float[] addUs)
    throws RemoteException;
  public float subtract(float[] subtractUs)
    throws RemoteException;
}
```

Notice that this interface fulfills its two requirements: it extends `Remote`, and its methods throw `RemoteException`. Now let's see how the remote interface is used.

Step 2: Create the Remote Class

The remote interface is implemented by the remote class and the stub. Here we'll look at the remote class. This class is constructed by the server and then made available for remote invocation.

There are two requirements on a remote class:

- It must extend `java.rmi.server.UnicastRemoteObject`.
- It must implement the remote interface.

The remote class is the workhorse of an RMI system. It is the class whose methods provide services to clients. Here is a remote class whose methods provide the services of our mathematical example:

```java
import java.rmi.*;
import java.rmi.server.*;

public class Mathematician
            extends UnicastRemoteObject
            implements MathServices {
  public Mathematician() throws RemoteException { }

  public float add(float[] addUs)
              throws RemoteException {
    return addUs[0] + addUs[1];
  }

  public float subtract(float[] subtractUs)
              throws RemoteException {
    return subtractUs[0] - subtractUs[1];
  }
}
```

The only tricky part of this class is the constructor. The no-args constructor of the superclass (`java.rmi.server.UnicastRemoteObject`) throws `java.rmi.RemoteException`, so a subclass must explicitly provide a constructor that also throws this exception, even if the constructor's body does nothing.

Now let's see how to make a stub.

Step 3: Create the Stub

A stub must be created for every class whose methods are to be made available for RMI calling. The stub and the remote class both implement the remote interface. On the client side, a remote reference points to an instance of the stub. Stubs are also used on the server side.

Stubs are created by using the `rmic` tool, not by writing and compiling Java source code. `rmic` resides in the JDK's `bin` directory, so it's already in your path if you can compile and execute. To create a stub, type **rmic *remote_class_name***.

To learn all of `rmic`'s command-line arguments, type **rmic**.

In our case, the remote class name is `Mathematician`, so the corresponding stub is created by typing **rmic Mathematician**.

If a remote class is in a package, the class' full name must be provided. So for example if `Mathematician` were in a package called `services`, then you would type **rmic services.Mathematician**.

The output from `rmic` is a classfile whose name is the remote class name with `_Stub` appended at the end. So in our example the stub is called `Mathematician_Stub`.

Now the three essential pieces have been created: the remote interface, the remote class, and the stub. The next step is to create server and client code.

Step 4: Create the Server

An RMI server is an application that creates one or more remote objects and makes them available to clients. Creating an RMI server is not completely straightforward, because of the need to interact with the RMI registry.

The RMI registry is a program that associates names with RMI services. A server specifies a name for every remote object it provides. A client accesses a remote object by specifying the server and the service name. In general, the names in the registry are descriptive of the services they represent. Choosing good service names is as important as choosing good variable names.

The RMI registry is a process separate from any individual JVM. It must be running before any Java applications try to interact with it. To start the registry, type **rmiregistry** on a command line. The program resides in the Java `bin` directory.

On a single machine, multiple Java applications can offer services through a single registry. An application accesses the registry via the `java.rmi.Naming` class, all of whose public methods are static. To associate a name with a remote object, a server should call `Naming.rebind()`, which has the following signature:

```
public static void rebind(String name, Remote obj)
```

The `name` argument is the name by which clients will access the remote object. The `obj` argument is the remote object itself; its type is `Remote` rather than `Object` because a remote object implements a remote interface, which extends `Remote`. You can look up the other methods of the `Naming` class in the API; it's possible to bind a new object to a name and to unbind a name (that is, to tell the registry that the name no longer corresponds to the object). A server continues to run as long as at least one remote object is bound.

An RMI server performs two tasks:

1. Create an instance of the remote object.
2. Bind the remote object to a name.

Here is a server for our example. The service name is `brainiac`.

```
import java.io.*;
import java.rmi.*;

public class MathServer {
  public static void main(String[] args) {
    try {
      Mathematician m = new Mathematician();
      Naming.rebind("brainiac", m);
    }
    catch (RemoteException x) {
      System.out.println("Remote Exception stress " + x);
    }
    catch (IOException x) {
      System.out.println("Other IOException stress " + x);
    }
  }
}
```

Recall that remote objects extend `UnicastRemoteObject`, so their constructors throw `RemoteException`. The `Naming.rebind()` call throws various subclasses of `IOException`.

Servers must always be prepared to handle multiple clients. You saw in the object streams server example that it's a good strategy for a server to spawn off a service thread as soon as possible after receiving a client connection on a server socket. With RMI you have no access to the server socket, but you still need to take precautions. No matter how many clients concurrently call a remote method, there is still only one object executing the method. If the method accesses critical data of the object, you need to use the techniques of Chapter 7 to protect the data.

Step 5: Create the Client

A client obtains a remote reference by contacting the RMI registry on the server machine. This is done by calling the static `lookup()` method of the `Naming` class. The signature of `lookup()` is

```
public static Remote lookup(String name)
```

Something seems to be missing from the signature. The object name is provided, but not the server hostname. How does the RMI infrastructure know which host to contact?

The name argument actually specifies both the server hostname and the object name, in a URL format. The format of this string is

```
rmi://server_hostname/object_name
```

The object name must be a name that has been bound to an object in the server's registry. It is optionally legal to omit everything except the object name. In this case the RMI infrastructure uses the local host as a server. This is very convenient for debugging, since you can develop code on a single machine.

The return type of Naming.lookup() is Remote, which is the superclass of the remote interface. The returned value should be cast to the remote interface type.

After the remote reference is obtained, calls made on the remote reference are automatically sent to the server. From a programmer's point of view the only difference between an ordinary call and an RMI call is that all RMI calls throw RemoteException. Here is a client application that uses RMI to remotely call the add() and subtract() methods of the brainiac service:

```java
import java.io.*;
import java.rmi.*;

public class MathClient {
  public static void main(String[] args) {
    try {
      // Get remote reference.
      String url = "rmi://" + args[0] + "/brainiac";
      MathServices ms = (MathServices)Naming.lookup(url);

      // Add.
      float[] addUs = { 12.34f, 56.78f };
      float sum = ms.add(addUs);
      System.out.println("Sum = " + sum);

      // Subtract.
      float[] subtractUs = { 99.99f, 76.54f };
      float difference = ms.subtract(subtractUs);
      System.out.println("Difference = " + difference);
    }
    catch (NotBoundException x) {
      System.out.println("Name stress " + x);
    }
    catch (RemoteException x) {
      System.out.println("Remote Exception stress " + x);
    }
```

```
    catch (IOException x) {
      System.out.println("Other IOException stress " + x);
    }
  }
}
```

The user supplies the remote server's hostname on the command line.

At this point all necessary code has been written. All that remains is to deploy and execute the client and server applications.

Step 6: Start the Programs

Before you start the programs that constitute an RMI application, you need to make sure that the right files are present on the right machines. Remember that the remote interface and the stub must be deployed on both the server and the client.

The various programs must be started up in the following order:

1. The server's RMI registry
2. The server
3. The client or clients

The RMI registry must be started first. If it is not running when the server application calls `Naming.rebind()`, an exception will be thrown. The server should be started next, so that the desired remote objects will be available when clients call `Naming.lookup()`. Clients should be the last applications to be started.

Summary

This chapter has discussed your two options for client/server communication: object streams and RMI.

Object streams use Java's `Socket` and `ServerSocket` classes. Although they are straightforward to use, choosing this design forces you to create a protocol and some kind of command class.

RMI, which is built on top of object streams, relieves you of many low-level tasks, including protocol design and command class maintenance. However, with RMI you take on some high-level tasks, including interaction with the RMI registry, as well as creation and deployment of stub classes.

Both approaches have advantages and disadvantages. If you are familiar with all the costs and benefits, you will be able to make a well-informed decision when the time comes to choose which strategy you will use in your project.

Chapter Review Lab

Client/Server Weather Forecasting

In this exercise you will create a weather station client/server application that produces weather reports. When clients contact the server they can request a forecast or a temperature. Of course, the point of this exercise is to practice network programming in Java, so the weather reports don't need to be based on reality. Feel free to choose forecasts at random from a group of strings like Rainy or Sunny or Oobleck. Generate random numbers for the temperatures.

Implement two solutions: one that uses object streams and one that uses RMI. This work will give you exposure to both technologies, so you'll be able to make a good choice when you decide which one to use in your project.

One possible solution set appears on your CD-ROM in solutions\Chapter_13.

Chapter 14

Putting It All Together

At this point you have the big picture. You know how to create a server that accesses data in a disk file. You know how to create a Swing GUI client. You know how to connect the server and the client, using object streams or RMI. This chapter discusses a number of small, unrelated issues that can affect your grade on the Developer's Exam in big ways. These issues are Javadoc, threading, extra credit, object streams vs. RMI, common-sense GUI design, and the `jar` tool.

Javadoc

Your code is required to provide Javadoc API pages for all the public parts of your classes. These pages are generated by the `javadoc` tool, which shares a lot of code with the compiler. To create your pages, make sure all your public data and methods are commented with Javadoc-style comments. Then run `javadoc` on your source.

By default, `javadoc` documents all the public and protected features of a class, even if they don't have Javadoc-style comments. Consider a class with no Javadoc comments at all, just a pair of variables and a method:

```
package xyz;
import java.util.*;

public class VectorOfStrings extends Vector<String> {
  public int  x;
  public int  y;

  public String toString() {
    return "Vector-o-Strings";
  }
}
```

javadoc processes source files, so to generate an API for this class you type **javadoc VectorOfStrings.java**.

The result is 13 professional-looking HTML files, including an index, a package overview (not that there's anything else in the package), and a page for the class. The class page displays the class hierarchy, the list of implemented interfaces, field/constructor/method summaries, and field/constructor/method details. In fact, `javadoc` automatically generates everything anyone could want from a class page, except for an overall class description and detailed information about the fields, constructors, and methods. This information has to be provided by the programmer, in the form of Javadoc comments.

A Javadoc comment begins with /** and continues through the next */. A Javadoc comment just before a class definition becomes that class' description in the API page. A Javadoc comment just before a field or method becomes that field or method's description. Here's our VectorOfStrings class with an added class description:

```java
package xyz;
import java.util.*;
import java.io.*;


/**
A Vector that contains strings and has very little to offer.
*/

public class VectorOfStrings extends Vector<String> {
  public int  x;
  public int  y;

  public String getString(int n) throws IOException {
    if (Math.random() > 0.5)
      throw new IOException();
    return "Vector-o-Strings";
  }
}
```

You can make a class description fancier by adding tags. These are special codes that appear inside the Javadoc comments that cause special formatting. For example, you might want a run of text to appear in a fixed-width font; this is generally done when referring to code. In our example, "Vector" should be in program font. To do this, insert <code> before the text run and </code> after the run:

```java
/**
A <code>Vector</code> that contains strings and has very little to offer.
*/
```

You can render a run of text in italics by inserting <i> before the run and <\i> after the run. So if the VectorOfStrings class really has *very* little to offer, you can use this comment:

```java
/**
A <code>Vector</code> that contains strings and has <i>very</i> little to offer.
*/
```

Another family of tags begins with @ and extends to the end of the line. The @ tags are

@author

@version

@see

@return

@param

@throws

The first three of these tags are for commenting a class. The last three appear in method comments. Here's a fully commented VectorOfStrings class that uses one of each kind of tag you've seen so far:

```java
package xyz;
import java.util.*;
import java.io.*;


/**
A <code>Vector</code> that contains strings and has <i>very</i> little to offer.

@author     Philip Heller
@version    1096.1
@see        java.util.List
*/

public class VectorOfStrings extends Vector<String> {
    /**
    Just an int.
    */
    public int  x;

    /**
    Just another int.
    */
    public int  y;

    /**
    @return   Returns a constant string that isn't the
              quite the class name.
    @param    <code>n</code> is ignored.
    @throws   IOException about half the time,
              randomly.
```

```
*/
public String getString(int n) throws IOException {
  if (Math.random() > 0.5)
    throw new IOException();
  return "Vector-o-Strings";
  }
}
```

As you can see, `@return` is for documenting a method's return value, `@param` is for documenting an argument, and `@throws` is for documenting exceptions. Use these codes to provide descriptions of all return values, all arguments, and all exceptions in all public methods. Since your assignment doesn't require you to document your protected fields or methods, use the `-public` command-line flag to tell `javadoc` to ignore all nonpublic features.

Thread Issues

Your server is required to be multithreaded. That is, it has to perform appropriately when servicing multiple simultaneous clients. There are several issues that you should keep in mind when designing this part of your project.

First, it's impossible to thoroughly test multithreaded code. With threads, some bugs manifest themselves only when a careless thread is granted the Java Virtual Machine (JVM) processor at a particular moment. Since you have no control over when the thread scheduler swaps in a new thread, you can't possibly test every scenario. So no matter how thoroughly you may have exercised your code, there might still be bugs lurking in the depths.

So if you can't simulate every possible condition, you need to *imagine* every possible condition. You need to go through every possible combination of "If thread A is waiting to execute a synchronized method of object X, while thread B owns the lock of X because it's running X's so-and-so method...." If your multithreading code is at all convoluted, the number of combinations is staggering, and the scenarios are so complicated that it's difficult to think clearly about them. Your only chance is to make sure your threading design is straightforward. Can you explain it to someone else without referring to your source code or your comments? If not, it's too complex to hold easily in your mind. And if it's that complex, you won't be able to think through every possible scenario.

It's possible that a very complicated threading design actually works flawlessly under all conditions. Nevertheless, the complexity will still bring your grade down. Your assignment spec can be implemented with a moderately simple threading model, and any additional complexity is unnecessary. It isn't enough to observe the absence of deadlocks. You need to convince yourself that deadlocks are impossible.

The second issue concerns thread priorities. Recall from Chapter 7, "Threads," that priorities are vaguely defined. At best, a thread's priority influences how much processor time that thread will receive, over a statistically large number of thread switches. If your thread code deadlocks and you solve the problem by adjusting a priority, you're moving in the wrong direction. There is no guarantee that two JVMs will treat priorities the same way. So if you have a complicated priority scheme, throw it away. Your deadlock is likely to appear on a different machine; it would be tragic if it appeared while your project was being graded. All deadlocks should be resolved by redesigning your waiting and notifying structure, not by adjusting priorities.

The third issue concerns waiting and notifying. It's important to make threads wait on appropriate objects. Imagine a server that provides a large number of clients with multithreaded access to a large number of resources. Never mind what the resources are or what the clients do with them. Each client connects to the server, then does *something* with a single resource, then possibly does something with a different resource, and so on until the client closes the connection. Clearly, while a client is doing its thing with a resource, other clients should not have access to that resource. The obvious way to enforce this in Java is to have a client acquire some object's lock while accessing the resource; another client that wants the same resource will have to execute `wait()` until the first client finishes its work and calls `notify()`. This is what `wait()` and `notify()` are for.

The question is, on what object should `wait()` and `notify()` be called? There are two possibilities. First, all threads could wait on a single object. This is a very simple approach, easy to understand and easy to implement. However, it has a serious drawback. Suppose thread A is accessing object X. The thread acquires the overall lock and begins to do its thing. Now suppose thread B wants to access some different object Y. There's only one lock, and thread A owns it. Thread B can't proceed until thread A is finished, even though it's perfectly safe to do so. The server slows down more and more as more clients connect, needlessly preventing one another from getting much work done. The system might as well not be multithreaded, since only one thread can proceed at a time.

The alternative is to provide a lock for every resource. Now a client thread needs to wait only if the desired resource is unavailable. The server is much more efficient. In particular, it has the virtue that all clients immediately get to make progress, even if that progress is slow. From a client's perspective, immediate slow progress is much better than no progress at all.

The only drawback to providing a lock for every resource is that your code can become complicated. But it doesn't have to. It's possible to create a server that locks appropriately without being too complex to think about.

Extra Credit

This point was made in Chapter 10, "About the Developer's Exam," but it bears repeating: *there's no extra credit*. The Developer's Exam assessors report that many candidates submit work that goes far beyond the requirements of the spec. Usually this is gratifying; it's good to know that people take pride in their work. However, the scoring guidelines don't provide a way to acknowledge the extra work by awarding extra credit points.

The only way extra work can affect your grade is downward. Suppose you add some brilliant functionality to your client GUI. If the code is poorly commented, if it's difficult to read, or if its public methods don't have Javadoc comments, your assessor is obligated to reduce your score, no matter how impressive your GUI is.

If your extra work is less than brilliant, your risk is greater. Now it's not just the implementation that can bring your grade down. The new functionality itself is subject to scrutiny. If, for example, you add GUI controls that make your client frame hard to use, you'll lose points.

This isn't to say that creativity is unimportant. Creativity is vital, but it must be expressed appropriately. Your Developer's Exam project isn't an appropriate place. It's okay to submit a boring project. You'll have plenty of opportunities throughout your career to express your brilliance in ways that can be appreciated.

RMI or Object Streams?

Object streams are an appropriate design choice for simple client/server systems. As complexity increases, Remote Method Invocation (RMI) becomes increasingly appropriate. There are two reasons for this.

First, object streams require a custom protocol. You need to invent a command object that tells the server what service is required, and you need a way for the client to supply arguments and receive results. This is easy if there are only a few services (as there will be in your project). However, as the server's services become increasingly broad, the cost of implementing the expanding protocol increases. With RMI, you just add more methods to the remote interface and then implement them on the server and call them in the client.

Second, RMI can be invoked from non-Java systems. It isn't easy or fun, but sometimes it's necessary. An object-stream server is not likely to be useful to a non-Java client, because only Java knows how to serialize and deserialize Java objects.

Somewhere between simple-enough-for-object-streams and complicated-enough-for-RMI is an area of overlap where either technology can be justified. Your project lies in this area. This is why you can choose object streams or RMI according to your taste, and neither is considered better. You won't gain or lose points for either choice.

So which should you choose?

If you have experience with one of the technologies but not the other, consider using the one you're not familiar with. The exam is a good opportunity to gain new experience. If you find you don't like using the unfamiliar technology, you can always fall back on the familiar one.

On the other hand, if you're equally experienced or inexperienced in RMI and object streams, RMI is probably more beneficial to you in the long run. Your choice won't affect your grade, but RMI experience looks better on a resume than object stream experience. Commercial applications (that is, those written by enterprises that have money to pay their programmers) increasingly use J2EE. J2EE is a jumble of technologies that includes JavaServer Pages, Enterprise JavaBeans, and much more. RMI is part of J2EE, so RMI experience is appealing to hiring managers.

Common-Sense GUI Design

You could spend years mastering the principles of modern GUI design. You probably don't want to make that kind of commitment, though, and the exam expects you only to show good common sense. You can't get into much trouble if you remember that the goal of a GUI is to make life easier for your users. With that in mind, we'll review three principles that are easy to understand and easy to implement: standardization, resizing, and disabling the impossible.

The first principle is standardization. Look at several programs that you use frequently: a web browser or a mail reader, for example. What features do they have in common? Do they share these features with many other less-used programs?

It's difficult to find a successful program that *doesn't* have most of the following:

- A menu bar at the top of the main frame
- A File menu at the far-left end of the menu bar
- One or more toolbars below the menu bar
- A work area below the toolbar(s)
- A status bar at the bottom of the main frame

Standardized features are good because they put expected functionality in expected places. People who approach your application for the first time can expend their energy learning how to use the unique parts of the program. If I try to use your program to create a new file of whatever type your program creates, and I don't find a New… menu item at the top of a File menu at the left end of a menu bar at the top of a main frame, then I have to spend time figuring out where you put the file-creation functionality. Every time I want to create a new file, my comfortable habit of looking in the File menu fails me. I would prefer to spend my time using your program to get useful work done.

This does not mean that you should implement all standard features whenever you create a GUI. Rather, if your GUI provides standard functions, then the controls for those features should appear in standard places. For example, every GUI needs a way to quit, and the Exit menu item goes at the bottom of the File menu. So you have to provide a menu bar to hold the File menu, which holds the Exit menu item. But not every GUI requires a status bar. You need to provide one only if your program generates helpful status information. Similarly, you might not need a toolbar. So the rule of thumb is, if your GUI supports standard functionality, then that functionality should be controlled in a standard way.

The second principle concerns resizing. You saw in Chapter 12, "Layout Managers," that Java provides sophisticated layout managers to ensure appropriate resizing of components. If components are too large, screen space is wasted. If components are too small, they are difficult to use.

But what makes a component too large or too small? Generally the best size for a component is its preferred size. Often components that aren't their preferred size look odd. This is especially true of text components, whose preferred height is determined by the font and preferred width is determined by the label. Consider the dialog created by the following code:

```
JDialog dialog = new JDialog();
Container cont = dialog.getContentPane();
cont.setLayout(new GridLayout(1, 2));
cont.add(new JLabel("Name:"));
cont.add(new JTextField(10));
```

The dialog is shown in Figure 14.1.

If you look closely at the text field, you'll see that it isn't quite as wide as they could be. There's a small area of wasted space between the label and the text field. The wasted space looks worse if the dialog becomes wider, as in Figure 14.2.

Figure 14.2 shows the downside of using a Grid layout manager for this dialog. When a user resizes the dialog, their intention is to get more space for typing in a name. They don't need a wider label, but that's exactly what they get, thanks to the Grid layout manager's blindly fair policy of sharing all new pixels among all child components.

It's even worse when the dialog becomes taller as well as wider. Look at Figure 14.3.

FIGURE 14.1   Slightly wrong component size

FIGURE 14.2   Truly wrong component size

FIGURE 14.3   Extremely wrong component size

In addition to the width problem, this dialog now has a height problem. The text field has become taller, but the font hasn't grown. The text looks lost and forlorn in the middle of all that white background.

As a general principle, it isn't enough to think about the size of a component at the moment it is displayed. You need to consider the consequences of resizing. In our example, a more sophisticated layout scheme is called for:

```
JDialog dialog = new JDialog();
Container cont = dialog.getContentPane();
cont.setLayout(new GridBagLayout());
GridBagConstraints gbc = new GridBagConstraints();
gbc.gridx = 0;
gbc.gridy = 0;
gbc.gridwidth = 1;
gbc.gridheight = 1;
gbc.weightx = 0;
cont.add(new JLabel("Name: "), gbc);
gbc.gridx = 1;
gbc.gridwidth = 1;
gbc.fill = GridBagConstraints.HORIZONTAL;
gbc.weightx = 100;
cont.add(new JTextField("        "), gbc);
```

Now even in its initial appearance the label's width is appropriate, as seen in Figure 14.4. When the dialog resizes, the components stay the right size, as seen in Figure 14.5.

FIGURE 14.4   Appropriate component size

FIGURE 14.5   Appropriate component size, after resizing

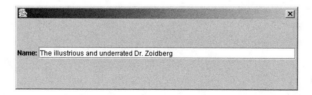

Our last principle of GUI design can be called "disabling the impossible." A GUI should make it impossible for a user to configure a request that the GUI can't fulfill. As a very simple example, think about typing a credit card number into a web page. What should you type after the first four digits? A space? A hyphen? The next digits? Have you ever guessed wrong and had to wait for an error-message page that tells you to type again, without explaining the required format? Then you have to remember what format you typed into the original page, which by now is gone forever. It would be better if the error-message page told you why your format was wrong. It would be even better if the original form page told you what format was expected. It would be best if the original form page made it impossible to type a bad format, either by accepting all formats or, best of all, by clearly prompting you as in Figure 14.6.

In the figure, it's obvious that the groups of digits are separated by hyphens, and it's equally obvious that the user shouldn't type any hyphens, because they're already there. The ultimate in user-friendliness would be if the text field accepted only digits as input.

As another example, consider a form for ordering ice cream. Suppose the online ice cream stand offers only chocolate, vanilla, and strawberry. Figure 14.7 would be the wrong way to prompt for input.

What happens if the user types an unavailable flavor or misspells an available flavor, as in the figure? This kind of GUI usually flashes a dialog box that says something irritating like, "Flavor unavailable, please try again." The design is a waste of the user's time. The GUI should make it impossible to specify an unavailable flavor or to misspell an available one. Since the program obviously has access to the list of available flavors, it should present users with all legal options and allow them to choose from those options. This can be done with a combo box if there are a lot of options or with a group of radio buttons as shown in Figure 14.8.

FIGURE 14.6   User-friendly credit card input

FIGURE 14.7   A wrong way to prompt for a flavor

FIGURE 14.8   One right way to prompt for a flavor

Now there's no possibility of misspelling, because the GUI doesn't require typing. There's no possibility of requesting a flavor that isn't sold at this virtual ice cream stand, because only the available flavors are displayed. Users have no way to request a service that the GUI doesn't provide.

Most error dialogs in most GUIs complain about invalid input. When your GUI code includes an error dialog, ask yourself whose fault the error is. It might really be your fault, for creating the conditions for the user to make an invalid request.

There is much more that could be said about creating great GUIs, but our purpose here isn't to make you the world's greatest user interface designer. We're just here to get you a good grade on your exam, and you'll be fine if you keep in mind the principles of standardization, resizing, and disabling the impossible.

Using the *jar* Tool

A *jar* file is a Java archive file. Its format is compatible with zip files and tar files. The `jar` command resides in the Java `bin` directory. You invoke it by typing a command line, for example:

```
jar -cvf sources.jar *.java
```

The `-cvf` is a cluster of options. The `c` is the most important option; it says that a new jar file is to be created. `jar` can create, extract, list the contents of, or update an archive file. To specify which operation is be performed, the first argument (after the optional hyphen) must be `c`, `x`, `t`, or `u`. Think of these four as primary options. The remaining options are secondary; they tell `jar` how to do its job.

Table 14.1 shows some of `jar`'s secondary options.

The `-v` option means that `jar` prints out detailed information about every file it adds to or extracts from the archive file. The `-0` option, which is used only when creating or updating, overrides `jar`'s compression algorithm, which is compatible with `zip`'s algorithm and produces nearly the same degree of compression. The `-M` option, also used only when creating or updating, tells `jar` not to create a manifest file inside the archive. A *manifest* is a file that provides information about the jar file's contents; by default `jar` creates one automatically for you.

The `-f` and `-m` options each require that you specify a filename in the command line. The `-f` specifies the name of the archive file to be created, extracted, listed, or updated. The `-m` option is used when you create your own manifest file, which you do when you want to make an executable archive.

Notice in our example that the option letters are clustered together, sharing a single hyphen. That's the preferred syntax. After the cluster (`-cvf`) come any filenames required by options in the cluster. In our case the f option requires a filename; `jar` will create an archive named `sources.jar`. The `.jar` extension is customary. If you use `.zip`, your archive can be read by all `zip`-compatible tools.

TABLE 14.1   Secondary jar Options

Option	Requires Filename	Function
-v	no	Verbose
-0 (zero)	no	Don't compress
-M	no	Don't create a manifest
-f	yes	Specifies jar file to create, extract, etc.
-m	yes	Specifies manifest file

After the last jar or manifest filename required by a secondary option, the command line ends with a list of content filenames (*.java in our example). These are the files to be inserted into or extracted from the archive. You don't need to specify them if you're doing a listing or an extraction; if no filenames appear, then jar will list or extract everything in the archive. If you're doing a create, then the listed files will be copied into the new archive. If you're doing an update, the listed files will be copied into an existing archive. If a directory name appears in the list, the directory's contents are processed recursively.

A jar file may appear in a classpath, in place of a directory name. Thus if you create several packages containing numerous class files, you can ship them to your customers in a single jar archive. Your customers can use them without extracting the archive, which is a messy alternative to keeping everything isolated inside the jar file.

Leaving class files in a jar is slightly less efficient than extracting them, because the JVM must extract and decompress them before they can be loaded. However, this inefficiency is slight and is incurred only once per file; after a class is loaded, its description is inside the JVM and the file need never be touched again.

If a jar file contains an application's main class, you can make the jar executable. This is a nice convenience for your users, because with an executable jar they don't have to remember the name of the main class. To run an executable jar file, you just use the -jar option and name the file on the java command line, like this:

```
java -jar the_executable_archive.jar
```

To make an executable jar, first create a manifest that tells which class file is the main class. To do this, create a text file that contains a line like the following:

```
Main-Class: x.y.MyMainClass
```

Note that you specify the class name, not the class filename, so there's no `.class` suffix. Be sure to specify the entire class name, including package prefixes (`x.y.` in this example). The text file can have any name at all. It is not inserted into the jar file. Instead, the `jar` program reads it and copies its information into the manifest file, which the `jar` program creates.

Now build your jar file, using the `-m` option to tell `jar` which file to look in for manifest information. For example, if your `Main-Class` line is in a file called `manny.txt`, your command line would be

```
jar -cvfm my_archive.jar manny.txt *.class
```

The `jar` program reads the main class declaration in `manny.txt` and builds a manifest inside the jar, containing the main class declaration and a bit of extra information. Inside the jar a directory named `META-INF` is created, and in `META-INF` is a plain-text file called `MANIFEST.MF`. Here's what `MANIFEST.MF` looks like for our example:

```
Manifest-Version: 1.0
Created-By: 1.5.0 (Sun Microsystems Inc.)
Main-Class: MyMainClass
```

Ease of use is an important part of software quality. A little familiarity with the `jar` program can significantly increase the ease of use of your project.

Summary

In the previous chapters you've read about the GUI, I/O, and communication technologies that you will need to complete your project. This chapter has reviewed some smaller miscellaneous concepts: you've read about Javadoc, threading, extra credit, object streams vs. RMI, common-sense GUI design, and the `jar` tool.

That's all you need! At this point you're ready to download your assignment and get to work. Good luck!

Appendix

A

Practice Exam

Questions

1. Given the following:

```
public enum Wallpaper {
  BROWN, BLUE, YELLOW;
}
```

   Which of the following are legal?

   A.
```
enum PatternedWallpaper extends Wallpaper {
    STRIPES, DOTS, PLAIN;
  }
```

   B. `Wallpaper wp = Wallpaper.BLUE;`

   C.
```
Wallpaper wp =
        new Wallpaper(Wallpaper.BLUE);
```

   D.
```
void aMethod(Wallpaper wp) {
        System.out.println(wp);
  }
```

   E.
```
int hcode =
        Wallpaper.BLUE.hashCode();
```

2. Given the following:

```
package pack;

class Sploo {
  public int            a;
  public static int     b;
  int                   c;
  static int            d;

  public void eee() { }
  public static void fff() { }
}
```

   Which of the following features of class `Sploo` may be accessed by a class, in package `pack`, as a result of the following import?

```
import static pack.Sploo.*;
```

   A. a

   B. b

   C. c

   D. d

   E. eee()

   F. fff()

3. Given the following:

```
public abstract class Abby {
  abstract provideMe();
}
public class SubAbby extends Abby { }
```

Which statements are true?

A. Abby generates a compiler error.

B. SubAbby generates a compiler error.

C. If SubAbby were declared abstract, it would compile without error.

D. If SubAbby were declared abstract, it could be instantiated.

E. Abby is a legal type for variables.

4. Given the following code:

```
class Xxx {
  int[]        ages;
  int[]        heights = new int[10];
}
```

Which statements are true?

A. ages is initialized to null.

B. ages is initialized to a reference to an array with zero elements.

C. heights is initialized to null.

D. heights is initialized to a reference to an array with zero elements.

E. heights is initialized to a reference to an array with 10 elements.

5. Given a class with a public variable theTint of type Color, which of the following methods are consistent with the JavaBeans naming standards?

A. public Color getColor()

B. public Color getTint()

C. public Color getTheTint()

D. public Color gettheTint()

E. public Color get_theTint()

6. Which of the following statements are true regarding the following method?

```
void callMe(String... names) { }
```

A. It doesn't compile.

B. Within the method, names is an array containing Strings.

C. Within the method, names is a list containing Strings.

D. The method may be called only from within the enclosing class.

7. Given the following:

```
public class Food { }
public class Fruit extends Food { }
public class Citrus extends Fruit { }

public class Pomelo extends Citrus { }

public class SuperDuper {
  public Fruit feedMe() { return new Fruit(); }
}

public class Subby extends SuperDuper {
  public ????? feedMe() { return new Pomelo (); }
}
```

Which of the following are legal return types for `feedMe()` in class Subby?

A. Object

B. Food

C. Fruit

D. Citrus

E. Pomelo

8. Given the following class:

```
class A extends java.util.Vector {
  private A(int x)  { super(x); }
}
```

Which statements are true?

A. The compiler creates a default constructor with public access.

B. The compiler creates a default constructor with protected access.

C. The compiler creates a default constructor with default access.

D. The compiler creates a default constructor with private access.

E. The compiler does not create a default constructor.

9. Which of the following types are legal arguments of a `switch` statement?

A. enums

B. bytes

C. longs

D. floats

E. strings

10. Given the following:

```
int[] ages = { 9, 41, 49 };
int sum = 0;
```

Which of the following are legal ways to add the elements of the array?

A. `for (int i=0; i<ages.length; i++)`
    `sum += ages[i];`

B. `for (int i=0; i<=ages.length; i++)`
    `sum += ages[i];`

C. `for (int i:ages)`
    `sum += i;`

D. `sum += ages[int i:ages];`

11. Which lines check that x is equal to four? Assume assertions are enabled at compile time and runtime.

A. `assert x == 4;`

B. `assert x != 4;`

C. `assert  x == 4 : "x is not 4";`

D. `assert  x != 4 : "x is not 4";`

12. Which are appropriate uses of assertions?

A. Checking preconditions in a private method

B. Checking postconditions in a private method

C. Checking preconditions in a public method

D. Checking postconditions in a public method

13. `EOFException` and `ObjectStreamException` both extend `IOException`. `NotSerializable-Exception` extends `ObjectStreamException`. `AWTException` does not extend any of these. All are checked exceptions. Suppose class `AClass` has a method `callMe()` whose declaration is

`void callMe() throws ObjectStreamException`

Which of the following may appear in a subclass of `AClass`?

A. `void callMe()`

B. `void callMe() throws IOException`

C. `void callMe()`
        `throws NotSerializableException`

D. `void callMe()`
      `throws ObjectStreamException,`
            `AWTException`

14. ObjectStreamException extends IOException. NotSerializableException extends ObjectStreamException. AWTException does not extend any of these. All are checked exceptions. The callMe() method throws NotSerializableException. What does the following code print out? Choose all lines that are printed.

```
try {
  callMe();
  System.out.println("I threw");
}
catch (ObjectStreamException x) {
  System.out.println("Object stream");
}
catch (IOException x) {
  System.out.println("IO");
}
catch (Exception x) {
  System.out.println("Exception");
}
finally {
  System.out.println("Finally");
}
```

- **A.** I threw
- **B.** Object Stream
- **C.** IO
- **D.** Exception
- **E.** Finally

15. While testing some code that you are developing, you notice that an ArrayIndexOutOf-BoundsException is thrown. What is the appropriate reaction?

- **A.** Enclose the offending code in a try block, with a catch block for ArrayIndexOutOfBoundsException that does nothing.
- **B.** Enclose the offending code in a try block, with a catch block for ArrayIndexOutOfBoundsException that prints out a descriptive message.
- **C.** Declare that the method that contains the offending code throws ArrayIndexOutOfBoundsException.
- **D.** None of the above.

16. How is `IllegalArgumentException` used? (Choose all correct options.)

   A. It is thrown by the JVM when a method is called with incompatible argument types.

   B. It is thrown by the JVM to indicate arithmetic overflow.

   C. It is thrown by certain methods of certain core Java classes to indicate that preconditions have been violated.

   D. It should be used by programmers to indicate that preconditions of public methods have been violated.

   E. It should be used by programmers to indicate that preconditions of nonpublic methods have been violated.

17. Suppose `shorty` is a `short` and `wrapped` is a `Short`. Which of the following are legal Java statements? (Choose all correct options.)

   A. `shorty = wrapped;`

   B. `wrapped = shorty;`

   C. `shorty = new Short((short)9);`

   D. `shorty = 9;`

18. Which of the following statements are true? (Choose all correct options.)

   A. `StringBuilder` encapsulates a mutable string.

   B. `StringBuilder` is threadsafe.

   C. `StringBuffer` is threadsafe.

   D. `StringBuffer` is generally faster than `StringBuilder`.

19. Suppose you know that a file named `aaa` was created by a Java program that used a `DataOutputStream`. The file contains 10 `doubles`, followed by a UTF string. Which of the following code snippets read the string correctly? Assume all code exists in an environment that legally handles `IOException`. (Choose all correct options.)

   A.
```
RandomAccessFile raf =
    new RandomAccessFile("aaa", "r");
for (int i=0; i<10; i++)
  raf.readDouble();
String s = raf.readUTF();
```

   B.
```
RandomAccessFile raf =
    new RandomAccessFile("aaa", "r");
raf.seek(10*8);
String s = raf.readUTF();
```

   C.
```
FileReader fr = new FileReader(fr);
for (int i=0; i<10*8; i++)
  fr.read();
String s = fr.readUTF();
```

D.
```
FileInputStream fis = new FileInputStream("aaa");
DataInputStream dis = new DataInputStream(fis);
for (int i=0; i<10; i++)
  dis.readDouble();
String s = dis.readUTF();
```

E.
```
FileInputStream fis = new FileInputStream("aaa");
DataInputStream dis = new DataInputStream(fis);
dis.seek(10*8);
String s = dis.readUTF();
```

20. Suppose you want to read a file that was not created by a Java program. The file contains lines of 8-bit text, and the 8-bit encoding represents the local character set, as represented by the current default locale. The lines are separated by newline characters. Which strategy reads the file and produces Java strings?

   A. Create a RandomAccessFile instance and use its readText() method.

   B. Create a RandomAccessFile instance and use its readUTF() method.

   C. Create a FileReader instance. Pass it into the constructor of LineNumberReader. Use LineNumberReader's readLine() method.

   D. Create a FileInputStream instance. Pass it into the constructor of LineNumberReader. Use LineNumberReader's readLine() method.

   E. Create a FileInputStream instance. Pass it into the constructor of DataInputStream. Use DataInputStream's readLine() method.

21. What interfaces can be implemented in order to create a class that can be serialized? (Choose all that apply.)

   A. No interfaces need to be implemented. All classes can be serialized.

   B. Have the class declare that it implements java.io.Serializable. There are no methods in the interface.

   C. Have the class declare that it implements java.io.Serializable, which defines two methods: readObject and writeObject.

   D. Have the class declare that it implements java.io.Externalizable, which defines two methods: readObject and writeObject.

   E. Have the class declare that it implements java.io.Externalizable, which defines two methods: readExternal and writeExternal

22. Suppose you are writing a class that will provide custom deserialization. The class implements java.io.Serializable (not java.io.Externalizable). What access mode should the readObject() method have?

   A. public

   B. protected

   C. default

   D. private

23. Suppose you want to create a class that compiles and can be serialized and deserialized without causing an exception to be thrown. Which statements are true regarding the class? (Choose all correct options.)

    A. If the class implements `java.io.Serializable` and does not implement `java.io.Externalizable`, it must have a no-args constructor.

    B. If the class implements `java.io.Externalizable`, it must have a no-args constructor.

    C. If the class implements `java.io.Serializable` and does not implement `java.io.Externalizable`, its nearest superclass that *doesn't* implement `Serializable` must have a no-args constructor.

    D. If the class implements `java.io.Externalizable`, its nearest superclass that *doesn't* implement `Externalizable` must have a no-args constructor.

24. Suppose you want to use a `DateFormat` to format an instance of `Date`. What factors influence the string returned by `DateFormat`'s `format()` method?

    A. The operating system

    B. The style, which is one of SHORT, MEDIUM, or LONG

    C. The style, which is one of SHORT, MEDIUM, LONG, or FULL

    D. The locale

25. How do you generate a string representing the value of a `float f` in a format appropriate for a locale `loc`?

    A.
```
NumberFormat nf =
    NumberFormat.getInstance(loc);
String s = nf.format(f);
```

    B.
```
NumberFormat nf =
    new NumberFormat(loc);
String s = nf.format(f);
```

    C.
```
NumberFormat nf =
    NumberFormat.getInstance();
String s = nf.format(f, loc);
```

    D.
```
NumberFormat nf =
    new NumberFormat(loc);
String s = nf.format(f, loc);
```

26. Given the following code:

```
1. String scanMe = "aeiou9876543210AEIOU";
2. Scanner scanner = new Scanner(scanMe);
3. String delim = ?????; // WHAT GOES HERE?
4. scanner.useDelimiter(delim);
5. while (scanner.hasNext())
6.   System.out.println(scanner.next());
```

What code at line 3 produces the following output?

```
aeiou
AEIOU
```

   A. `String delim = "d+";`

   B. `String delim = "\d+";`

   C. `String delim = "\\d+";`

   D. `String delim = "d*";`

   E. `String delim = "\d*";`

   F. `String delim = "\\d*";`

27. Which line prints double d in a left-justified field that is 20 characters wide, with 15 characters to the right of the decimal point?

   A. `System.out.format("%20.5f", d);`

   B. `System.out.format("%20.15f", d);`

   C. `System.out.format("%-20.5f", d);`

   D. `System.out.format("%-20.15f", d);`

28. Suppose MyThread extends `java.lang.Thread`, and MyRunnable implements `java.lang.Runnable` (but does not extend `Thread`). Both classes have no-args constructors. Which of the following cause a thread in the JVM to begin execution? (Choose all correct options.)

   A. `(new MyThread()).start();`

   B. `(new MyThread()).run();`

   C. `(new MyRunnable()).run();`

   D. `(new Thread(new MyRunnable()))`

   E. `   .start();`

29. What will be the outcome when the following application is executed?

```
public class ThreadTest {
   public void newThread() {
      Thread t = new Thread() {
         public void run() {
         System.out.println("Going to sleep");
            try {
               sleep(5000);
            } catch (InterruptedException e) {}
            System.out.println("Waking up");
         }
      };
      t.start();
      try {
```

```
      t.join();
    } catch (InterruptedException e) {}
    System.out.println("All done");
  }
  public static void main(String [] args) {
    new ThreadTest().newThread();
  }
}
```

A. The code prints "Going to sleep," then "Waking up," and then "All done."

B. The code prints "All done," then "Going to sleep," and then "Waking up."

C. The code prints "All done" only.

D. The code prints "Going to sleep" and then "Waking up."

E. The code does not compile.

30. Given the following class:

```
class Classy {
  synchronized void notStaticMethod() {
    for (long n=0; n<100000000000L; n++)
      System.out.println(n);
  }

  synchronized static void staticMethod() {
    for (long n=0; n<100000000000L; n++)
      System.out.println(n);
  }
}
```

Suppose thread A and thread B both have references to each of two instances of Classy. These references are named classy1 and classy2. Which statements are true? (Choose all correct options.)

A. If thread A is executing classy1.staticMethod(), then thread B may not execute classy1.staticMethod().

B. If thread A is executing classy1.staticMethod(), then thread B may not execute classy2.staticMethod().

C. If thread A is executing classy1.notStaticMethod(), then thread B may not execute classy1.staticMethod().

D. If thread A is executing classy1.notStaticMethod(), then thread B may not execute classy1.notStaticMethod().

E. If thread A is executing classy1.notStaticMethod(), then thread B may not execute classy2.notStaticMethod().

31. Suppose threads aThread and bThread are both accessing a shared object named sharedOb, and aThread has just executed:

sharedOb.wait();

What code can bThread execute in order to get aThread out of the waiting state, no matter what other conditions prevail?

A. aThread.notify();

B. aThread.notifyAll();

C. aThread.interrupt();

D. sharedOb.notify();

E. sharedOb.notifyAll();

32. Suppose class Car has public variables forceOnGasPedal and forceOnBrakePedal, and a public method respondToPedalChanges(). Class Driver manipulates an instance of Car by changing the variables and then calling the method. Which statements are true? (Choose all that apply.)

A. The Car and Driver classes are loosely coupled.

B. The Car and Driver classes are tightly coupled.

C. This degree of coupling is desirable.

D. This degree of coupling is undesirable.

33. Suppose class Home has methods chopWood() and carryWater(); it also has a method called chopWoodAndCarryWater(), which just calls the other two methods. Which statements are true? (Choose all that apply.)

A. chopWoodAndCarryWater() is an example of appropriate cohesion.

B. chopWoodAndCarryWater() is an example of inappropriate cohesion.

C. chopWoodAndCarryWater() is an example of appropriate coupling.

D. chopWoodAndCarryWater() is an example of inappropriate coupling.

34. Suppose class Lemon extends class Citrus. Given the following code:

Lemon lem = new Lemon();
Citrus cit = new Citrus();

Which lines compile without error? (Choose all that apply.)

A. lem = cit;

B. cit = lem;

C. lem = (Lemon)cit;

D. cit = (Citrus)lem;

E. cit = (Object)lem;

35. Suppose classes `Lemon` and `Grapefruit` extend class `Citrus`. Which statements are true regarding the following code?

```
1. Grapefruit g = new Grapefruit();
2. Citrus c = (Citrus)g;
3. Lemon lem = (Lemon)c;
```

    A. The cast in line 2 is not necessary.

    B. Line 3 causes a compiler error.

    C. The code compiles, and throws an exception at line 3.

    D. The code compiles and runs without throwing any exceptions.

36. Suppose class `aaa.Aaa` has a method called `callMe()`. Suppose class `bbb.Bbb`, which extends `aaa.AAA`, wants to override `callMe()`. Which access modes for `callMe()` in `aaa.AAA` will allow this?

    A. public

    B. protected

    C. default

    D. private

37. What happens when you try to compile the following code and run the `Zebra` application?

```
class Animal {
  float weight;
  Animal(float weight) {
    this.weight = weight;
  }
}

class Zebra extends Animal {
  public static void main(String[] args) {
    Animal a = new Animal(222.2f);
    Zebra z = new Zebra();
  }
}
```

    A. Class `Animal` generates a compiler error.

    B. Class `Zebra` generates a compiler error.

    C. The code compiles without error. The application throws an exception when the `Animal` constructor is called.

    D. The code compiles without error. The application throws an exception when the `Zebra` constructor is called.

    E. The code compiles and runs without error.

38. Given the following code:

```
1. class Xyz {
2.    float f;
3.    Xyz() {
4.      ???   // What goes here?
5.    }
6.    Xyz(float f) {
7.      this.f = f;
8.    }
9. }
```

What code at line 4 results in a class that compiles?

A. super();

B. this(1.23f);

C. this(1.23f); super();

D. super(1.23f); this(1.23f);

39. What relationship does the **extends** keyword represent?

A. "is a"

B. "has a"

C. Polymorphism

D. Multivariance

E. Overloading

40. When should objects stored in a Set implement the `java.util.Comparable` interface?

A. Always

B. When the Set is generic

C. When the Set is a HashSet

D. When the Set is a TreeSet

E. Never

41. Given the following class:

```
class Xyzzy {
  int a, b;

  public boolean equals(Object x) {
    Xyzzy that = (Xyzzy)x;
    return this.a == that.a;
  }
```

Which methods below honor the hash code contract?

A. `public int hashCode() { return a; }`

B. `public int hashCode() { return b; }`

C.
```
public int hashCode() {
    return a+b;
}
```

D.
```
public int hashCode() {
    return a*b;
}
```

E.
```
public int hashCode() {
    return (int)Math.random();
}
```

42. Give the following declarations:

```
Vector plainVec;
Vector<String> fancyVec;
```

If you want a vector in which you know you will only store strings, what are the advantages of using `fancyVec` rather than `plainVec`?

A. Attempting to add anything other than a string to `fancyVec` results in a compiler error.

B. Attempting to add anything other than a string to `fancyVec` causes a runtime exception to be thrown.

C. Attempting to add anything other than a string to `fancyVec` causes a checked exception to be thrown.

D. Adding a string to `fancyVec` takes less time than adding one to `plainVec`.

E. The methods of `fancyVec` are synchronized.

43. The declaration of the `java.util.Collection` interface is

```
interface Collection <E>
```

The `addAll()` method of that interface takes a single argument, which is a reference to a collection whose elements are compatible with E. What is the declaration of the `addAll()` method?

A. `public boolean addAll(Collection c)`

B. `public boolean`
`        addAll(Collection c extends E)`

C. `public boolean`
`        addAll(Collection ? extends E)`

D. `public boolean`
`        addAll(Collection<? extends E> c)`

44. The `java.util.Arrays` class has a `binarySearch(int[] arr, int key)` method. Which statements are true regarding this method? (Choose all that apply.)

   A. The method is static.

   B. The return value is the index in the array of **key**.

   C. The elements of the array must be sorted when the method is called.

   D. After the method returns, the elements of the array are sorted, even if they weren't sorted before the call.

45. Given the following class:

```
package ocean;
public class Fish {
  protected int size;
  protected void swim() { }
}
```

Which of the following may appear in a subclass of `Fish` named `Tuna` that is not in the `ocean` package?

   A. void swim() { }

   B. public void swim() { }

   C. `size = 12;`

   D. `(new Tuna()).size = 12;`

46. Given the following class:

```
public class App {
  public static void main(String[] args) {
    System.out.println(args.length);
  }
}
```

Assuming `App.class` is stored in an appropriate location in file `appjar.jar`, what is printed when you type the following command line?

`java -cp appjar.jar -ea App  1 2 3 4`

   A. 4

   B. 5

   C. 6

   D. 7

   E. 8

   F. 9

47. Given the following classes:

```
public class Wrapper {
  public int x;
}


public class Tester {
  private static void bump(int n, Wrapper w) {
    n++;
    w.x++;
  }

  public static void main(String[] args) {
    int n = 10;
    Wrapper w = new Wrapper();
    w.x = 10;
    bump(n, w);
    // Now what are n and w.x?
  }
}
```

When the application runs, what are the values of n and w.x after the call to bump() in the main() method?

A. n is 10, w.x is 10

B. n is 11, w.x is 10

C. n is 10, w.x is 11

D. n is 11, w.x is 11

48. When does the string created on line 2 become eligible for garbage collection?

```
1. String s = "aaa";
2. String t = new String(s);
3. t += "zzz";
4. t = t.substring(0);
5. t = null;
```

A. After line 3

B. After line 4

C. After line 5

D. The string created on line 2 does not become eligible for garbage collection in this code.

49. Suppose you want to run the following command line on a Windows system:

`java -classpath somewhere;elsewhere aaa.bbb.MyApplication`

On a Unix system the command line would be:

`java -classpath somewhere:elsewhere aaa.bbb.MyApplication`

Assume the CLASSPATH variable is not set. Which must be true in order for the application to run?

A. Class MyApplication must contain the statement `package aaa.bbb;`.

B. Class MyApplication must be in a directory named aaa and must contain the statement `package bbb;`.

C. Class MyApplication must contain either the statement `package somewhere.aaa.bbb;` or the statement `package elsewhere.aaa.bbb;`.

D. The file MyApplication.class must be found either in `somewhere\aaa\bbb` or in `elsewhere\aaa\bbb`. (Substitute forward slashes for backslashes on a Unix system.)

50. What is -15 % -10?

    A. 0

    B. *5*

    C. 10

    D. *-5*

    E. -10

Answers

1. B, D, E.   A and C are illegal because an enum may not be extended or instantiated. B is a legal use of one of the enum's constants. D legally passes an enum into a method. E legally calls a method that all enums inherit from `Object`.

2. B, D, F.   A static import does not apply to non-static features, so A, C, and E are ruled out. Since the class performing the import is in the same package as `Sploo`, all static features (data and methods) that have public, protected, or default access are imported into the importing class' namespace.

3. B, C, E.   `Abby` is a valid class; it contains an abstract method, so the class must also be abstract. `SubAbby` must be declared abstract because it doesn't provide an implementation for the abstract method of its parent class. An abstract class may not be instantiated but is a legal type for variables.

4. A, E.   `ages` is a reference, so in the absence of initialization code it is initialized to `null`. `heights` is initialized; the array contains 10 floats that are initialized to 0f.

5. C.   The method's name is `get` followed by the name of the variable. The variable name's first character is converted to uppercase.

6. B.   The method declaration demonstrates standard use of a variable argument list, which is accessed inside the method as an array.

7. C, D, E.   Covariant returns are legal in 5.0, so in addition to the exact return type of the super-class' version, any subclass of that type is also legal.

8. E.   The compiler creates a default constructor only if a class has no explicit constructors.

9. A, B.   The only legal arguments of `switch` statements are enums and primitives that are compatible with `int`s.

10. A, C.   A is the standard pre-5.0 way to add the elements. B throws an exception because it loops one time too many. C uses the enhanced `for` loop notation. D uses an illegal made-up notation.

11. A, C.   The boolean that follows the `assert` keyword is the condition that must be met. The condition may optionally be followed by a colon, followed by a message that is displayed if the assertion fails.

12. A, B, D.   Assertions are appropriate for checking postconditions in all methods and for checking preconditions in most methods. They are not appropriate for checking preconditions in public methods, however, because public methods are often called in environments where assertions are not enabled.

13. A, C.   All exceptions declared by an overriding method must be compatible with types thrown by the overridden version.

14. B, E.   When the exception is thrown, the current pass through the `try` block is abandoned, so "I threw" isn't printed. The first `catch` block that is compatible with the exception's type is executed. This is the block for `ObjectStreamException`, which is a superclass of the thrown type. Only one `catch` block is executed per thrown exception; execution then continues at the `Finally` block, which prints "Finally".

15. D.   Since `ArrayIndexOutOfBoundsException` is a runtime exception, it indicates a faulty algorithm that should not be released. The only appropriate response is to find and fix the bug.

16. C, D.   The purpose of `IllegalArgumentException` is to indicate a precondition violation in a public method. The core Java classes use it this way, and so should we. The JVM does not throw `IllegalArgumentException`.

17. A, B, C, D.   All four statements are legal. A and C are examples of unboxing, which allows assignment from a wrapper to a primitive. B is an example of boxing, which allows assignment from a primitive to a wrapper. D is assignment of a literal `int` to a `short`, which is legal because the right-hand side of the assignment is a literal rather than a variable.

18. A, C.   `StringBuilder` is nearly identical to `StringBuffer`. The main differences are that `StringBuilder` is not threadsafe, and its methods are generally faster than those of `StringBuffer`.

19. A, B, D.   A and B correctly use a random access file. A reads and discards the leading doubles; B just seeks past them. C doesn't work because readers are for files that contain only 8-bit text; they don't work on UTF files. D and E use a file input stream. D correctly reads and discards the leading doubles and then reads the UTF string. E doesn't work because the `DataInputStream` class doesn't have a `seek()` method.

20. C.   For a file that contains only 8-bit text, use a reader. By default, a reader interprets 8-bit text according to the current default locale. Readers read their input character by character; to assemble the characters into lines of text, chain on a `LineNumberReader` and call its `readLine()` method.

21. B, E.   There are two ways to ensure that a class can be serialized: you can implement `Serializable`, which is a tagging interface that defines no methods, or you can implement `Externalizable`, which defines the `readExternal` and `writeExternal` methods.

22. D.   Default deserialization is only bypassed if the `readObject()` method has private access.

23. B, C.   If a class implements `Externalizable`, it must have a no-args constructor. If a class implements `Serializable` and does not implement `java.io.Externalizable`, its nearest non-externalizable superclass must have a no-args constructor.

24. C, D.   Date formatting is determined by the locale and by the style. Style constants are defined as static `int`s in the `DateFormat` class: SHORT, MEDIUM, LONG, and FULL.

25. A.   `NumberFormat` instances should be obtained by calling the static `getInstance()` method, not by calling a constructor. To format a number, pass the number (and no other arguments) into the `NumberFormat`'s `format()` method.

26. C.   The goal is to create a regular expression that matches the run of digits in the middle of scanMe. The "d" in a regular expression indicates "digit." Two escaping backslashes are necessary: one is consumed by the Java compiler when it compiles the literal string. The second tells the useDelimiter() method that the "d" is a special character. The "+" quantifier matches one or more occurrences, which is what we want. The "*" quantifier matches zero or more occurrences; there are zero digits between the vowels, and that is considered a "*" match, so using "\\d*" splits the string into "a", "e", "i", etc.

27. D.   The minus sign in the format string causes left-justification. The number to the right of the decimal point in the format string controls the number of digits to the right of the decimal point in the output.

28. A, D.   A is correct because the start() method of Thread (which is inherited by MyThread) causes a thread to begin execution of the thread object's run() method. Calling run() directly as in B and C just causes the run() method to execute in the current thread. D creates a new thread whose target is an instance of MyRunnable; this is the typical way to use the Runnable interface.

29. A.   With the call to join() after the new thread is created and started, the main thread will wait for the new thread to finish its execution before continuing any processing after the call to join().

30. A, B, D.   There are three locks to consider: the class lock, which controls access to the static synchronized method, and the individual object locks, which control access to the non-static synchronized methods. A and B are true because staticMethod() is controlled by the class lock. C is false because classy1.notStaticMethod() is controlled by classy1's object lock, while classy1 .staticMethod() is controlled by the class lock. D is true because both threads are trying to execute code controlled by classy1's object lock. E is false because thread A is executing code controlled by classy1's object lock, while thread B wants to execute code controlled by classy2's object lock.

31. C, E.   The notify() and notifyAll() methods affect the threads that are waiting for the object on which the call is made. In other words, you notify the object, not the thread. So A and B don't work. When a thread is interrupted, it leaves the wait state and enters the InterruptedException handler, so C is correct. D does not work because there might be multiple threads waiting for sharedOb. E works because it guarantees that all waiting objects are moved out of the waiting state.

32. B, D.   Tightness of coupling expresses the degree to which one class relies on knowledge of the internals of another class. Tight coupling is undesirable because if class Car changes the way it stores its data, class Driver (and any other similarly coupled classes) needs to be rewritten.

33. B.   Cohesion is the degree to which a class or method resists being broken down into smaller pieces; it is a desirable quality. chopWoodAndCarryWater() can obviously be broken down into its two constituent parts, so it has inappropriate cohesion. This question does not concern coupling, which is an object's reliance on knowledge of the internals of another entity's implementation.

34. B, C, D.   A cast is required when assigning from a superclass to a subclass, so A requires a cast but B does not. The cast in C is required; the cast in D is not but does no harm. The cast in E turns the right-hand side of the assignment into an Object, which may not be assigned to a Citrus without a cast.

35. A, C.   Line 2 is an assignment from a subclass to a superclass, so the cast is not necessary. Line 3 compiles because it obeys the compile-time casting rules. At runtime, the JVM notices that the class of the object referenced by c is not compatible with the Lemon class, so an exception is thrown.

36. A, B.   Public and protected methods may be overridden by any class. A default method may be overridden only if the subclass is in the same package as the superclass.

37. B.   Class Animal has no no-args constructor. Class Zebra has no constructor at all, so the compiler creates one that just calls the superclass' no-args constructor. Since there is no such constructor, compilation fails.

38. A, B.   A legally invokes the superclass' no-args constructor. The call is unnecessary, since the compiler inserts it in the absence of a call to any other superclass constructor. B legally invokes the constructor at line 6. C and D are illegal because in a constructor any call to super() or this() must be the first line of the constructor; so there's no room for both, in either order.

39. A.   Java's extends and implements keywords represent the "is a" relationship between types.

40. D.   TreeSet stores its elements in natural order, which is determined by casting the elements to Comparable and invoking their compareTo() methods. If you add an element that isn't comparable to a tree set, you'll eventually get an exception.

41. A, E.   The hash code contract states that if two objects are equal, they must have equal hash codes. In this case two objects are equal if their a values are equal. If two such objects have different b values, then answers B, C, and D will return unequal hash codes for equal objects, which violates the contract. E always returns 0; it's strange and inefficient, but it doesn't violate the contract.

42. A.   fancyVec is a generic collection, so the compiler checks the types of arguments to add().

43. D.   The notation Collection<? extends E> c means that c is a generic collection whose type is compatible with type E.

44. A, B, C.   The method is static, and it returns the index of key. The array must be sorted before the method is invoked.

45. B, C.   A is illegal because it attempts to override the swim() method with a more restricted access mode. B overrides with a less-restricted access mode, which is legal. C is legal because it accesses protected superclass data of the current instance. D is illegal because it accesses protected superclass data of a different instance.

46. A.   The args array contains command-line arguments that are not directives to the java command. Only the strings "1", "2", "3", and "4" are passed into args, so args.length is 4.

47. C.   Primitives are passed by value, so bump() increments a copy of n, not n itself. Object references are also passed by value, so bump() uses a copy of w, not w itself; since that copy points to the same object as the one pointed to by w, changes made in bump() are permanent.

48. A.   Line 3 creates a new string that contains "aaazzz" and assigns t to point to that new string. At that moment there are no references to the string created on line 2 ("aaa"), so it becomes eligible for garbage collection.

49. A, D.   Since the application class name is `aaa.bbb.MyApplication`, it must declare that it is a member of package `aaa.bbb`. The class file must appear in a subdirectory named aaa\bbb in one of the directories of the classpath.

50. D.   15 % 10 is 5, so the magnitude of the result is 5. The sign of the result is the sign of the left-hand operand, so the result is -5.

Glossary

A

access modifier   Access modifiers dictate which classes are allowed to use a feature.

anonymous class   A class without a name is called an anonymous class. An anonymous class can be declared to extend another class or to implement a single interface. The syntax does not allow you to do both at the same time, nor to implement more than one interface explicitly.

arithmetic promotion   Automatic conversion to an int of a byte, short, or char arithmetic operand.

assertion   Assertions provide a convenient mechanism for verifying that a class' methods are called correctly. This mechanism can be enabled or disabled at runtime. Typically assertions are enabled during development and testing and disabled in the field.

assignment conversion   Conversion of a primitive or reference value to a new type, during execution of the assignment operator.

autoboxing   The automatic assignment of a primitive value to a compatible wrapper type. Aka *boxing*.

auto-unboxing   The automatic assignment of a wrapper type to a compatible primitive value. Aka *unboxing*.

automatic variable   A variable defined in the scope of a method. It ceases to exist when the method returns. Contrast with instance variables, whose lifetime is the life of the enclosing class.

B

bitwise operators   Operators that operate on int and long data. Bit *n* of the result is a function only of bit(s) *n* of the operand(s). Java's *bitwise operators* are inversion, AND, XOR, and OR.

blocking   A thread blocks when, on detection that it cannot proceed because of the absence of a needed resource, it gives up the CPU.

boxing   The automatic assignment of a primitive value to a compatible wrapper type. Aka *autoboxing*.

C

casting   Explicit data type conversion using the cast operator: (*newtype*).

***catch* block**   A block of code that deals with an exception that might arise during execution of the try block.

character literal   An explicitly specified value for a char variable. The value is enclosed in single quotes.

checked exception   Exceptions that describe unavoidable environmental problems encountered by a program. They must be handled by the try-catch mechanism or by declaring that the method calling the exception-throwing methods throws the same exceptions.

class invariant   A constraint on a class's state that must be met before and after execution of any nonprivate method of a class. (Private methods might be used to restore the required state after execution of a nonprivate method.)

class variable   A *static variable*, created when the class is loaded and destroyed when the class is unloaded. There is only one copy of a class variable, and it exists regardless of the number of instances of the class, even if the class is never instantiated.

compilation units   Three top-level elements known as *compilation units* may appear in a file. None of these elements is required. If they are present, then they must appear in the following order: package declaration, import statements, class/interface/enum definitions.

concatenation   The joining together of string objects.

concurrency   Apparent simultaneous execution of multiple threads. The simultaneity is actually an illusion caused by the rapid swapping of the threads in and out of the CPU.

conditional operator   The ?: operator. Also called the *ternary operator*.

constants   An enum's constants are the values declared in its first statement.

container components   Swing components that can contain other components (including other containers).

conversion   Implicit change of date type.

coupling   An object's reliance on knowledge of the internals of another entity's implementation.

D

deadlock   A waiting thread is deadlocked when the condition for which it is waiting never arises.

default access   One of Java's four access modes. It may be assigned to a class, a variable, or a method when no access modifier is explicitly provided. A feature with default access is accessible to any class in the same package as the class that owns the feature.

default constructor   A constructor created by the compiler when a class has no explicitly programmed constructors. It invokes the default constructor of the superclass.

default package   An unnamed package, consisting of all classes in the current working directory that do not contain a package declaration.

E

encapsulation   The aggregation into a class of data and behavior.

enclosing class   A class that contains an inner class within its scope.

enum   A compilation unit similar to a class but using the enum declaration. Used for typesafe enumeration.

enumerated constants   A design pattern in which state or similar values are represented by arbitrarily assigned primitives. Prone to bugs.

error   A nonrecoverable condition, similar to an exception, but arising from problems in the JVM rather than in the environment.

event   A change in state, usually due to user input in a GUI component.

event listener   An object that receives notification (via a method call) of an event.

exception   A condition that prevents normal execution of a method. Represented by java.lang.Event and its subclasses.

exception chaining   Handling an exception by creating and throwing a new exception of a different type. The new exception contains a reference to the original one.

F

feature   A class, a method, or a variable.

floating-point literal   An explicit value that can be assigned to a float or double variable. A floating-point literal expresses a number that contains one or more of the following: a decimal point; the letter E or e, indicating scientific notation; the suffix F or f, indicating a float literal; or the suffix D or d, indicating a double literal.

framework   A group of interfaces that define the semantics of some functionality, along with the classes that implement that functionality.

G

garbage collector   A thread that reclaims inaccessible memory. Memory that represents an object is considered inaccessible when there are no references to the object.

generic collection   A collection that performs compile-time type checking on the objects it contains.

graph   An object, as well as all objects referenced by that object, as well as all objects referenced by *those* objects, etc. When an object is passed to an Object Output Stream, its entire graph is serialized.

I

identifier   The name of a variable, method, class, or label. Keywords and reserved words may not be used as identifiers. An identifier must begin with a letter, a dollar sign ($), or an underscore (_); subsequent characters may be letters, dollar signs, underscores, or digits.

inheritance   The availability to a child class of a parent class' data and methods.

inner class   A class defined within the scope of another class, known as the enclosing class.

instance variable   A variable defined in the scope of a class. Its lifetime is the lifetime of the enclosing instance of the class.

integral literal   An explicitly specified integral value, consisting of an optional sign followed by a sequence of digits.

iterator   An object that returns the elements of a collection one by one.

J

jar file   A Java archive file, generally created by the `jar` tool. The file format is compatible with the zip and tar formats.

K

keyword   A word whose meaning is defined by the programming language.

L

late binding   Runtime determination of how to perform a method call.

List   An ordered collection of data, represented by the `java.util.List` interface.

listener   An object that receives notification when another object, which is typically a GUI component, sends an event. An object becomes a listener by implementing a listener interface and registering with the event source.

lock   An entity that permits access to the synchronized instance methods of an object or to the synchronized static methods of a class. At any moment, at most one thread may own a lock.

M

manifest   A file within a jar file that describes the jar's contents. Useful for creating executable jars.

Map   A collection that associates unique keys with values. Represented by the `java.util.Map` interface.

member class   See *inner class*.

member variable   See *instance variable*.

metadata   Data associated with a file but not part of the file's contents, such as creation date and owner.

method-call conversion   A conversion that happens when a value of one type is passed as an argument to a method that expects a different type.

model-delegate   A design pattern in which each view can visually describe the model according to the set or subset of data it is most interested in.

modifiers   Java keywords that give the compiler information about the nature of code, data, or classes.

monitor   Any object that has synchronized code.

N

narrowing conversion   Conversion of a primitive value to a narrower type.

O

object equality   A definition of equality, implemented by the `equals()` method, wherein two possibly distinct objects are considered equal if their variables are equal.

object reference   A handle for accessing an object.

overloading   Reuse of a same method name with different arguments and perhaps a different return type.

overriding   Reuse of a method name in a subclass, with identical arguments and compatible return type.

P

package   A group of related classes, interfaces, and enums.

port number   A number that identifies a service on a TCP/IP server.

postcondition   A constraint that must be met on return from a method. Postcondition violations should be indicated with assertions.

post-decrement   The post-decrement operator is positioned after an expression and reduces the value of the expression by 1.

post-increment   The post-increment operator is positioned after an expression and increases the value of the expression by 1.

precondition   A constraint that must be met on entry of a method. Precondition violations in nonpublic methods should be indicated with assertions. Precondition violations in public methods should be indicated with runtime exceptions.

pre-decrement   The pre-decrement operator is positioned before an expression and reduces the value of the expression by 1.

preferred size   The default size of a GUI component, barring conflict with a layout manager.

pre-increment   The pre-increment operator is positioned before an expression and increases the value of the expression by 1.

primitive   A non-object data type. Java's primitive types are `boolean`, `byte`, `short`, `char`, `int`, `long`, `float`, and `double`.

priority   An integer from 1 to 10 that determines the amount of CPU time allocated to a thread over a statistically significant amount of time. Higher priority corresponds to more CPU time. Implementation may vary among JVMs.

private access   One of Java's four access modes. A private feature may be accessed only by the class that owns the feature.

property   In the JavaBeans naming convention, a property XXX of an object is data accessed by the object's `get`XXX`()` method and modified by the object's `write`XXX`()` method.

protected access   One of Java's four access modes. A protected feature may be accessed by classes in the same package as the class that owns the feature, as well as by subclasses of the class that owns the feature, regardless of the subclass' package.

protocol   An agreement among programmers regarding the interchange of data between two programs, typically in a client/server relationship.

public access   One of Java's four access modes. A public feature may be accessed by any class.

R

reference   A handle for accessing an object. Similar to a pointer.

reliable protocol   A low-level protocol in which all data is eventually delivered to its destination.

remote interface   In RMI, an interface that describes the services offered by a remote object.

Remote Method Invocation (RMI)   A method call in which the calling object and the executing object reside on different JVMs.

remote reference   A reference to an object on a different JVM. Used by RMI.

reserved words   Words that may not be used as identifiers, even though they are not keywords and have no meaning in the programming language.

runtime exception   An exception that describes a condition that should never arise in a correct program, such as the use of a `null` reference or integer division by zero. Represented by subclasses of `java.lang.RuntimeException`.

S

serialization   Writing an object, along with its graph of references, to an Object Output Stream.

Set   An unordered collection in which all members are unique. Sets implement the `java.util.Set` interface.

signed data type   A numeric primitive type that may take both positive and negative values. All Java's numeric types except `char` are signed.

static   A static feature belongs to a class, rather than to an individual instance of a class.

static initializer   Code that appears inside curly brackets that are preceded by the `static` keyword, but not inside a method. Static initializer code is run when a class is loaded.

string literal   A sequence of characters enclosed in double quotes.

stub   An object that implements a remote interface and communicates with a remote object. Generated by the `rmic` tool.

synchronized code   Code that may be executed only if the executing thread holds the lock of the object that owns the code.

T

tagging interface   An interface that defines no methods.

ternary operator   The `?:` operator. Also called the *conditional operator.*

threadsafe   A class or group of classes is considered threadsafe if any thread can call any method of any instance at any time.

thread scheduler   The part of the JVM that determines which thread is running at any given time.

throw   To present an exception or error to the JVM, terminating normal execution through the current block or method.

transient   A transient variable is not stored as part of its object's persistent state.

***try* block**   A block of code that might throw an exception and is preceded by the `try` keyword.

typesafe enumeration   A design pattern in which state or similar values are represented by instances of a dedicated class. When properly implemented, the pattern makes it impossible to represent illegal or undefined values. Java's enums provide language-level support for typesafe enumerations.

U

Unicode   A standard for representing characters with 16-bit patterns.

unsigned data type   A numeric primitive type that may not take negative values. Java's `char` type is signed.

unary operator   An operator that takes one operand.

unboxing   The automatic assignment of a wrapper type to a compatible primitive value. Aka *auto-unboxing.*

W

waiting state   A nonexecuting thread state, entered when a thread executes an object's wait() method and terminated when the object's notify() or notifyAll() method is invoked.

weight   A GridBag property that determines the amount of space allocated to a component when its container resizes.

widening conversion   Conversion from a narrower to a wider numeric data type.

wrapper class   A class that encapsulates a single, immutable value. Each Java primitive data type has a corresponding *wrapper class*.

Y

yield   To voluntarily give up the CPU. A thread yields by executing its yield() method.

Index

Note to the Reader: Throughout this index **boldfaced** page numbers indicate primary discussions of a topic. *Italicized* page numbers indicate illustrations.

You Can Never be <u>TOO</u> Prepared

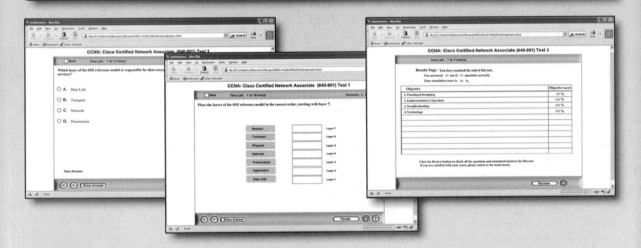

Tools, Skills, & Strategies
for Software Engineers

Designing Highly Useable Software
By Jeff Cogswell • ISBN: 0-7821-4301-6 • **US $39.99**

"Highly useable" software is easy to use. It does what you expect it to. And it does it well. It's not easy to build but as this book demonstrates, it's well worth the effort. Highly useable software is highly successful software—and everyone wins.

Inside, an accomplished programmer who has made usability his business systematically explores the world of programming, showing you how every aspect of the work is implicated in the usability of the final product.

Effective Software Test Automation:
Developing an Automated Software Testing Tool
By Kanglin Li; Mengqi Wu • ISBN: 0-7821-4320-2 • **US $44.99**

Whatever its claims, commercially available testing software is not automatic. Configuring it to test your product is almost as time-consuming and error-prone as purely manual testing.

There is an alternative that makes both engineering and economic sense: building your own, truly automatic tool. Inside, you'll learn a repeatable, step-by-step approach, suitable for virtually any development environment. Code-intensive examples support the book's instruction.

Effective GUI Test Automation:
Developing an Automated GUI Testing Tool
By Kanglin Li; Mengqi Wu • 0-7821-4351-2 • **US $44.99**

Have you tried using an "automated" GUI testing tool, only to find that you spent most of your time configuring, adjusting, and directing it? This book presents a sensible and highly effective alternative: it teaches you to build and use your own truly automated tool. The procedure you'll learn is suitable for virtually any development environment, and the tool allows you to store your test data and verification standard separately, so you can build it once and use it for other GUIs.

Coder to Developer:
Tools and Strategies for Delivering Your Software
By Mike Gunderloy • ISBN: 0-7821-4327-X • **US $29.99**

Are you ready to take the leap from programmer to proficient developer? Based on the assumption that programmers need to grasp a broad set of core skills in order to develop high-quality software, this book teaches you these critical ground rules. Topics covered include project planning, source code control, error handling strategies, working with and managing teams, documenting the application, developing a build process, and delivering the product. All of the techniques taught in this unique book are language and platform neutral, and were selected to help you effectively design and develop complex applications.